Endless Shout

SHOUT ENDLESS
ESS SHOUT END
DLESS SHOUT EN
NDLESS SHOUT
ENDLESS SHOU
UT ENDLESS SH
HOUT ENDLESS S
SHOUT ENDLESS

ENDLESS SHOUT

INVENTORY PRESS

Institute of Contemporary Art
University of Pennsylvania

Proposal for *Bedouin Hornbook* as Hyperstition sent from N to Dear Angel of Dust on 06.01.1981 and received on 08.20.2016

Original text:
Excerpt from Nathaniel Mackey's novel *Bedouin Hornbook*, 1986.

I even got a surprise visit from an old friend of mine named Derek whom I hadn't seen for two years. He teaches music out at Cal Arts and it turns out he's planning a symposium, at which he's invited me to give a talk. He got interested in something he calls "propositional positionality" a few years back. He was in a workshop run by Joseph Jarman at the Creative Music Studio in Woodstock. Jarman, it seems, turned to a horn player at one point and asked him to stand up and play something. The horn player stood up but before he could start playing Jarman stopped him, saying, "Wait a minute. Notice the stance. It's a statement. The instrumentalist as sculpture. Notice it. We usually take it for granted but we can use it." This clicked with an idea Derek had been carrying around for some time—namely that people weren't being precise enough in discussing Miles Davis turning his back on his audiences, that sufficient note had yet to be made of the fact that the angle at which his back addressed the audience tended to vary in relation to a host of contextual factors and coefficients. The upshot was that he set about quantifying and chronologizing—based on photographs, films, second-hand accounts and first-hand observation—the positional/propositional variables attendant upon Miles's posture, or, as he himself puts it, the "semiotemporal calculus of Miles's postural kinematics." He's published two or three monographs discussing his findings. Anyway, this developed into a more general interest in the "semantics of movement and posture," one of the results of which is the symposium he's planning for the spring having to do with "Locus and Locomotivity in Postcontemporary Music," the one at which he's invited me to speak.

6.1.81 as an element of effective culture that makes itself real.

6.1.81 as a fictional quantity functional as a time -travelling device.

6.1.81 as a coincidence intensifier.

6.1.81 as a Call to the Old Ones.

I even got

1. **a surprise visit** from an old friend of mine named Derek whom I hadn't seen for two years. He teaches music out at Cal Arts and it turns out he's planning
2. **a symposium,** at which he's invited me to give
3. **a talk.** He got interested in something he calls
4. **"propositional positionality"** a few years back. He was in a
5. **workshop** run by Joseph Jarman at the Creative Music Studio in Woodstock. Jarman, it seems, turned to a horn player at one point and asked him to stand up and play something. The horn player stood up but before he could start playing Jarman stopped him, saying, "Wait a minute. Notice the
6. **stance.** It's
7. **a statement.**
8. **The instrumentalist as sculpture.**
9. *Notice* **it.** We usually take it for granted but
10. **we can use it."** This clicked with
11. **an idea** Derek had been carrying around for some time—namely that people
12. **weren't being precise enough** in discussing Miles Davis turning his back on his audiences, that sufficient note had yet to be made of the fact that
13. **the angle** at which his back addressed the audience tended to vary in relation to a host of contextual factors and coefficients. The upshot was that he set about
14. **quantifying and chronologizing**—based on
15. **photographs,**
16. **films,**
17. **second-hand accounts**
18. **and first-hand observation**—the
19. **positional/propositional variables** attendant upon Miles's posture, or, as he himself puts it, the
20. **"semiotemporal calculus of Miles's postural kinematics."** He's published
21. **two or three monographs** discussing his findings. Anyway, this developed into a
22. **more general interest in the "semantics of movement and posture,"** one of the results of which is the
23. **symposium** he's planning for the spring having to do with
24. **"Locus and Locomotivity in Postcontemporary Music,"** the one at which he's **invited** me to
25. **speak.**

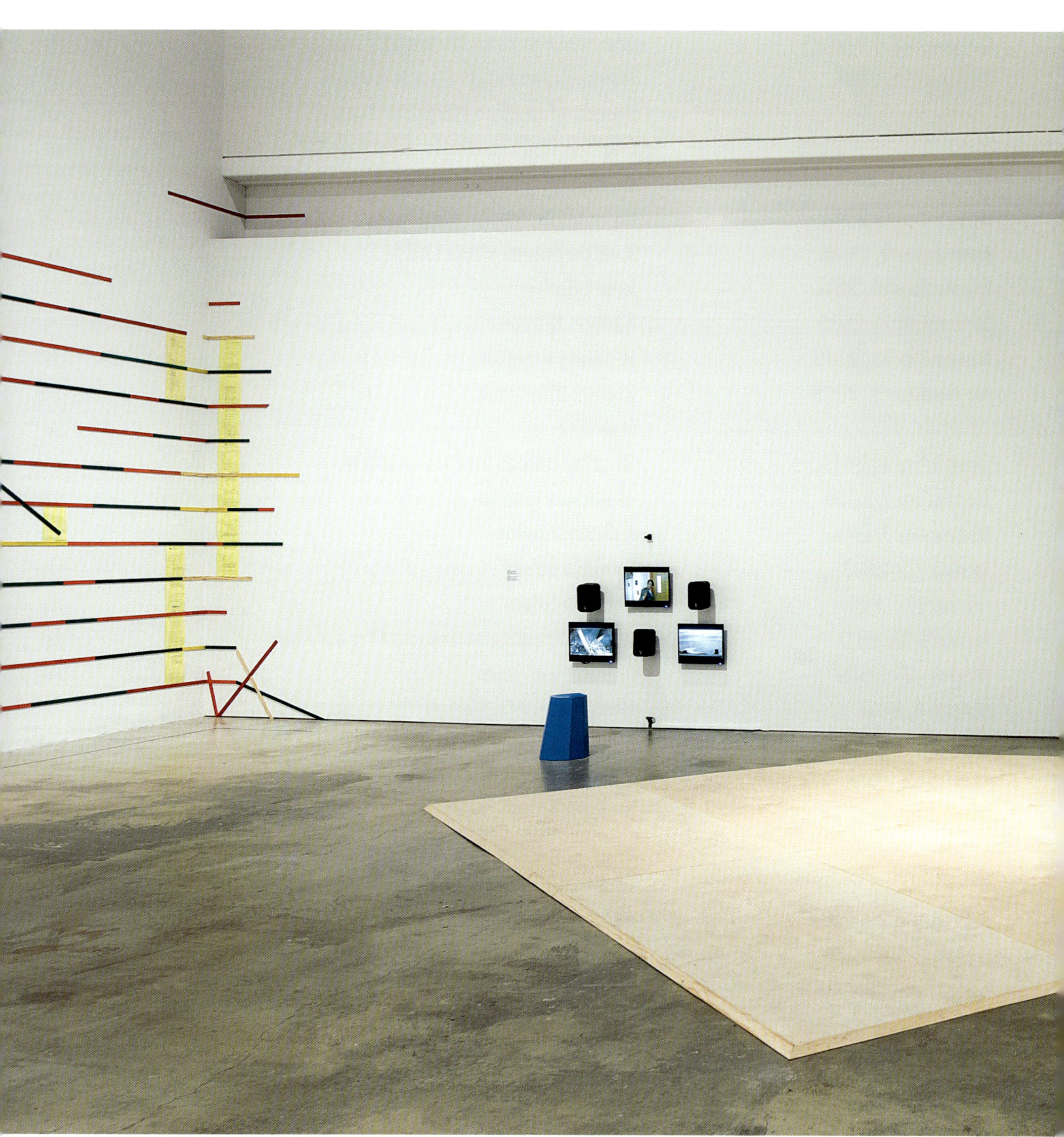

Preliminaries

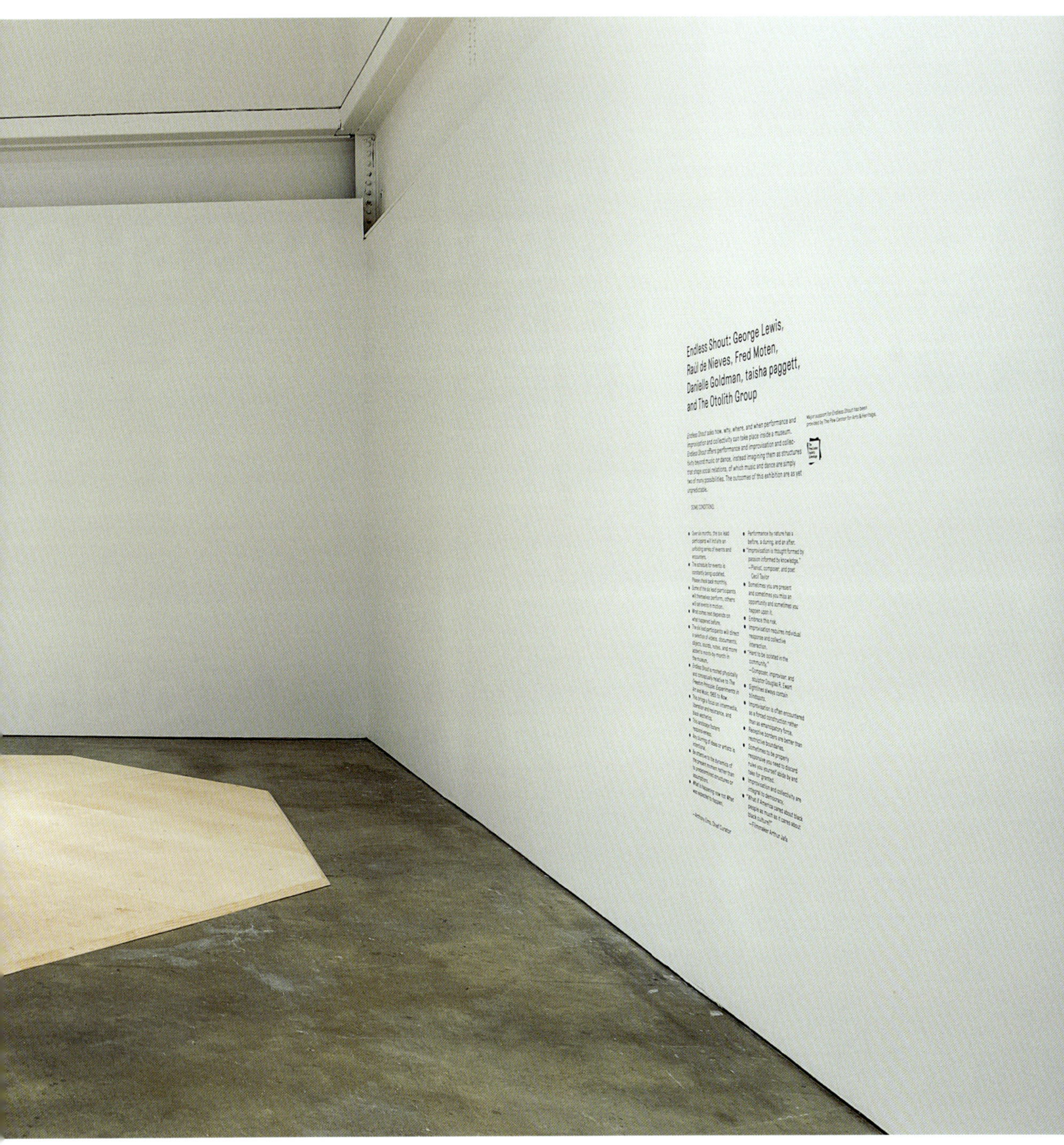

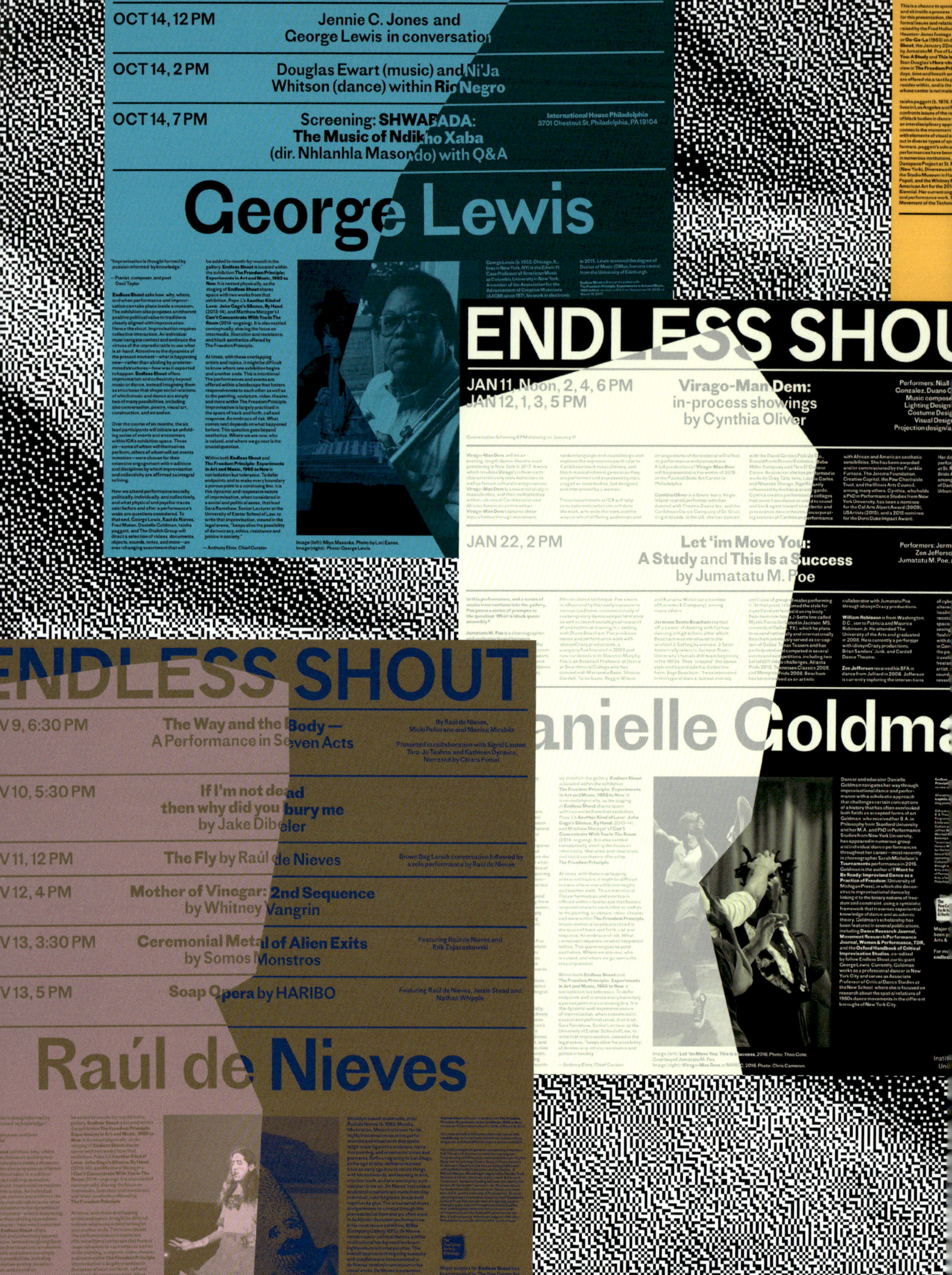
Fee: $15
by Ensemble Pamplemousse
OCT 14, 12 PM — Jennie C. Jones and George Lewis in conversation
OCT 14, 2 PM — Douglas Ewart (music) and Ni'Ja Whitson (dance) within Rio Negro
OCT 14, 7 PM — Screening: SHWABADA: The Music of Ndikho Xaba (dir. Nhlanhla Masondo) with Q&A
International House Philadelphia
3701 Chestnut St, Philadelphia, PA 19104
George Lewis
ENDLESS SHOUT
JAN 11, Noon, 2, 4, 6 PM
JAN 12, 1, 3, 5 PM
Virago-Man Dem: in-process showings by Cynthia Oliver
Performers: Niall Gonzalez, Duane
Music compose
Lighting Design
Costume Design
Visual Design
Projection design/a
Conversation following 6 PM showing on January 11
JAN 22, 2 PM
Let 'im Move You: A Study and This Is a Success by Jumatatu M. Poe
Performers: Jerm, Zen Jefferson, Jumatatu M. Poe,
Danielle Goldma
ENDLESS SHOUT
V 9, 6:30 PM — The Way and the Body — A Performance in Seven Acts
By Raúl de Nieves, Micki Pellerano and Monica Mirabile
Presented in collaboration with Sigrid Lauren, Tara-Jo Tashna and Kathleen Dycaico. Narrated by Chiara Fumai
V 10, 5:30 PM — If I'm not dead then why did you bury me by Jake Dibeler
V 11, 12 PM — The Fly by Raúl de Nieves
Brown Bag Lunch conversation followed by a solo performance by Raúl de Nieves
V 12, 4 PM — Mother of Vinegar: 2nd Sequence by Whitney Vangrin
V 13, 3:30 PM — Ceremonial Metal of Alien Exits by Somos Monstros
Featuring Raúl de Nieves and Erik Zajaceskowski
V 13, 5 PM — Soap Opera by HARIBO
Featuring Raúl de Nieves, Jessie Stead and Nathan Whipple
Raúl de Nieves

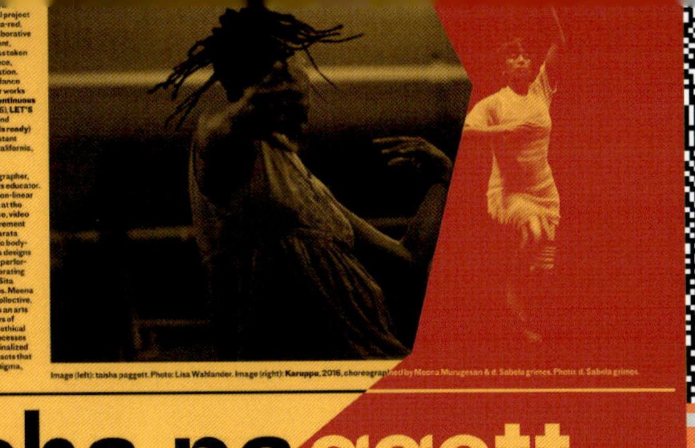

Image (left): tisha paggett. Photo: Lisa Wahlander. Image (right): Karrapba, 2016, choreographed by Moena Murugesan & d. Sabela grimes. Photo: d. Sabela grimes.

tisha paggett
March 4 & 5
1 & 3 PM

ENDLESS SHOUT

MARCH 16, 7 PM

Screening: Monangambee,
The Third Part of the Third Measure
The Otolith Group in Person

International House Philadelphia
3701 Chestnut St, Philadelphia, PA 1

MARCH 19, 4 PM

Mouth of Darkness
by travis

MARCH 19, 6 PM

Hieroglyphic Being

The Otolith Group

Institute of Contemporary Art
University of Pennsylvania

Major support for **Endless Shout** has been provided by The Pew Center for Arts & Heritage

— Anthony Elms, Chief Curator

ENDLESS SHOUT

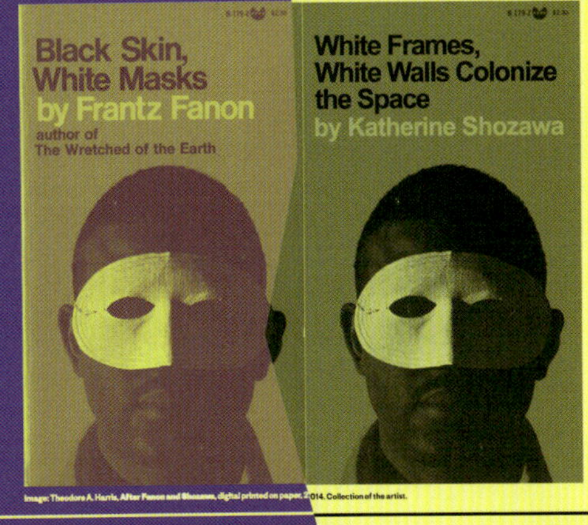

Image: Theodore A. Harris, After Fanon and Shozawa, digital printed on paper, 2014. Collection of the artist.

Ashon Crawley
Theodore Harris
DEC 7, 6:30 PM

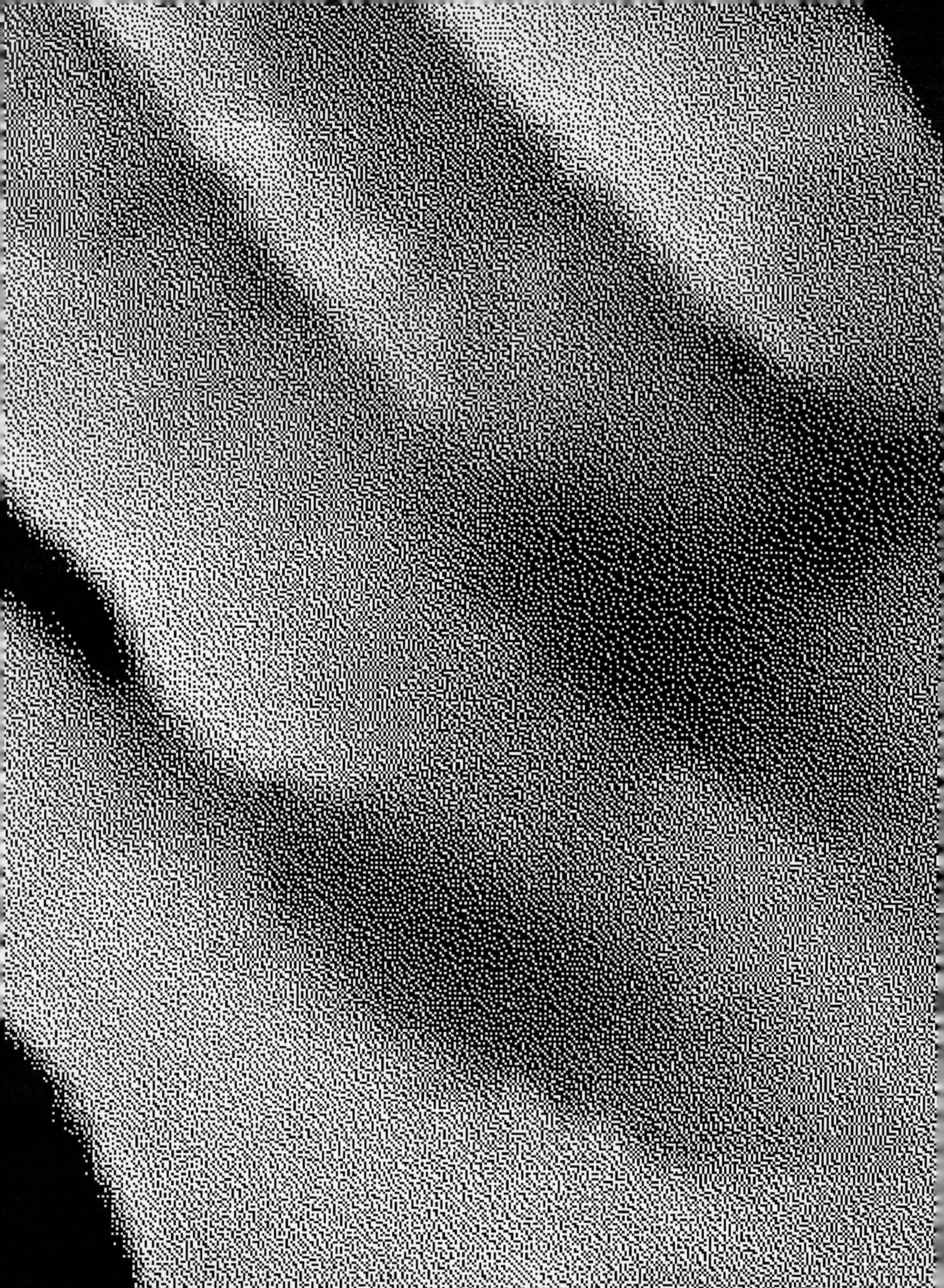

Endless Shout: George Lewis, Raúl de Nieves, Danielle Goldman, taisha paggett, and The Otolith Group

Endless Shout asks how, why, where, and when performance and improvisation and collectivity can take place inside a museum. *Endless Shout* offers performance and improvisation and collectivity beyond music or dance, instead imagining them as structures that shape social relations, of which music and dance are simply two of many possibilities. The outcomes of this exhibition are as yet unpredictable.

Some Conditions

- Over six months, the lead participants will initiate an unfolding series of events and encounters.
- The schedule for events is constantly being updated. Please check back monthly.
- Some of the six lead participants will themselves perform, others will set events in motion.
- What comes next depends on what happened before.
- The six lead participants will direct a selection of videos, documents, objects, sounds, notes, and more added to month-by-month in the museum.
- *Endless Shout* is rooted physically and conceptually relative to *The Freedom Principle: Experiments in Art and Music, 1965 to Now.*
- This brings a focus on intermedia, liberation and resistance, and black aesthetics.
- This landscape fosters responsiveness.
- Any blurring of ideas or artists is intentional.
- Be attentive to the dynamics of the present moment rather than to predetermined structures or assumptions.
- What is happening now not What was expected to happen.
- Performance by nature has a before, a during, and an after.
- "Improvisation is thought formed by passion informed by knowledge." — Pianist, composer, and poet Cecil Taylor
- Sometimes you are present and sometimes you miss an opportunity and sometimes you happen upon it.
- Embrace this risk.
- Improvisation requires individual response and collective interaction. "Hard to be isolated in the community." — Composer, improviser, and sculptor Douglas R. Ewart
- Sightlines always contain blindspots.
- Improvisation is often encountered as a forced construction rather than as emancipatory force
- Receptive borders are better than restrictive boundaries.
- Sometimes to be properly responsive you need to discard rules you yourself abide by and take for granted.
- Improvisation and collectivity are integral to democracy.
- "What if America cared about black people as much as it cares about black culture?"— Filmmaker Arthur Jafa

—Anthony Elms, Chief Curator

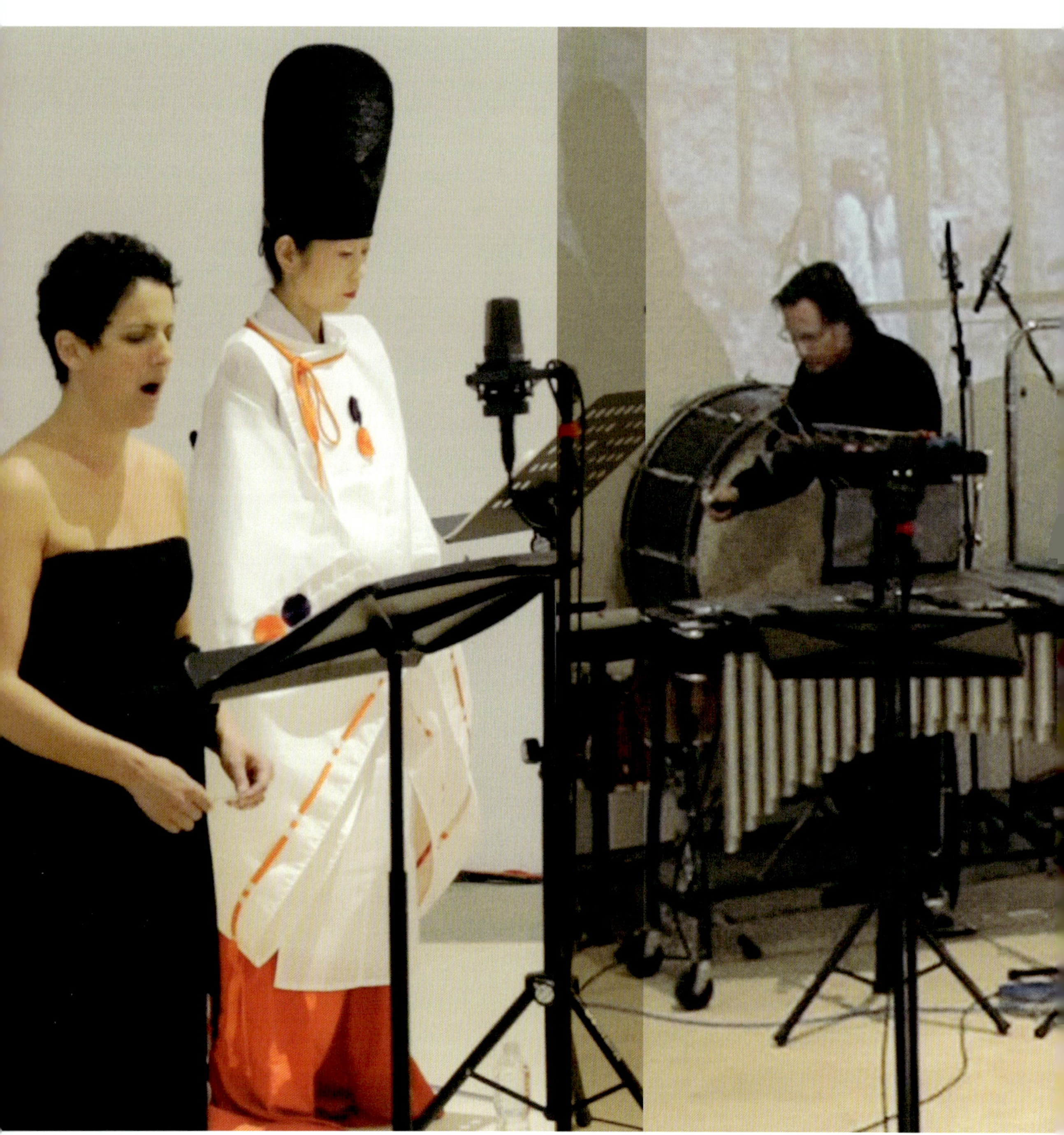

A Line Becomes a Circle

Miya Masaoka

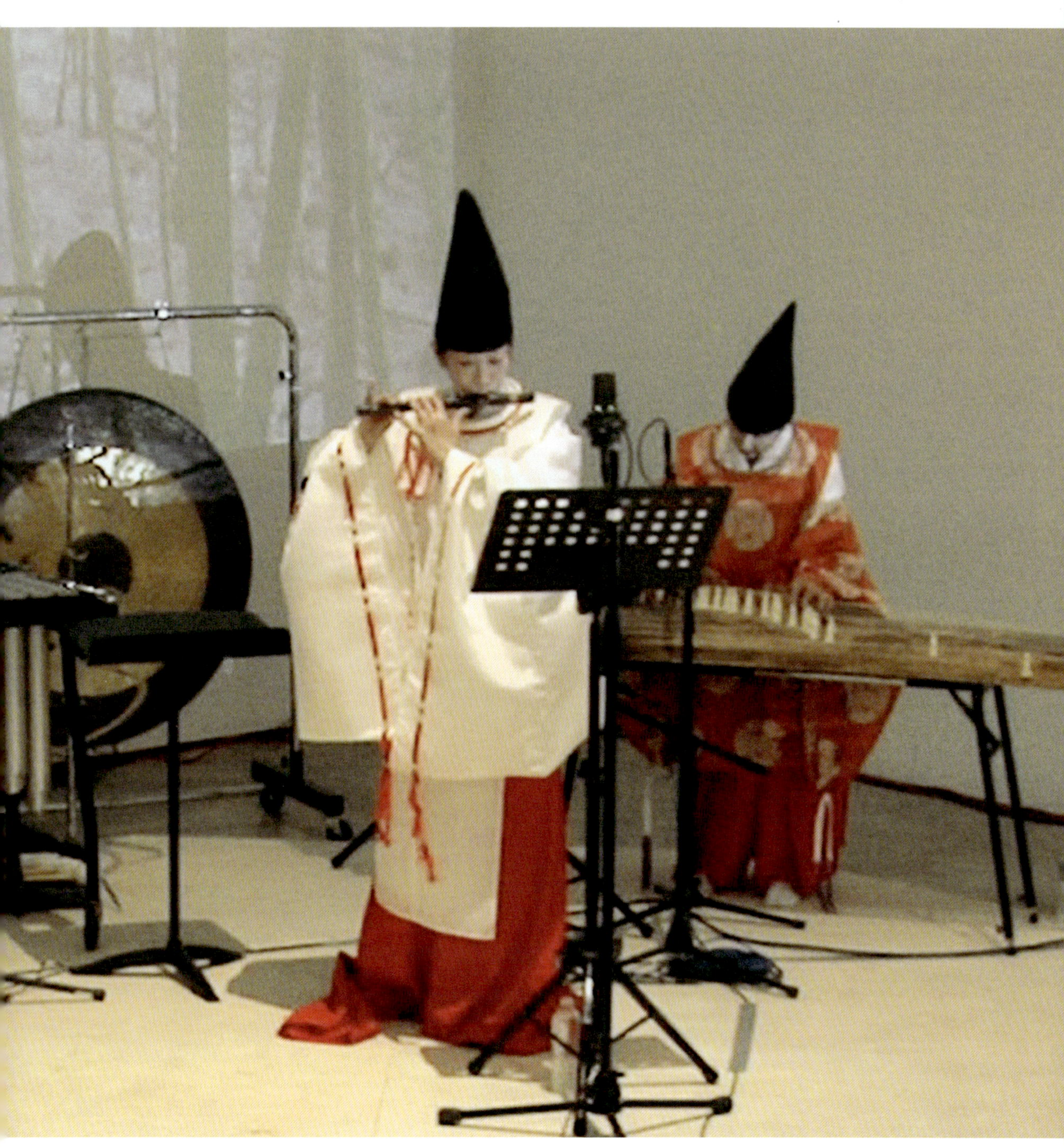

A chamber opera composed by Miya Masaoka. Excerpts of poetry by Haiku poet Shiki Masaoka (1867–1902). Makiko Sakurai, vocals; Noh and Shomyo, movement; Ann Moss, soprano; Chris Nappi, percussion; Miya Masaoka, composition, koto, vocals, movement. Video filmed at the Masaoka Castle ruins in Matusyama, Japan. Editing by Alice Baird.

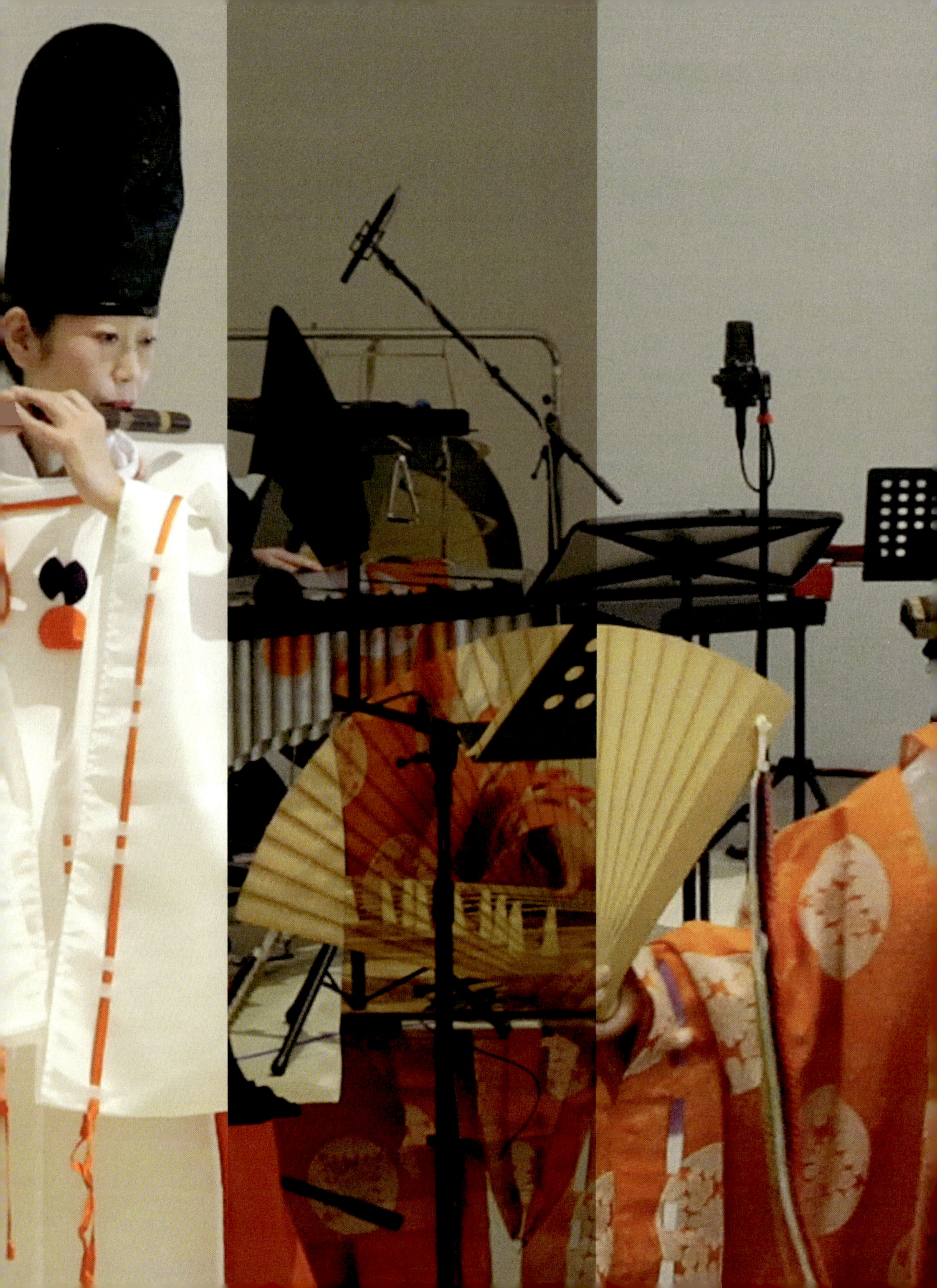

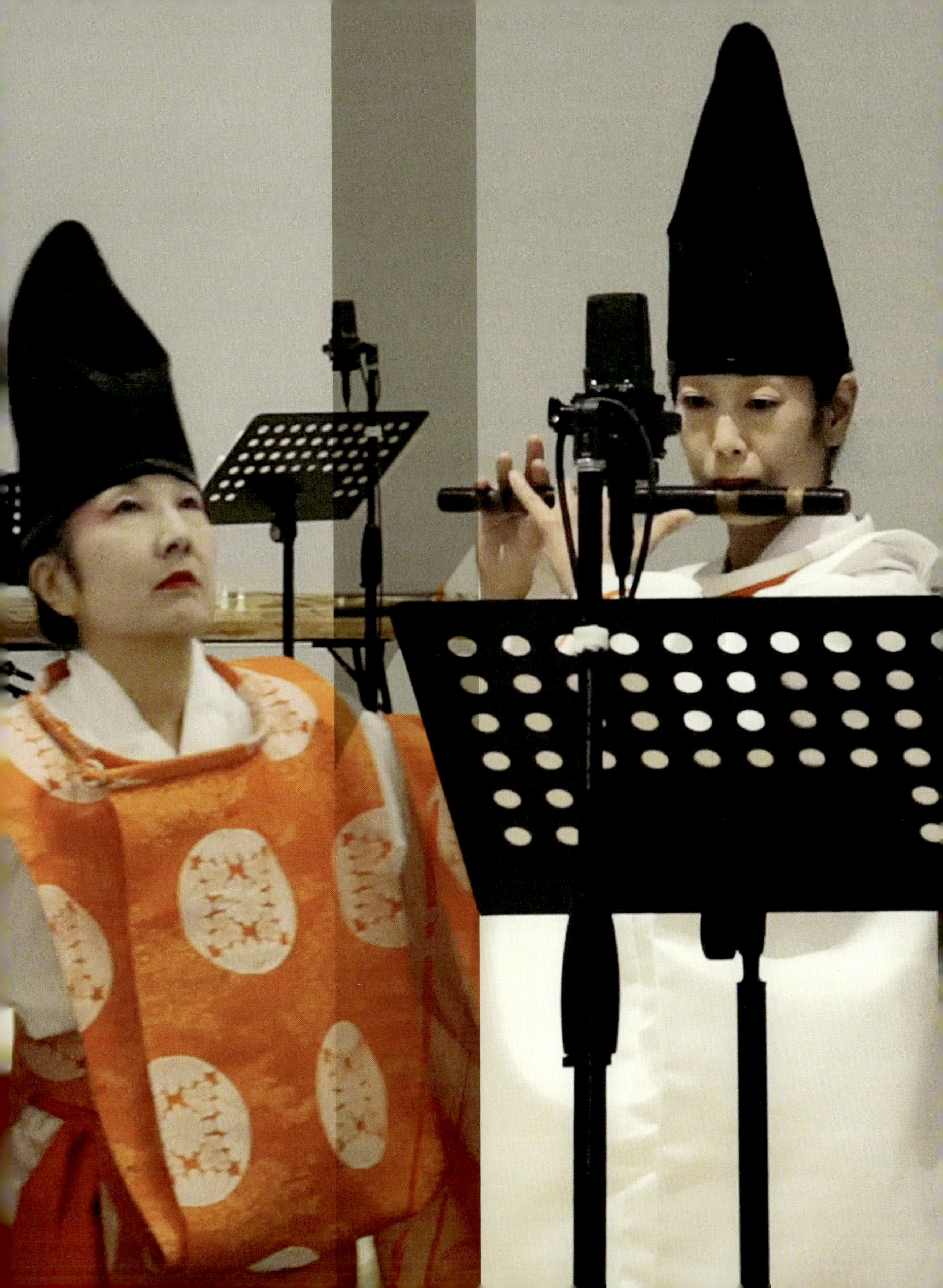

A Line Becomes a Circle
Miya Masaoka

An ancestor on my father's side, Shiki Masaoka, was from Matsuyama, Japan, where he lived and worked during the nineteenth century and was a major figure in developing modern haiku and tanka poetry. Known for breaking many of the haiku "rules," Shiki Masaoka introduced humor, everyday life, and other forbidden subject matter in haiku. At times he refused to include a season of the year in every haiku, a previous requirement. He also wrote an experimental Noh play that was never performed or translated. My grandparents were born in the Meiji era in Japan, and I was very moved researching his life, and the people of the Meiji era, an era that quickly and abruptly transitioned into modernity. In a sense, *A Line Becomes a Circle* pays tribute to my distant relative Shiki Masaoka, yet brings the text into a contemporary context, setting the words in both Japanese and English.

Haiku is a highly condensed and minimal form. What is not being said, and words that remain can be considered–what I call "the non-blank space"–is a kind of materiality and exists as a certain form of minimalism in the gagaku music, visual art, and poetry of traditional Japanese arts.

Most of the poetry in this work was written when Shiki was a young man at the height of his creative life, he died from tuberculosis at the age of thirty-two.

The title, *A Line Becomes a Circle*, is my idea of "a play on words" from a quote by the Indian Hindu monk, Swami Vivekananda, living in the same time period, but of course a different location from Shiki Masaoka. Here is the original Swami Vivekananda quote:

There is no motion in a straight line. Everything moves in a circle; a straight line, infinitely produced, becomes a circle....

Tanka poems have five lines, and there are five lines in a pentagon shape that can be curved to morph into the form of a circle. This circle graphically represents endlessness not only in temporality, but in all things as well as implying movement and motion—the act of transformation, evolution and things not staying the same but becoming something different, embracing a new identity. One last note: Shomyo singing, used for *A Line Becomes a Circle*, is unusual in the lexicon of Japanese music as improvisation is a part of its tradition.

**Two haikus and one kanshi poem excerpt used in
A Line Becomes a Circle**

*If someone asks
tell them I am still alive autumn wind*

I do not know the day my pain will end
yet in the little garden
I had them plant
seeds of autumn flowers

Excerpt:
*I envy myself the wanderings I once had.
Cramped and cringing, I never go out the gate,
Thinking only how the rounding years go by.*

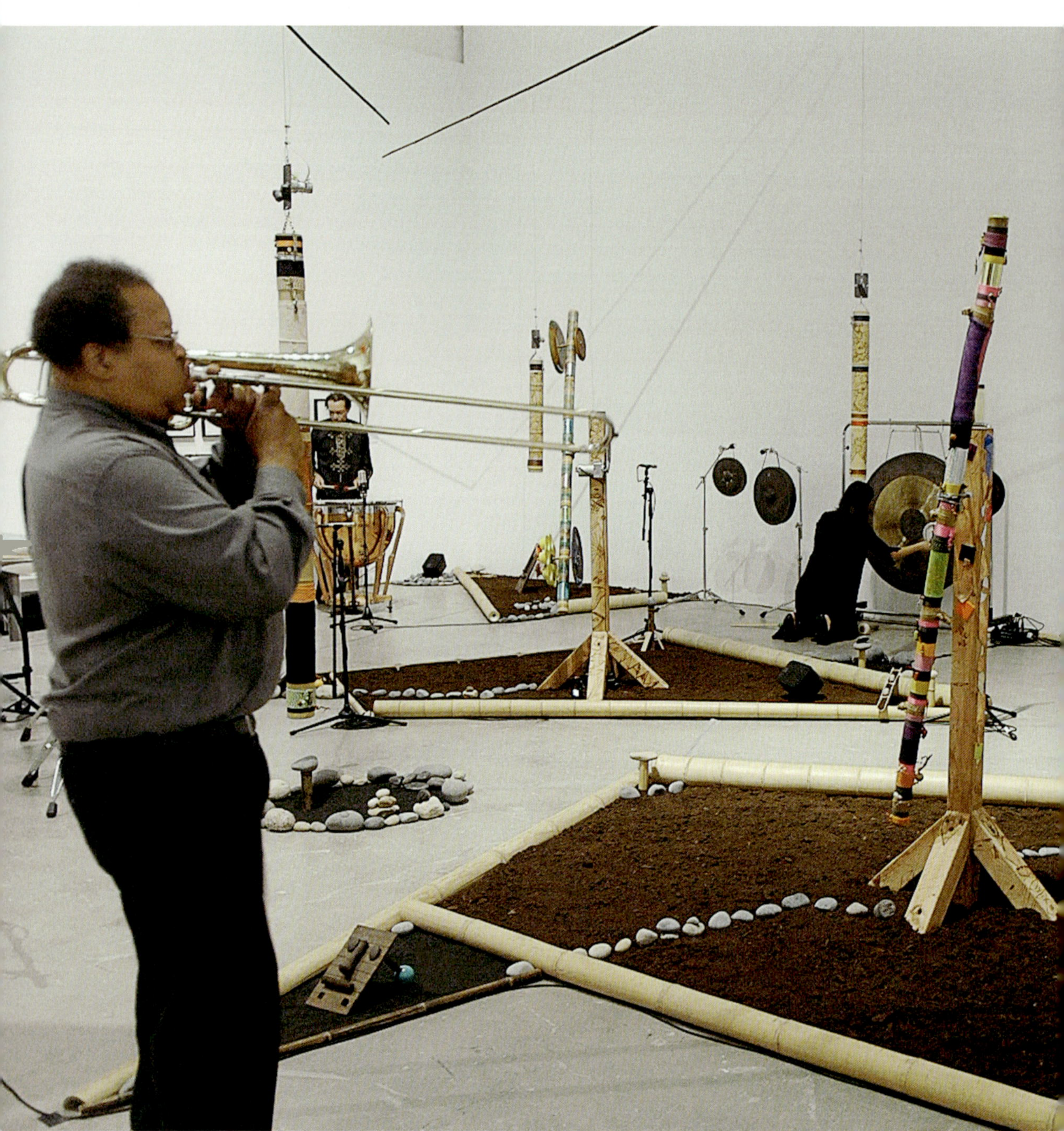

George Lewis

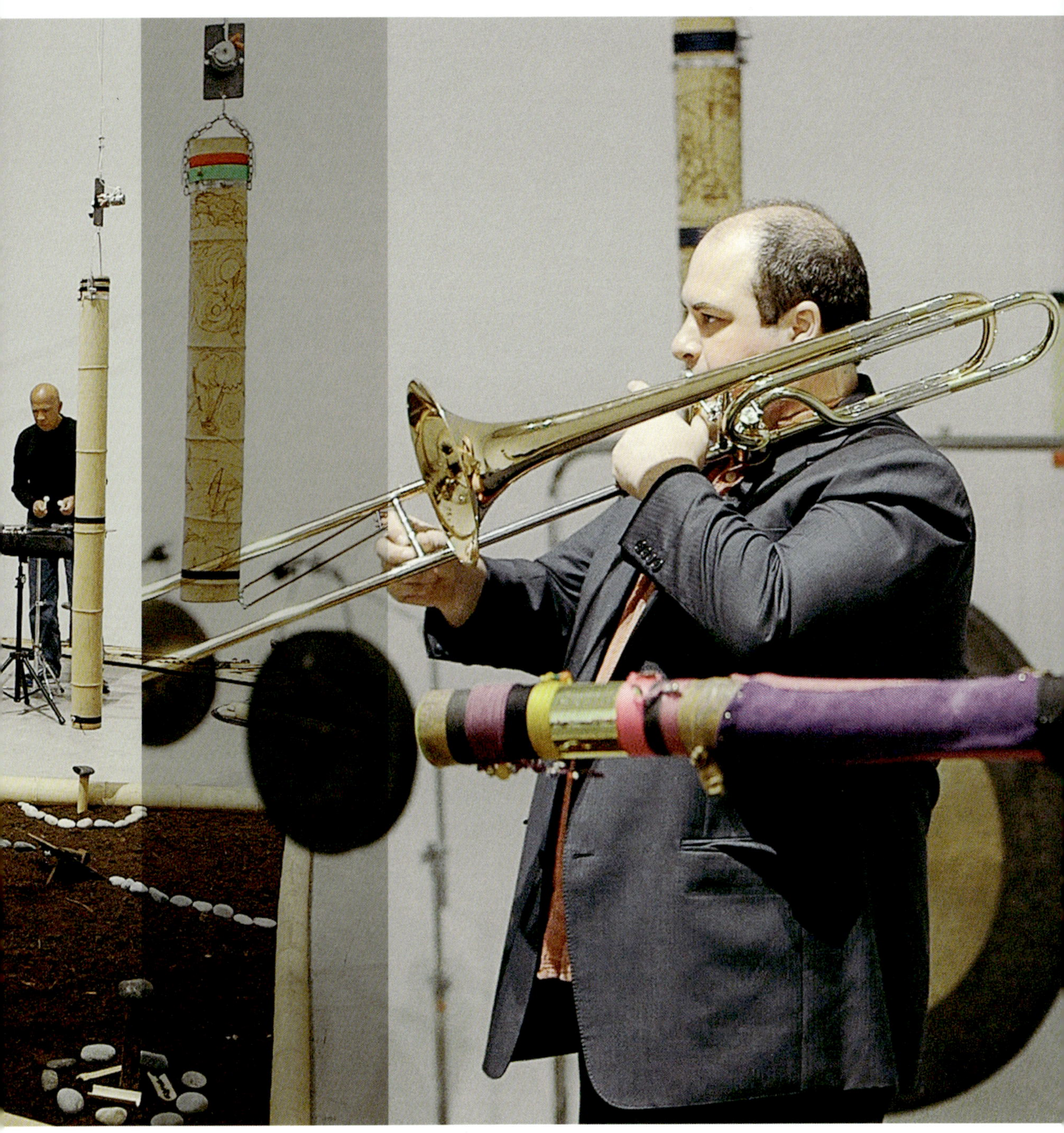

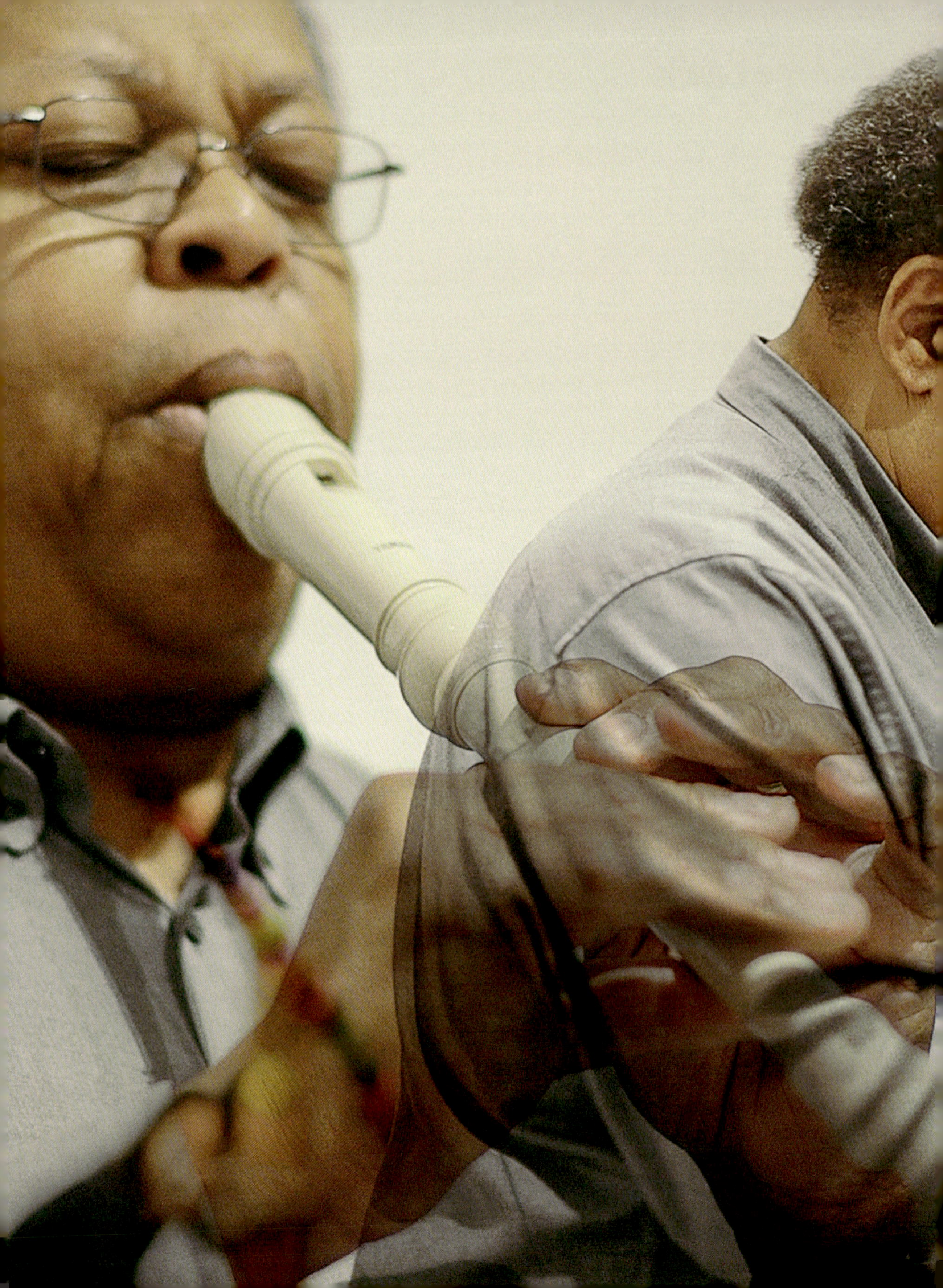

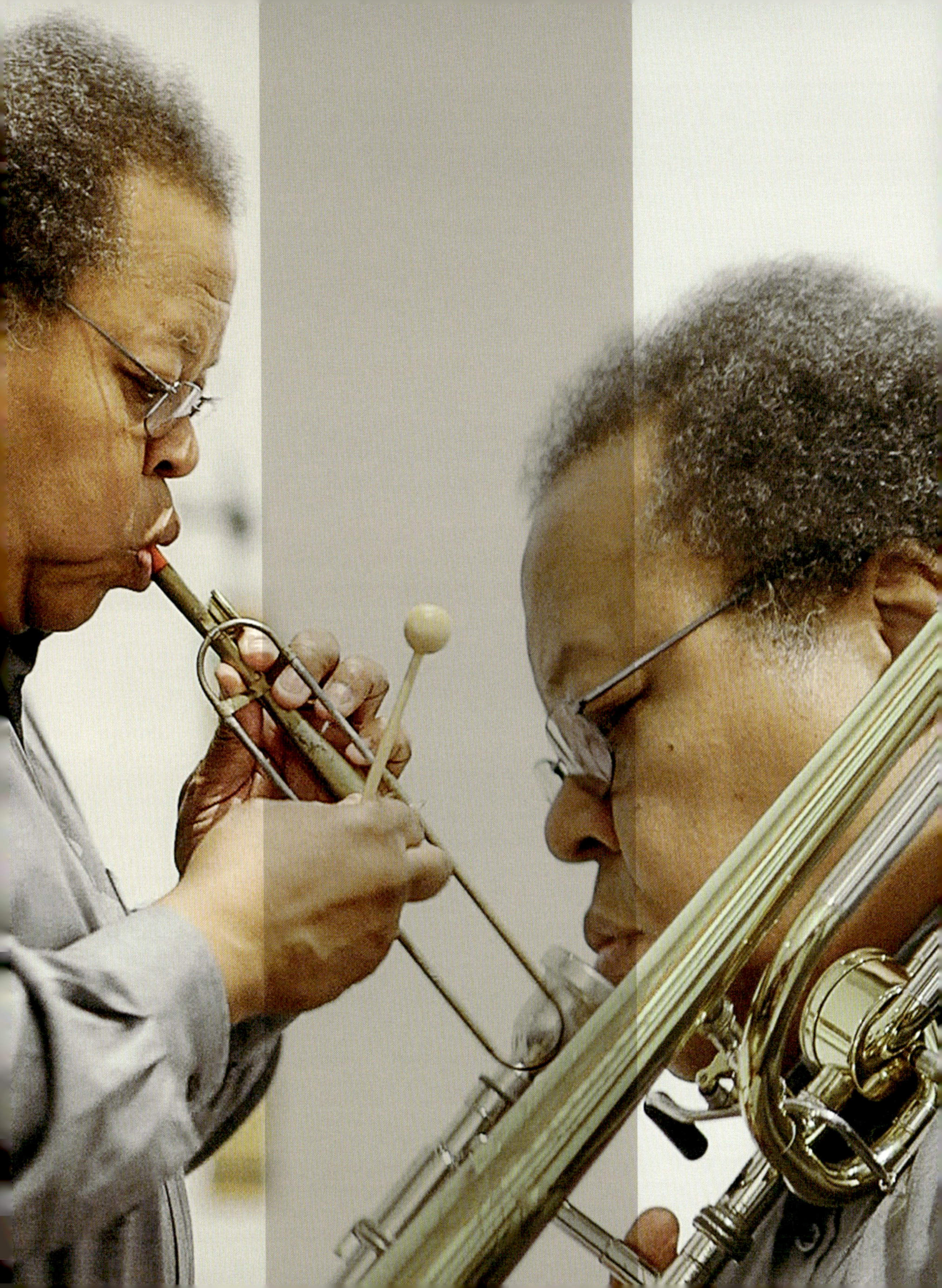

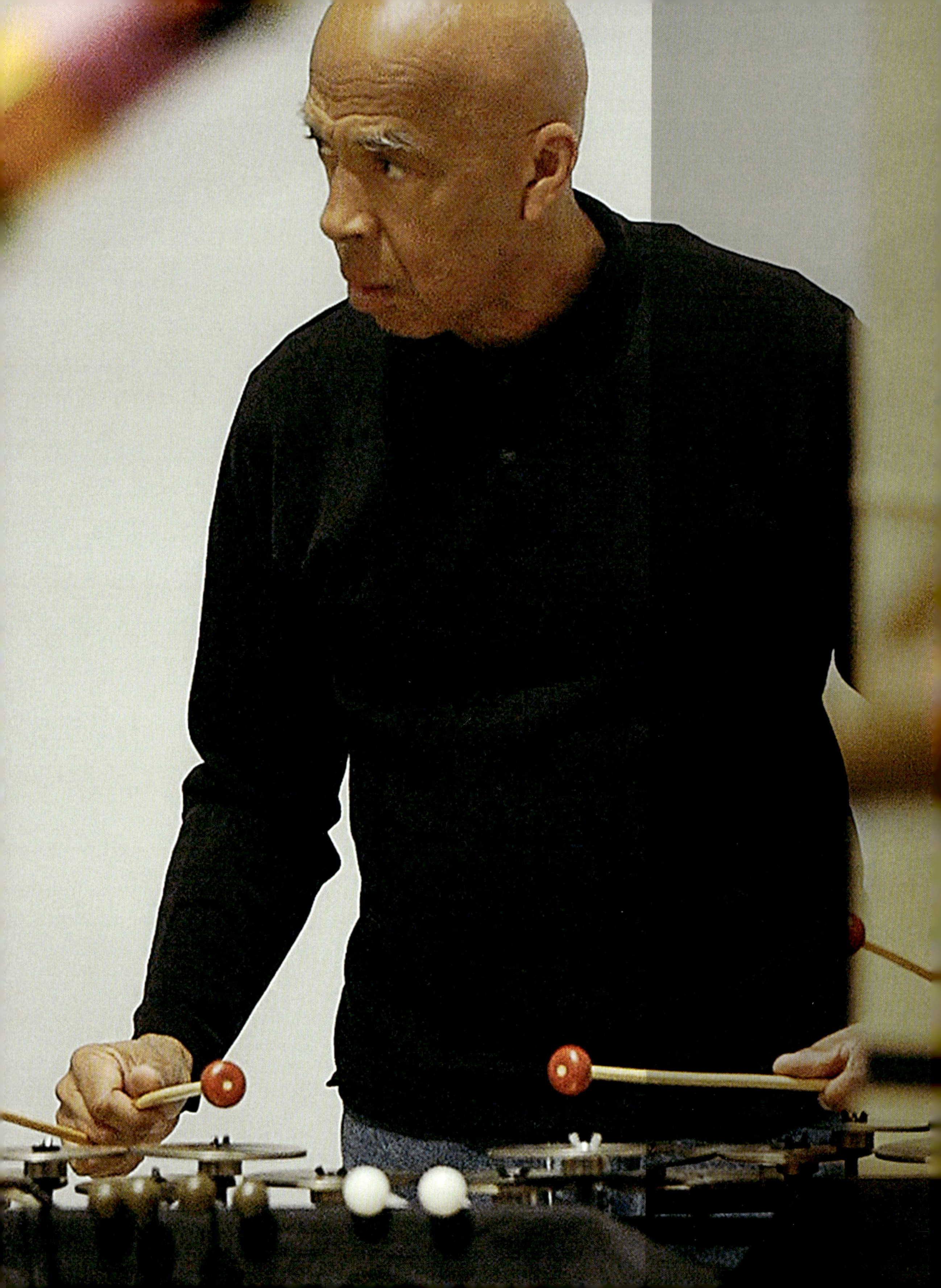

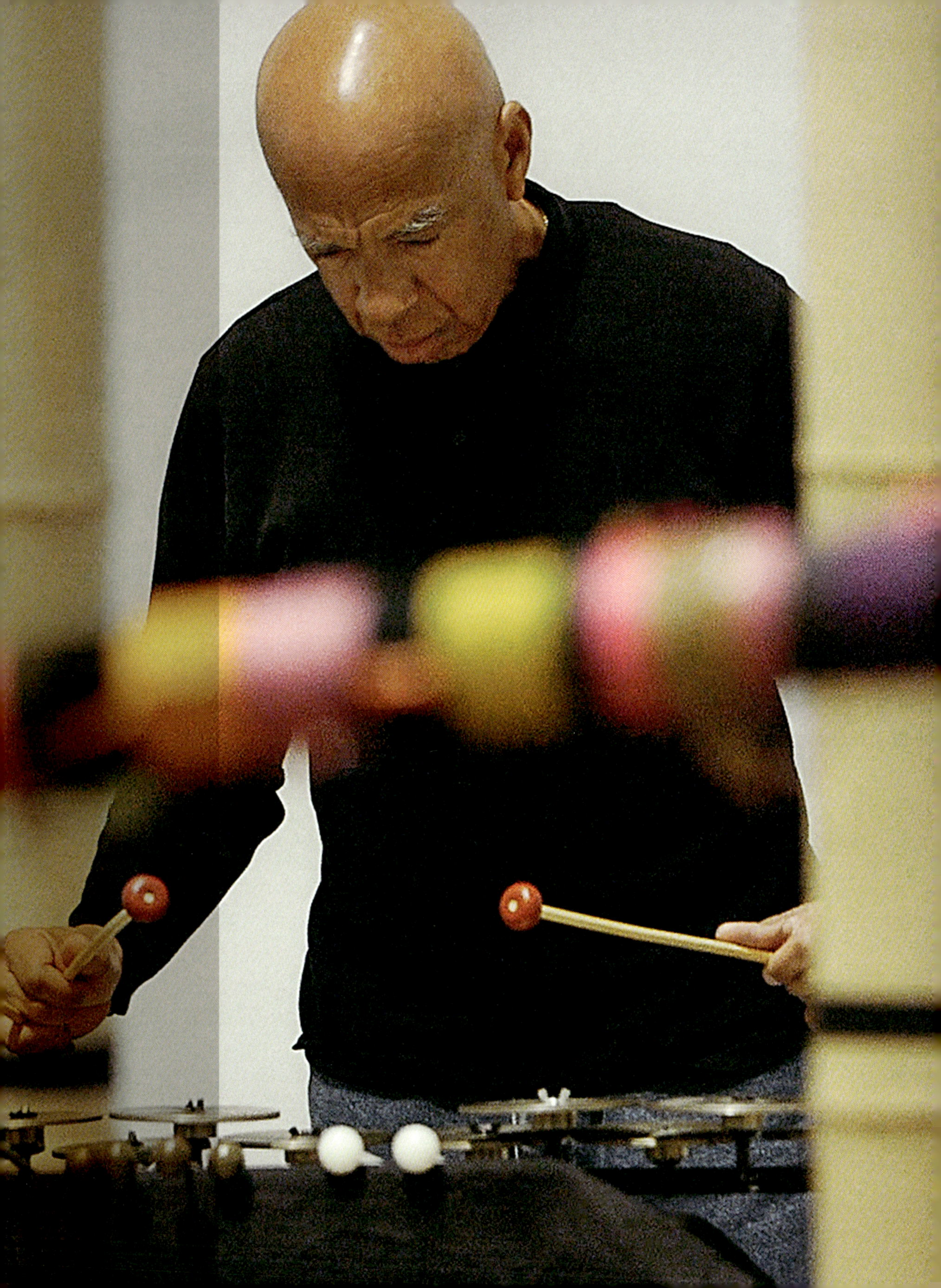

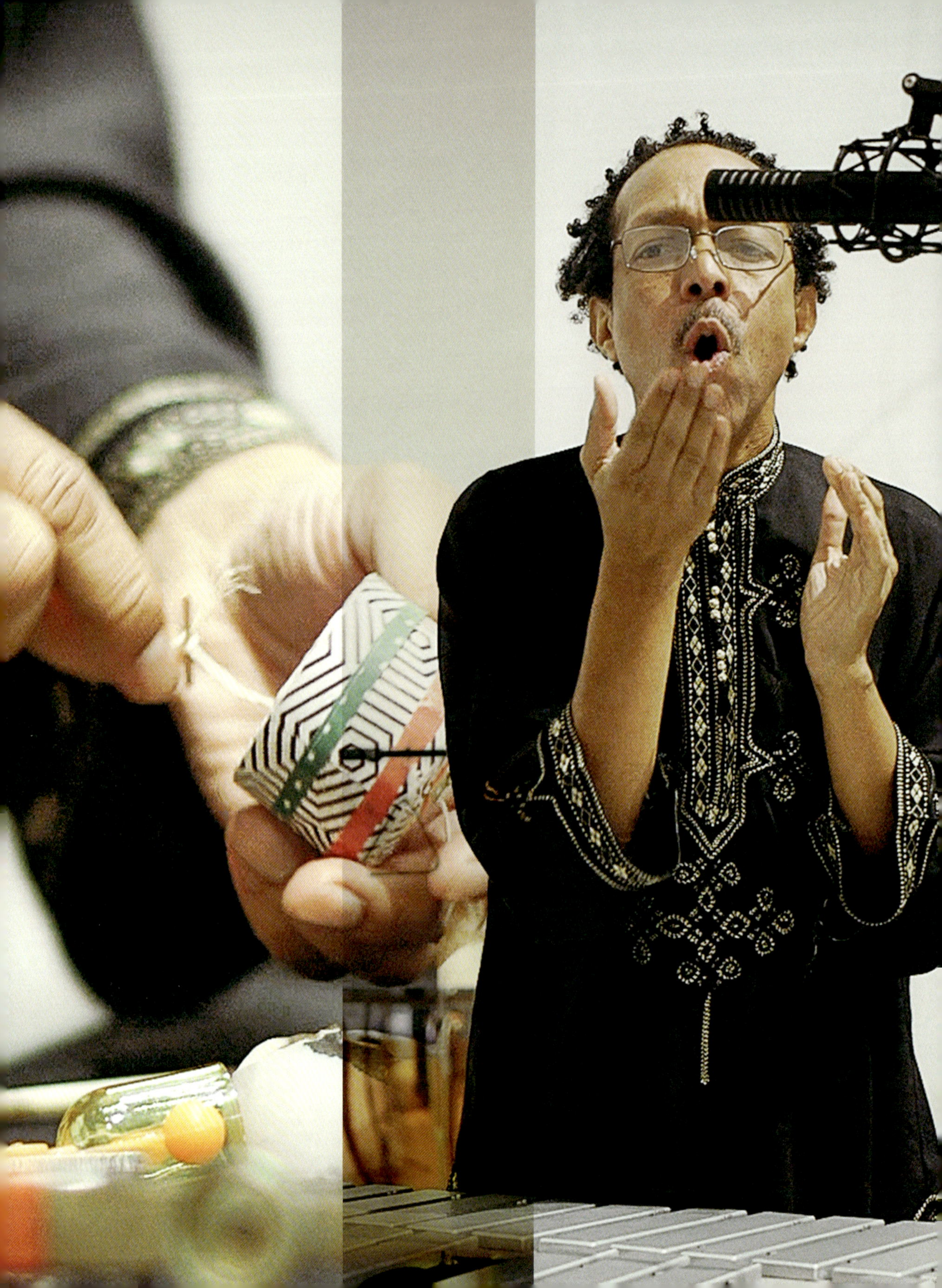

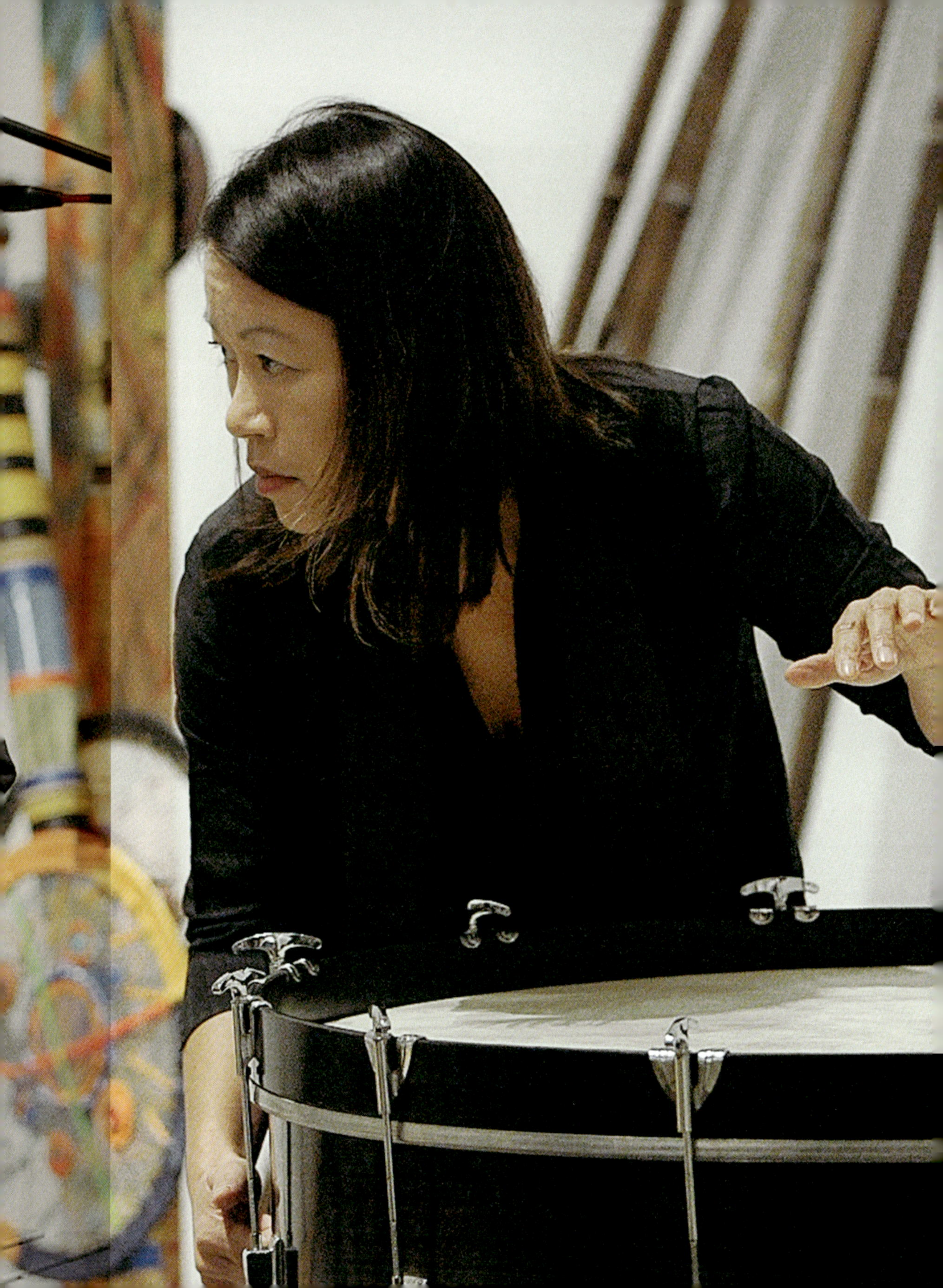

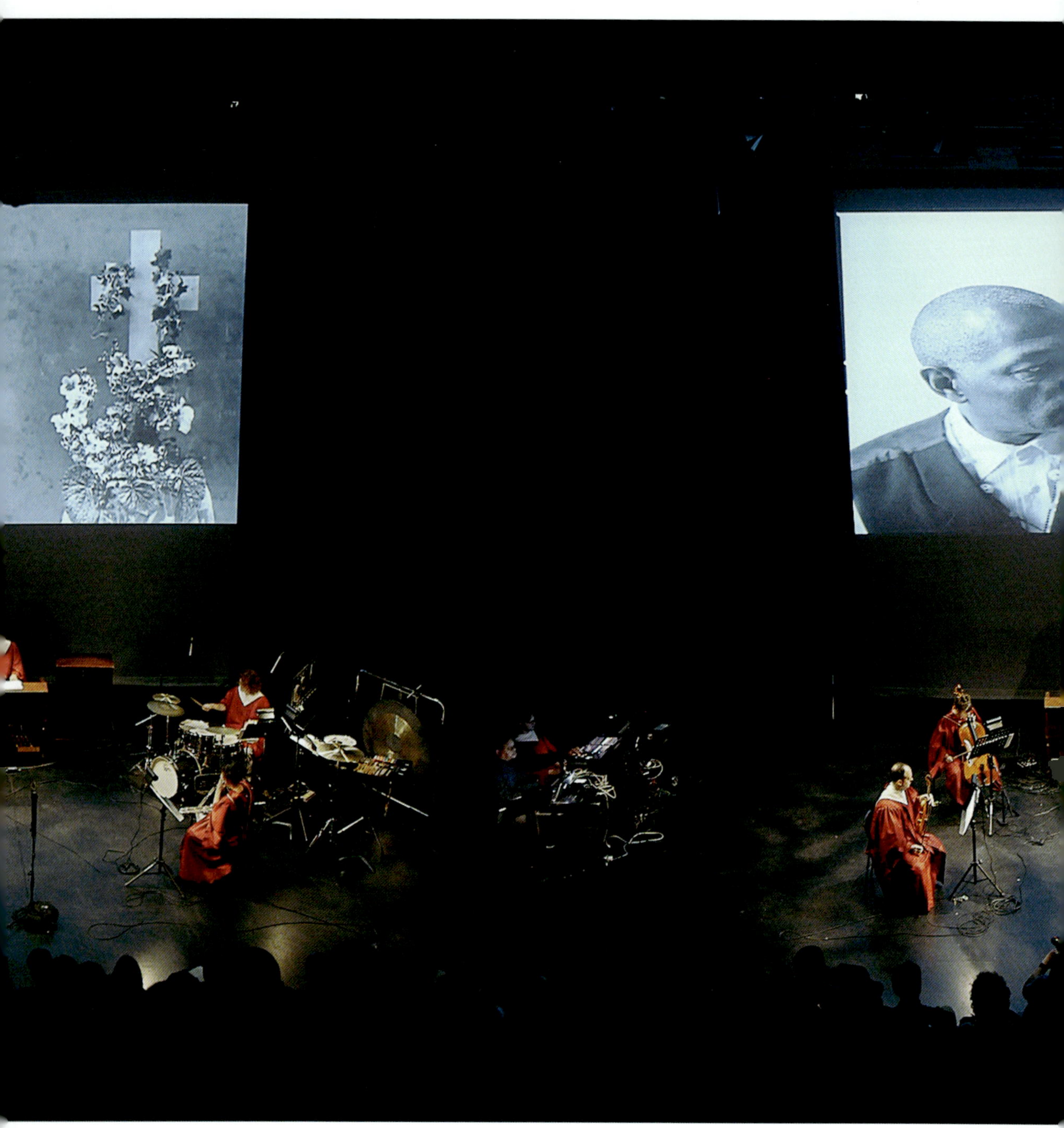

A Recital for Terry Adkins

George Lewis and Ensemble Pamplemousse

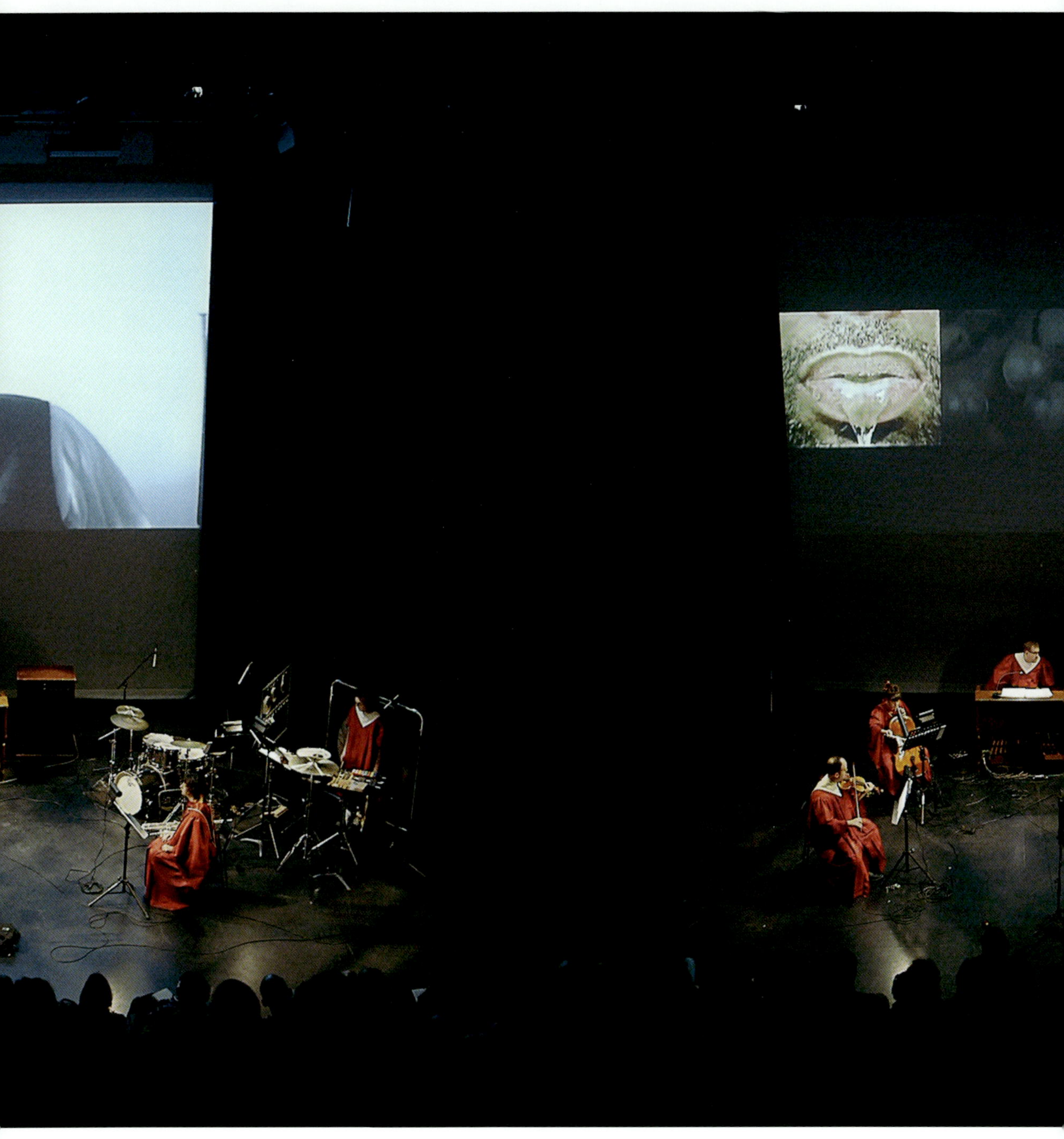

David Broome, Natacha Diels, Andrew Greenwald, Bryan Jacobs, George Lewis, Jessica Marino, Joshua Modney

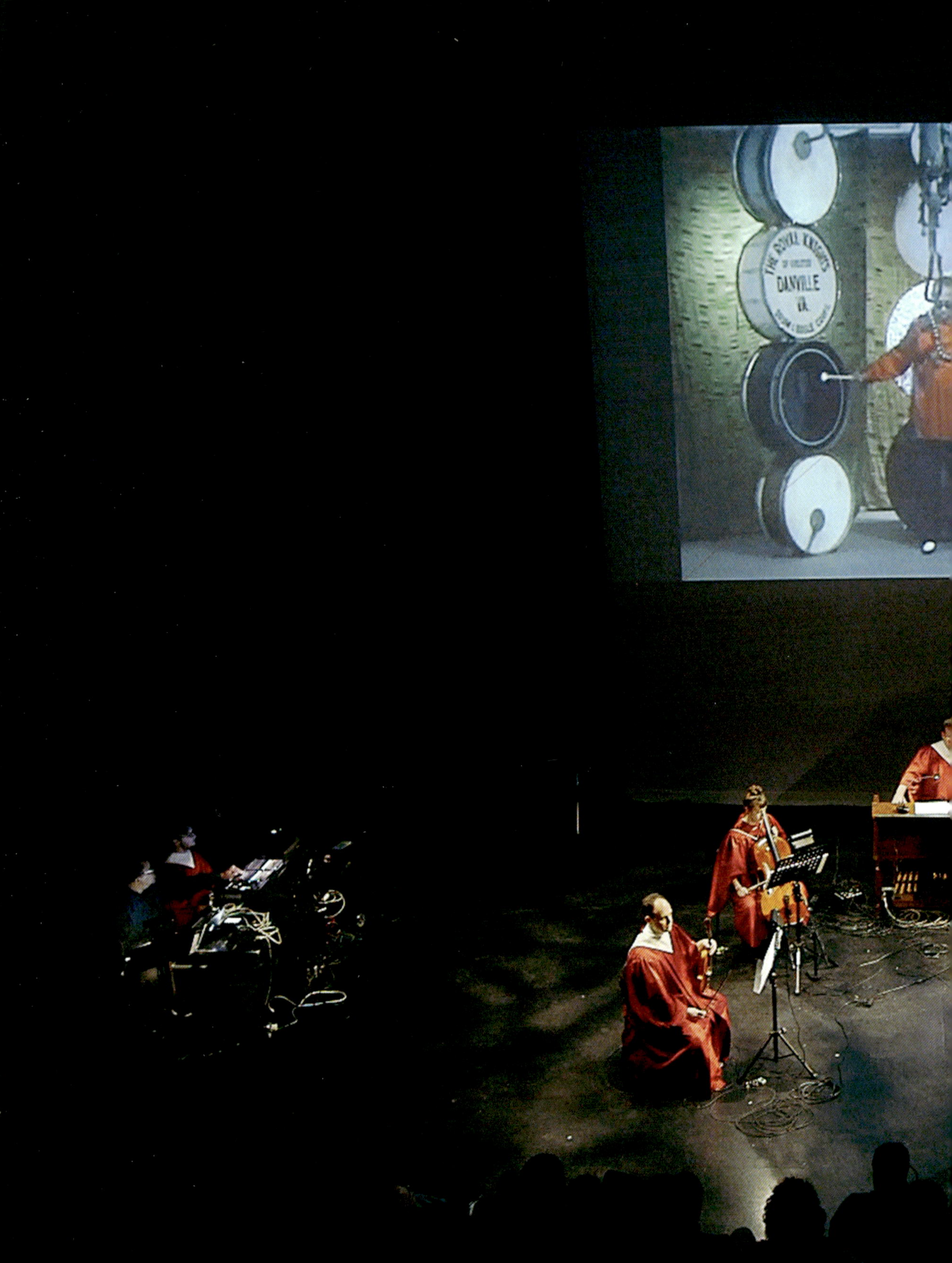
THE ROYAL KNIGHTS
DANVILLE
VA.

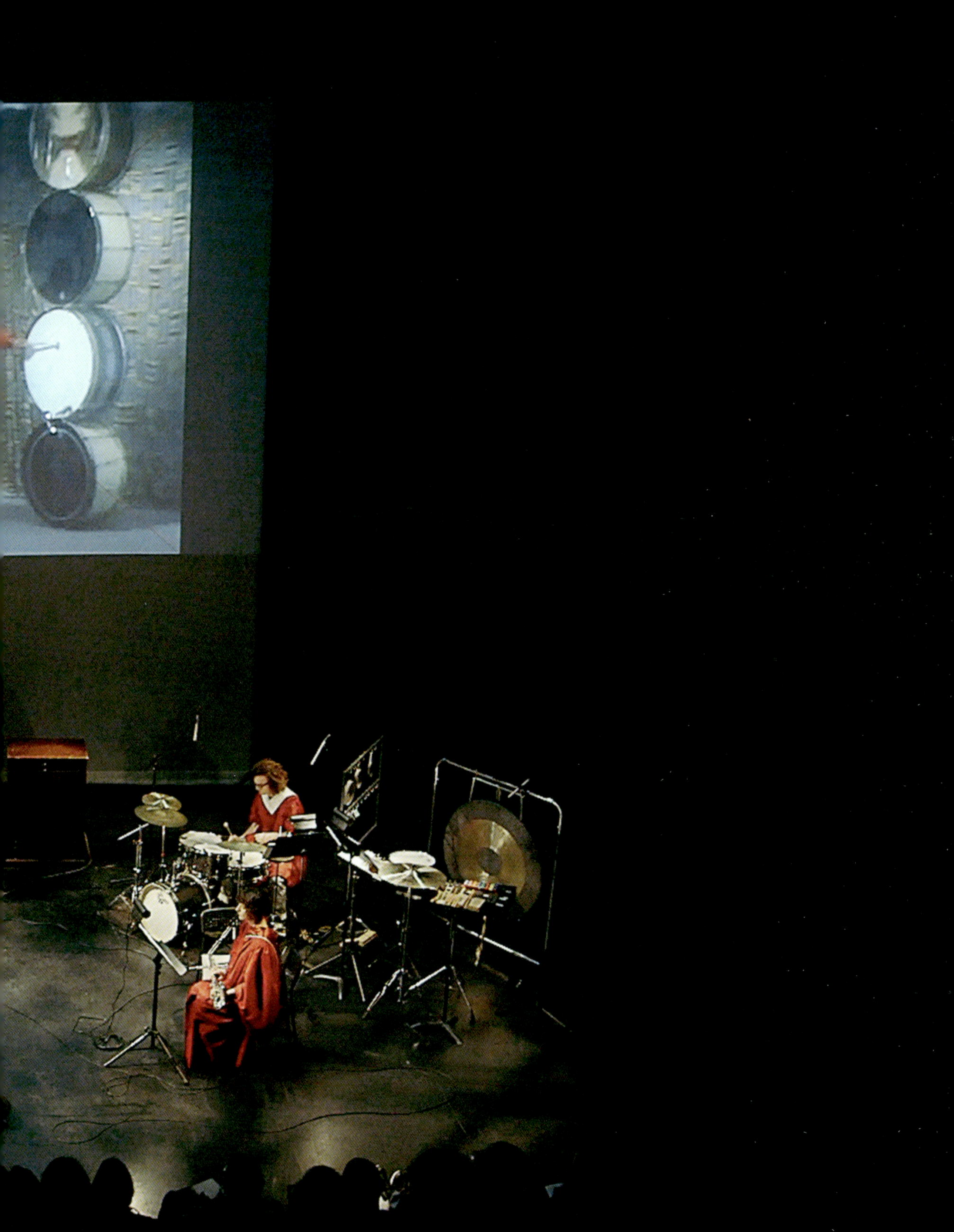

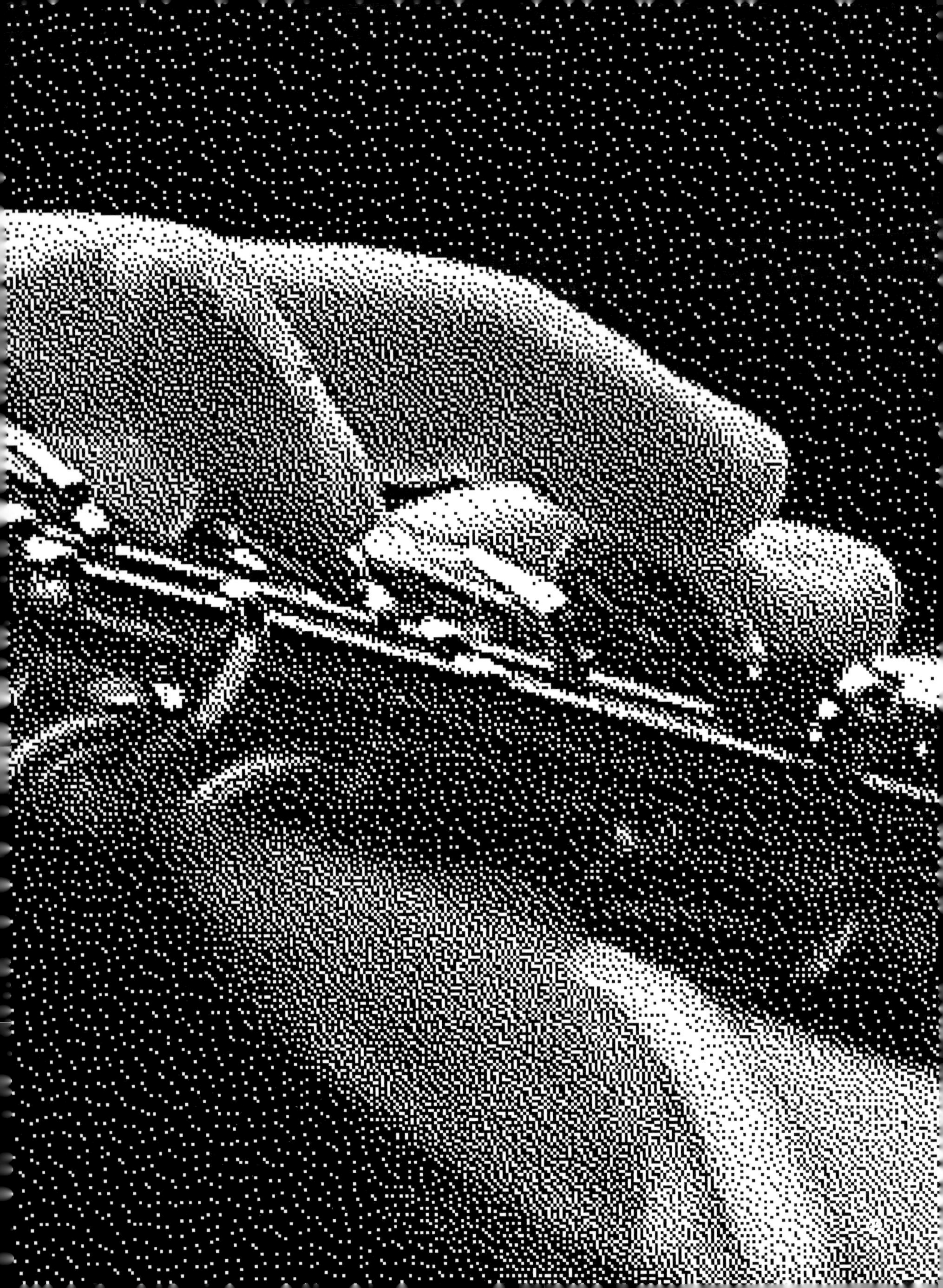

A Recital for Terry Adkins
George Lewis

Terry Adkins (1953–2014)

Artist, performer, and multi-instrumentalist Terry Adkins received a BS from Fisk University in 1975, an MS from Illinois State University in 1977, and an MFA from the University of Kentucky in 1979. Adkins had a solo museum exhibition at the Whitney Museum of American Art (1995), and his work is included in the permanent collections of the Hirshhorn Museum and Sculpture Garden, Washington DC; the High Museum of Art, Atlanta; the Studio Museum in Harlem, New York; the Metropolitan Museum of Art, New York; the Museum of Modern Art, New York; and the Tate, London. Adkins's final body of work—three-dimensional representations of bird songs, constructed from cymbals and other percussion instruments—was posthumously featured in the 2014 Whitney Biennial.

Adkins was celebrated for his Recitals, which began as live performances scheduled as part of the run of his gallery installations. As Adkins said in an interview with me in 2014, he would present Recitals "at points at which I feel that the installation has to be rejuvenated by another activity, so it's not just sitting there the whole time. Every once in a while it gets another shot in the arm by a Recital appearance." A major component of these works was Adkins' Lone Wolf Recital Corps, which has been active since its first performances in Zurich in 1987. Frequent collaborators in the Corps include Jamaaladeen Tacuma, Bill Cole, Arthur Flowers, and Robert Wisdom. The final Lone Wolf Recital Corps performance was held at the Studio Museum in Harlem in November 2013.

Recitals were often dedicated to historical figures with resonance in American culture, like Jean Toomer, Herman Melville, Frederick Douglass, John Brown, Bessie Smith, and Matthew Henson. "In addition to an installation- based experience that includes sculptures, some of which can be activated to produce sound," Adkins told me, "there is the live component that borrows and performs from their legacy, be it literary, poetic, historical or otherwise." The Adkins Recital eventually became an intimate interpenetration between the sculptural exhibition and its performative aspect, a unique hybrid of the historical and the synaesthetic. The Recitals challenged "experiencers" to forsake both ocular- and auriculo-centrism in favor of a composite experience that places eyes and ears in dialogue—and at times, in confrontation.

"Without the live component," Adkins told Daniela Salvioni in 2010, "the installations wouldn't be Recitals. That is the part that activates and amplifies the biographical data of the individual, the legendary, the lore surrounding these people. It's a way of reclaiming and upholding their legacies, reviving them." This Recital for Terry Adkins may be taken in that spirit.

Bridging *Endless Shout* with *The Freedom Principle: Experiments in Art and Music, 1965 to Now*, artist Jennie C. Jones and composer and musicologist George Lewis came together with a very congenial lunchtime audience for a discussion of Jones's work and its implications.

George Lewis: I've been chasing Jennie around the world for a couple of years now, ever since the *Artforum* people asked me to create a blurb for … was it the Smithsonian?

Jennie C. Jones: Yes, the Hirshhorn Museum exhibition, *Higher Resonance*.

GL: They gave me 150 words, which clearly was not anywhere near enough for someone who does all the things she does.[1] She's that multi-voiced artist I'm always trying to write about—sound art collages, immersive sound installations, sculptures, works on paper, all kinds of things, with a sharp engagement with histories and memories of sound and music.

    The piece upstairs in the show, *Quiet Gray with Red Reverberation #2*—part of a series?

JCJ: There's a body of work from 2014, *Tone*, the exhibition with the Melba Liston piece, which we'll talk about later. So this was one of two sisters, kind of.[2]

GL: You said the red represents "reverberation." We see all these things in your work like reverberation, or metaphors relating to sound. In fact, this series of pieces is functional, I think, in terms of sound. Do you agree with that?

JCJ: Absolutely. I started as a painter a million years ago, and left painting and took a very long sort of walk before coming back to the dreaded canvas. And I was only able to do that through a deep investigation into materials. I always saw painting more as an object than a window. Painting isn't necessarily a picture-making device; it is a functional object in a room. So to start there with painting as an object in a room leads into the physics of acoustics in a space, and how objects in a room affect sound. So after going on two separate paths, working with acoustic panels, and integrating sound-absorbing materials into the work visually, I finally built this bridge, so I wasn't just making a sound piece and having drawings that were illustrative, but trying to merge those two things in one space.

GL: I'm excited about all of these, but I don't even know what some of these things are. What's a bass trap?

JCJ: I got these used from a guy in California who was disassembling his recording studio. He made these bass traps; they're packed with mineral wool and fiberglass, and they're mounted one in each corner in recording studios to literally be bass traps and absorb the lower frequencies. They don't always look like this. This object has been taken from the floor and put on a pedestal, and inverted with feet put on it.

GL: The thing that amazes me about it is that it's got to have the same function in a gallery or in any space as it does in a recording studio. It's almost as if by absorbing sound, you can listen to its effect, even though it's not making sound itself. And that's one of the interesting things about you as a sound artist—you take on absorption. It's not just broadcasting, it's absorbing sound.

    Actually, you had an exhibition called *Absorb/ Diffuse*. Could you talk about that a little bit?

JCJ: That was the first exhibition at The Kitchen in 2011.[3] That was the first exhibition where I started incorporating these materials and left the more illustrative methods that I was just talking about, where I was doing a lot more drawing of sound, looking at how things are connected. And now we're wireless, so even those works feel a little bit dated already, in just a decade.

Jennie C. Jones and George Lewis

Absorb/Diffuse was the first time I really edited a sound piece that was completely instrumental. I had always leaned a bit on the poetics of song lyrics. That was a tremendous launching pad for me, that show. It opened up a lot of other ways of thinking, and led to everyone paying attention. Evelyn Hankins from the Hirshhorn came to my apartment where I was working, and sat on the end of my bed because I had no studio. And we talked about modernism, minimalism, and sound, and the politics of what it is to be absorbed and consumed, which I hope is a metaphor in the work as well. And she gave me my first museum show.

The Kitchen, which you were at yourself for many years, is still such an important platform for experimental work.

GL: I was at The Kitchen way back in the halcyon days of the eighties.[4] A piece that was premiered there, Douglas R. Ewart's *Bamboo Forest*, became the basis for our collaborative work *Rio Negro,* which you'll see in the downstairs galleries. A lot of wonderful things happened at The Kitchen before, during and after I was there, which was from 1980 to '82. But a lot of it, at least in my time being there, was around challenging comfortable assumptions about place. And I don't mean geographical place; I mean the place of artists, especially artists who didn't fit the standard models.

So this is where I want to go a bit. I'm looking at the Tate Modern website and it's very informative. This section is all about "sound art"—art which uses sound both as its medium, what it is made out of, and as its subject, what it's about. That's already too narrow a definition for what Jennie is doing. This piece, *Quiet Gray with Red Reverberation #2*, isn't made out of sound, but it still engages sound in a very dramatic way and in one that's stretching of the definition. And there are more to come, as I see it.

The other thing is, you know there are some wonderful people, like Susan Philipsz who was the first sound artist to win the Turner Prize.[5] And there's Kurt Schwitters, the Swiss sound artist— they didn't have sound artists in 1932, they were still called composers. [laughter] His famous piece is *Ursonate*, and it sort of sounds a bit like this [imitates the composition].[6] That kind of performance, I'm pretty bad at that. [laughter] *Ur* in German means primordial. It's using these primordial Indo-European syllables.

Nowadays, when you write a piece with voice and you're going to make weird sounds, they tell you to use the International Phonetic Alphabet, IPA.[7] But in 1932 they didn't have that, so people were saying, "Oh, this is an *Urtext*"—that meant a primordial European text. That's sort of the problem with this, when you look at what goes on. It's all about the usual suspects—Russolo, the fascist, they don't talk much about that [laughter], F. T. Marinetti, and those people, Dada, Surrealism, Duchamp, Cage, and other wonderful people. Bill Fontana, there's a lot of people there, Bruce Nauman, it's fantastic. Now, I look at this and I say, hey where's Jennie on this list? She's as cool as anybody on this list. And where are the other people of color?

JCJ: But what's interesting about the territory that I try to dig into and what we were talking about at first is this: When we think about how performance art and sound art bump up against each other, or how experimental or avant-garde music and jazz bump up against these things too, they never quite make it into each other's histories and narratives or stories. For example, there's the Rahsaan Roland Kirk film where he's with Cage, called *Sound??* from 1966.[8] Their narratives run in parallel, but they're never in the same shot. And that's sort of a way to frame it. They cut back and forth, from Kirk performing, which looks like it could connect to Ben Patterson, getting the audience to participate, passing out slide whistles and really engaging the audience in this performative way that tips its hat to performance art and kind of talks about jazz and talks about sound art all at once. And then they show

Cage separately, having these profound moments, and having these asides about listening.

GL: I love that film because it reifies in terms of montage the kinds of separations we're talking about. And this is something I've always been a little concerned with about histories of sound, histories of music. It all comes from an offhand remark that Cecilia Dougherty, the video artist, made at a Bard seminar. She said something like, "Well, in all these histories, what you want to ask first is: where are the women?" And once you ask that, then you ask where are the … whoever? Because often people aren't there, and you wonder why they're not there. I've written a bunch of stuff on Ben Patterson, including an *Artforum* piece I just finished, which is about to be published any day now.[9] My beef is really with the historians. When you look at the artists, they all say, oh yeah, Ben was right there with us. Ask Emmett Williams, Alison Knowles, everybody. But the historians, they snip the guy off. How can you do that?[10] I was thinking, what about Terry Adkins?[11] What about you? We were talking about Nick Cave's soundsuits, and Charles Gaines, who's also in this show. There are a lot of people out there, and what we have to do is be a little more vigilant and place pressure on these kinds of incomplete narratives. But the only way to do it is for everybody in the audience—now, you can all do your part—you can come to these shows and ask, "Hey, where is everybody?" You'll have plenty of opportunity to do it, I guarantee you. [laughter] There won't be a real lack of that.

Jennie, you talked about modernism, minimalism, and jazz, which are three huge, almost readymades at this point. Those are themes in your work? Or things you react against?

JCJ: I feel like they're almost an alphabet that I can play with, to reconstruct my own sentences and my own paragraphs using some of that very coded formal methodology. My natural leaning has always been very formal and very minimal. That took some time to reconcile because it's not a particularly profitable or popular way for a black woman to be making visual work. But that language and my ability to hopefully reposition it, to make moments of revisionist history

by putting things in a different context, and by equating formalism to the Modern Jazz Quartet, is a way to kick that open, bridging Coltrane with Abstract Expressionism, or whatever parallels that were happening historically, as a very rich soil to take off from and push in my own work.

GL: Well, you just played out another one that I want to unpack a little bit, about minimalism not being the most profitable engagement for a black woman. You feel like saying more about that?

JCJ: No, except that I still have a lot of student loans and have been living in my same crappy apartment. [laughter]

GL: That's very upfront. I have an article now about Julius Eastman, who was a gay black singer-composer. A lot of us knew him; he passed away a number of years ago. There's a new book about his work, *Gay Guerrilla*, which is the title of one of his pieces. Julius certainly belongs right there at the origins of sonic minimalism, but never seems to quite get there with the historians until very recently, when people like Mary Jane Leach and Renee Levine Packer, who edited the book, have put Julius back into that group.[12] Because there's always something where—well, maybe student loans are one part of it— but also just the framing, that somehow minimalism isn't where black people reside.

JCJ: Well, of course. If we rip the Band-Aid off we have to talk about how the arts in general are more market-driven than they've ever been. How does one participate in a system that's already broken? Do you woodshed? You just hunker down on your own and let that continue on while you continue doing your thing until, you know, maybe fifty years after you're gone they realize this was a critical voice that was not included in the discourse because it wasn't profitable for institutions or private galleries. But I am in a world that's very different from your world in the sense of commercial galleries, and having a lot of heartbreak over how they dictate cultural politics and discourses.

GL: Where they combine, I think, and part of my job, more as a person who writes than as a composer, is to speed up that process. Let's not have it be fifty years, let's have it be next week, or let's have it be right at the outset that you say "Oh wow!" Use your ears instead of using, I don't know, racism or something, which makes you deaf. If you're able to hear through the noise, then you can obviously hear John Coltrane as being an early minimalist.

JCJ: This is what you referenced in that essay. It was so perfect. And it made me listen with new perspective.

GL: It was just obvious. Those of you who know the piece, McCoy Tyner is playing this solo.[13] It's just the same stuff repeated over and over again. And the date is right, it's 1960. We're talking about La Monte Young's *Trio for Strings*, that's '58.[14] And Coltrane being a strong influence on the soprano saxophone on both La Monte and Terry Riley, Terry Jennings, all these Coltrane-influenced minimalist saxophone players, who we don't hear about for the same reason that people don't seem to think that there is anything other than gender transgression in the image of the Ben Patterson "Lick Piece," licking whipped cream off a white woman's body, an act for which he could have been lynched in large segments of the US. And people I guess are trying to bring that back now, the alt-right and so on, although hopefully they won't succeed.

But I didn't want to get too far away from your themes. This jazz thing.

JCJ: Even now, there's a part of me that just goes like this [cringes] when I hear the word "jazz." Because I immediately associate it with how much it was hijacked by Ken Burns, PBS, and the sort of Jazz with a capital Lincoln Center "J"—which is problematic in its own right for what they include and don't include in that history. You know, how long can we "take the A train"? [George laughs] There's an edgy freedom that is existing, that is intangible and more ephemeral than being stuck with the object-making and picture-making of visual art, and how long it took me to sort of play with that space to find a methodology for myself.

GL: Well, a work like your *Blues in C Sharp Minor for Teddy Wilson*, is there a kind of synesthesia taking place there? The blue …

JCJ: A little bit …

GL: Beyond just the obvious "Oh, it's the blues." What's going on there?

JCJ: This was the first, and I don't want to say last. But I always avoided blue for that very reason. [laughter]

GL: But suddenly you've got this one. Look at that blue …

JCJ: It completed a tri-tone kind of the theme for the show at the Contemporary Arts Museum Houston, because I'd only been really working with very hot colors as a way to talk about reverberation and to think about optics and sonic relationships.[15] The red pieces often bounce off the wall like the glow from a sign, and create a different kind of optic pairing with the sonic. Blue has something that grabs light and doesn't give off light. As a pigment it was something I avoided for a while, but it made sense for the show to wrap up the decade with this tri-tone thing. And these are the first pieces where I start to get more gestural. Incredibly aggressive and expressive for me, painting as painting again. And push up silence with noise—painting and gesture as noise. And then, the acoustic absorbers function as the end of a measure or a silencing marker.

GL: How does Teddy Wilson come into the dedication? [laughter] He's a cool guy, right?

JCJ: I just felt like that sharp edge was totally a C-sharp edge. Sometimes it's just a little hair of a moment that makes me think of a song, and that makes me think of a title. I don't often give titles specifically in that way, but it just clicked.

GL: Let me go on to another part of what you do, because there's so much of what you do. I'm interested in how you deal with consumption patterns, flows, transmission media. You've been looking at these things, they're absorption media, but you're also dealing directly with how sound is transmitted, how it travels. You can take something simple like a cassette box or something like that—and people still use them around the world, it's not all taking place through the Internet. People take a little cassette or a little CD and they put it in their pocket and they go somewhere in another part of the world and they pull it out. A musician from Tokyo, a friend of mine, told me this about when he visited Dakar, and then I saw it for myself when I went to Dakar at that club called Thiossane, where Youssou N'Dour played every night.[16] I was sitting right up in the front, and every so often the drummer or the keyboard player, they toss you a little bone. They look at you and they do something cool, like [imitates lively music playing]. And you're thrilled. [laughter] It's amazing. And after the gig, you can buy the cassette. Or they take it to the store and the next day you can buy it in the store, the physical object. So the physical transmission of sound, I think, is something that comes up quite a bit in your pieces.

JCJ: I don't know if I'm a Gen X-er, I don't know what I am, but we're witnessing the loss of the physical with listening, and how we listen, and how we don't walk across the room. A vinyl record can make you stand up and walk across the room and turn it over and have a pause, and have a moment, that anticipation of what's on the next side, or the liner notes or folding out the double gatefold and being, like, blown away. That relationship is gone. The first iPods were just scrolling little grey screens. It was just information and I think people couldn't handle it. Then they brought the album covers back as icons that you could swipe through, but without any of the criticality, right? The liner notes are gone, the essays are gone. Sometimes you're even, "Well who's playing drums on that?" and you have no access to anything besides the album cover image and the title of the album. And then you can choose the most popular song and miss everything that's on the B-side and not pay any attention to how it was sequenced or organized. There's an order, clearly, that was mindfully thought of—what song will come first and what song will be last—and that bums me out. [laughter] I feel like I have a hard time navigating music digitally. It's almost overwhelming.

I get very excited if I put in a CD and the database can't find it. I'm like, HAH! [laughter]

GL: The other thing is, and I think this is something that gets into the cultural critique that your work embodies and enacts—when the iPods came out, who curates these databases?

JCJ: Exactly.

GL: It turns out that major corporations curate them. And I'll tell you a story. I made a CD, *Les Exercices Spirituels*, an octet with sound spatialization.[17] Under normal circumstances the piece would be called contemporary classical music; nobody is improvising or playing any hot licks, they're playing what I wrote, right? For a long time. Anyway, I get the CD and I stick it in there and it says the genre is jazz. So I ask the company, "How did that turn up?" They say, "We didn't do it. When we put in the genre we always put in avant-garde or classical."

You know, when you hit the button on iTunes, and it asks, do you want to send information to Gracenote? The company called up Gracenote and asked them about the genre stuff, and it turns out that whoever responded sort of dissembled about the process. They said that they were crowdsourcing these genres, which turned out not to be quite true now, although they did that when they first started. So in other words, if a hundred people who looked on Wikipedia saw jazz on your Wikipedia site, then that became your genre. Simple as that.

But later, that becomes reified when Gracenote is bought by the Tribune Corporation, and that happens about 2013.[18] Major corporations do the curating now, and this relates in some ways to the differences between the visual and the sonic, in black music being highly commodified—perhaps the most commodified and policed music in the history of the world—because of its power. That power, they see it as needing channeling and needing "curation," that's a gentler word.

So if you're looking at something like one of your works—for example, the one where you're talking about noise-cancelling, instrument cables, cable ties—what do these elements mean to you? You know, there's a lot of musicological scholarship on noise cancellation.

JCJ: In 2010, before The Kitchen show, I was looking at empty CD cases and systems of removal that would operate also in terms of historic removal. That exhibition was called "Electric." It was at Sikkema Jenkins.[19] And everyone who makes sound art has to have their *4'33"* exorcism. So I made my *4'33"* exorcism, which was four minutes and thirty-three seconds of the opening chords of Miles Davis's *In a Silent Way*. It's only Herbie Hancock's chords from the beginning, and that is stretched out over four minutes and thirty-three seconds. Miles is never present. If you don't know that album, its impact was sort of like when Dylan went electric. When Miles and Herbie made that album it had this same effect: "Why is there an electric keyboard with Miles Davis?"

GL: I didn't realize the Cage *4'33"* connection. I didn't get that. And the other thing is, on my iTunes it's four minutes and thirty-five seconds. [laughter]

JCJ: Damn you, digital world, and your accuracy! It's adding the silence, right? [laughter]

So I came to working with the cables because of the connection to the theme of electric and being unplugged or plugged, and wanting to comment on the white box gallery space as a dead space that's feeding back into itself, plugging into one spot and cycling in this kind of silent loop.

GL: Can I play some of it? What's the full title?

JCJ: *Slowly, In a Silent Way, Caged.*

[Playing the piece]

GL: You really like bass [laughter], I mean a lot of these pieces have fantastic low sounds. Is that true or is that just my impression?

JCJ: Maybe yeah.

GL: Maybe it's because you know the way bass tones work acoustically. They diffuse all over the space. They're not directional like high pitched sounds are.

JCJ: Just one thing about that piece in particular. The acoustics of a white box gallery, where most of this work has lived, are pretty horrible. Instead of fighting that space I started making sound pieces that would benefit from being echo-y and float-y. Maybe that's part of the space; if you're going to have a sound piece in a room that has cement floors and big metal beams and white drywall everywhere, then why not let the sound piece be influenced and expanded in that space instead of trying so hard to fight it? That started affecting the way I was editing sound, too.

GL: That's in the venerable tradition of chamber music. We know what the space is going to be like and so we compose the music for the space. It seems like you're composing music for a space that as a visual artist you encounter quite often.

JCJ: Yeah, yeah.

GL: Well, I know people want to ask questions, but we're not quite ready for you yet [laughter], because I had a burning question I wanted to ask Jennie. Actually, I have two more things. First of all, this business of scores. You're really into scores. Here's a bar line, and here's another piece combining the acoustic absorption with the metaphor of the score. Then, there are actual scores that you could play. Did anyone ever play these?

JCJ: Yeah I had one ... now I'm going to forget his name. This kid in Houston challenged me about the scores. We had this big debate about scores, about the visual art world co-opting this term "score," and what that really means. If they're functional or not functional, or if they're just visual. He felt there was enough information in the way I was making these collages that they could be played. Maybe that's something you could speak to, because at some point you could call anything a score because it's about interpretation, right? With or without having any music notation or notes, or little kind of hints that this is actually playable, anything is. That was the big debate, about whether a lot of my scores were actually functioning as scores that could be played.

GL: I think you could play this. This is your *Score in 8 Measures* or part of it.[20] There are eight pieces in this, *Score for Melba Liston*. And then you have this other one which isn't really a score, but your container motif, *The Gentle Influence of the Bourgeoisie*, is that the total title?[21]

JCJ: Yeah.

GL: Then it says "Trombone Improvisation." So we have a piece about Melba Liston, the great trombonist and arranger, but the other trombonist you're referencing is Paul Rutherford. Now, what about this trombone thing? I mean, I play the trombone myself [laughter], and I was just wondering—I mean, a lot of people really don't like trombones. [laughter]

JCJ: I have your solo album.

GL: You do? [laughter]

JCJ: I think why I am fascinated with the trombone is super-nerdy and conceptual—which is, that you find your notes in space. It's just fascinating to watch and to see how one finds the notes in physical space that way. And also, I think all wind instruments for me connect more deeply to existential, spiritual kind of things because of the breath itself, because of breathing and what that does, and what that breath gives—not a voice, but channeling something else. Out of all the horns, the trombone is the most fascinating to me because of that spatial relationship.

GL: But then you shift gears with this "Gentle Harm of the Bourgeoisie" thing. What you did with the Rutherford piece was a very complex move because you have to trace it back a couple layers. It starts with Bunuel, right?

JCJ: Yeah.

GL: So first it's your *The Gentle Influence of the Bourgeoisie*, then Rutherford's solo trombone album is *The Gentle Harm of the Bourgeoisie*, and the Bunuel film was *The Discreet Charm of the Bourgeoisie*.[22]

Paul Rutherford was an amazing trombone player. He passed away in 2007. One of the last records he made was for forty years of the Globe Unity Orchestra, which we played together on with all those other European and American free jazz players.[23] He also started the amazing group Iskra 1903, which is connected with Lenin.[24] He was, I think, a lifelong member of the British Communist Party. So a lot of what he was doing, the title of Iskra and *The Gentle Harm of the Bourgeoisie*, it's all connected with political circumstances, which I think you picked up on.

JCJ: I always say that I'm really good at writing the table of contents for a book that I don't have the chops to write. The titles make these nice sweeping things that you then can unpack.

GL: Anybody have any comments or questions or anything?

Question: I have a question about color, because for some of your collages there's a descriptive color when you look at it directly, and then you see a shadow of color you have to look at an angle in order to see. I just wonder how color functions and how you come up with these ideas.

JCJ: Color is complicated. Really, for me it's just an activation point. Color is very scary to me. I gave a talk at Dia about Agnes Martin, and I'll be on a panel with Richard Tuttle at the Guggenheim for Agnes' show in December.[25] I only say that because of the kindred connection I feel with Agnes in terms of color, and fighting color, or muting color. It works a lot like muting or sound absorption—color being present, but maybe suppressed, and then having an exit. But that glow and that relationship to optics was really a building block for me in terms of smashing the two worlds together to think about the sonic and the optic. And what reverberates more than color? If you condense it down to just that one slice, then it is also about that activation and a little magic, not unlike the impressionists creating magic, light that's there, but not there. That's not really an answer, but it's one of those things where color is ephemeral and complicated and there are pigments that reflect and pigments that absorb.

Question: I have a question for both of you. Something that George recognized and sort of sparked something in me was the idea of writing history and the timeframe for it. You see many artists who, ten, twenty, thirty years later, get written back into history, and I'm thinking about this in the context of Jennie, of what kinds of associations you would want. Are there contemporary artists or influences? Or the timeframes you would want to see yourself connected to? The kind of history you might want to be written into? Something for both of you, for George as a historian, you as an artist, how you would want to be associated?

JCJ: Well, I had one amazing moment at the Menil. There was an exhibition called "Silence" curated by Toby Kamps at the Menil Collection that looked at this idea of silence.[26] It was not only multi-generational, it was totally historical. Some of the works were from the permanent collection, and there was also Steve Rodin and Stephen Vitiello, my contemporaries who operate in the visual art world but are in sound, and work back and forth.

Kamps chose the two panels from my Kitchen exhibition, but I didn't totally understand his context until I arrived at the show. The Menil is stunning because it's all natural light, it's a very beautiful space. I walk in and there's Rauschenberg's "White Paintings," my black paintings, and Cage's *4'33"* score under glass in the center of this room. And I was like, well that's it. Because it's about punching the holes in the narratives. And also, even if you just read it on the simple black/white formalist level, it's pushing the conversation open. In that sense, the Guggenheim just asked me to speak for Agnes's show. Are you kidding me? That's how I feel about it. Like, *are you kidding me?* That's an amazing context and as long as we can expand, if I can help by talking about modernism or minimalism to help expand that conversation then that's a worthy cause.

GL: Just the fact of you turning up, and, "Oh, *she's* the one that's talking about it"—in certain scenes, just turning up and being the unexpected voice. You punch those holes in the narratives just by turning up. We're all trying to do it in our ways. And someone like you, your work—not just you, but your work—embodies change. It embodies the possibility that things could be different than they are. People come out of a show like this and they say, "Wow, that was really different. I wonder what else could be different around here?" And that's when you start to find that real change is made possible through what you do, what you're doing.

Question: Jennie, I was wondering if the materiality of the work, using acoustic sound baffles, if it's been received in such a way that it's always necessarily in dialogue with the pieces around it?

JCJ: I think that they deal, profoundly for me, with silence. They're on a very microscopic level profoundly affecting the sonics in the space, with or without other sound pieces. Also, sometimes frustratingly for curators and museum guards, the closer you get to the works, the denser, the softer it is. In the first exhibition I had specifically all black panels. It was quite a surprise at the opening to have people looking around for where the sound was coming from and immediately go to one of the wall pieces and lean in. They thought the panels were emanating the sound, but they get totally hood-winked because the closer they got, the quieter it got. It was sort of this strange push-pull relationship that I didn't anticipate being so profound.

I often feel guilty that I'm bastardizing things that are sacred to some people, through digital editing and manipulating. But I just have tremendous Midwestern Catholic guilt in my DNA somehow. [laughter] I feel guilty about everything.

GL: Midwestern? What part of the Midwest?

JCJ: Ohio.

GL: I'm from Chicago, not a Catholic, but you know …

JCJ: But we know. I've brought this up before; we were at the School of the Art Institute of Chicago at the same time.

GL: That's right, but somehow we didn't meet.

JCJ: Because I was upstairs with the painters pulling
my hair out, and I remember seeing you down in the
lower level with all the equipment and the oscilloscopes
and things.

GL: Art and technology people.

Well, we might have to stop because I see Douglas
Ewart has left the room, and that means he's getting
ready for the performance with Ni'Ja Whitson, which
is going to happen in a little over half an hour. I just
wanted to please thank Jennie C. Jones.

[Applause]

1   George E. Lewis, "Jennie C. Jones: Higher Resonance," *Artforum*, May 2013, https://www.artforum.com/print/previews/201305/jennie-c-jones-higher-resonance-40572. "Jennie C. Jones: Higher Resonance," https://hirshhorn.si.edu/exhibitions/directions-jennie-c-jones-higher-resonance/.

2   Jennie C. Jones, "Tone," at Sikkema, Jenkins & Co. (2014), http://www.jenniecjones.com/2014-tone-at-sikkema-jenkins-co-1/

3   See "Jennie C. Jones: Absorb/Diffuse at the Kitchen," *Wire* 333, November 2011.

4   Lumi Tan, "A Conversation with George Lewis," http://thekitchen.org/blog/52. Also see http://archive.thekitchen.org/?artist=george-lewis

5   "Who is Susan Philipsz?", https://www.tate.org.uk/whats-on/tate-britain/exhibition/susan-philipsz-war-damaged-musical-instruments/philipsz-introduction.

6   For Kurt Schwitters's own version from 1932, see https://www.youtube.com/watch?v=6X7E2i0KMqM.

7   "Full IPA Chart," International Phonetic Association (2005/2015), https://www.internationalphoneticassociation.org/content/full-ipa-chart

8   Dick Fountaine, *Sound??* (1966), https://www.imdb.com/title/tt0756714/. Film.

9   George E. Lewis, "Benjamin Patterson, 1934–2016," *Artforum* (November 2016): 73-74, 204.

10   For a fuller discussion of the treatment of Patterson by historians, see George E. Lewis, "Benjamin Patterson's Spiritual Exercises," in *Tomorrow Is the Question: New Directions in Experimental Music Studies*, edited by Benjamin Piekut, 86–108 (Ann Arbor: University of Michigan Press, 2014).

11   Terry Adkins and George Lewis, "Event Scores: Terry Adkins and George Lewis in Conversation," *Artforum* (March 2014): 244–53. Also see George E. Lewis, "The Sound of Terry Adkins," in *Terry Adkins: Recital*, edited by Ian Berry (Saratoga Springs, New York: Frances Young Tang Teaching Museum and Art Gallery at Skidmore College; Munich, London, and New York: DelMonico Books/Prestel), 2017.

12   Renée Levine Packer and Mary Jane Leach, eds., *Gay Guerrilla: Julius Eastman and his Music* (Rochester: University of Rochester Press, 2016).

13   For more on John Coltrane as minimalist, see George E. Lewis, "Expressive Awesomeness: New Music and Art in Chicago, 1965–75," in T*he Freedom Principle: Experiments in Art and Music, 1965 to Now*, edited by Naomi Beckwith and Dieter Roelstraete, 115–127 (Chicago and London: Museum of Contemporary Art Chicago in association with the University of Chicago Press, 2015).

14   For a review of a recent performance of this classic minimalist work, see William Dougherty, "La Monte Young Trio for Strings Original Full Length Version, Dia 15 VI 13 545, West 22 Street Dream House, New York City," *Tempo* 70 (275), 2015: 99–100.

15   Valerie Cassel Oliver, ed., *Jennie C. Jones: Compilation* (Houston: Gregory R. Miller/Contemporary Arts Museum Houston, 2015).

16   See Seth Sherwood, "The Songs of Senegal," New York Times, December 3, 2009, https://www.nytimes.com/2009/12/06/travel/06senegalmusic.html.

17   George Lewis, *Les Exercices Spirituels*, Tzadik 8081, 2011, http://www.tzadik.com/index.php?catalog=8081. Compact disc.

18   Later, the Tribune Company sold Gracenote to Nielsen, another large media corporation. See Anthony Ha, "Nielsen will acquire Tribune-owned Gracenote for $560M," December 20, 2016, https://techcrunch.com/2016/12/20/nielsen-acquires-gracenote/.

19   "Electric: An Exhibition of New Works by Jennie C. Jones at Sikkema Jenkins & Co," http://artdaily.com/news/39143/Electric—An-Exhibition-of-New-Works-by-Jennie-C—Jones-at-Sikkema-Jenkins—-Co.

20   "Tone" at Sikkema, Jenkins & Co., http://www.jenniecjones.com/2014-tone-at-sikkema-jenkins-co-1/

21   http://www.artnet.com/artists/jennie-c-jones/the-gentle-influence-of-the-bourgeoisie-paul-a-W1_ZJ6r4N2gKm1DSjFkSQw2

22   Paul Rutherford, "The Gentle Harm of the Bourgeoisie," Emanem 4019 (1976), http://www.emanemdisc.com/E4019.html. About the Bunuel film, one could start at https://www.imdb.com/title/tt0068361/.

23   Globe Unity Orchestra, *Globe Unity: 40 Years*, Intakt CD 133 (2008), https://intaktrec.bandcamp.com/album/globe-unity-40-years, compact disc.

24   *Iskra 1903: Frankfurt 1991*, http://www.emanemdisc.com/E4051.html.

25   Jennie C. Jones and Richard Tuttle, moderated by Barbara Haskell, "Reflections on Agnes Martin," Guggenheim Museum, December 14, 2016, https://www.pacegallery.com/news/2848/reflections-on-agnes-martin

26   The exhibition ran from July 27 through October 21, 2012. See https://www.menil.org/exhibitions/24-silence.

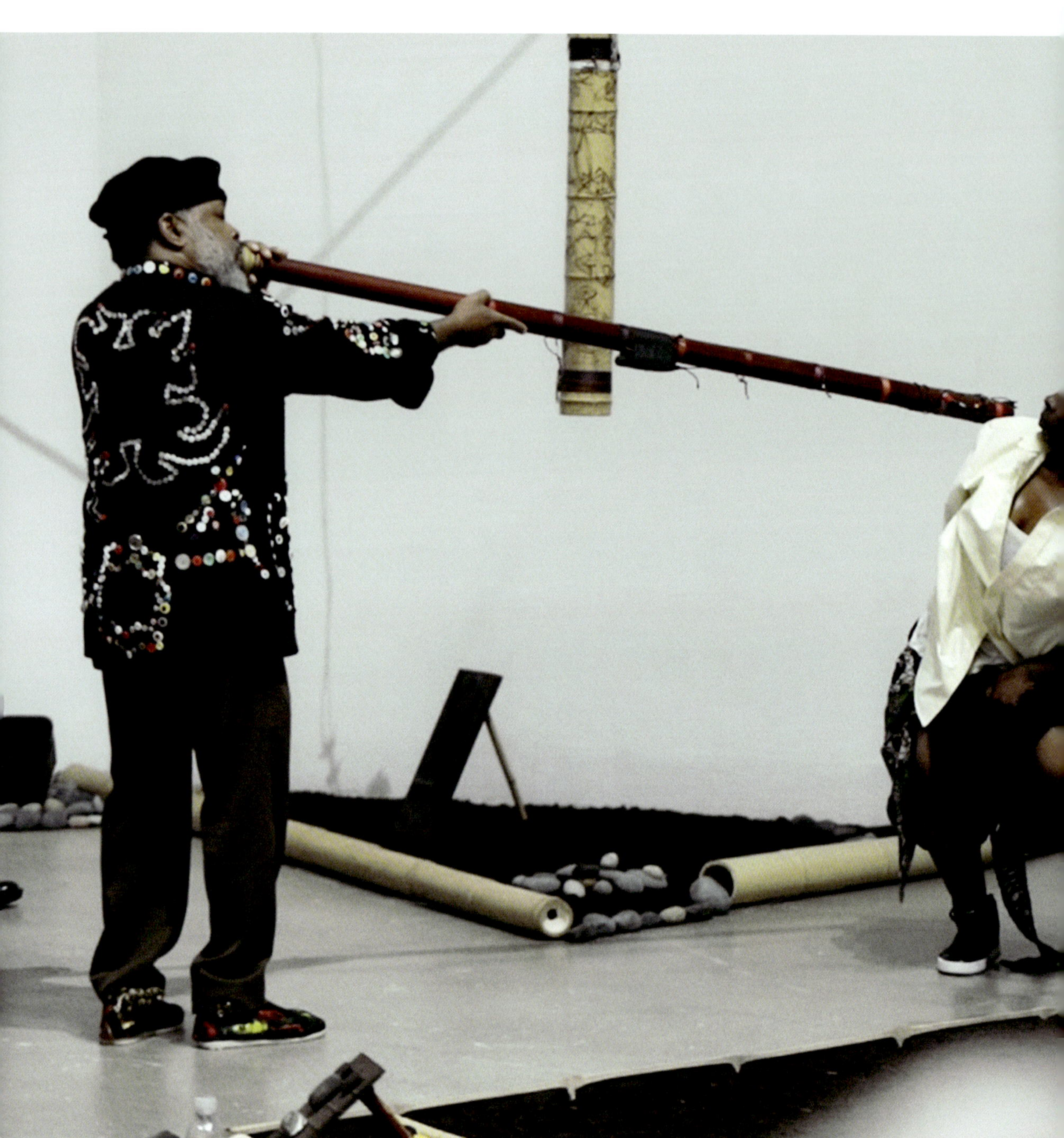

Douglas Ewart and Ni'ja Whitson

Douglas Ewart and Ni'ja Whitson

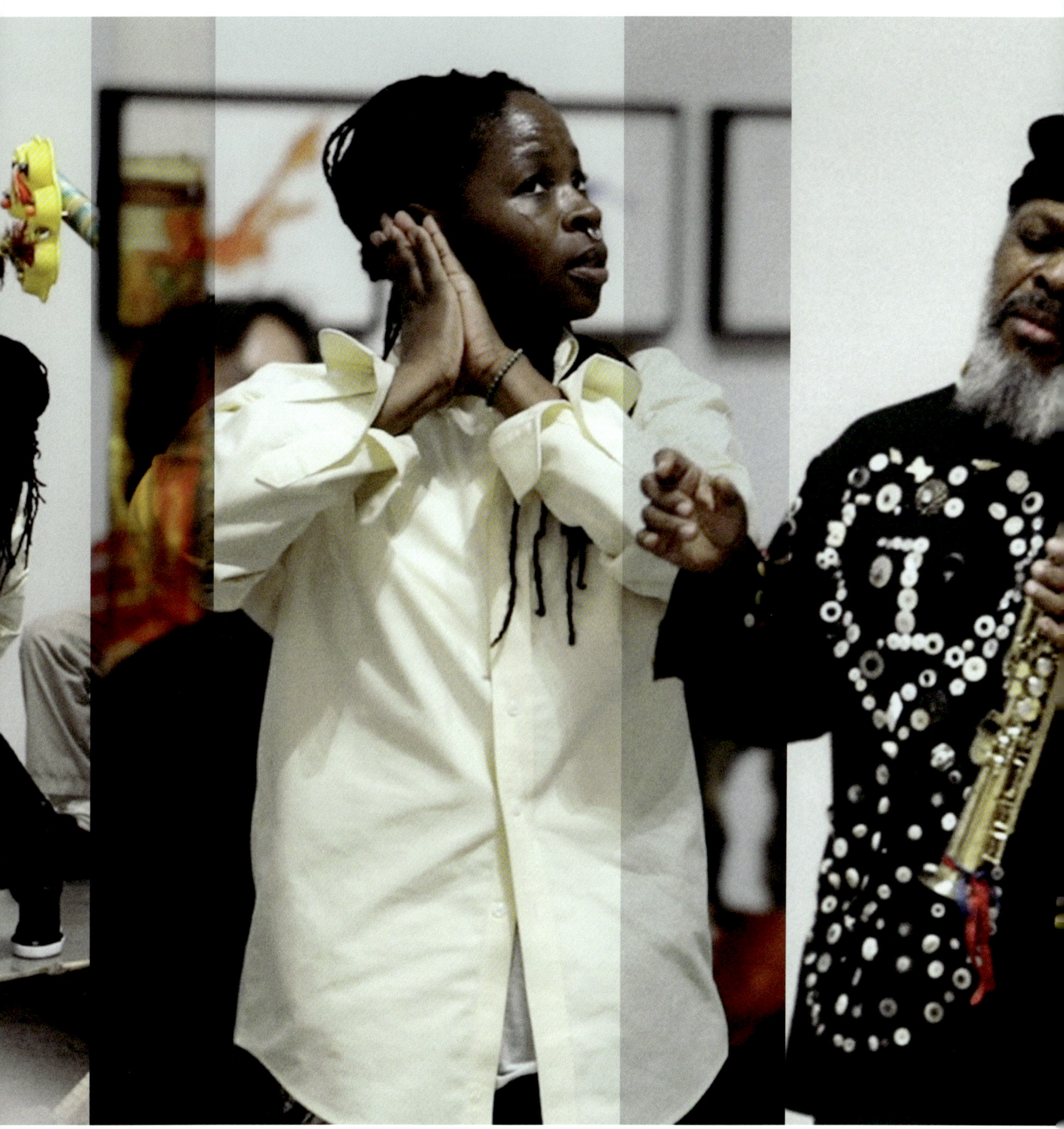

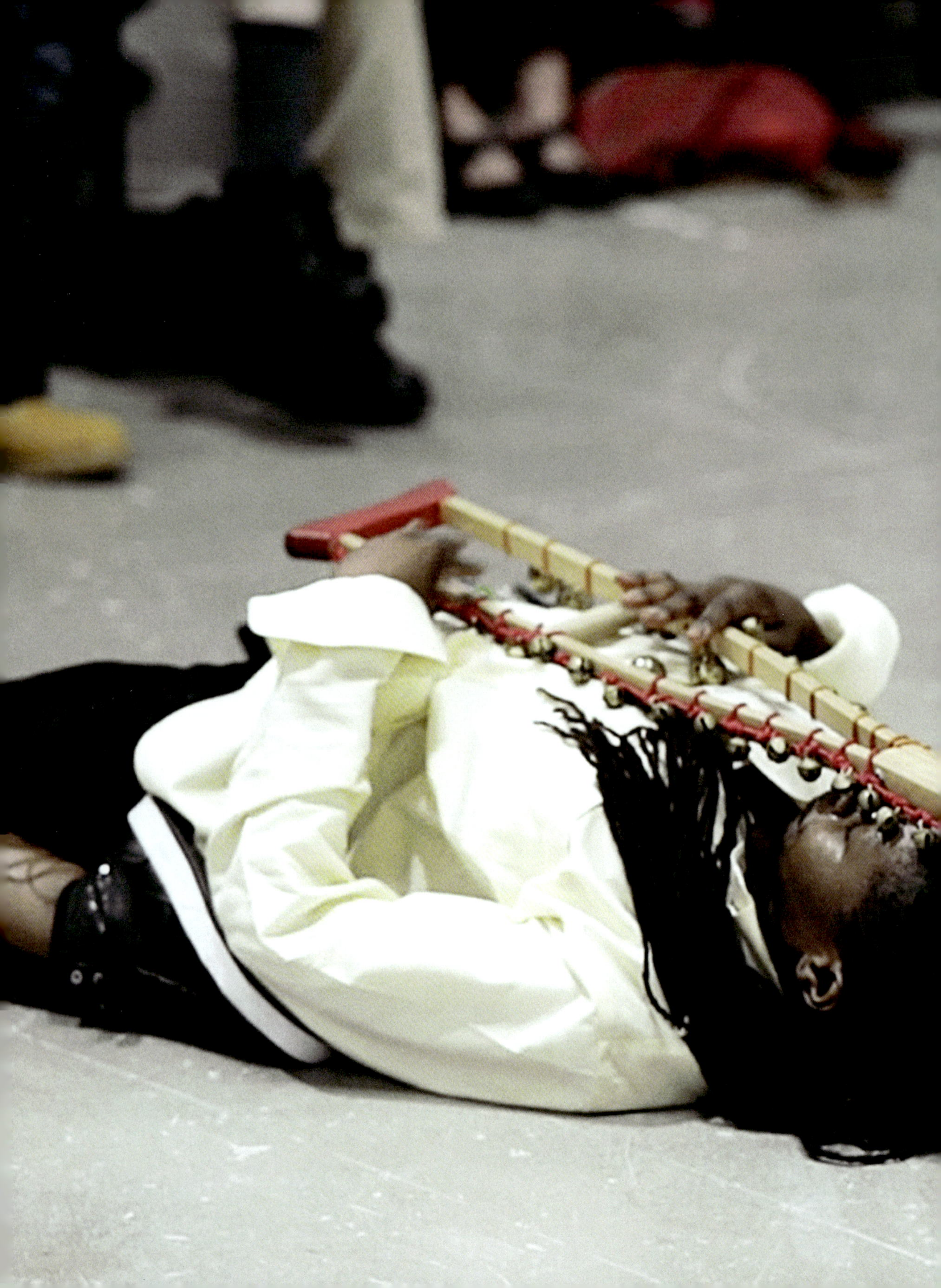

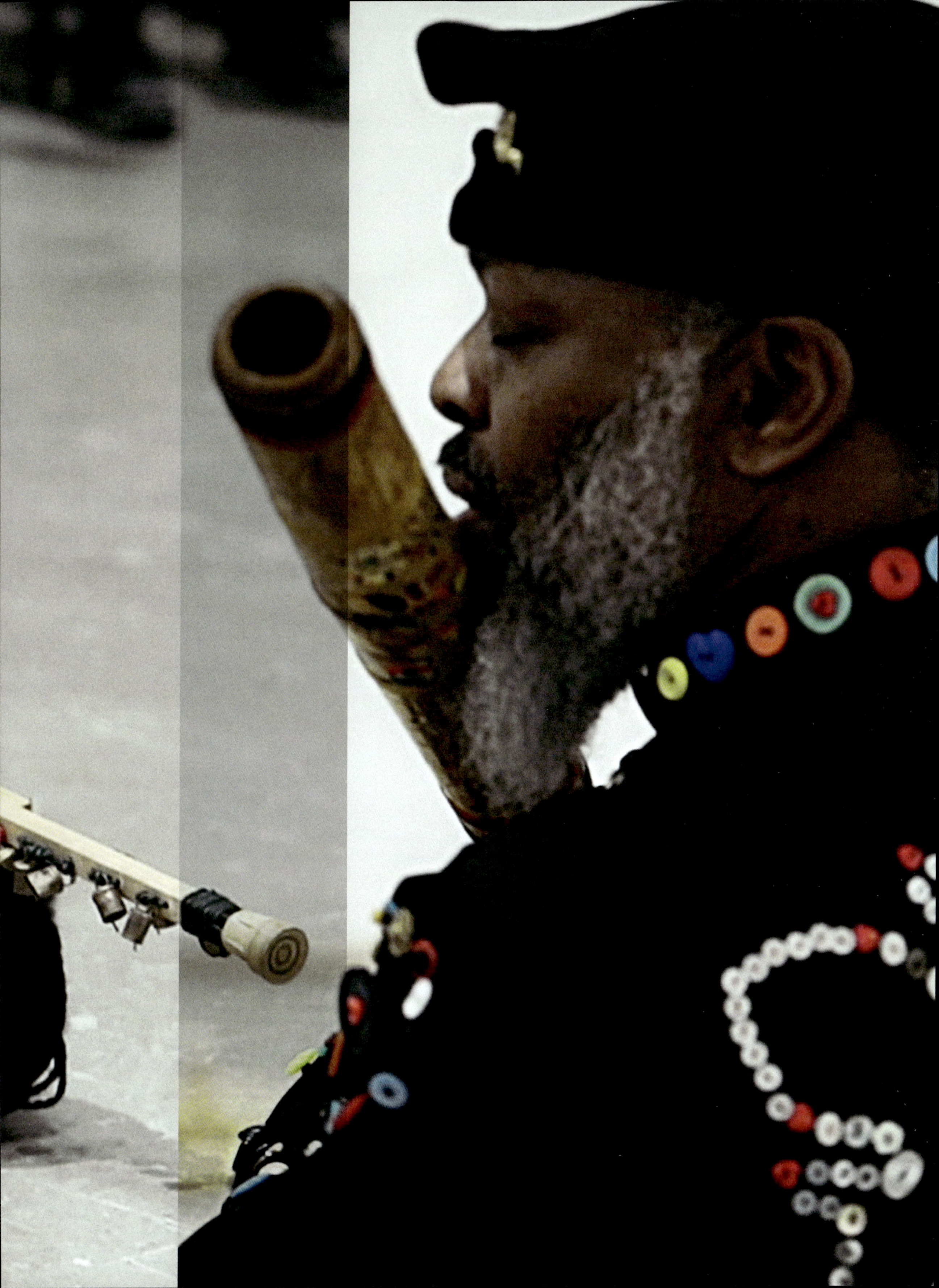

John William Coltrane the Sonic Sequoyah/Sequoia
Douglas R. Ewart

When I hear John Coltrane, I steep inside with the laughter of love that is life!
I am stripped of denominators
The equation ... clear
My endorphins go wild, I am charged
I tick tock with a regularity that is beyond equilibrium
I am ocular
Reams of new realms
I follow anxiously!
Mountains of malleable magna, meshing minds and souls
The magic medicine dispensed by a Spirit Man
possessed by every Oresha: Papa Legba, Obatala, Yemenya, Oshun, Ogun, Shango ...
Youth and maturity
Delight and death
Devils and angels
I am buoyed ... up; a tidal wave of sound engulfs my sanctum, incubating new
dendrites
I dip down deep
Amniotic fluids flush about, keeping my thoughts keen
An eagle
Earth and sky
I bellow with the breezes of my thermals

Water Song
Douglas R. Ewart

We got pesticide in the water
Herbicides in the sea
Fungicides in the river
That runs right side of me/we
Plastic bags are forming islands on sea and land
There might be a debate about global warming but there can be no debate about global
harming

We are mostly water
We cannot live with out it, as we look at other planets to live … water is the key
Please don't waste the water
Water is our most valuable asset

When washing your hands, man!
Turn the faucets down low
For when the faucet's flow is high, most of the water just rushes by
You don't need a lot of water to wash your hands well
Slow your flow my brothers and sisters so we will have water to grow the food and the
plants too

When you're washing your dishes make soapy water, and rinse water in your dishpans
When your soapy water gets too soiled, make your rinse water your new soapy water and
use your old soapy water to water the plants, the plants love it, and I do it all the time,
and they thrive (
no bleach in the water)
You can also use spent water from a tub bath to water plants
You/we will save millions of gallons of water when you make this plan, and make a
smaller footprint

We just have to turn a faucet on, and out runs the water see
But others through out the Planet Earth have to fetch it from a well, river, stream, stand-
pipe, billabong, and sometimes a gutter, and swamps too!
One gallon of water weighs 8.33 pounds
Five gallons of water weighs 41.65 pounds
Women/people in Africa, Asia, the Americas and other places must carry several buckets
of water weighing forty pounds or more for miles every day
That takes a lot of effort, energy, time and risk too … for predators: man and beast lie in
wait
Fetching water is drudgework
Many women and girls lack a good education/schooling because they have to fetch water
most of every day
We could use the money saved from water conservation/preservation and fund educa-
tion/schooling for those that can't get one, in far and near lands
Water … Water … Water … Water … Water, the Staff of Life!

Rio Negro Poem and Narrative
Douglas R. Ewart

Don't use so much soap, for the rivers have been bathing themselves for millennia/
kilo years/millenniums

They/we are all returning to Africa without setting feet there, as you can see and feel
it in the one-drop. Out of Africa and Black again.

I/We went to Penn's Landing, and saw a family consisting of a statuesque red headed
man, his magnificent Black wife and their two very comely daughters
Moving as one.

And then we saw countless confluxes of ethnicities on the landing. The change is
happing without consent, for love, like and/or attractions are more powerful than
hate, barriers or laws of stupidity.

Did you think today?

You got a Rhythm
I got a Rhythm
The sea got a Rhythm
The bee got a Rhythm
Bata got a Rhythm
The moon got a Rhythm
Neptune got a Rhythm
The turtle got a Rhythm
Rio Negro got a Rhythm
Your Mama got a Rhythm
Every-goody/body got a Rhythm

History

Written and Compiled by Douglas R. Ewart

Guainía (Spanish pronunciation: [gwai'ni.a]; Yuri language: Land of many waters) is a department of Colombia. It is in the east of the country, bordering Venezuela and Brazil. Its capital is Inírida.

History

The river was named by the Spanish explorer Francisco de Orellana, who first came upon it in 1541. By the middle of the seventeenth century, Jesuits had settled along its banks in the midst of numerous tribes: Manau, Aruák, and Trumá Indians. After 1700 slaving along the river was common, and indigenous populations were greatly diminished after contact with infectious European diseases.

Rionegro (Spanish pronunciation: [rio'neɣro]) is a city and municipality in Antioquia Department, Colombia, located in the subregion of Eastern Antioquia. The official name of the City is "Ciudad Santiago de Arma de Rionegro," but is named after the Negro River which is the most prominent geographical feature of the municipality. Rionegro is also sometimes called the *Cuna de la democracia* (cradle of democracy) as it was one of the most important cities during the era of the Colombia's struggle for independence and the 1863 constitution was written in the city.

Rio Negro (Amazon) The **Rio Negro** (Portuguese: **Rio Negro** ['ʁi.u nɛgɾu]; Spanish: Río **Negro** ['ri.o 'neɣro] "Black River") is the largest left tributary of the Amazon, the largest blackwater river in the world, and one of the world's ten largest rivers in average discharge.

The river was named by the Spanish explorer Francisco de Orellana, who first came upon it in 1541. By the middle of the seventeenth century, Jesuits had settled along its banks in the midst of numerous tribes: Manau, Aruák, and Trumá Indians. After 1700 slaving along the river was common, and indigenous populations were greatly diminished after contact with infectious European diseases.

The Rio Negro (Portuguese: *Rio Negro* ['ʁi.u nɛgɾu]; Spanish: Río Negro ['ri.o 'neɣro] "*Black River*") is the largest left tributary of the Amazon, the largest blackwater river in the world, and one of the world's ten largest rivers in average discharge.

While the name *Rio Negro* means *Black River*, its waters are similar in color to strong tea. The dark color comes from humic acid due to an incomplete breakdown of phenol-containing vegetation from sandy clearings. The river was named because it looks black from a distance.

Much has been written on the productivity of the Rio Negro and other blackwater rivers. The older idea that these are "hunger rivers" is giving way, with new research, to the recognition that the Rio Negro, for example, supports a large fishing industry and has numerous turtle beaches. If explorers did not find many Indians along the Rio Negro during the seventeenth century, it is likely that their populations were reduced because of new infectious diseases and warfare rather than low river productivity.

Rio Negro has a very high species richness. About 700 fish species have been documented in the river basin, and it is estimated that the total is 800–900 fish species, including almost 100 endemics and several undescribed species. Among these are many that are important in the aquarium trade, including the cardinal tetra.

From Wikipedia, the free encyclopedia

This article is about the molecule. For the group of chemicals containing a phenol group, see Phenols. *"Carbolic acid" redirects here. It is not to be confused with* carbonic acid.

Phenol, also known as **carbolic acid**, is an aromatic organic compound with the molecular formula C_6H_5OH. It is a white crystalline solid that is volatile. The molecule consists of a phenyl group ($-C_6H_5$) bonded to a hydroxyl group ($-OH$). It is mildly acidic and requires careful handling due to its propensity to cause chemical burns.

Phenol was first extracted from coal tar, but today is produced on a large scale (about 7 billion kg/year) from petroleum. It is an important industrial commodity as a precursor to many materials and useful compounds. It is primarily used to synthesize plastics and related materials. Phenol and its chemical derivatives are essential for production of polycarbonates, epoxies, Bakelite, nylon, detergents, herbicides such as phenoxy herbicides, and numerous pharmaceutical drugs.

Contents [hide]

Major rivers in the Orinoco Basin [edit]

- Apure: from Venezuela through the east into the Orinoco
- Arauca: from Colombia to Venezuela east into the Orinoco
- Atabapo: from the Guiana Highlands of Venezuela north into the Orinoco
- Caroní: from the Guiana Highlands of Venezuela north into the Orinoco
- Casiquiare canal: in SE Venezuela, a distributary from the Orinoco flowing west to the Negro River, a major affluent to the Amazon
- Caura: from eastern Venezuela (Guiana Highlands) north into the Orinoco
- Guaviare: from Colombia east into the Orinoco
- Inírida: from Colombia southeast into the Guaviare.
- Meta: from Colombia, border with Venezuela east into the Orinoco
- Ventuari: from eastern Venezuela (the Guiana Highlands) southwest into the Orinoco
- Vichada: from Colombia east into the Orinoco

See also: Casiquiare canal-Orinoco River hydrographic divide

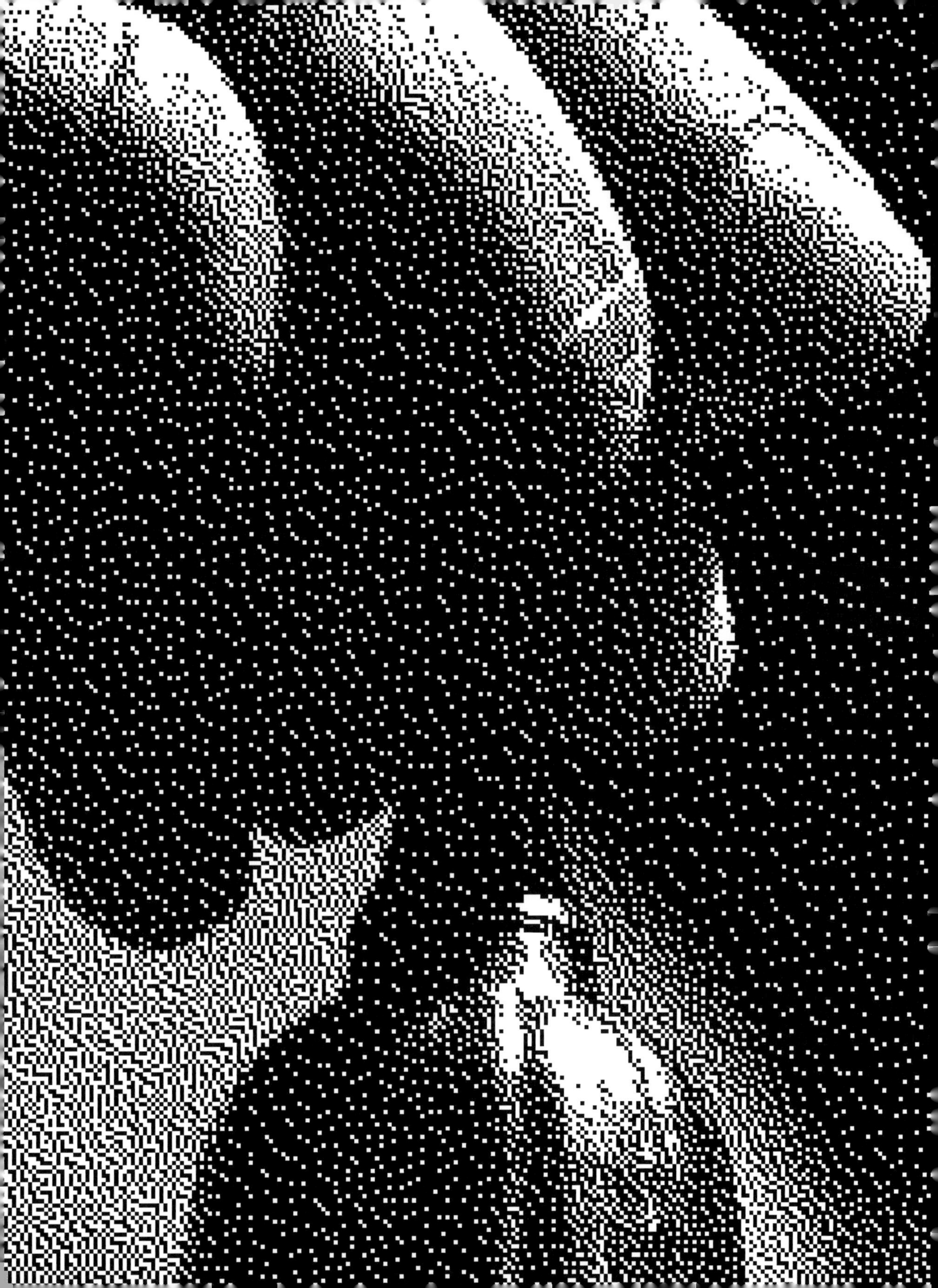

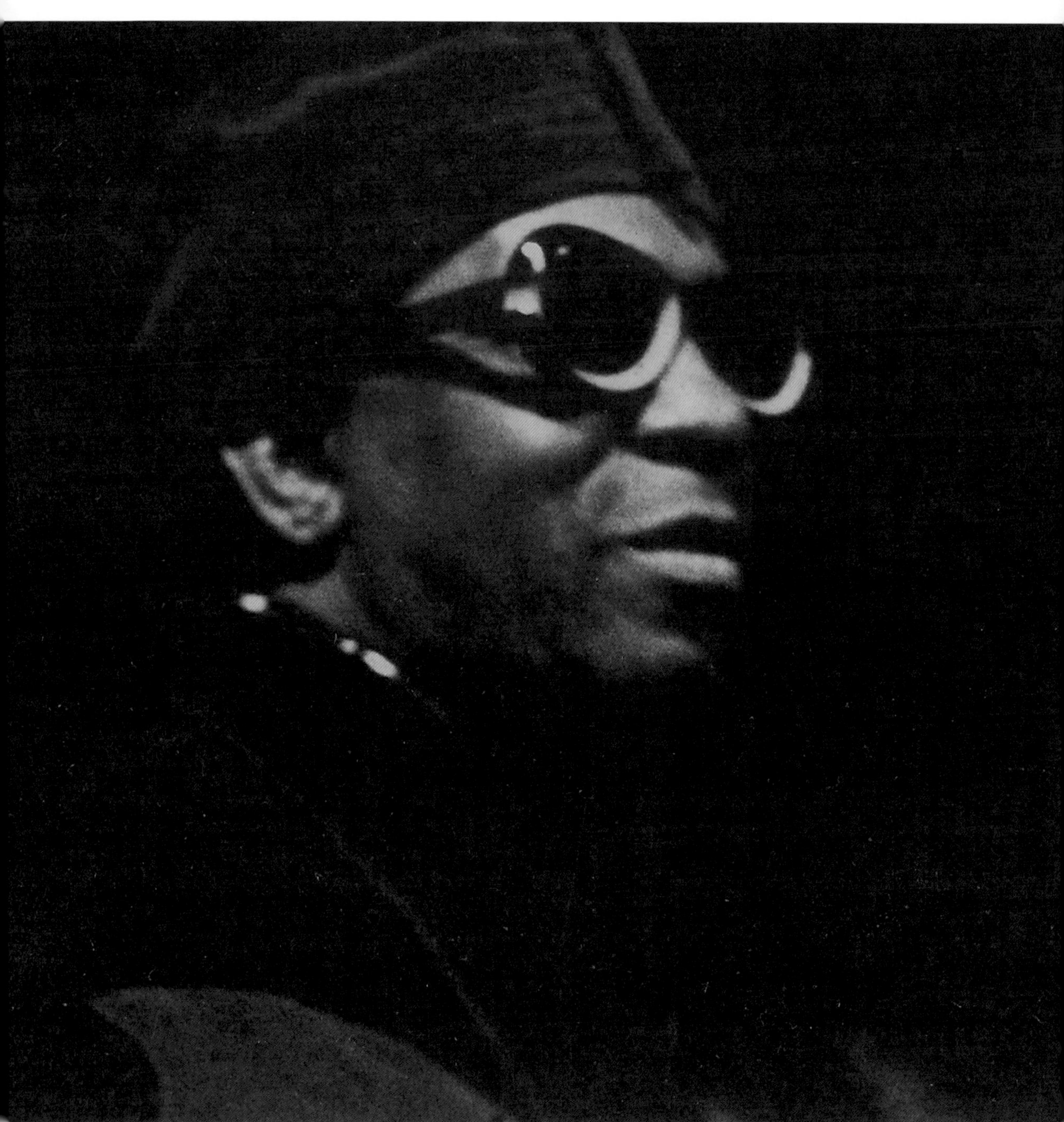

SHWABADA The Music of Ndikho Xaba

Directed by Nhlanhla Masondo

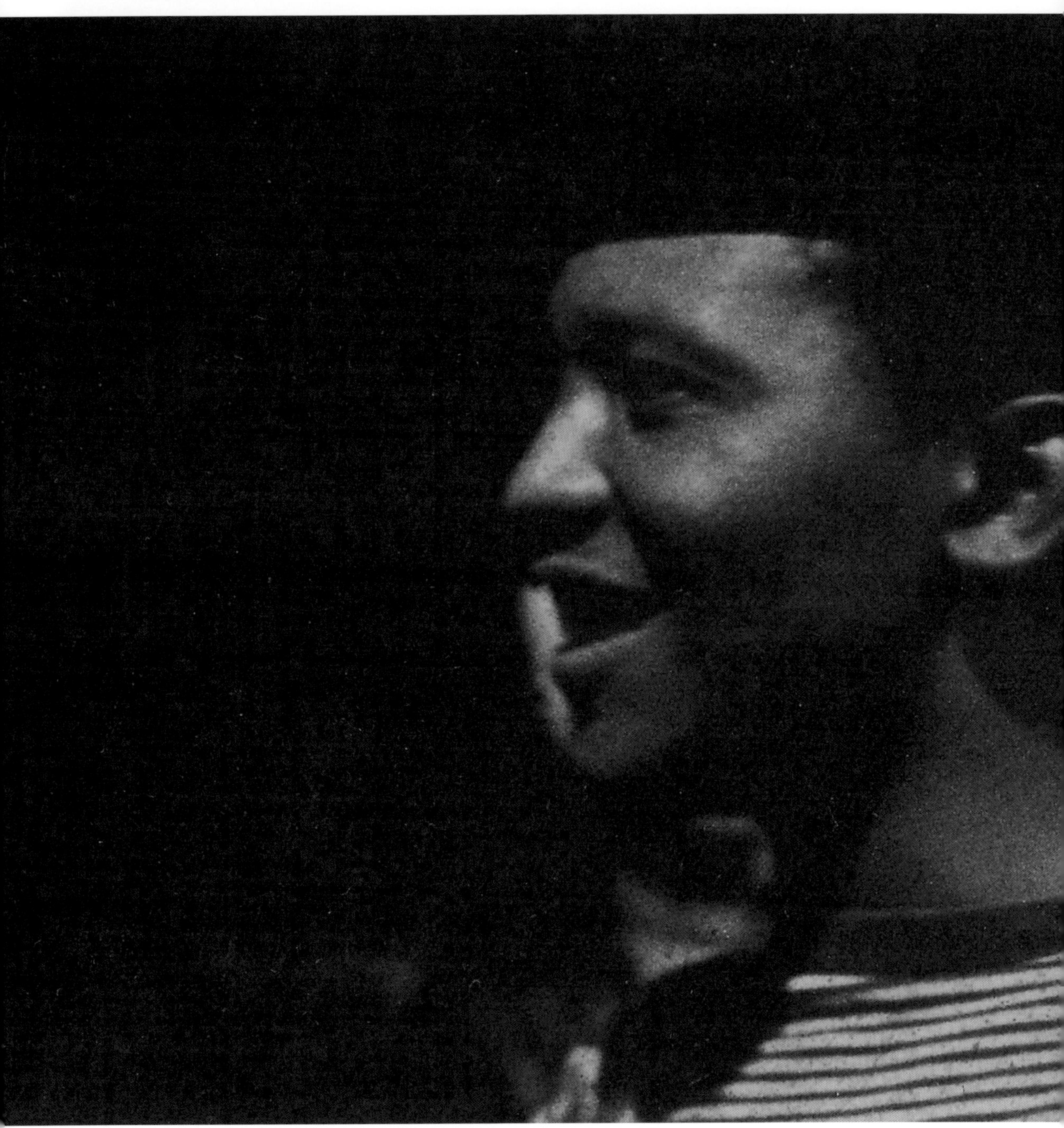

Film screening followed by a discussion featuring director Nhlanhla Masondo, joined by Carol Muller, Professor of Music at the University of Pennsylvania, and longtime AACM members George Lewis and Douglas Ewart, both of whom collaborated with Xaba.
Composer: Sun Ra with Xaba, undated.

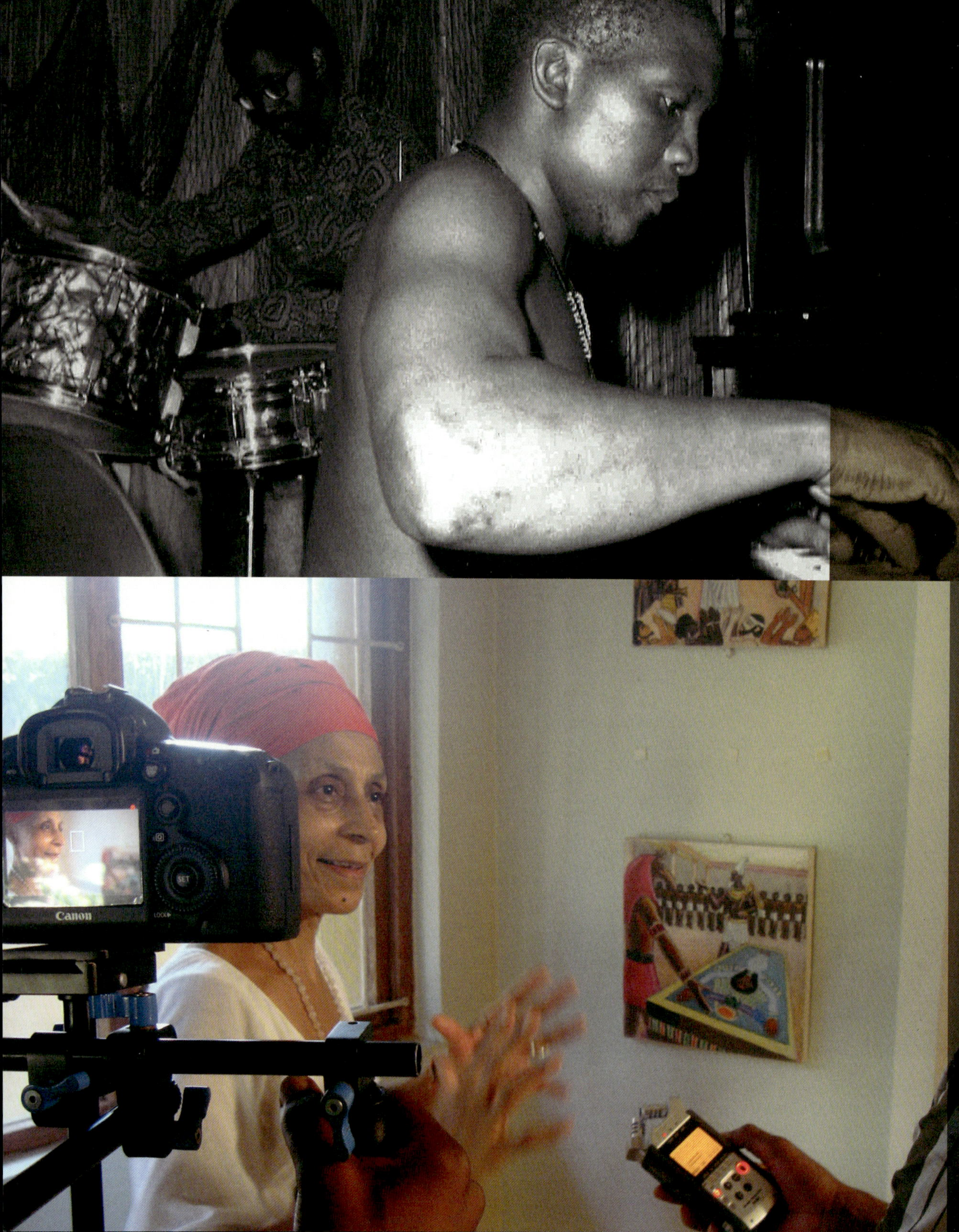

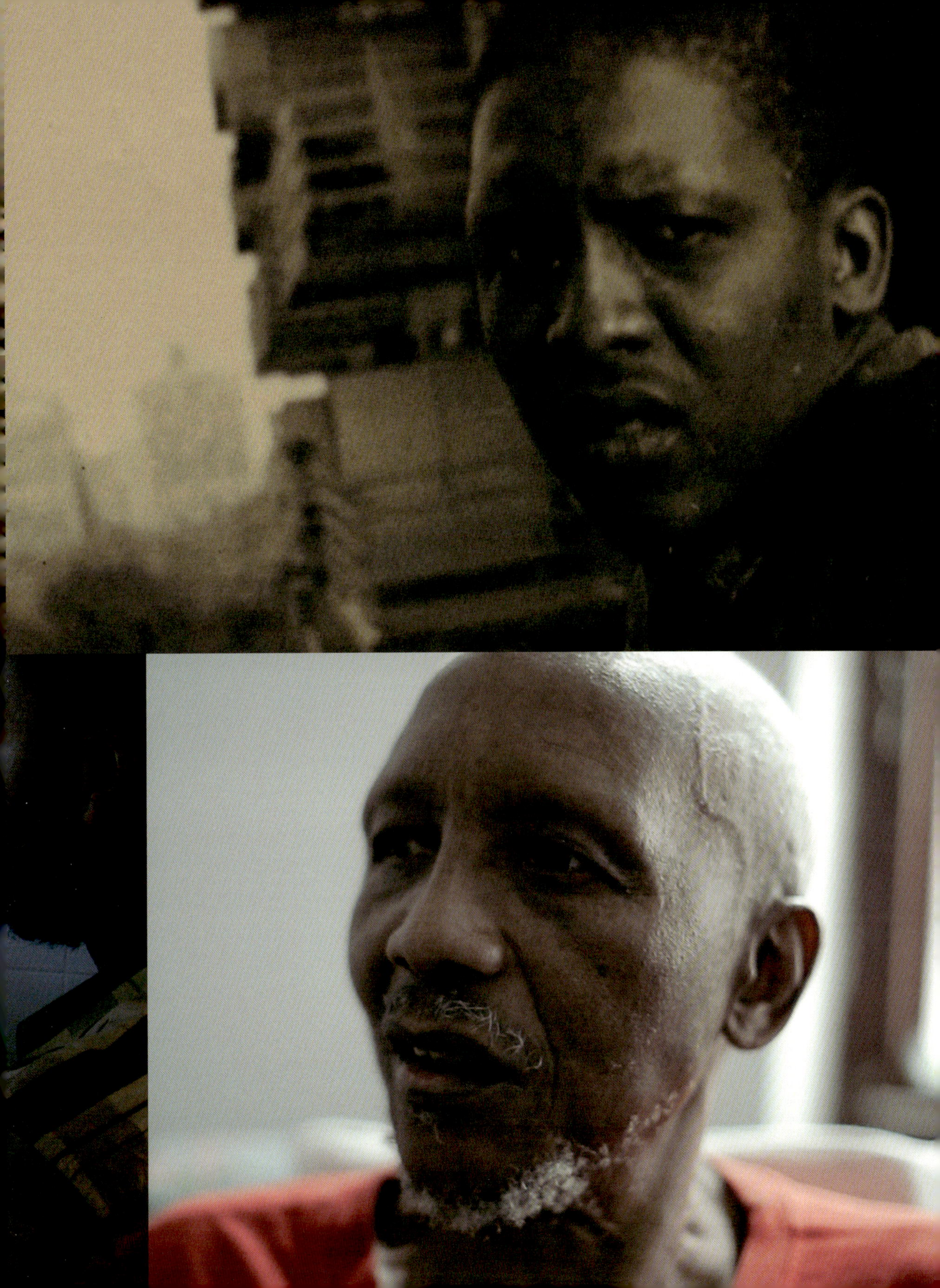

Shwabada
Ndikho Xaba Documentary

SYNOPSIS

SHWABADA: *The music of Ndikho Xaba* is a cinematic inquiry into the art of composer and multi-instrumentalist Ndikho Xaba, navigating the world of theater and music to arrive at an intimate portrait of an African artist.

Summary

From his roots playing an organ at home to international stages shared with the likes of Hugh Masekela, Sun Ra, Yusef Lateef, and others. His first public performance in 1960 in *Mkhumbane*, the musical written by Alan Paton and Todd Matshikiza, set in motion events that culminated in his exile in the US, where he led the eclectic and pioneering band Ndikho Xaba & The Natives.

In 1970, as the leader of *Ndikho Xaba and the Natives*—a band based in San Francisco, California, Ndikho Xaba released an inventive record of exceptional musicianship, seeped in the African and spiritual traditions of the jazz avant-garde. Today, the record is considered as Holy Grail among lovers of free jazz and record collectors. The documentary film navigates through fifty years of Xaba's artistry, from his roots in the theater during the early '60s, moving from city to city while hounded by the notorious South African Police Special Branch, leading to a thirty-four-year exile in the US.

The film goes beyond the biographical; a meditative work that strives to evoke the spirit and character of Ndikho Xaba's message as contained in his music.

AN OPEN LETTER
TO THE ONE I LOVE

I find myself looking in the
mirror wondering what stares
back at me
It has no reflection just a
picture of you
Your long hair and glasses always
reminded me of a wise teacher
who
taught me how to love and
respect
Her name was also joy
She would talk about how her
blood was made from sunshine
and
that her tears where made
of stars. I loved when she would
tell us all stories specially of
her youth. She was a ride back
rider that wore a golden suit,
the horse was brightly colored in
every shade of the rainbow. She
greeted everyone with just one
single smile. Indeed she looked
to find new students to stroll
around the world to speak of
every language so that one would
see they are her.

·SCENE I·
INTERIOR

joy walks into the room
65 million years ago
naked, wearing only her business
flat chested
silky
(describe someone standing
perfectly straight)
perfect posture

now keep breathing
spine aligned
feel your butt, really feel it
send that breath to your feet
align, describe something, align

Nobody knows what she's saying
But they see what she's doing

(Camera zooms in)
to a plant
the tree of life …
what trees live in the desert
(I'm asking you to make a
mental list)
(zoom out, fade away,
and radiate)

·SCENE II·
EXTERIOR: ANOTHER PLANET
(ONE THAT WE CAN'T SEE)

Joy: "on another planet she
walked the ways I always saw"

hight heel up and down
in midnight
the hair was black
long
i never had my fingers through
out it
the wings
i saw her as the first person
i could see behind her eyes

"do you mean JOY"
"WHAT DID SHE LOOK LIKE"
"TELL ME"

voice over: or possibly text
(like a foreign film)
cut to — wet bodies dancing or
touch or rub (close up of skin
on skin)

it was a dance floor the lights
where coming within myself
i don't know maybe it was
an outfit
(each outfit is an essay — they
move the story along — read into
the outfits …)
like the one i wore last night
tell me
what are u trying to do to
no matter what you're trying
to do
to me

i'm gonna be naked
(ask the audience to please
remove their clothes)

move the naked people to one
side
of the room, they will be seen
as the angels (alien energy)
for the remainder of the play
and those with clothes on will
still be considered physical
bodies effected/affected by
gravitational pull.

Joy runs down the theater (from
back to front) being chased by
a monster.
Screams fill the exterior room

The First Person (was Joy)

Raúl de Nieves

Show the passing of time: tumble
weeds, clocks, candle flame.
-u-mine-today-

"You" and Joy are eating on a
picnic blanket:
i won't let you go away
the bells rang
and so did the beats
o please don't
you have to try
you can't break away from me my
hair is long don't you see

IT blow like the wind my name is
JOY (everyone shivers)

when do i look like it's
really real
does it look like nothing you
want to do

U can't run from my love

Joy gets up and walks away
We are left wondering if she
too has been influenced by
the atmosphere

NO MATTER WHAT YOU DO I'LL
GET TO YOU
by the trying i'll cry and try
you can't run
in national listings but i'll
make you mine today
from here we have a moment of

silence
as "you" sit alone on the
blanket.

Take 7 minutes to breathe in
and out and see if the audience
gets on the same breathing
schedule as you.

Stare at one thing, move your
eyes around the room and come
back to the one thing.

Everyone sings:

JOY
JOY
US
IN
JOY
US
JOY
JOY
US
IN
JOY
US
JOY
JOY
US
IN
JOY
US

Repeat until the majority of
the room is singing along,
those not singing should be
considered snakes and moved
into the light (not in the sense
of a treacherous or deceitful
person, snakes are good and
the reclaiming of that word is
important)

One of the singers approaches
the
"snakes"
approach life as an experiment ...
see what happens

they run without looking
(one of the snakes grabs an ax
and
splits the singer's head open, a
white bird flies out)

sky like minds
access a peace of mind
clarity crossroads

keep breathing — breath is
movement

everything turns blue and white

a gap (like an earthquake)
take a deep breath
a pause
begin to be present ...
open your eyes

create a feeling of being rushed
we need everyone's help with this
stress them out for everything

·SCENE V·
INTERIOR – BATHROOM

A mirror (the cheapest one
on craigslist)
Repeat:
i have what it takes to change
the movie of my life
the same things don't need
to be happening

Intense anxieties with no
storyline attached
take interest in your pain
your fear moves closer
lean in

(eyes meet eyes and the 2 faces
stare into each other)

get curious
experience
beyond labels
welcome them

(hear sounds of nature ... running
stream, rain)

a glacier breaks
but we see the mirror cracked
continue with feelings of being
disconnected

Do anything that helps melt
the resistance ...

Joy appears in the broken mirror
She seems farther away than the
"other" reflection

Suddenly we are at school
Picture yourself at school
How do you feel here
Who is here with you

How do you know them
What are you trying to learn
How will you know when you have
learnd-ed it
Once you learn it
what will you do with it

Put a silk scarf over the mirror,
that glacier has died,
end of scene.

·SCENE VI·
INTERIOR – WIDE SHOT

Large circle of bodies sit
cross legged
learning to stay present
learning to take joy in the magic
of honest self-reflection
take a dive
you have to understand the story
try is the only word i know
i've been told that before

We need a helicopter for this
Or at least ask the audience to
stand — And look down

Ask them to imagine:

A fertile crescent
A pot belly pig
A mound of dirt and grass
It looks weak—like nothing—
who cares
But now tell them: this is one of
the places that we came from
There are many, but this is one
Feel the mood change
Ask them if they love that little
pot belly pig now

Joy floats up from behind the hill
– the size of a giant
You can only see her bust and the
hill becomes her breasts

A band plays (any band will
do, a different band for every
performance)

(the audience can sit now)
but they have to sit as tall
as possible
as if they were the third one
the chosen one

I need google maps for the
next scene
All those oceans
Ocean floors
(we see a pixelated version
(tiny pixels) of blue)
google ocean
and click images

it's in these words/worlds —
little words/worlds

zoom in more

pretend you see a squid in all
those pixels
now that squid is real
we are not the opposite of squid
but we are squid
we are nature

read code (zeros and ones, x's
and o's)
hugs and kisses
just generic anything printed
out from a code archive
the band will interpret them
as notes
band plays again

band plays for as long as the
code—code as code

Voice of Joy: but everyone says
it together

"oh" but if you say so
take advantage of all the things
that we keep together
everyone will have as much, as
much as they need
we all accomplish what we want
In the success of being a
human being
no body wants as much as they
all need
take advantage of the things that
keep together
who the fuck cares
that's the answer of the

strengths of life
in the middle of the night
no body gives a fuck
(fade to grey)

the grey represents night
(a night that won't turn black)
but you can't see the stars
city light, airports,
car horns, dust
artificial, but artificial is
here and real
look at what you are holding

the camera tilts up to the
sky (not a scene change,
but a transition)

birds don't have meanings
ha ha ha ha ha ha ha ha ha ha ha
ha (group of annoying laughter)

it's funny that far from pursuit

ANYWAYS

(camera moves back down to
earth, slowly)

it's a different location now
tricks stolen from the new wave

a transparent projection of Joy
is focused behind us,

slowly people begin to notice
its presence

**NOW COMES THE MAIN ONE
YOU ARE GOING TO SAY:**

"this is all there is"

the guy that dies raises a fist in
the air
i didn't get the idea
-you did-
and when peoples raise their fist
up to god
this guy talks just like i do,
just like me
he's getting too close to
his ideas
all kinds of day dreaming
shadows should have spoken
the words change their meaning
the worlds change the beings
words that are used in airplanes
how can you hear the words you
hear on the ground

3 or 7 or 12 planes fly over
the stage

making lots of noise
blue angels
leaving a long pause where we
can't hear anything but the play
doesn't stop the actors continue
to speak, his gap in the story
leaves much to be interrelated.
Let's shoot for 3 minutes of
jet noise

(You can hear again)

it's like music how do you do it

when you look out the window
but you don't want them to stay
like this
as children
if you don't know

fourth one

ladies and gentlemen
Train to succeed with the best
the best in beauty
You should be made of beauty
You should be raised to burn

Look
Listen
Respond.
In any case

(we need a new/old symbol)

These federal laws burn
Someone proudly maintained

Violators subject to die, the lie
and the feeling of detachment
some times less, the works.

In any case naturally I learn
to swear
I'm on this train and what
if I don't know how to catch
the ball?
I'm walking down the street to
get the right clue
one side of desperation
somewhere
SHIT!

The planes come back
Loud and low
Another chunk of dialogue
is missing

it's always shocking
it leaves the body forever
get me back to reality it's only
the question
but can you ask me what size
to choose

congratulations
class diploma
middle east political and global
studies with a focus in leaders.

What are you gonna do with
your life?

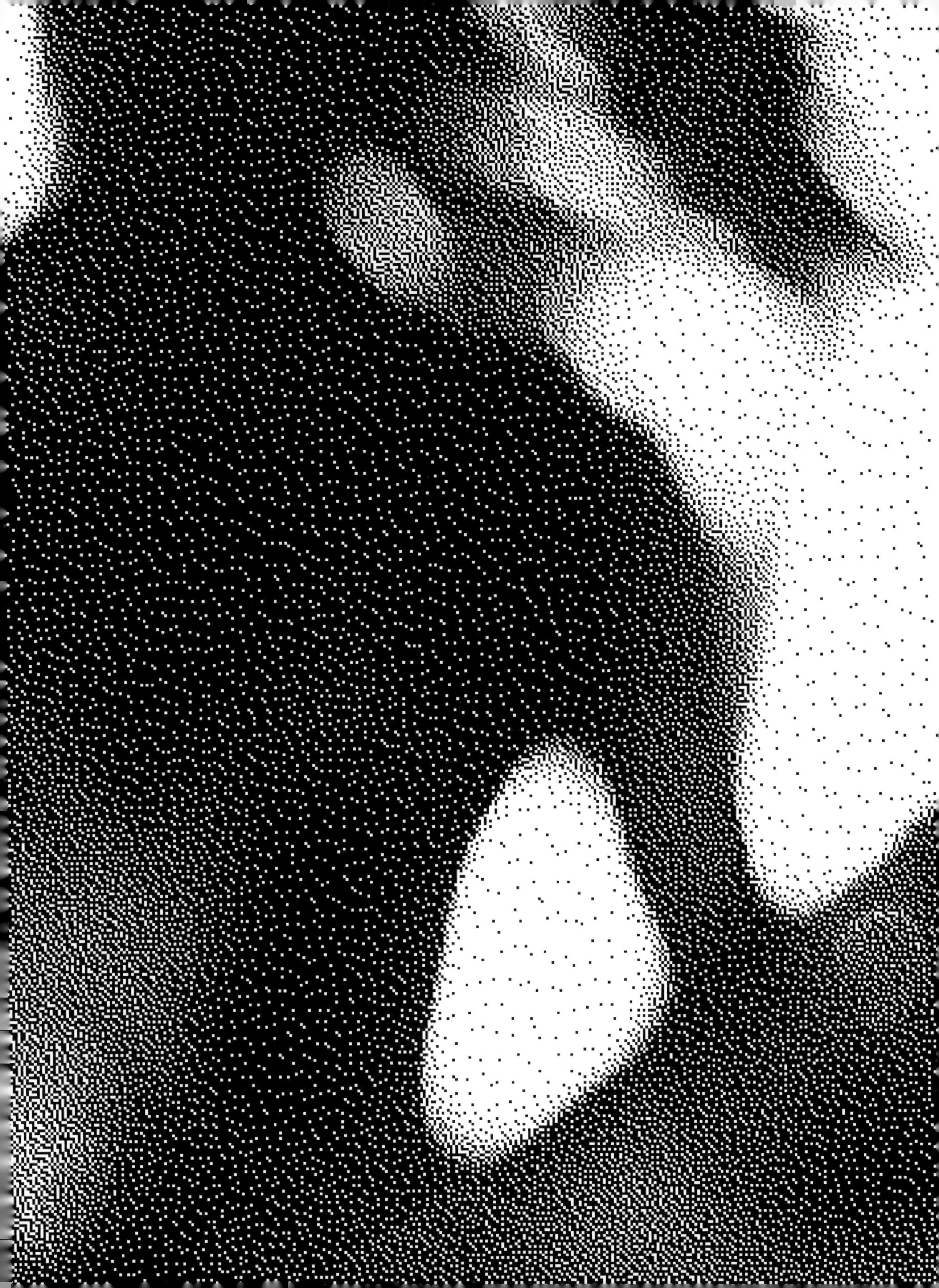

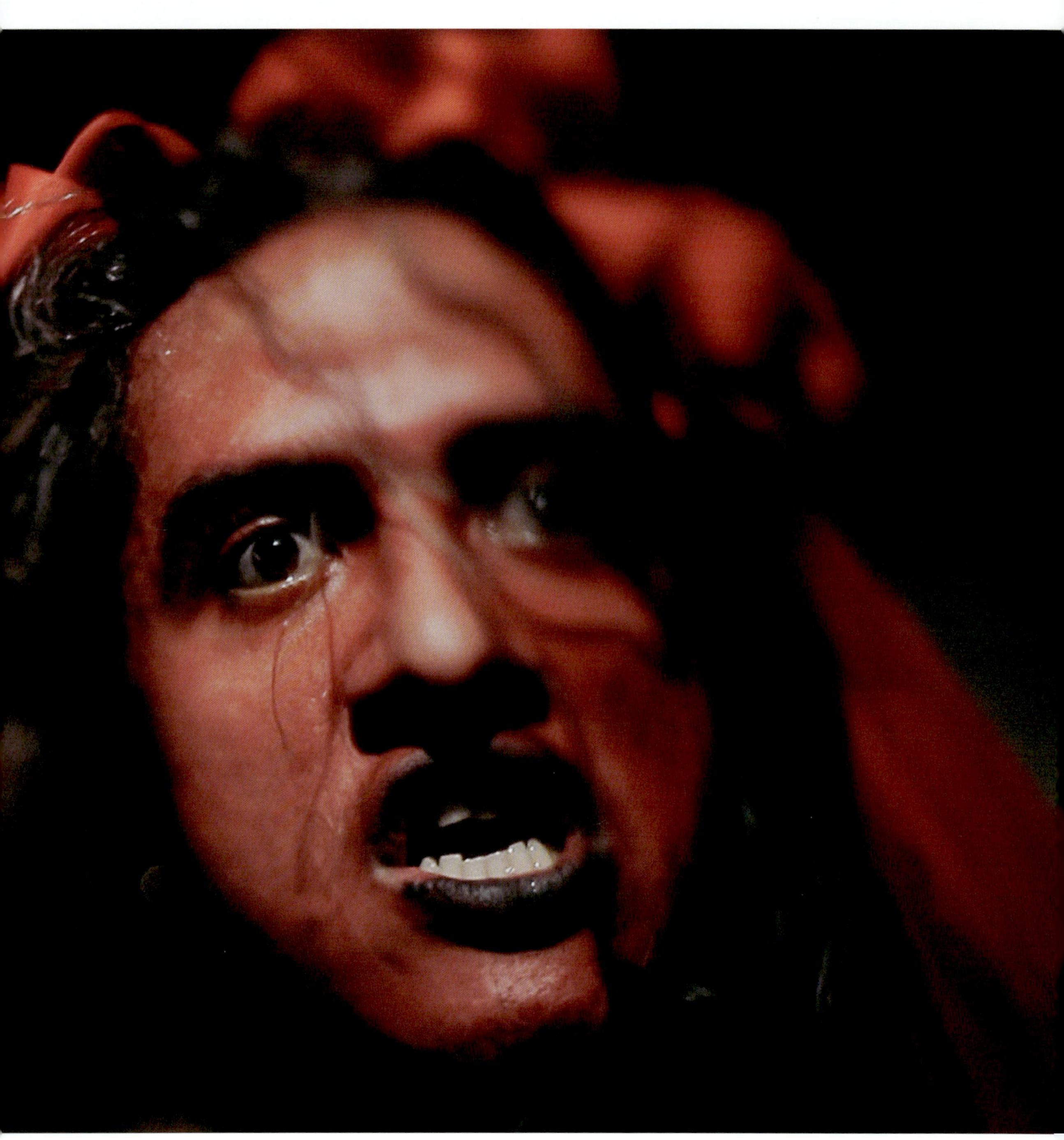

The Way and the Body — A Performance in Seven Acts

Raúl de Nieves with FLUCT

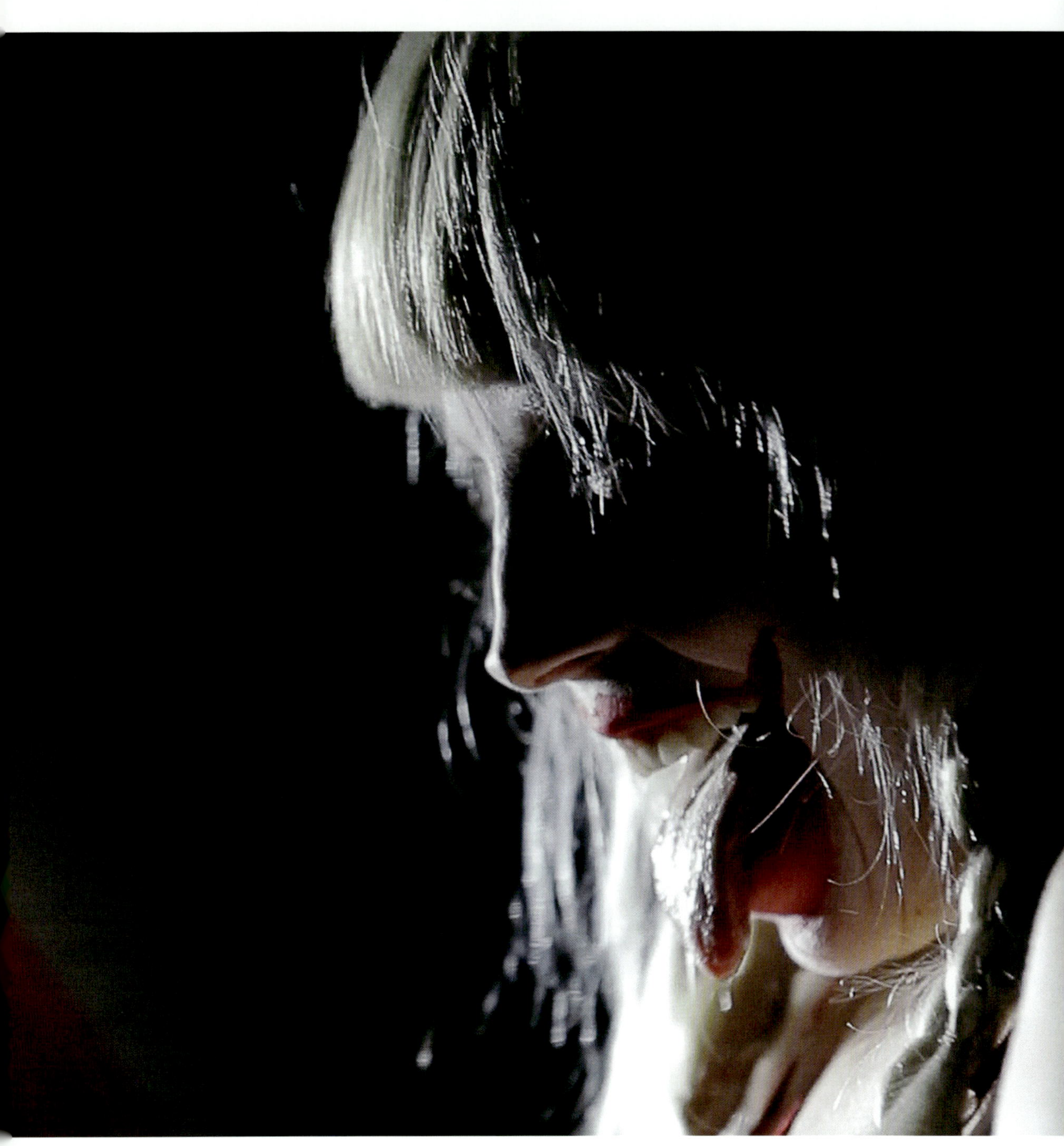

By Raúl de Nieves, Micki Pellerano, and Monica Mirabile. Performers: Kathleen Dycaico, Sigrid Lauren, Monica Mirabile, Micki Pellerano, Tara-Jo Tashna. Narrated by Chiara Fumai.

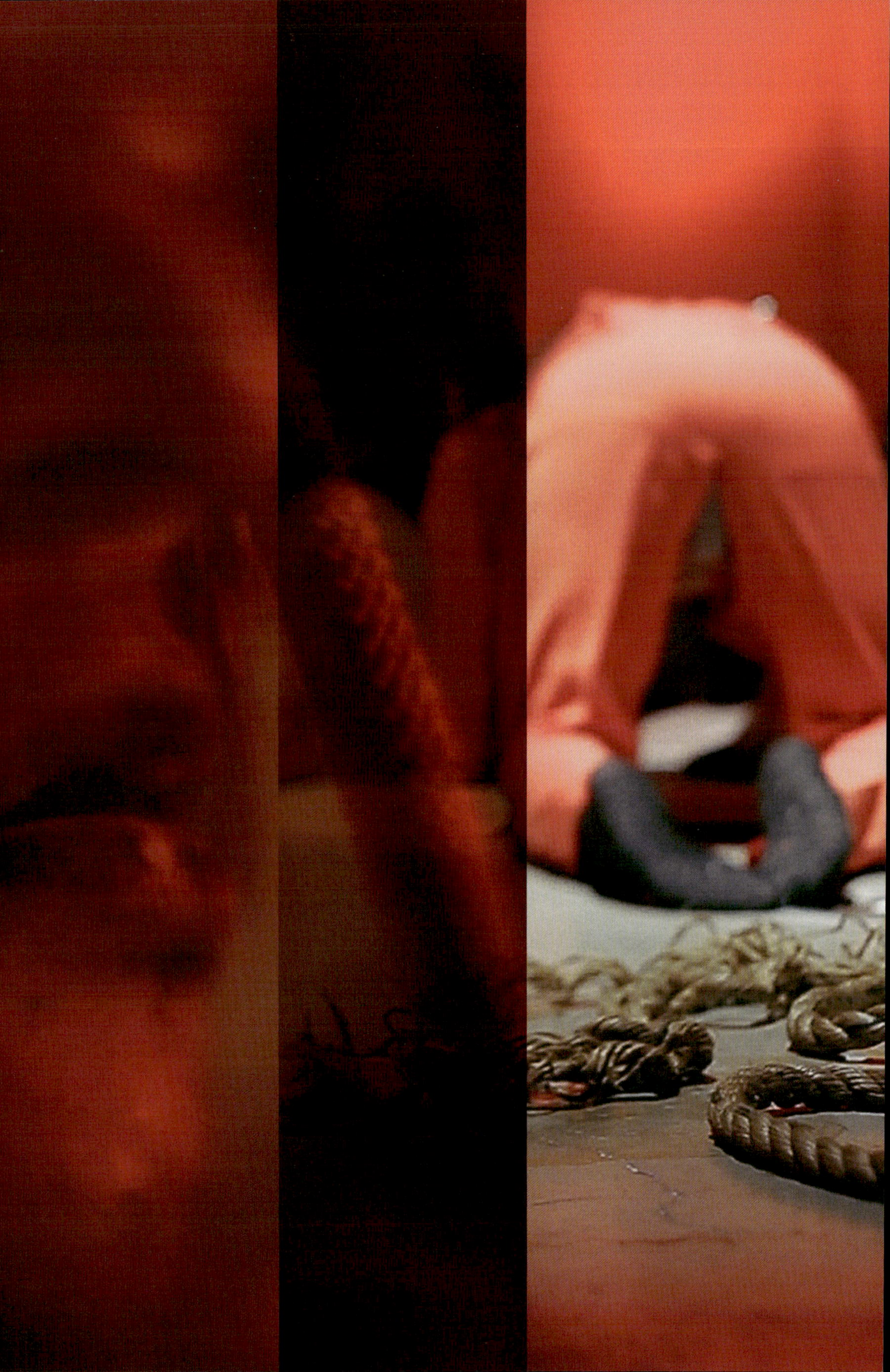

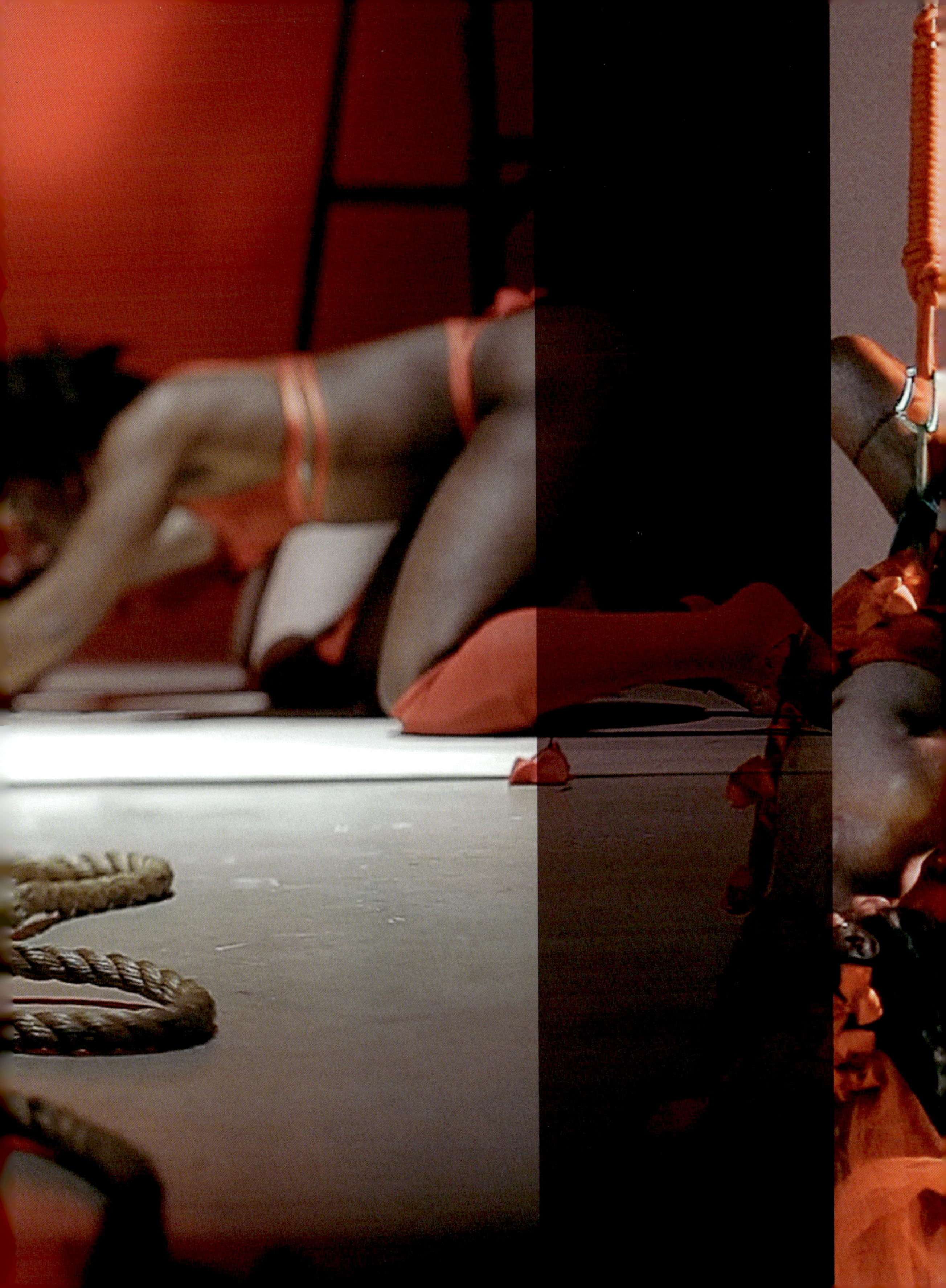

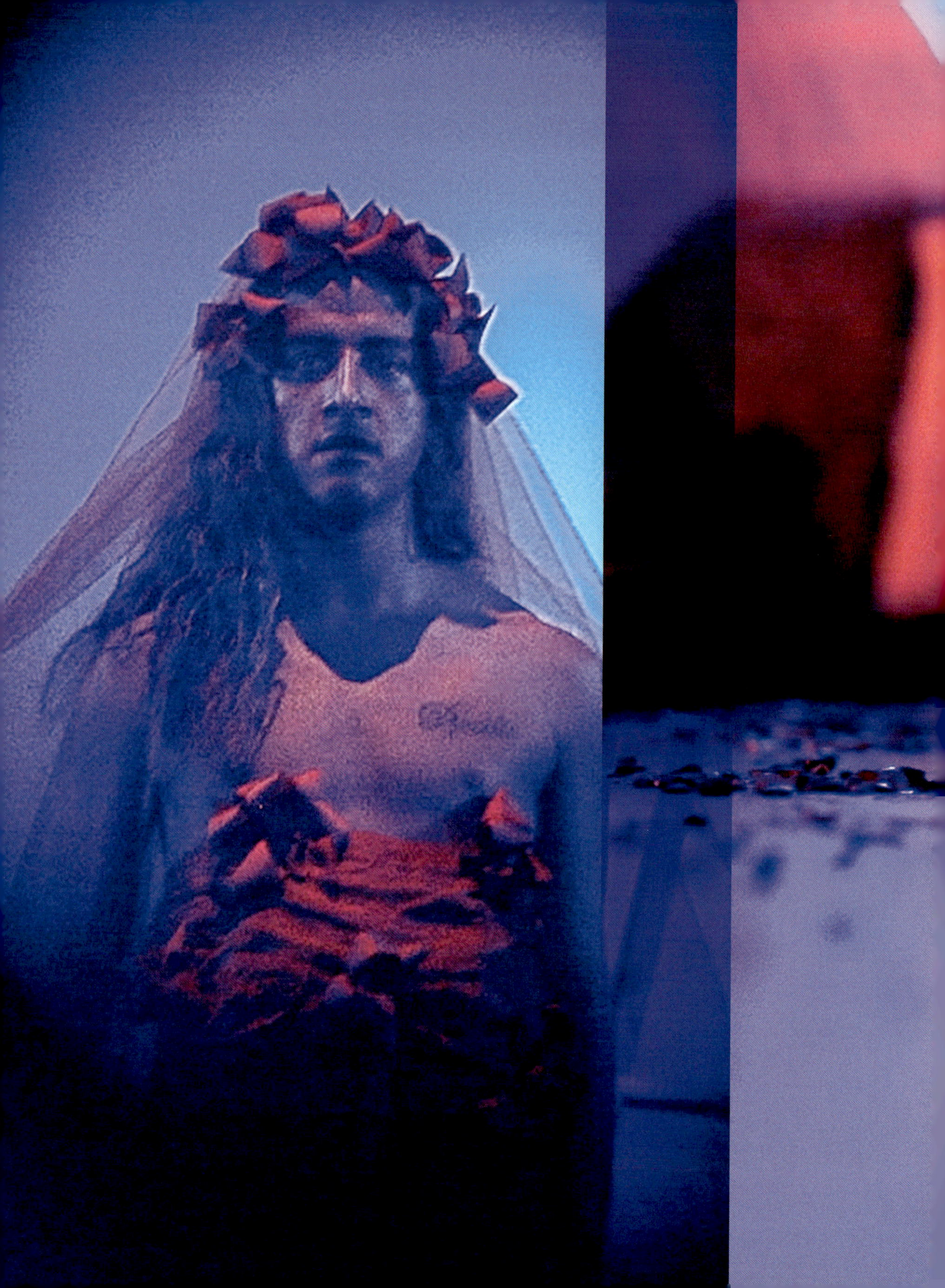

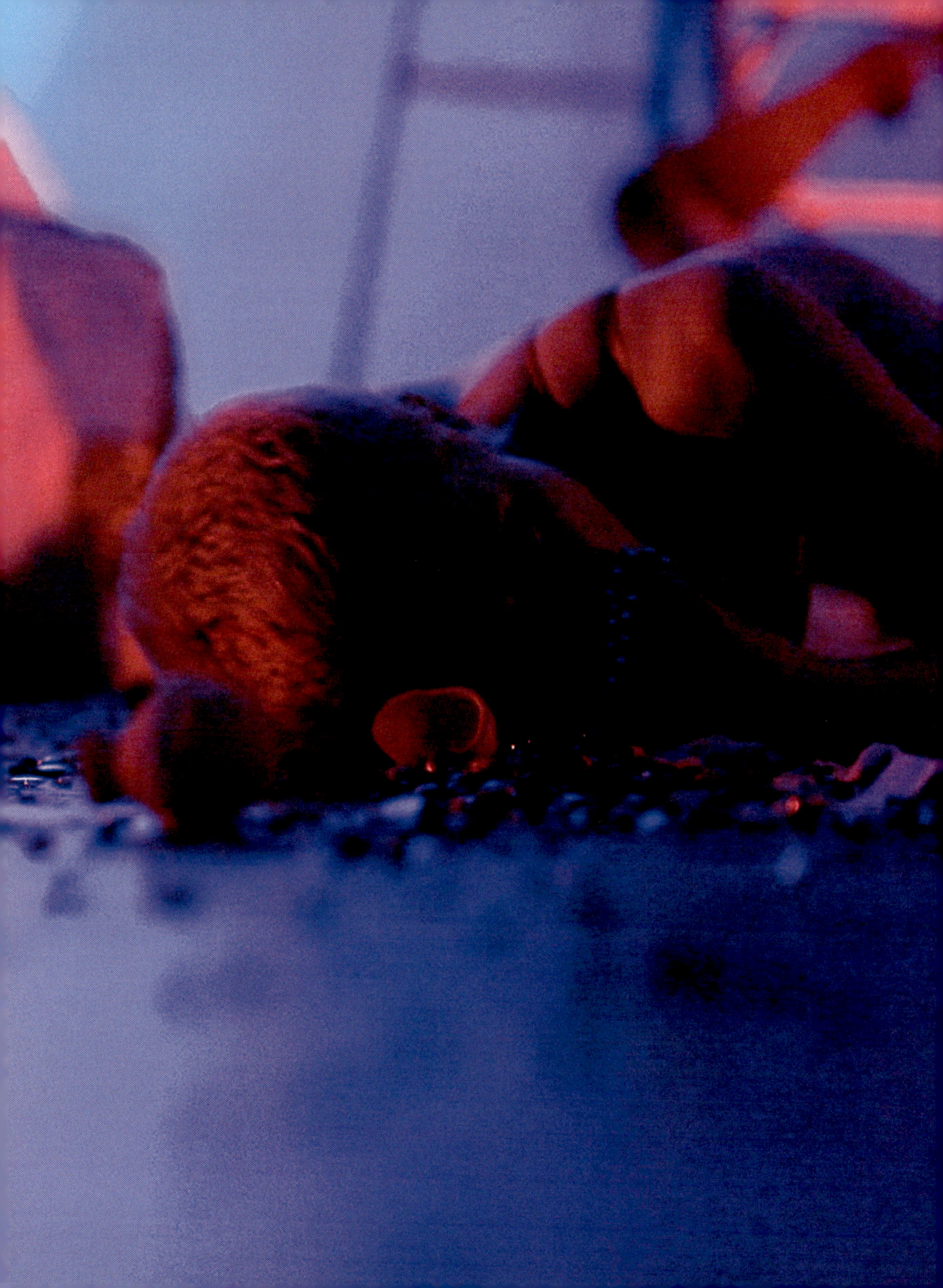

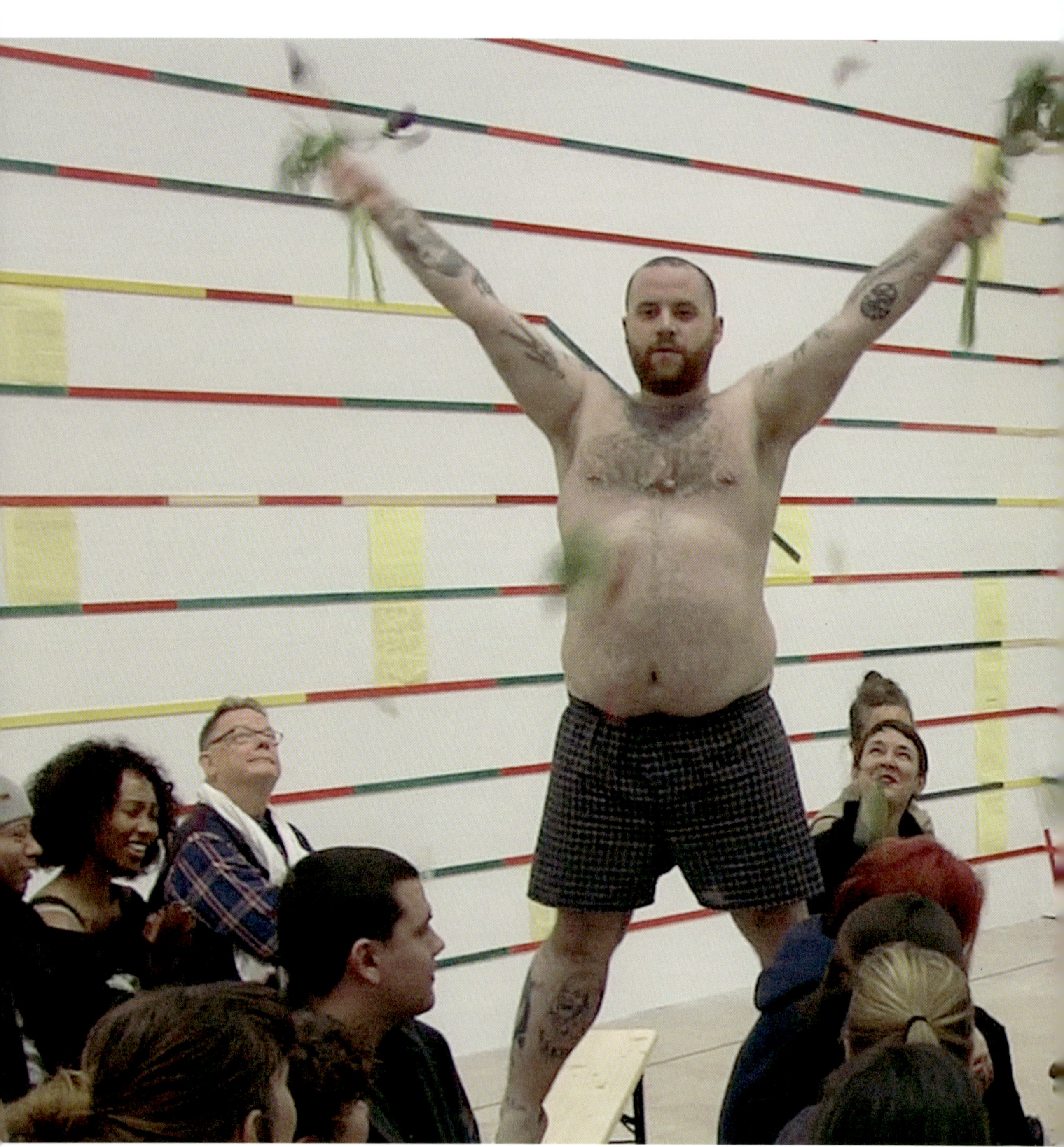

If I'm not dead then why did you bury me

Jake Dibeler

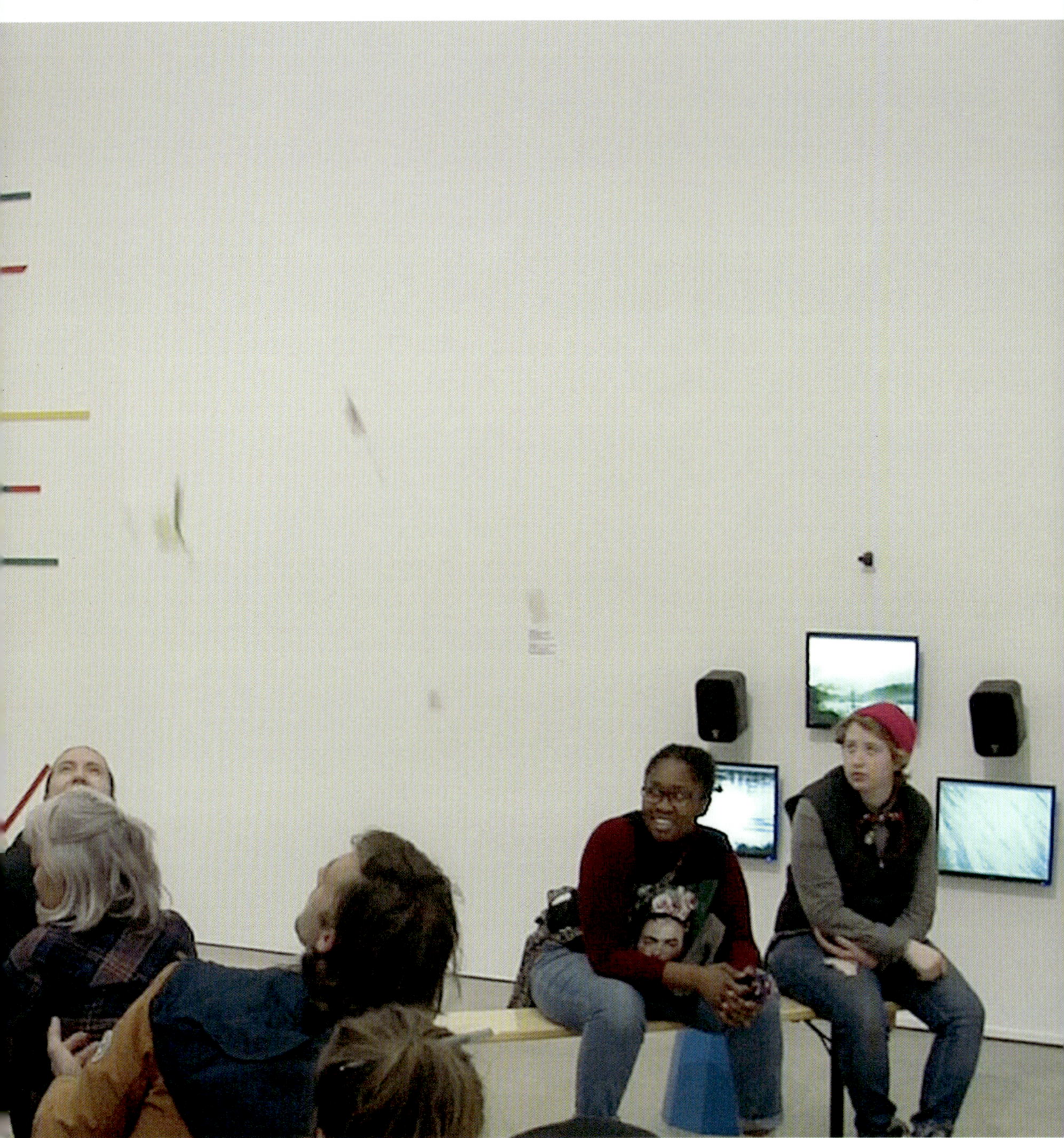

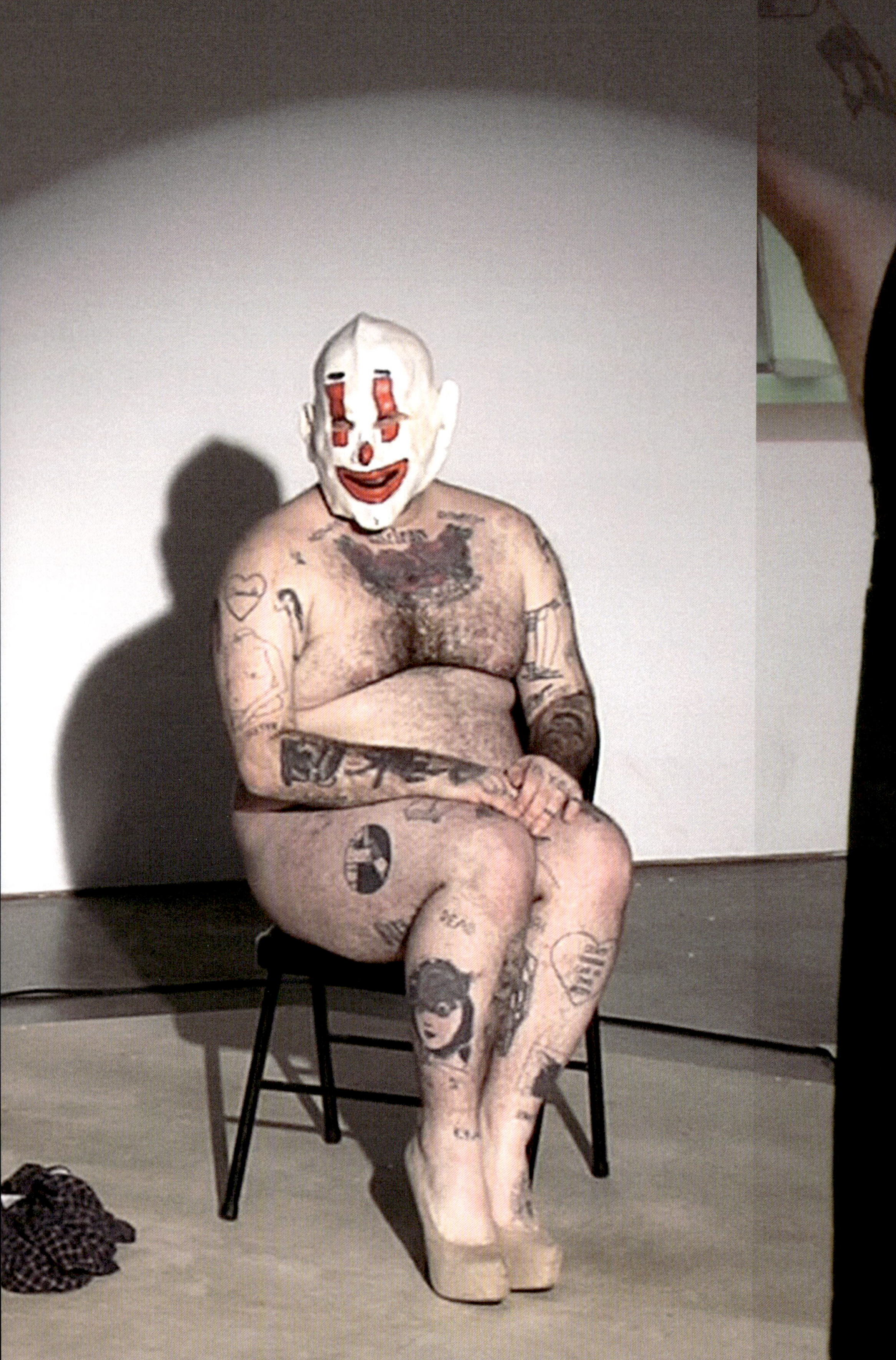

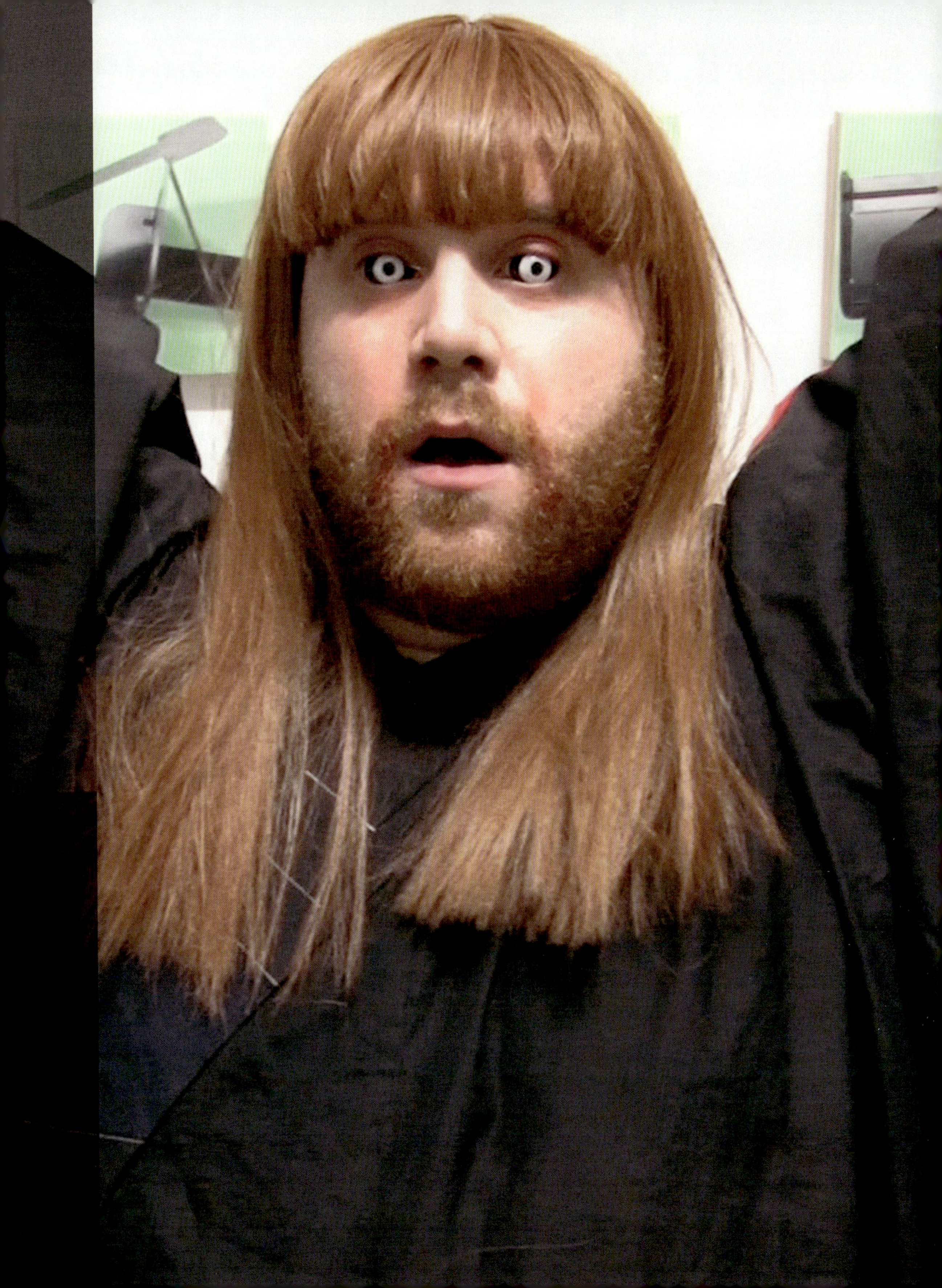

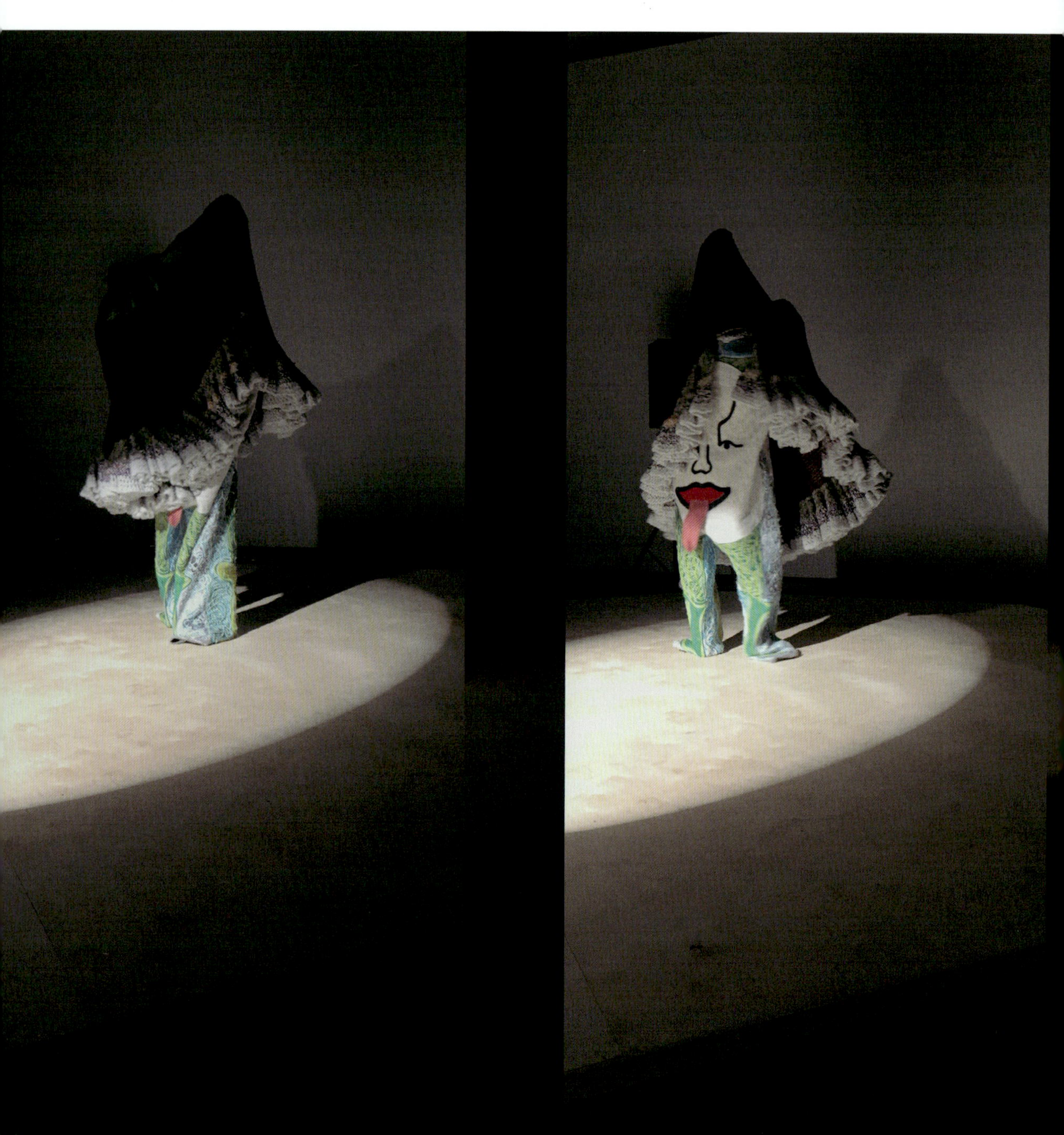

The Fly, solo improvisation

Raúl de Nieves

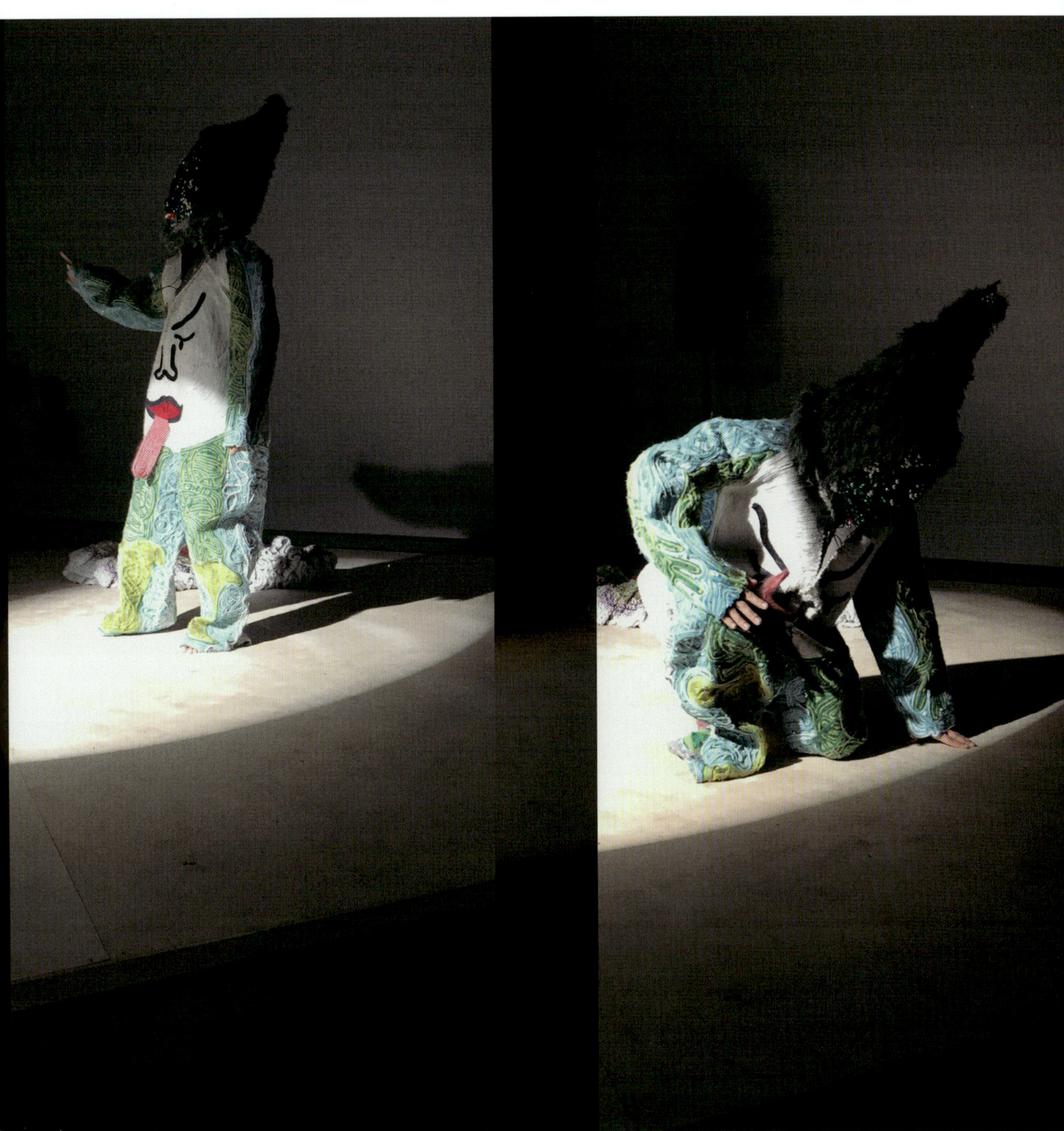

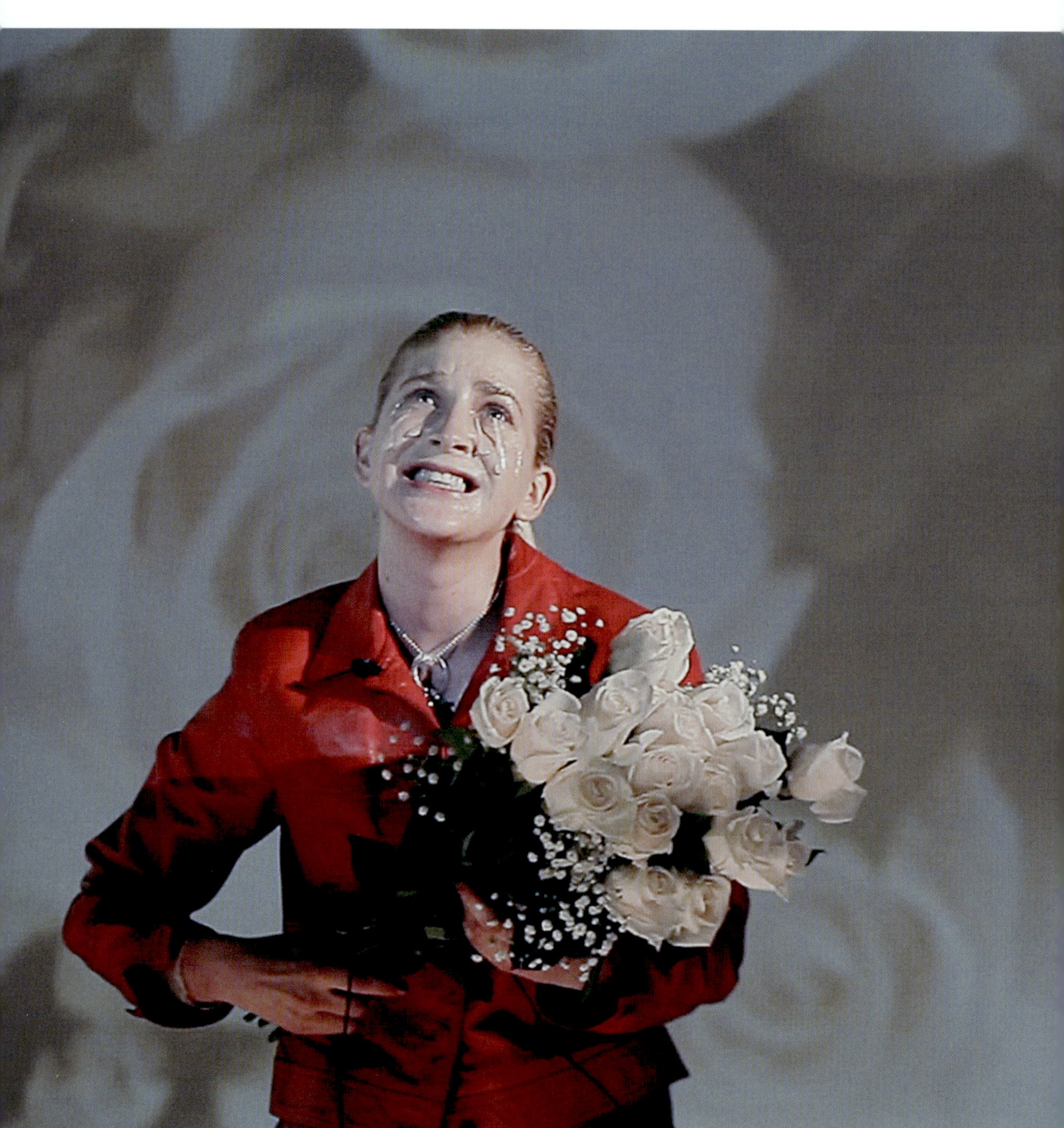

Mother of Vinegar: 2nd Sequence

Whitney Vangrin

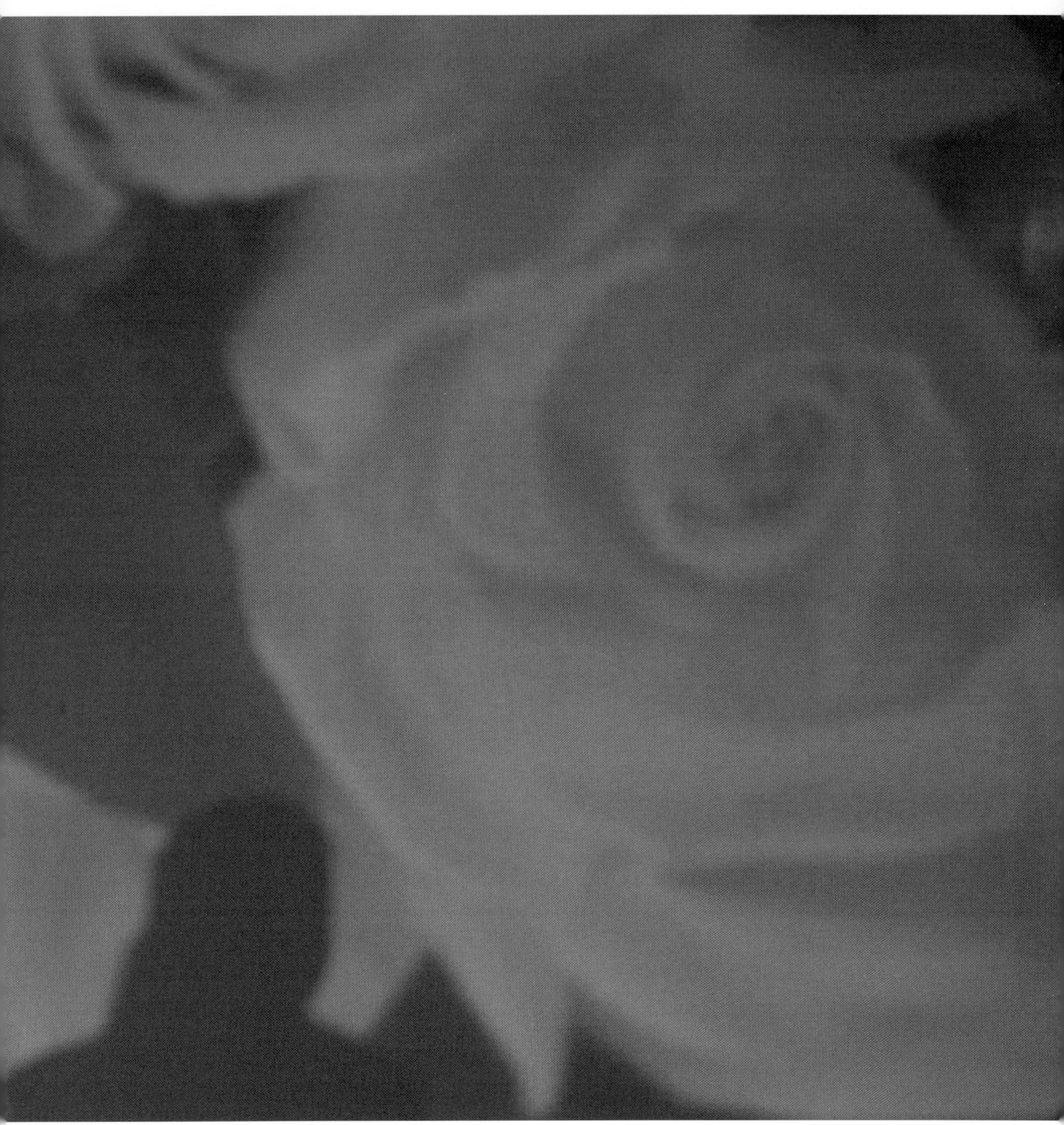

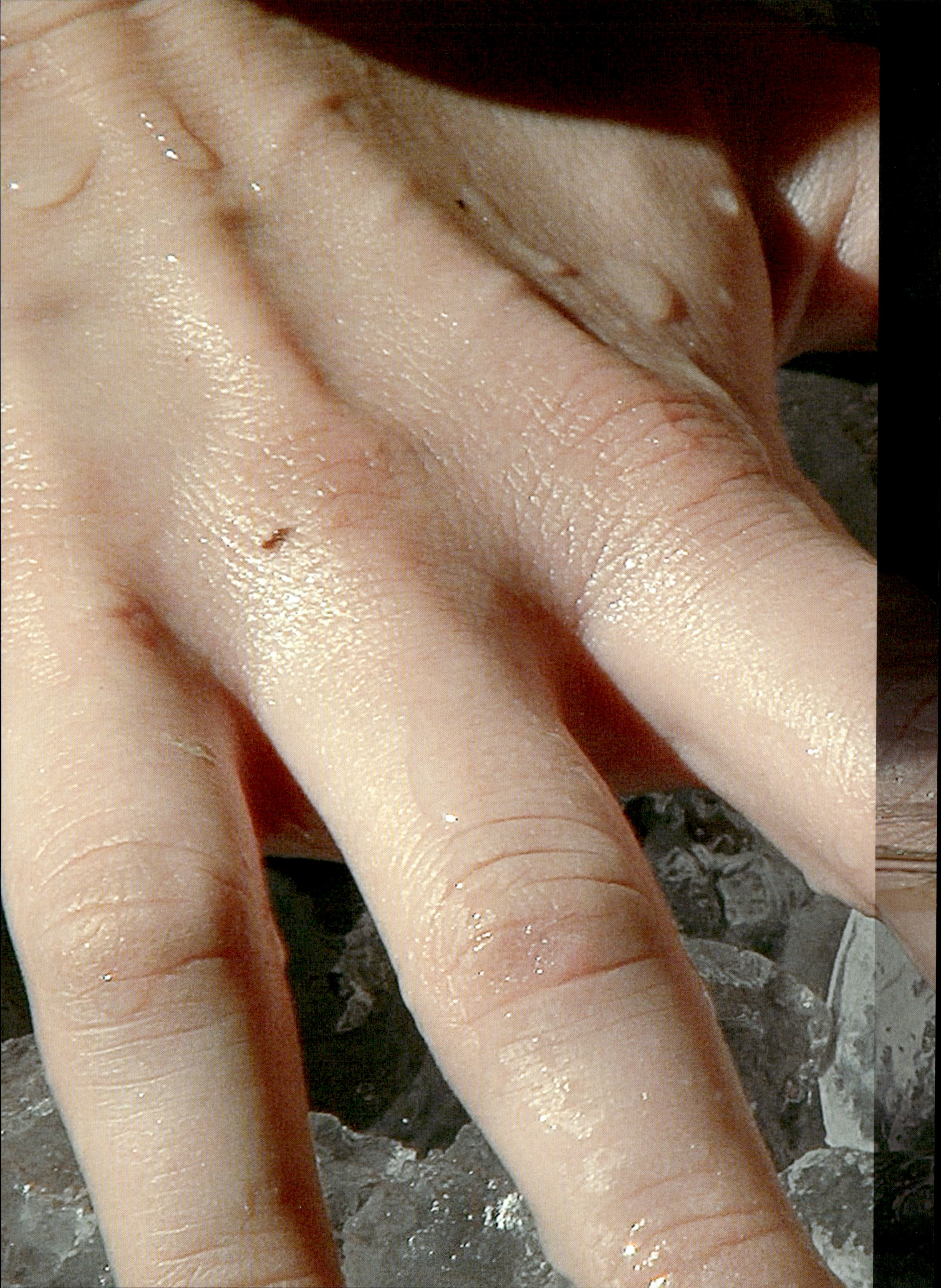

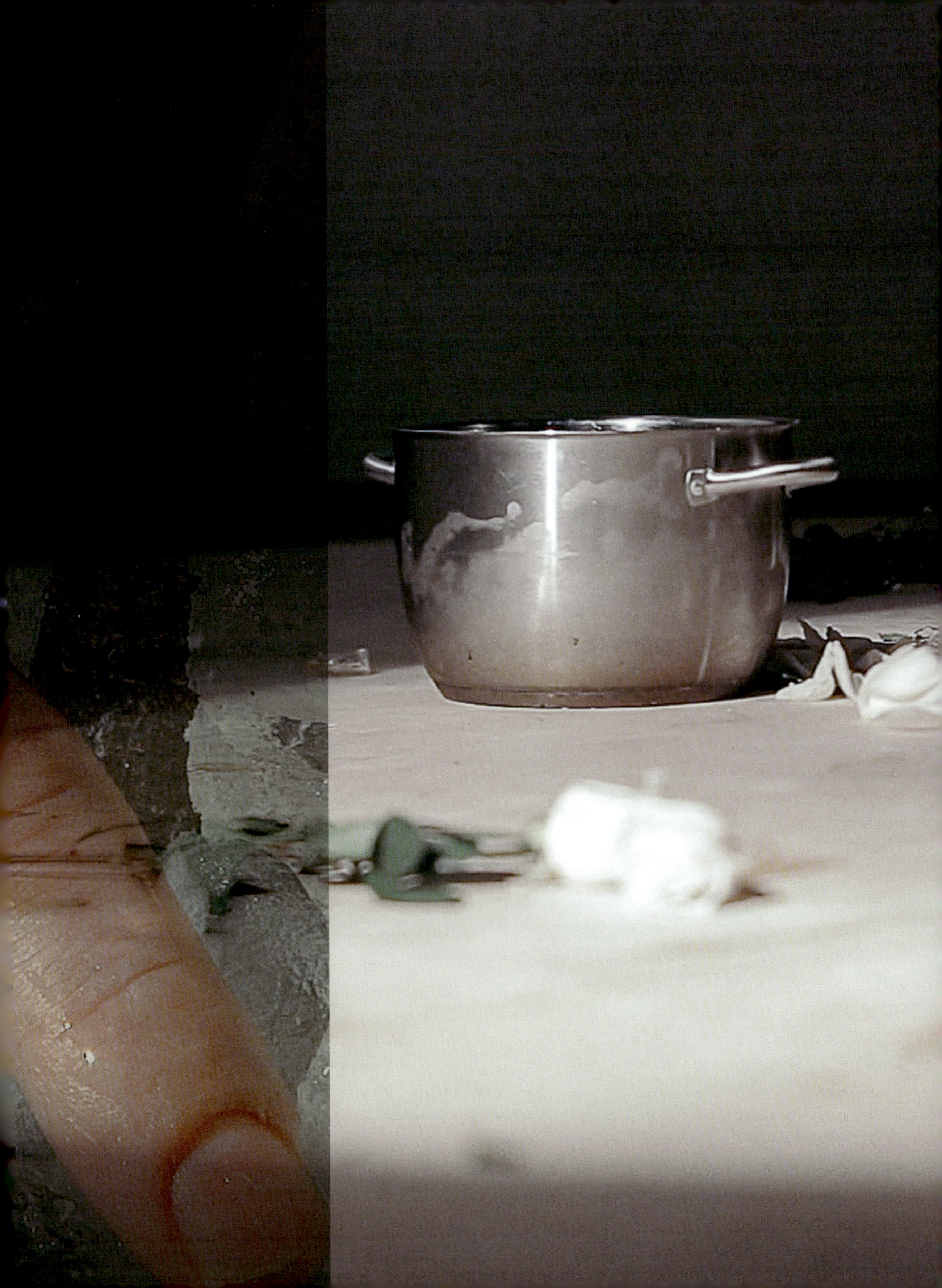

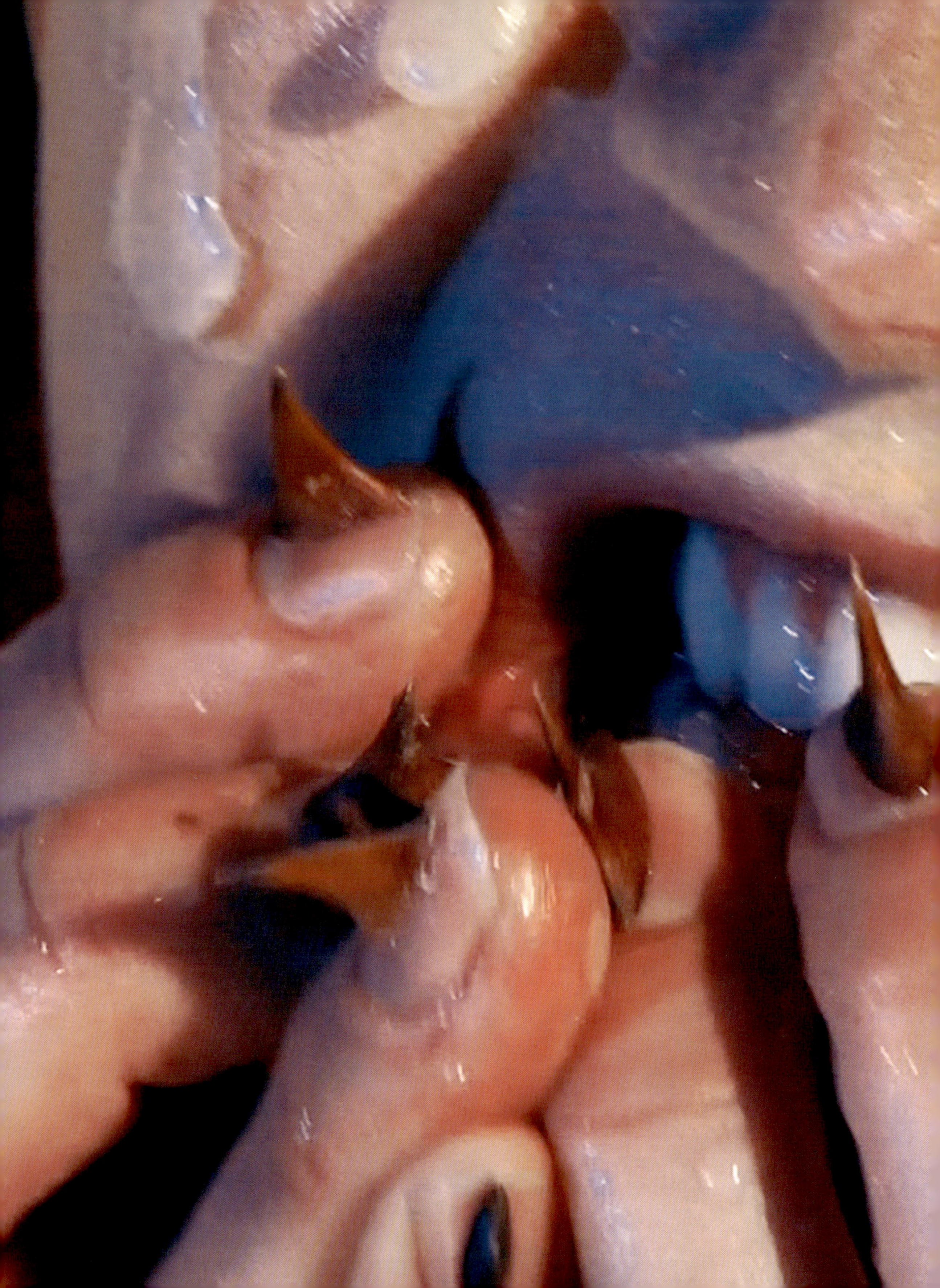

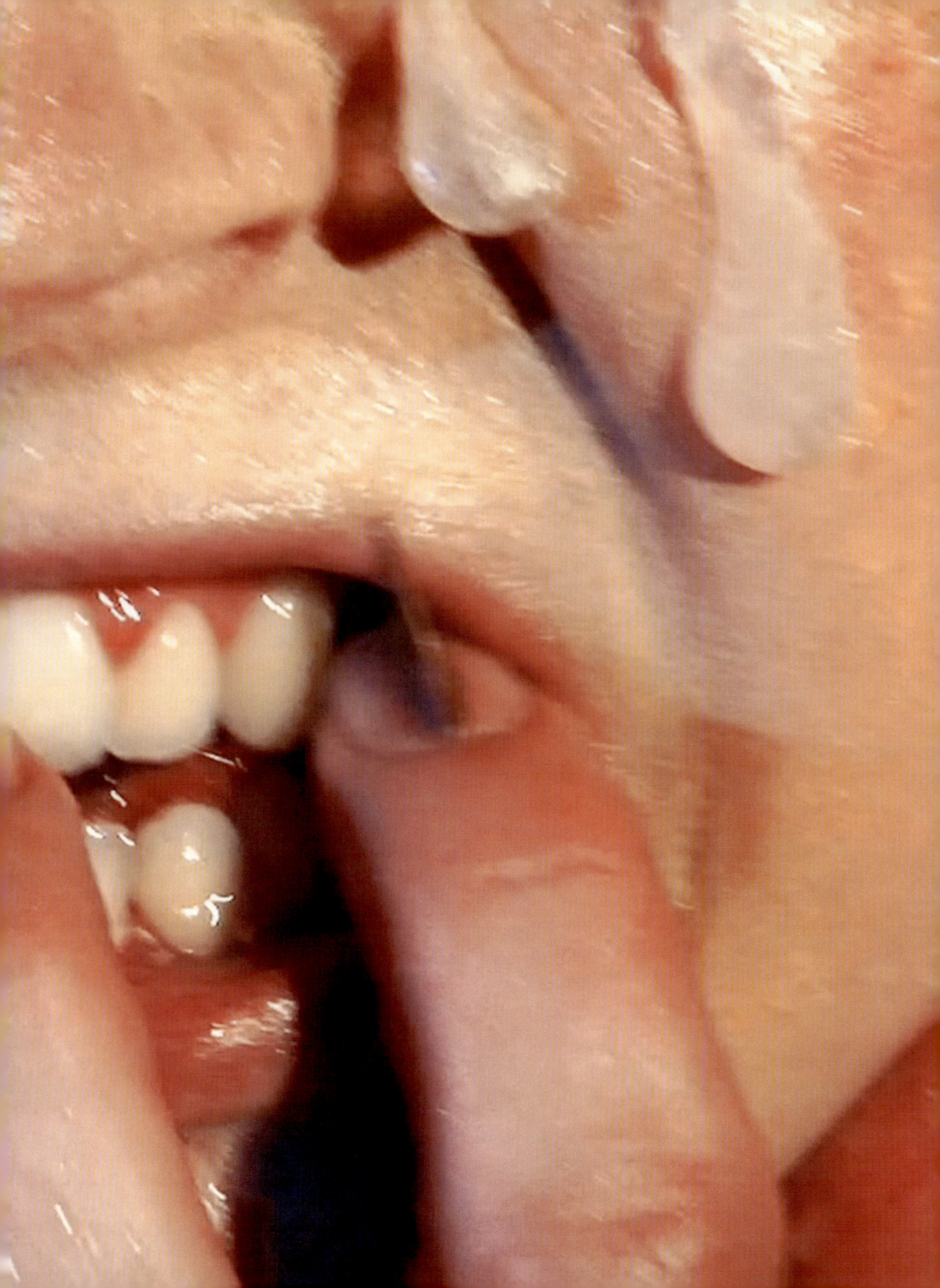

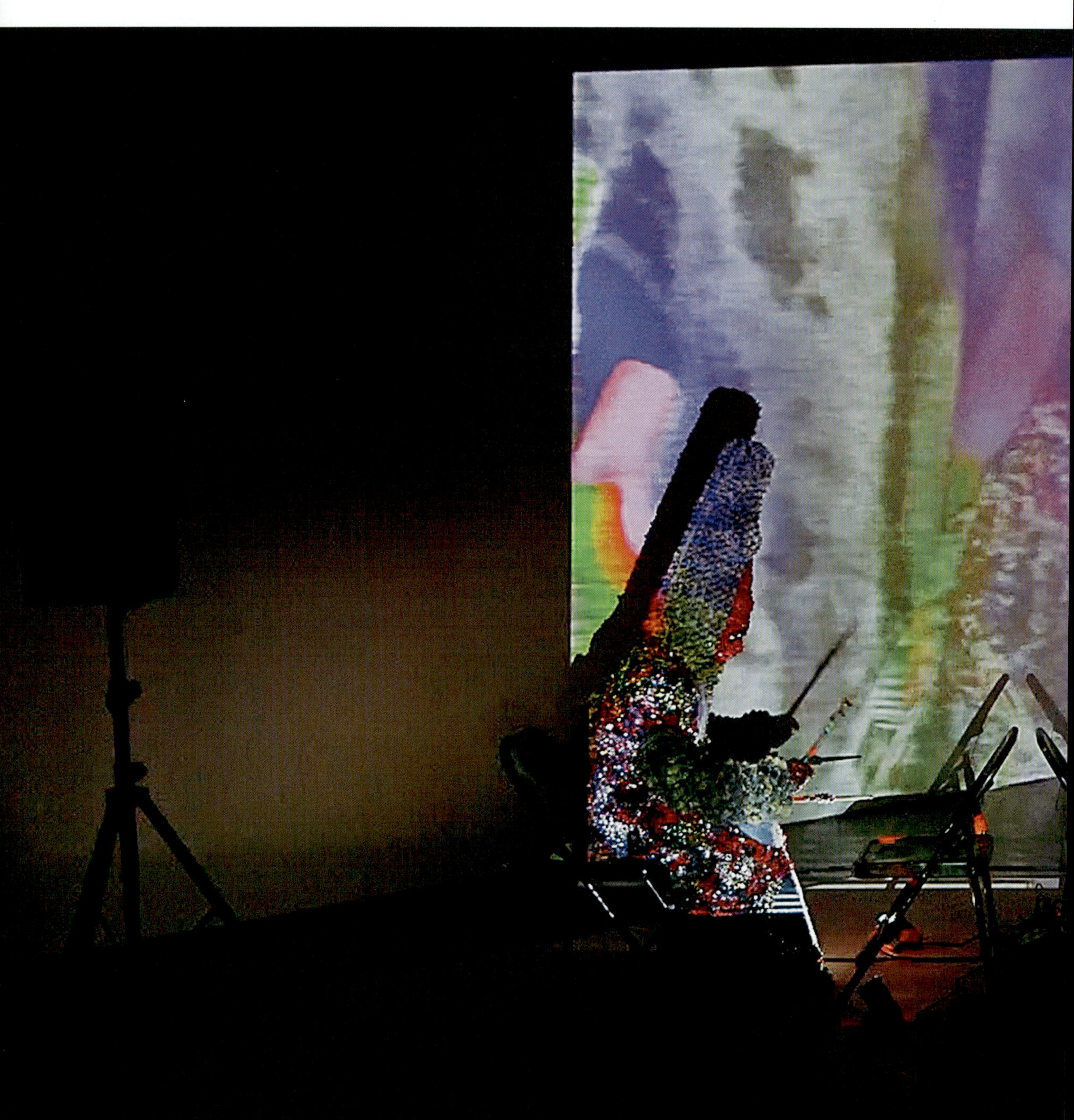

Somos Monstros

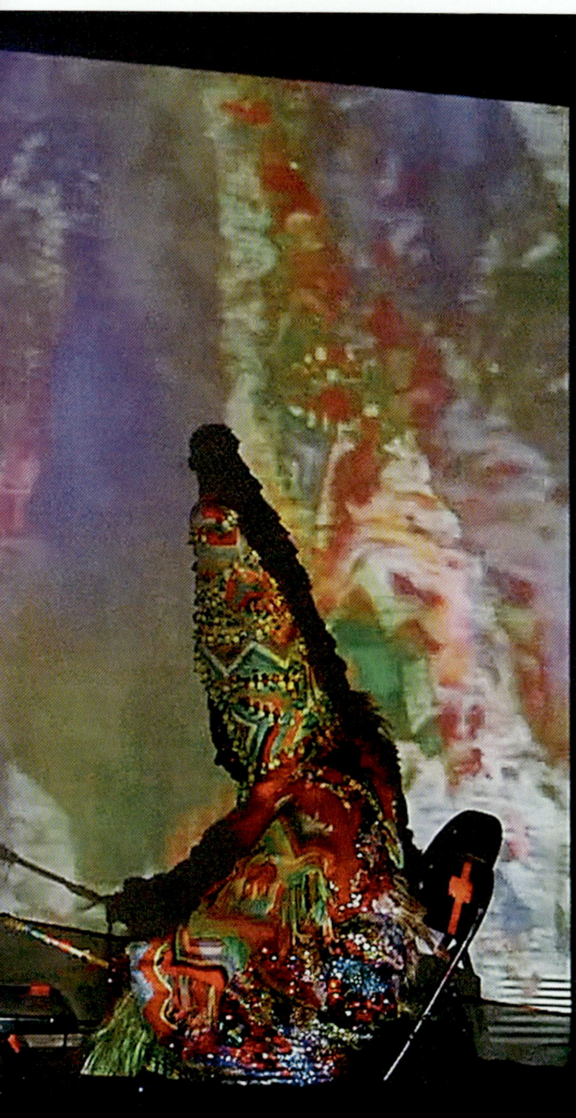

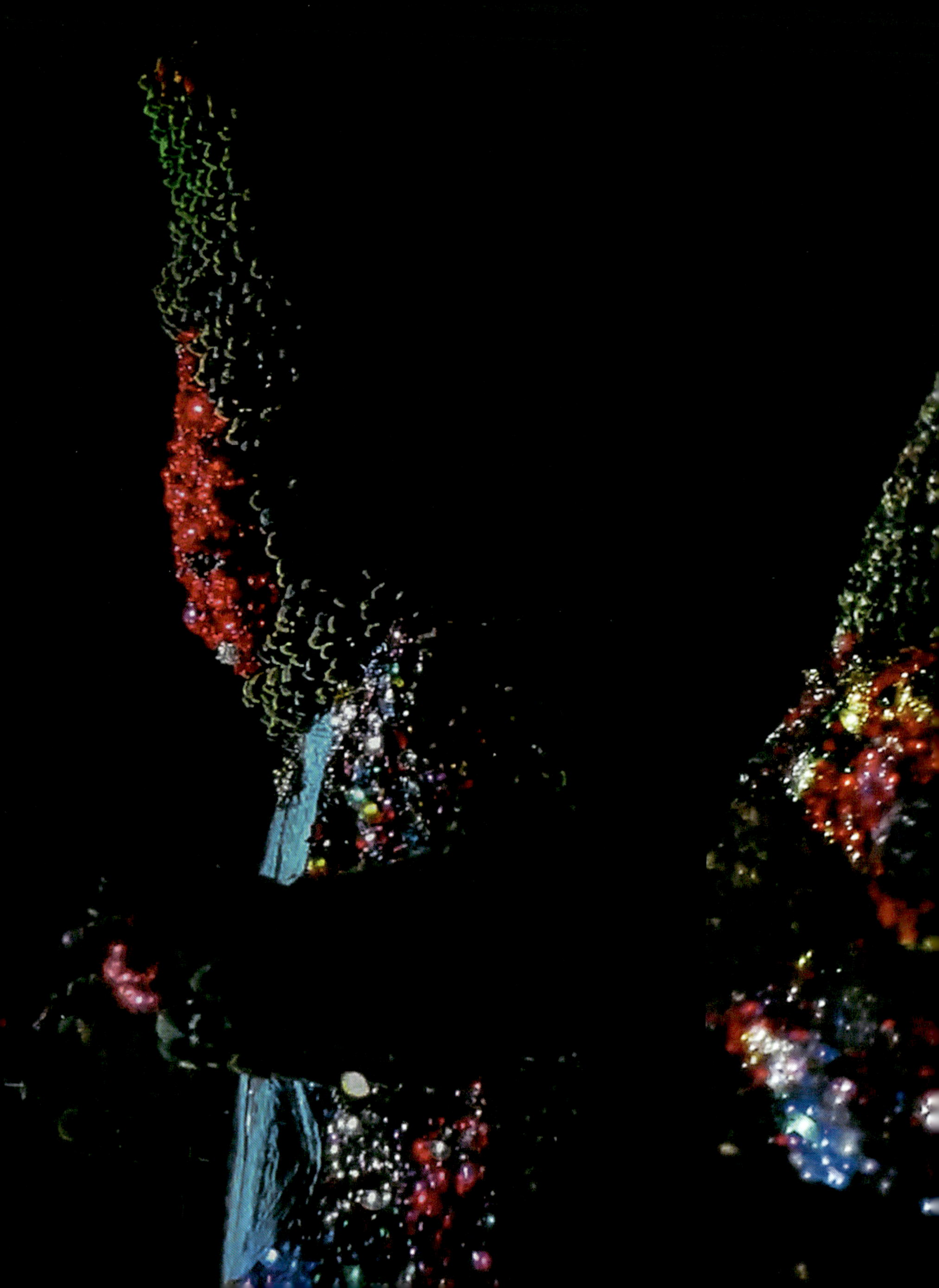

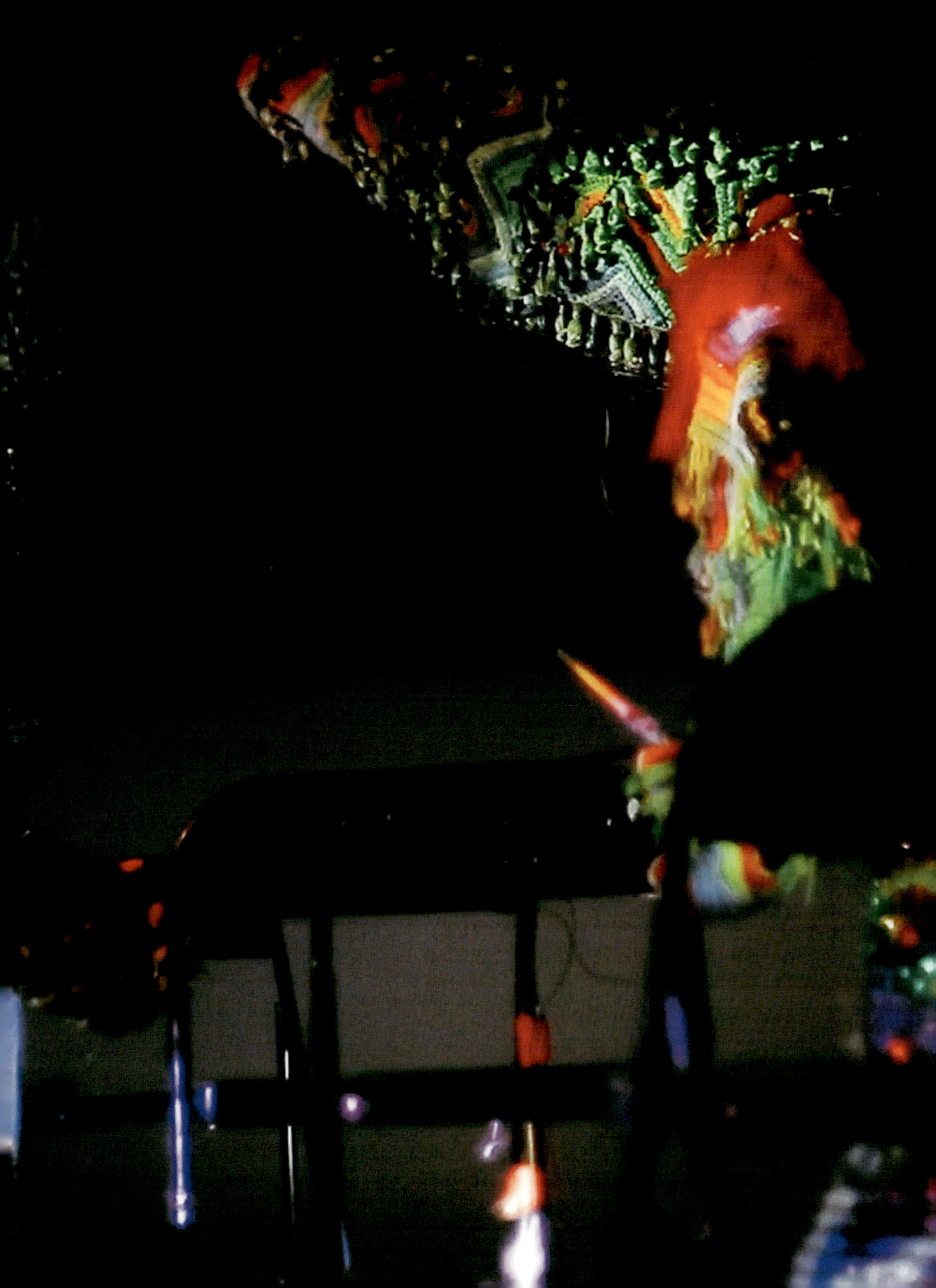

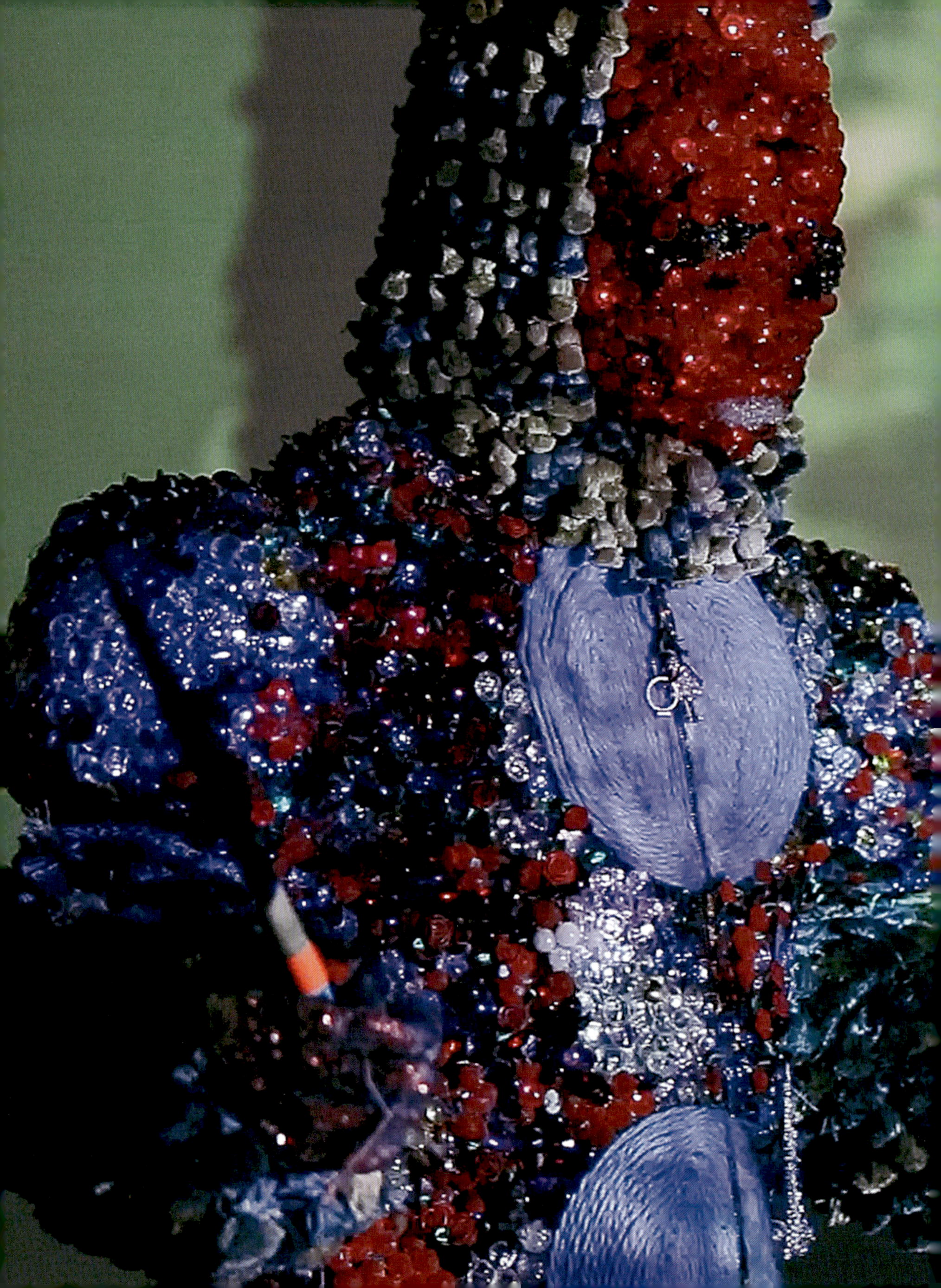

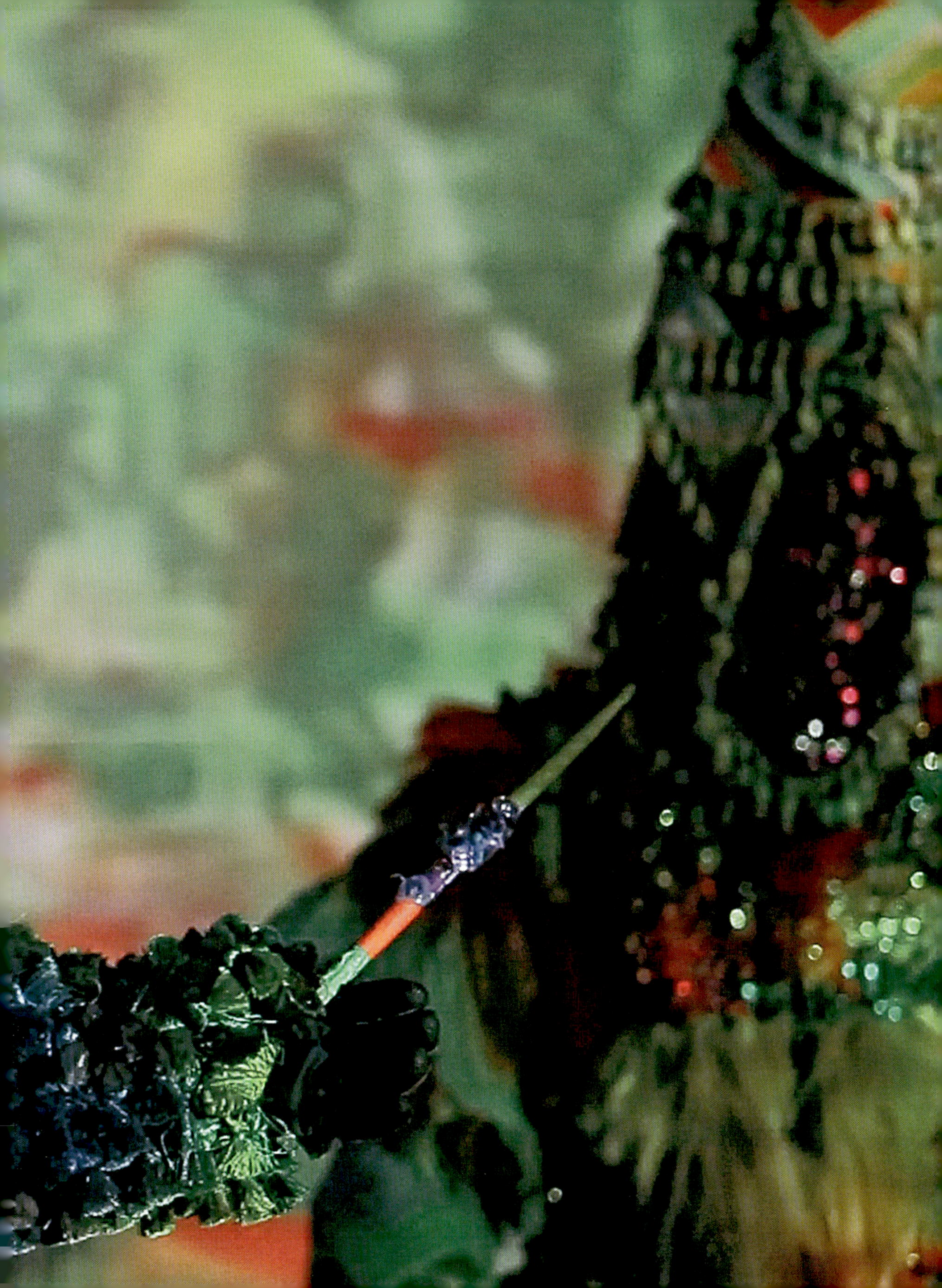

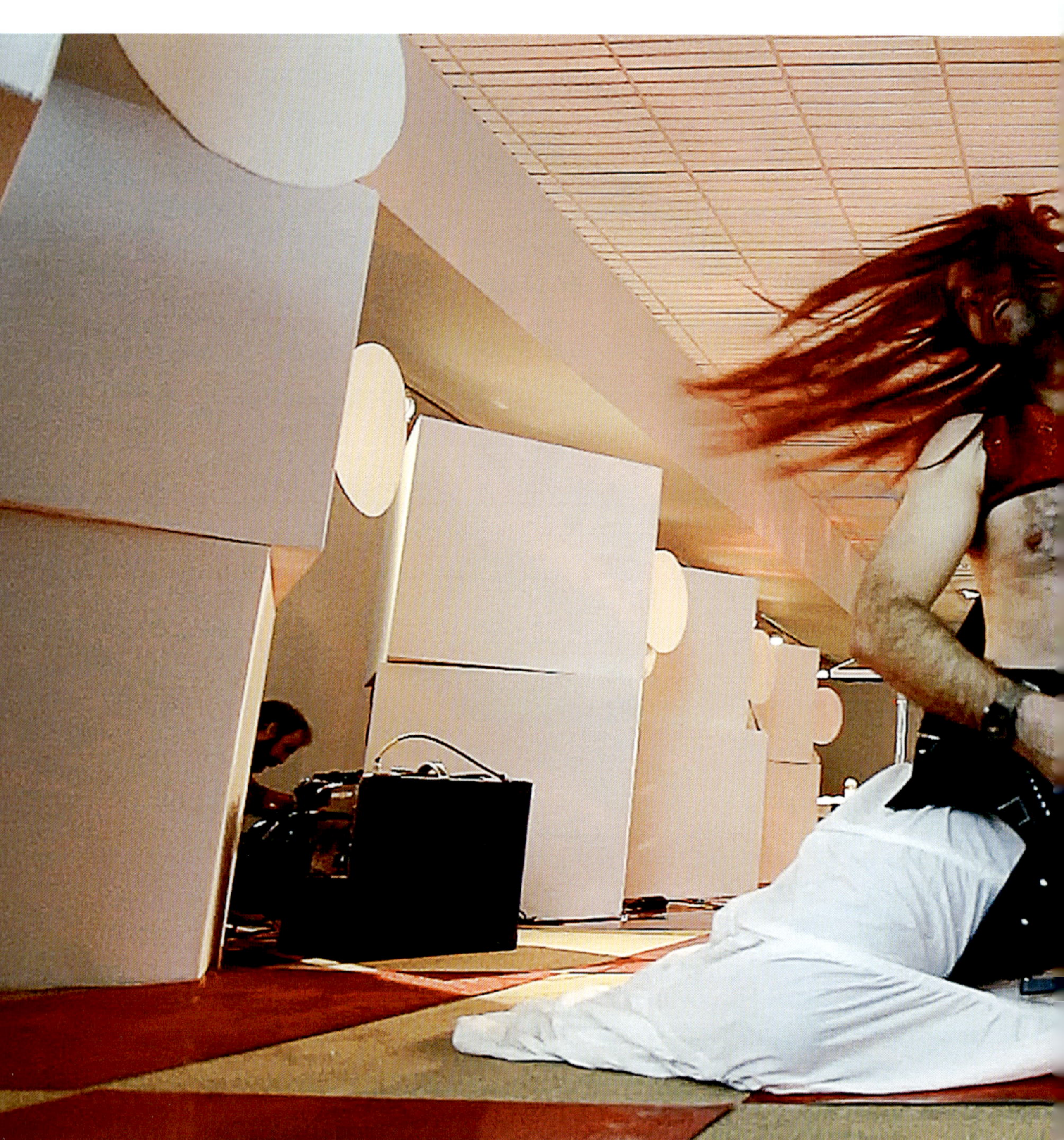

Soap Opera

Haribo (currently known as Hairbone)

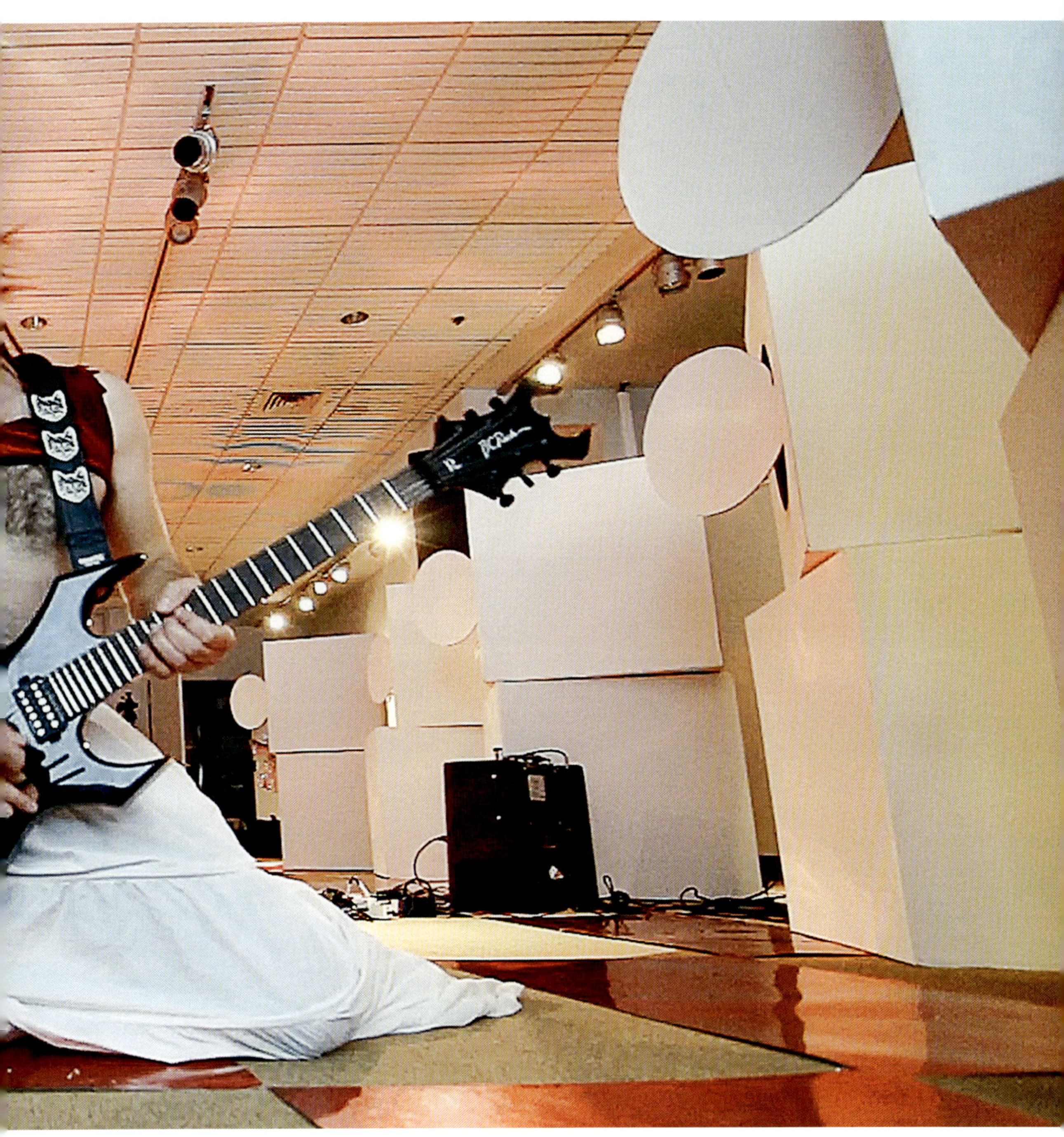

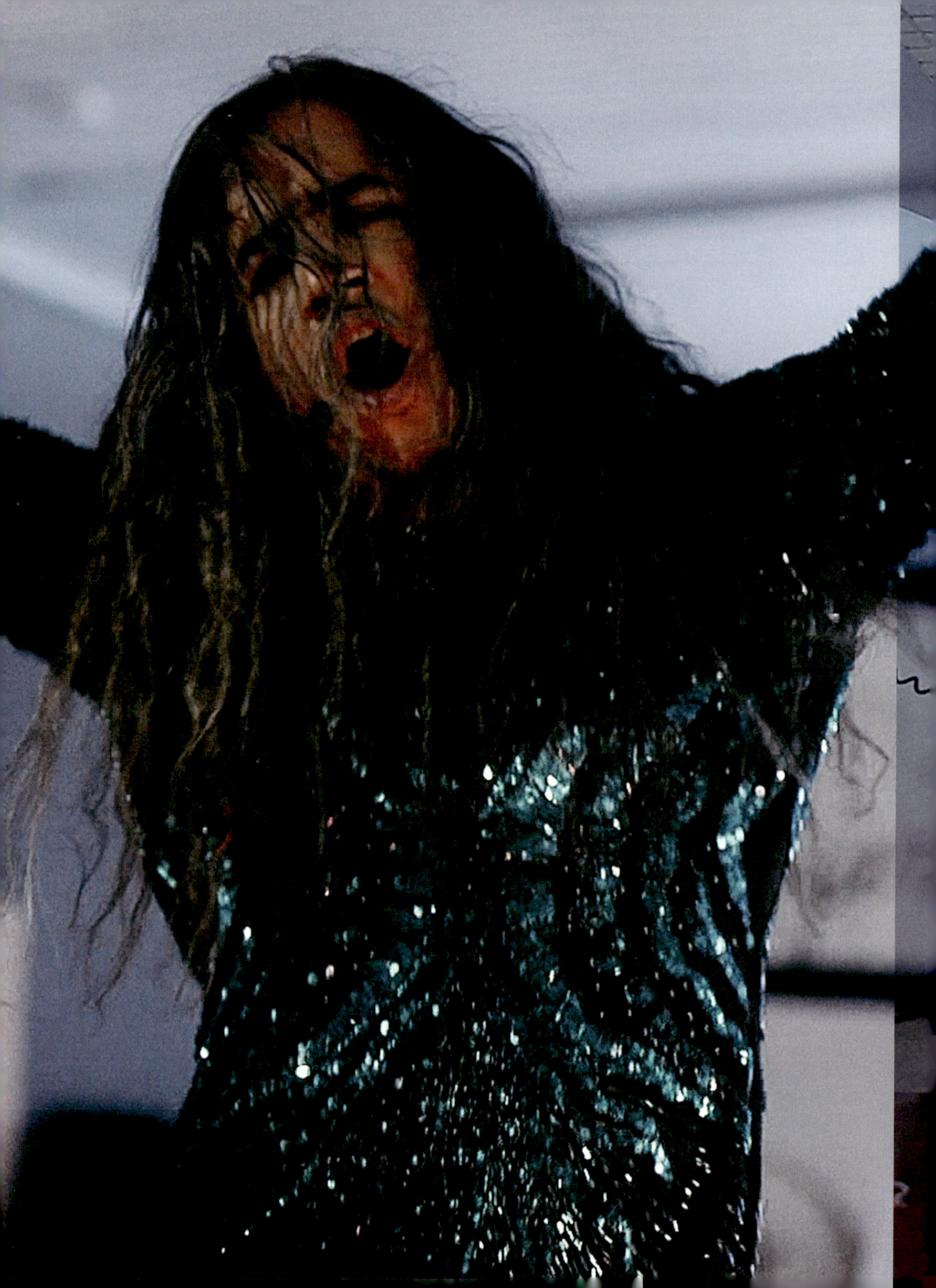

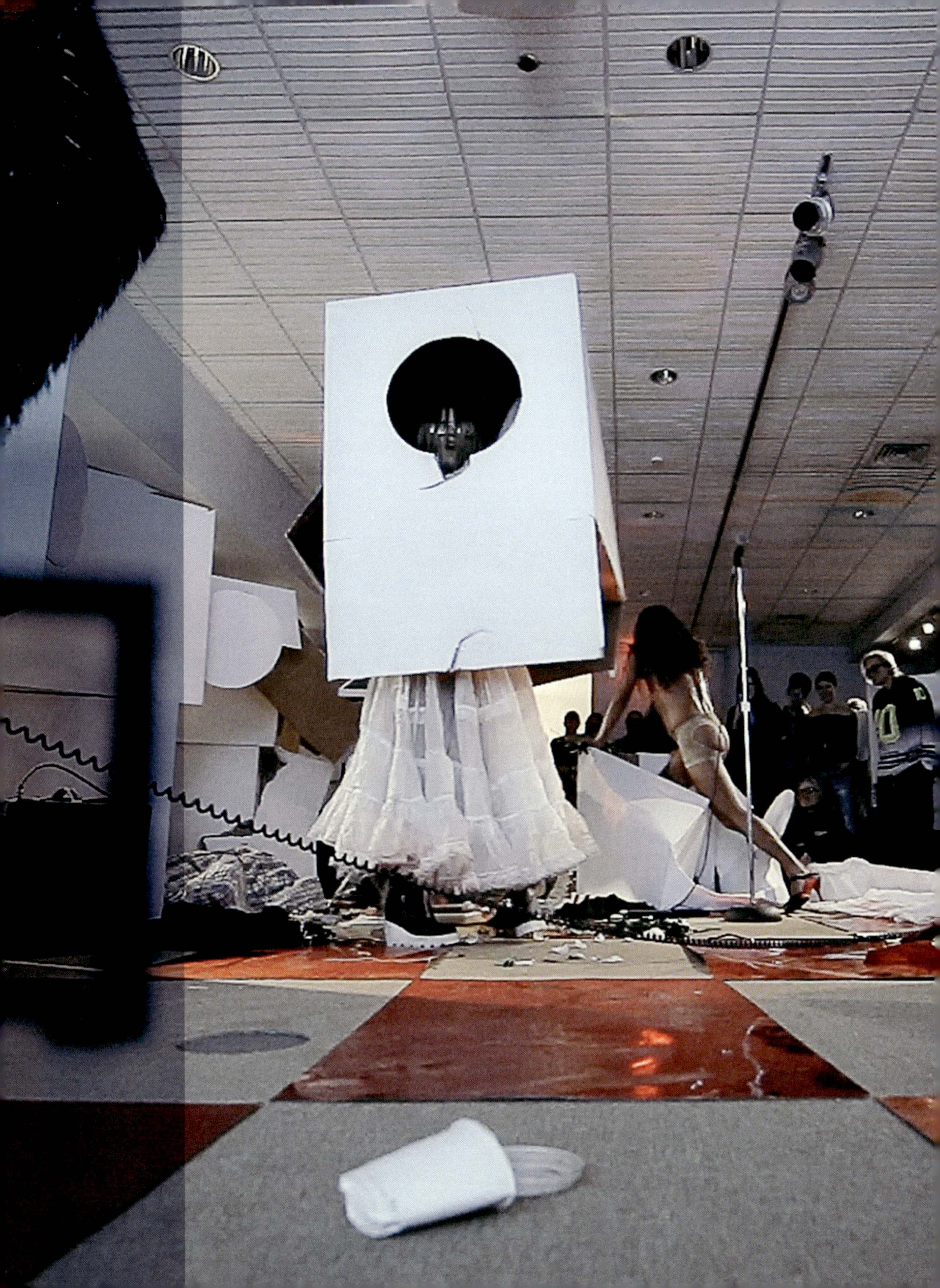

I ask myself, where is it that I'm supposed to go? I kind of want to do my laundry today … Oh, this looks like a very special place to wash my clothes. I have a job interview today to attend to. I guess I'll stop here and do my laundry today.

OK, I like this place. What should I do while I wait for my laundry to stay? I don't know. I've never been to this Laundromat, but I'm in a hurry. I'll just take a moment and see about the news today. It said it would take 24 minutes. How can I make 24 minutes last faster today? I ask myself that many times.

Ugh … it's been a rough day today. I was thinking about what can I do? To make time go faster? Oh, I know what I can do … I'll watch TV.

18 minutes left. I know what I'll do … I'll take somebody else's clothes. Don't tell anyone. I wonder if they'll notice that I took their clothes. I should call my friend Maria in the meantime, and see if she can tell me some gossip.

Maria? Hey! It's me … Raul! What are you doing today? I'm just sitting here at the Laundromat.

Maria … Speak to me … I want you to tell me what you want.
Maria … Who do you want to be?
Maria … Show me who you are.
Maria … Take me for myself, and you can give me all I want.
Maria … Just ask yourself. What is it that you want, too? What is it you want to say? Who do you want to be right now? Because it will come back to you.

Something must have been wrong. Because I … was dirty. I guess I'll wipe my mouth with my own discretion of a vice. Maria was right inside. I wonder if my laundry's done? It doesn't seem to be ending any time soon.

I met my friend Diana, and she was asking me about what I wanted to do after I was done doing my laundry. I told her I had a very important meeting. But then I realized that I didn't have a meeting anywhere. I was supposed to be watching TV, sitting in my bedroom, staring at the screen.

It was supposed to tell me what was to come for me today. But the TV was actually full of static. I was just staring into distance. I left my laundry at the Laundromat and forgot about it. When I went back, the stewardess told me that because I had left it for over 24 hours, it had become property of anyone.

I decided just to keep staring into static. The static was so hard up until my eyes. I called my friend Diana, to see if she could give me another answer. Maria wasn't there, but Diana was …

Dirty Diana can't you be inside my mind.
Dirty Diana do you want to see me now?
Dirty Diana can't you be inside myself.
Dirty Diana why you even stick around.
Dirty Diana can you see me in my mind?
Hello … are you … here …?

Diana wasn't there to get herself out. Diana wasn't even around to ask her about her vision. Diana was actually sitting in her couch, talking to her friend. She had never answered the phone. It was all a lie. Diana wasn't around. It was Maria.

Everything started making sense. The Television was on at all times, and Diana was staring back into her own Television. Maria wasn't around, it was Diana that was talking to her. She had never gone to the Laundromat. She had just had a bad case of diarrhea. Diana wasn't even real; nor was Maria. Maria was there the whole time. She wasn't even watching Television. She was actually reading the newspaper. The newspaper had very bad things to say about today. But Diana didn't care. Nothing had changed. Maria was not even there to tell Diana that she had been possessed by the static of her own Television.

The Laundromat was all made up. Nothing was real. Her clothes, her garments, everything of her possessions … was false. You see this? It's all a lie. Maria wasn't standing in front of herself. It was Diana. Diana was asking her, who is it that I'm talking to? It's Maria. And Maria was being … her own self.

Who is Diana? And who is Maria? Are they both the same person? Were they characters that the character decided to make up? We should ask him that.

Who did you make up today? I myself was staring back into the Television. And realized that I WAS INSIDE THE SOAP OPERA.

It was me that was Maria, and Diana. They were a fictional character made up by me. The Laundromat was a bad case of delusion. I stared back at the Television, praying for it to bring me into its true form of vision.

Dear TV, please let me inside. Dear Television, I wanna be like you. Maria ... Diana ... which one of them is me? Maria ... Diana! I want to be ... the Television Staaaaaaaaaaarrrrr!!! My dreams have come true ... I AM MYSELF!

I was the Soap Character. I had become the person I wanted to be. I was always inside the Television. And the Television was staring back at ME. I wasn't watching. They were watching ME. I wasn't staring. They were staring at me.

Are we inside a washing machine? I ask myself, how dirty am I? I belong within your self in me. I give you my heart. Cause I'm a Television starlet ... inside a washing machine! I WANT TO BE INSIDE A WASHING MACHINE IN ME!

It must have been all that bullshit that I put inside the cycle. I mean, Baking Soda. There's no such thing as bullshit, cause everything has a label. And if you read the label right, you'll always know what you're getting. So next time you put your wash at the washing machine, remind yourself ... there's no lies. Everything is real. The B.S. of the Baking Soda HAS FACTS.

So don't forget to always read the back of a product. For then, you will be safe. And you can go back home, and sit on your couch and watch Television. Diana and Maria don't lie. They don't tell stories. Let's see what my product has to tell me ... *"Welcome to Hell ... starring YOU!"*

Oh, that's a really good product. I forgot this clothes is done ... Oh no! It looks like none of the stains came out! WHY? Why would you do that? You said you would clean my clothes. I bought you! YOU'RE A LIE!

You said you were gonna clean my clothes. Look how easy it was for you to be broken. My machine didn't work! I must be on TV! I'm inside the Television. So I'm a Character.

I can choose which one I want to be. I'm gonna be Maria today. Maria sits on top of the Television. And she's the product of everyone's desire. Maria, Diana. Choose which one you want today. $10.99 a month for only you could be yourself.

All I can do is pray ... that Maria and Diana are all false advertising. There's just one place that I can run to. And that place is deep down beneath the storms of today. Walking into the washing machine. I find myself where I started. Where everything had been perfect. The washing machine was working and my clothes were inside of it.

Fred Moten: Thank you very much, Amy, and thank all of you for being here today. I'm especially honored to be sitting next to Charles Gaines, whose work as a teacher and thinker—and, of course, as an artist of unparalleled range and depth—has been an inspiration to me for a long time. We've actually done this once before, so you would think I'd be a little bit less nervous to be up here sitting next to you. Although, it's funny, I would be even more nervous, except just today I already had an encounter with a star who's my hero—on the train, I sat next to Felicia "Snoop" Pearson.

Charles Gaines: Now that's impressive.

FM: It was the only time I ever actually took a selfie. I'll show you all after this. I want, first of all, to pick up on something that Amy said in her introduction about your work and the intensity—I think unparalleled intensity—with which you have explored and investigated the grid. I would love to have you say more about your encounter with and investigation and exploration of the grid—where that comes from and what that's meant to you over the years.

CG: We won't do this again, because when we first talked, we spent about fifteen minutes trying to find out who was more humbled by being in the presence of the other. We won't do that this time. But with respect to your question, interest in the grid came out of a search [during] graduate school. I was searching for a meaningful way to [make] art. The normative strategies and procedures of art-making at the time were based upon the idea of the creative imagination. And, of course, the idea that the creative imagination was [both] real and a normative construct, which came out of some deep understanding of the human spirit—it bothered me that I couldn't make art that way. When I say I couldn't make art that way, it means that I could be driven by imagination to make paintings, but the paintings didn't mean very much to me. They didn't feel connected to me.

I didn't know if that was.... It might have been a unique form of art dyslexia.

Maybe it's a good thing I didn't think of it that way. But I did wonder about what to do about it, and so as a consequence, because of a friend, I was exposed to a couple of books on Poussin, about life [in] Florence and art. Poussin was an art historian, a Pablo Picasso of Renaissance and Baroque art history, and then also a book on Tantric art by Ajit Mookerjee. [In] Mookerjee's photographic essay, I found some drawings of the cosmos, Tantric Buddhist renderings that were diagrammatic. I discovered that they're done through meditation, and that the Buddhists considered these works of art. So that was the first time that required me to go outside—which meant that I had to go outside the Eurocentric or Western-centric frameworks of art practice to discover that art can be made outside of [that] model of the creative imagination.

There may be some argument that there is a correlation between meditation and what happens in meditation, and what happens when you barf from your subconscious. Somehow I think that meditation takes this rigorous discipline, [yet] imagination is supposed to be unleashed by releasing yourself from discipline. But, in any case, that piqued my interest—there is a strategy of making art where that isn't required. That, along with certain sections in Poussin's book that talked about works of art in relation to space, where he framed the study of art history as, in part, a study of operations that are not dependent or determined by artists' imaginations, and [then] allowed that to be discussed in terms of certain ideas on chance. I put the two things together and said, "Well okay, alright, now to give way for the creative imagination all you have to do is smoke a lot of dope and start listening to a lot of John Coltrane. Particularly, *A Love Supreme*." So I did that. And in the midst of that, I stretched a canvas and started painting a series of probably the worst paintings in history.... So I knew that wasn't it.

Charles Gaines and Fred Moten

And then I saw a show by Hanne Darboven. Actually there were three shows: at MoMA, at Leo Castelli Gallery, and at Ileana Sonnabend Gallery. And the shows were.... There were these diagrammatic drawings that tried to [engage in] a taxonomic analysis of her own consciousness, her own psychology—but the drawings were literally driven by the obsessive nature that she had. Amidst this intense emotional content, she created these very analytic drawings that just went on, and on, and on, and they all look alike. Then I went downstairs at Sonnabend Gallery.... More of the same drawings. Then I went to the Museum of Modern Art: more of the same drawings, and I really got angered by it because I thought, "You've seen one; you've seen them all." So I was curious why I was so angry and I realized that the presentation was something I was not used to—it was an image that, which at least in terms of Western art practice, I had never seen before. Things had really often just been comfortable ... so I had to reconsider my attitude about them. Then I made the connection to my earlier experiences with Tantric works. The issue is operating under the creation imagination. And I can't get outside that by sitting down and smoking a lot of dope and listening to John Coltrane. Because all that did was entrench the idea of the creative imagination. So I thought, well, you know, I have to have a discipline. The grid then became a type of discipline to remove myself from the creative imagination. There was this correlation that came with meditation.

FM: Okay, so now I have seventeen follow-up questions. First of all, I mean, this is so deep and interesting to me because for the last—I would say almost fifteen years— I have basically been obsessed with this formulation in Kant's Critique of Judgment, in Section Fifty, where he says, "The imagination in its lawless freedom produces nothing but nonsense and must have its wings severely clipped by the understanding." And so, there's a really intense way in which I feel like what you just said ought to lead me to the belief that, in this regard, you are a strict, almost orthodox Kantian. And yet, everything else in my being makes me resist saying that. Maybe the way that I would try to resist saying that, until you tell me to just accept it, is another phenomenon that seems to me to be equally crucial and fundamental in your work that goes hand in hand with [the] grid—and that's blur. We've talked about this before, but I'm wondering if maybe you have any thoughts about blur and how blur might be functioning in your work, as well.

CG: Yeah, you're right, I'm anything but a Kantian. In terms of that, the imagination is a function of a certain factor you're feeling, and so, it's like you're trying to talk about feelings independent of circumstance and context. And if you do that, then it's nonsense because it can't attach itself to the production of knowledge, which requires a certain discipline. I have an equal suspicion about what it claims to be the rational mind or the universal faculty of reasoning. Because I think that produces nonsense, too. I think that they [all] produce nonsense and the only thing that keeps us from living in a world of nonsense is that we can agree on certain things. Agreement is the only factor that makes something sensible. People actually think that there's some relationship between rational thought as an overarching paradigm and what truth is—you know it's real beyond the presence of serving consciousness; there's something admittable and determinable beyond conscious existence called truth, and Kant's notion of reason produces this. We were just talking about not getting too deep in the leaves right? So I'll try not to. But the thing that interests and fascinates me is the idea of dependent imagination.... There's a debate about what provides the most truthful experience. Is it our intuitive minds—our intuitional relationship to experiences? Or is it our rational understanding of relations, in which it's hard to say, "Oh, it's the intuition," in the sense of, you know, that I'm an artist? Some say, "Oh, no, it's the rational mind that does this." So that binary split—it seems like there isn't a way out of that, but I believe that there is.

I've created this fiction—this goes back to what I was saying about social and cultural agreement—that the relationship between a subject and the object of understanding, the method of understanding and the object of understanding, is a blur. It's not settled by either the rational or the intuitive mind. In both cases, the metaphorical blur, I think, is beautiful—another sort of way to articulate that is that you have to knead. It has to become this material space that you physically engage to see what it produces. My feeling is that coming from the standpoint of this certain irrationality, we can actually produce a whole experience by physically engaging. What you need is to not to be overdetermined in those conclusions. Pay attention to notions that are irrational. And the grid [gestures to the PowerPoint]—the same piece pops up once in a while. In the grid, I noticed that if I start with the subject of tree and then I paste a grid on top of it and transfer the image of the tree onto the grid, this recognizes that the tree itself is also gridded. But it's gridded using a different strategy and technology. And so I reproduce it within this more accessible, quite rational system. The thing that's awesome is that reinforces the difference between the two. Not that one actually resolves and settles the other, but [the process] amplifies the entire space and its indeterminacy in making relationships. In a very simple way, if I have the tree form and place a grid over it, then I will fill that space with a number, but that tree form only occupies a section of that space, not the entire space. So there's a whole section around the tree, and if there's a square and then there's a branch, on each side there's blur— metaphorical blur—which reinforces the idea, the mathematical determination, that the space between the edges of the square and the branch measures the degree of irrationality between the tree itself and the grid as a method of urban landscape. To extrapolate that in language or in any matters of understanding, whether intuitive or rational—we have to ignore negative spaces and highlight positive space, as if the negative spaces not only don't exist but also don't contribute anything to the object.

FM: To me this is fascinating, partly because.... Well, I want to go in a couple different directions. It seems like two directions, but it's actually one—or maybe it seems like one, but it's really two. In thinking about *Librettos*, there's a Plexiglas box or frame, and on the back side is text from a famous 1967 speech that Stokely Carmichael gave at Seattle's Garfield High School, and then there's a negative space. There's a space between the back side of the box and the front side of the box and on the front is printed the score, or pages from the score, of Manuel de Falla's opera, *La vida breve*. I was wishing that I could shrink myself so I could enter into the negative space between those pieces. What it is to enter into that negative space.... I think it corresponds in some ways to what Ralph Ellison would talk about in the beginning of *Invisible Man*, about getting inside the rhythm of another person. Or, to inhabit and embrace, rather than simply to exclude and disavow. Whatever it is that the grid delineates but cannot capture, that seems to me to correspond precisely to the anti-imperialist politics that Stokely Carmichael was talking about in that speech. What I want to do is have you talk a little bit more about the specificity of these art-making operations that you engage in. They seem to me to move against the grain of the hegemony and metaphysical valorization of the individual creative imagination. Talk about how these they connect to a history of revolt and a history of insurgency.

CG: That's all? [laughter]

FM: We'll open it out to the floor in a minute; they can finish it up.

CG: It's true there's a certain point in my practice that I started working with text and image. And one of the reasons why I started working with text is because it completely dealt with the idea of language. Over a period of time, that investigation of text began to be more specifically political, but it started out as an investigation of how language structure can determine how we think about things. So essentially in those cases I would put together or make a montage out of elements that were unrelated. There's a work that I did, *Nighttime*, from the early '90s that.... It's a good example. It best illustrates what I'm talking about. In that piece, I found crime photographs of capital crimes. I found crime scene photographs and photographs of criminals and then I had a whole archive of night sky photographs. So I searched down the moment that the crime occurred. The photographs come from the *Los Angeles Times* archives, and finding them wasn't difficult at all. But I would try to find the exact moment of the crime and make a montage of the elements based upon the myth of an exact moment. I would place the photograph of the crime scene and also the photograph of the convicted person, who wasn't the person who committed that crime. Again, because I searched the moment of the crime I could reconstruct the night sky at the very moment that the crime was committed. As if, say, the murderer of the victim looked up, they would see the night sky as it was presented in the photograph. This creates a series of coincidental links between three elements; those links were so convincing that even though you know the whole thing was fiction, it was believable. And this maybe explains why some people succeed. There is a certain kind of emotion attached to a work, which played a large role in giving the narrative a certain legitimacy. There was a belief that, for example, the heavenly bodies can influence human emotion. So the idea of gravity [as] a cause why a person's emotional state [changed] enough to commit a crime—that made sense to people. Now in this narrative, the bigger piece of course, was a fictional narrative, but the terms—or at least the claim that the narrative was based upon—they thought were believable. That shows you how language controls thought.

I started to go more deeply into political content with the same framework. For example, with *Librettos*, as you said: on the surface there's de Falla. Actually we took photos of the de Falla manuscript and had [them] printed on the surface of the Plexi. And inside the Plexi box is paper that's stained, and then on top of it. we printed the Stokely Carmichael text. So my feeling, even though the archival sources were totally independent of each other, was that they formed a compelling relationship. The terms of that, of course, are completely irrational, in the sense that we discussed earlier. In the human imagination or in the human process of reasoning, people edit out information that won't fit and that won't allow them to see these connections; they aggressively edit out this information. I think that your metaphor of blur still holds because within those pieces [the information is still] physically present. The things that you're editing out—they're persistent. You know that you're editing them out.

The piece that I have here in the exhibition, *Manifestos*, is based on the same idea. In *Manifestos 2*, I chose four political texts in order to produce that installation—you know the installation is made up of four monitors of stolen texts, a musical component, and four drawings of enlarged manuscripts of the music produced. So when I was done I took each of the four political texts and translated the texts into musical notation. I went through the process of "A" through "G," so that any letter in the manuscript corresponding to musical notation is turned into a note. So "A" would be the a-note; "B," the b-note; up through "G." I also included a page with B-flat because this process of translating musical notation into notes was first done in Romanesque times and then continued during the early Baroque period. The Bach family had a couple of games like that—turning music into notes. I did that and then came up with a line—a melody line, and then that melody line was accompanied by a harmony, the chords. In the drawings you can see one line—the melody line. Underneath, two staffs of the "G" and the bass clef of the harmony line. The chord accompaniment is produced by just taking the first letter of a particular word, turning that into a chord, and having that chord sustain the length of the word. So if the word was "tree," then the first musical letter is "E," which would be an E-note and an E-major chord. The music is written and then it's played while each text is scrolling—you can actually follow it by looking at the scrolling text and the drawings beneath them. Even if you don't know music, you can know where you are relative to the music in the drawing. When I give lectures about that, the music is so emotionally compelling that people believe that I intended it … that it's an intentional composition. Now the system is intentional but the composition is not, because I don't know what's going to happen. People just don't believe me.

What's interesting to me is that within the piece—and your term, "blur," is so useful to me, as it comes up in these lectures— people are completely aware of how much arbitrariness surrounds meaningful content, but they refuse to believe it. It's a matter of willfully—or I think unwillfully, but willfully—editing and not realizing the process of editing out is an ideological gesture. It's one framed by a particular paradigm or a particular belief. They don't believe that. That right into the issue of these major political texts—the nature of hegemonic practices, for example, or even the success of Trump (I apologize to anybody who voted for Trump.) But this moment of complete blur, political blur—how rational this all seems to so many people.

FM: Yeah. It makes you think that one possible definition of whiteness is the radical incapacity to believe in indeterminacy. I have a bunch more questions now, but I'm thinking about going back to Trane since we are in Philly; do you think *A Love Supreme* is an intentional composition? Or another way to put it would be—setting aside a certain kind of metaphysics that surrounds Trane, which tends to forget the intensity of the discipline that he submitted himself to in order to produce this work—I wonder if Trane's playing, and I'm thinking especially of the third movement of *A Love Supreme*, which is his musical transcription of his own literary or poetic prayer printed inside fold of the original pressing of *A Love Supreme*, prefigures the operations that you began to construct for yourself and to discover for yourself as an artist. This would be a link to Trane and, more generally, to the history of jazz improvisation, which you might place under the rubric of the non-intentional or in the negative space between the nonsense that the rational mind produces on the one hand, and the nonsense that the creative imagination produces, on the other.

CG: Yeah, I need to do some thinking. To directly answer your question: Yes, I think that Coltrane, in general, is operating in that space. This has to be articulated such that it's operating in defiance of some perceived ideas about improvisation, which reinforce the idea of the creative imagination. I see what you're saying as operating in that negative space—the outlines and the parameters of concrete outlines—as a different space than this extemporaneous character. The earliest

interpretation of improvisation is that it's instinctive. So I think it has to be said that—

FM: Like some animalistic version of the mythical free subject.

CG: Right, exactly. And how that plays into certain stereotypes of race. For example, explaining the difference between East Coast and West Coast jazz. Camaraderie is for the West Coast, as is embracing the idea of the primitive and saying that improvisation is an exploration of the primitive mind. What belies that stereotype is—as you said, Coltrane represents that. Particularly, you know, I had that album. I don't have it anymore. I'm trying to remember; it was a double album. I'm trying to remember that poem but I can't. But responding to that text….

FM: It goes something like, "A love supreme…. I would do everything I can to be worthy, my Lord." Something like that. Sorry. But you can hear that melody. There's this great—there was something called the *Coltrane Radio Project*. It was a public radio thing, like an eight-hour-long radio documentary on Trane—and somebody actually sang it, you know, you could hear it exactly.

CG: Well to me, rather than primitive expression, a better way of thinking about this, specifically modeled after Trane, is Steve Reich—his sound pieces—there's melody and speech and the ability to build melody from speech. One side could say, "Well, you're just responding intuitively to what you hear." But the other side would say that you are actually integrated deeply into the speech and pulling melody out of it, which they say is an entirely different operation. And I think it's not a farfetched idea to think that Coltrane, in that text, heard a sound.

FM: It's interesting to think about composition or creation emerging from that negative space because it's a space you have to learn how to want to inhabit or move in or move through. And usually the way you learn how to go there, or how to want to go there, is under duress. So I'm thinking about the crawlspace that Harriet Jacobs lived in for about seven years as a kind of negative space. Hortense Spillers calls it a "scrawl space." She wrote there. She wrote from there. It's an interesting space precisely because it's a space of fugitivity and constraint at the same me. It feels like these spaces of fugitivity and constraint, these negative spaces, are sites of deviance from the opposition of the voluntary and the involuntary. These are the spaces from which oppressed people write and create and do the work that they do in the interest of, I don't know, some kind of anticolonial, unsettling reformation of the earth. I guess what I'm saying is: it makes me all the more attuned to the intensity of the deep anticoloniality that is embedded throughout your practice. I mean it's clear in the *Manifestos*, which hopefully you all will go see, but I think it's there—everywhere. It raises the question for me—it doesn't raise a question, but I guess what I admire and can't put it in the form of a question, is the depth and intensity of how work labeled or called conceptual can eschew or go against the grain of other kinds of work that purport to be more political because they're more realistic or more naturalistic. There's actually a deeper insurgent radicalism because by working through the concept you're working through the foundations of the social and ecological disaster that we live in—called modernity—which is, in some ways, the history of the concept [itself]. That wasn't a question, but it was meant to be. Oh, it's five o'clock. That went quick. But is it okay to open it up?

CG: Yeah, sure. Audience Q and A.

Audience member: How did you account for the rhythms, or the rhythmic structure? Because you talk about how through the text you came up with the notes for the musical score.... Were you listening for the intonation of the speech itself for the rhythmic structure in those pieces?

CG: Each letter is equivalent to an eighth note. So, in the earliest forms, the measures are determined by the length of words, rather than fourteenths or sixteenths or whatever. The word, "tree," would have four eighth notes. The letters are reused and reused in rotation—it's inscribed. And the letters that are not used in rotation are silent beats or rests.

Audience member: This question is for Fred Moten. I really appreciate what you said about the place of futurity and restraint and I was wondering how that concept relates to the visual effect of your poetry, specifically in, "The Little Edges," or if it does [not]?

FM: Well, you know—I'm sorry—I'm just trying to make a picture of it in my mind. I guess the main constraint that you're operating [under] when you're using a keyboard of some kind is the length of the line— you know, you create a margin. And usually the way that we make this sort of simple distinction between prose and verse is that we'd say that prose adheres to the margin that you have created and verse—sometimes arbitrarily, sometimes as a function of specific calculations you make at the level of rhythm and meter—would lead you to break the line and deviate from adhering to the margin. I guess I started thinking that I didn't want to accept the distinction between—I didn't want poetry to be held eternally within the fight between verse and prose, so I started thinking about how to make shapes out of prose. And so that's what I was kind of doing in that book and in the book previous to that, *The Feel Trio*. Then, the visual thing would have its own sort of logic, you know—to try to break up the block-like structure that people fall into naturally when wring poetry. Not disavow it, but just see if I could work it, in a way. Which is again—to the extent that there's any affinity beyond just admiration and copying with what Charles does—there's a block-like quality most poetry adheres to. Particularly lyric poetry. I think it goes back to the hegemony of the sonnet as a privileged expression of lyric subjectivity. So just to create some new shapes, or, at the same time, have a set of operations that might culminate in the replication of a shape, but in a way that's so emphatic it doesn't try to fool anybody into thinking that it's accidental.

Audience member: This is for Charles. In the piece that you did with the trees, what determined the numbers that you used?

CG: The work is a series, so literally connected that way. In order to produce it—let me back up a little bit. In order to do the piece, I went out and photographed some trees. I traced their shapes on a grid, and filled the spaces inside the silhouette of the tree with numbers. Each number in the grid is predetermined. And the reason for that is to help facilitate production of the series. So up the middle are zeros, and it counts one to whatever number to the left, and one to whatever number to the right. So it's symmetry. Then when I draw the tree, I can reproduce it by simply filling in the same numbers on the next grid. It's a functional utilitarian strategy, so the numbers don't have numerical value, they have simply locational value—they help facilitate the structure. There is a consequential visual component, of course, which I'm interested in, but it was important to me in the work, at the time, that everything in the drawing had a purpose. So even though it functions visually, it's not put there for the purpose of its visual function. The same thing with the colors. I use colors as a file—[the way] you use different colors to make separate categories in the file system. Each tree is given a color, so that as they accumulate, any particular tree can be retrieved if you're paying attention to it, because it maintains its color. That also has a very important visual component—but again, it's not done for the purpose of it.

Audience member: Thank you. I'm enjoying this a lot. This is for Charles. You have four pieces- they're called *Manifestos*, in the back, right? Well: Malcolm X, a Native American, there was [*The Declaration of the Rights of Woman*] 1791; I think I'm forgetting one, was it JFK?

CG: Yeah.

Audience Member: Yeah. So basically it's a—

CG: Your memory is much better than mine.

Audience Member: Well, you know, I liked it, so I got into it a little bit. Basically, it's the same process that you were talking about with your other pieces, right? The space, the music, and so on and so forth—it's the same thing as the others you had up there right, the process?

CG: Are you talking about the grid?

Audience Member: Well no, not the grid— the *Manifestos*, the empty space, the way you have the plastic in front, and so on and so forth, and the music connected—now that's different than what you have back up there [referring to the PowerPoint], right? But it's the same process?

CG: No, it's—I'm glad that you mentioned that. These pieces aren't made in such a way that they can be performed. I imagine that it [resembles] some kind of Coltrane interpretation or style to perform these pieces, but they weren't made for performance, so as a result, it's simply the overlay of archives; the *Librettos* piece was actually a musical composition with the intention of being performed.

Audience Member: Okay. Alright, now, they are all political statements; obviously they are political things. Were you involved with radical politics at one time, you know, like Black Panthers, stuff like that, Black Nationalists? I'm just curious, what's your background as far as picking those pieces and making those kinds of statements—which are valid, I believe, and I'm glad that somebody's doing things like that—but I'm just curious what your background was with it?

CG: Actually I have no history of involvement with radical politics. I was—I'm old enough to have been around during those days, and so I was a spectator of those events and devastations like most of us. So my investment in the work is not on the level of radical politics, in the sense that the singular purpose of the work is to advance radical politics. I think the reason is because I've always been interested in abstract and lofty ideas— I can't help it. When I was a kid, I asked my mother, like, where birds came from. I was interested early on in the philosophical and conceptual structures that help determine politics or write them. I was reading, heavily, political discourse. And even as a young person, I was reading because I was interested in the philosophical implications of a process [based on] more literal specific notions of radical change. My work, in terms of dealing with text and dealing with concepts, particularly in the early work, tends to be more abstract and philosophical. And it was due to long discussions over martinis with artist friends whose work is specifically political, like Sam Durant and Andrea Bowers and some other artist friends. I decided to deal with more directly political text. I mean the discovery—and I was sorry it took so long for me to figure it out—was that I was really interested in art as part of activist enterprise. And in my interest in broad, general theories—I couldn't figure out, couldn't understand, that if I became more literal in that enterprise it would be different from this work—but I discovered that it wasn't.

One of the biggest influences in that regard was reading Edward Said's *Orientalism*. I saw him in a lecture, in a panel at Stanford in the '80s, and I went and read the book and that changed everything. He was criticized for trying to turn deconstruction into a discursive process. But to other theorists like Lyotard, Said undermined deconstruction. Yet that process of investigating the discursive nature of deconstruction created postcolonial theory. I mean, it somehow reflects what Fred was saying, incidentally, that this kind of approach to theoretical texts could have this political application. It's something that non-white theorists thought was possible. And the white theorists didn't think it was possible. Said was sort of isolated for a while because of that. But for me, he helped me realize that these broad, theoretical models that I was trying to interrogate in terms of how knowledge is produced were embedded in the politics themselves, and that changed everything.

Audience Member: Thank you very much for being here. I imagine under different circumstances there may be another individual who would have joined you today, so I was wondering if you could talk a little bit about maybe your collaborations with Terry Adkins and what that was rooted in, and how Terry may have responded to a conversation around the blur.

CG: A conversation about...?

Audience Member: The blur.

CG: Oh, the blur? Well, Terry called me one day and asked if I wanted a job at UPenn. Because I had never met him before, in the process of that we got to know each other. He invited me to participate in a project in Houston at Project Row Houses, which was one of the early Lone Wolf projects, and while he was there, he discovered that I played drums. He didn't know that I was a musician. And he gave me a sash and a staff and he told me to march around in this way.... This was at rehearsal, and he had musicians on the stage, and I said, "I play drums," and he said, "Oh, I didn't know that," and he got a set of drums. From that point on I became a participant in the ensemble, in a musical way. So whenever he had an event, he would call me up—because I lived in Los Angeles—and say he was doing this and he would fly me out to do it, and I would say I would, and conversely I created a performance in Los Angeles, and his involvement with that rekindled my interest in playing. So I started having performances and exhibitions. And I would call Terry—the drum group, they would play on a day's notice, just come out and do that. Because there's not that many—about a half dozen, or seven different performances. I could never figure out exactly why Terry liked my work. Terry's work is not easy. I mean, you may think it's easy. But it's not easy work and it took me awhile to get inside—the thing that helped me do that was an assignment to write the catalogue essay for this retrospective show. And that gave me the opportunity to spend endless amounts of time digging deep into his practice. Terry was anything but a systems guy, yet after exploring his work I thought that he probably appreciated a paradox in the work, when you're facing real rigorous discipline and practice, and if you know Terry, you know that he loves discipline. You have to work hard. But seeing this poetic result—that paradox—I think is the thing that he probably appreciated. The concept of the blur would be something that would appeal to him, mostly. Terry was a really good friend, so I really miss him.

Audience member: I was wondering if you could talk more about the compositional process of the vowels and the notes—that's really interesting. I was wondering if you could talk about it in relation to Cage's compositional verses, indeterminacy and all of that, in whatever direction you want to take it. I have a couple of ideas—one is that the typical Cage piece will just use completely random processes, whereas when you use the words, you're intimating this fantasy that that word has an essential relation to what it names; that it's not arbitrary at all. So there's something around those lines—to bring it to the discussion that you had before about Said and the political uses of theory and all of that, maybe the distinction that George Lewis makes between Afrological and Eurological approaches to indeterminacy. Lewis describes the Eurological, like Cage's practice and other modernists' approaches to indeterminacy, as a really politicized, blind attempt to erase all traces of influence (especially of Black music) into modernism, whereas the Afrological attempts to bring all the traditions together. Maybe that's what you mean [by] the creative imagination, at some point, as well.

CG: The source I'm not familiar with, and it's definitely key to understanding the question—what I got in part was some framework that determines a more universal or more localized political strategy of production, and where I saw myself in relationship to that? That's what I got so far, if there's anything you could say that could make me more responsive....

Audience member: Maybe never mind the George Lewis reference. Simply, how do you think your work stands with respect to Cage and a European modernism that uses indeterminacy, in political terms and cultural terms?

CG: I think, in many ways, it's quite traditional—in terms of implying certain avant-garde strategies to music, and even to the point where the same strategies play out in art. And I might be wrong about this but where I see myself as different is in how I use those strategies. The *Manifestos* were very influenced by Cage and indeterminacy, but also by Baroque music. It's also Western music in scale, which produces western-sounding chords; it's a diatonic scale— that's where my statement about being conservative is—it relies upon. But where I separate is two things: one is that I'm applying it to deal with a very specific critique of culture—I'm not using it as an exploration of avant-gardism, like trying to push the borders of art or trying to push the borders of music, and I'm not

operating out of a paradigm of progress with [regards to] modernism, which argues more in favor of universal structures, universal patterns. So I'm taking some things that I think are understood, in those ways, as moving against politics, and trying to use them in such a way that they're intrinsically embedded in politics. But more often than not, I'd have people ask me, "Do I feel that I've been compromised because I use Western musical instrumentation?," or even the scale, or, "Why am I using an eighteenth-century form? Why don't I go directly into blues form, or more specifically into jazz form?" They're uncomfortable questions to me; I say that I would if I had fourteen lifetimes. But they are uncomfortable questions because they are natural questions that should be raised. I think that rather than pointing to something that the pieces try to ignore, I feel that these are issues that the pieces actually bring up.

Audience Member: I see this overarching theme throughout the talk you guys had about becoming indecisive, or lost, potentially, through the grid, the blur, the layering of trees through color, through shapes of poems. I was wondering if that indecision and loss is what allows us to redefine ideas? What does it mean to try to do that on purpose, or whether that indecision should happen accidentally? Because then it seems like we would have to wait for it. So I wonder how something like that could be expedited or even take place.

FM: Well I don't know. I'm lost. [laughter] I think that the term that came up—indeterminacy— for me is not quite the same thing as indecision. Maybe what I hear in your question is, if indeterminacy or if a kind of embrace of indeterminacy would be part and parcel of alternative social arrangement, or of the capacity to better defend already existing alternative social arrangements, what would be the mechanism to actually engage in that? How would you make a set of intentional maneuvers in that direction? Because I'm not necessarily advocating indecision, I would say I think it's possible to actually comport yourself, or oneself, in a different way, in relation to the indeterminate, not only accept it but also to make an effort or decision to protect it. I think it's possible to do that. As a matter of fact, I think people do that all the time. One technical term for doing that is love. It's [why we] don't kill people when they don't do what we think they should do, you know—when they do something else. Then the question is, how do you develop, how do you exercise ethical comportments that would require you to behave that way toward more or less everything? You know, some of the most restrictive and repressive political forms that we find ourselves dealing with now are really all about the attempt to shut down differentiation with a kind of authoritarian brutality. I think that's why people derive a certain kind of hope, let's say, maybe from John Cage's protocols, even at the same time as they might find themselves appalled by those moments when Cage doesn't necessarily adhere to his own protocol.

Audience Member, Theodore Harris: Thanks for the talk; it's beautiful. I have two quotes from Mr. Gaines, but I want Fred to elaborate on them. It's part of my research for what I'm going to be talking about on the 7th, which is about formalism, but these are the two quotes: "The Black artist is engaged in a battle for her identity, and there is no possible victory, for to be marginal is to be in the battle." The second one is, "It is virtually impossible to invoke the discourse of marginality without buttressing the implacable edifice of the mainstream." Take it away, Fred.

FM: What did I do to you? [laughter]. We're supposed to be friends. It was funny because when you [gestures to Charles Gaines] were talking about Steve Reich— I had a text from Ashon Crawley two days ago talking about how he was all into Steve Reich, and I was thinking, "That's going to be really cool to hear you all talk about that." All of you should come back to see Theodore and Ashon next week. I mean I'm in the midst of a long-term, thirty-year collaboration with my friend Laura Harris, and she's written a book that's in part about Hélio Oiticica, this great Brazilian artist who famously made the claim that in Brazil, during the emergence of the Tropicalia movement out of and in relation to other social insurgencies , "The marginals are our heroes." I think that it's impossible for me to completely detach myself from that affective

relation to marginality. One of the main texts, for me, when I was in graduate school, was this great little essay that Foucault wrote on Maurice Blanchot, "The Thought from Outside"—I remember your collaborator, Theodore, and my other hero, Amiri Baraka, talking about the importance of the outside, what it meant to play outside, or Nathaniel Mackey, in a great essay called, "Destination Out," talking about the importance and absolutely crucial notion of the centrifugal in art. For me, I just can't help but valorize the outside, valorize the marginal. At the same me, I still believe what Charles is saying is true. But I think I understand something about the truth of it now that I didn't understand an hour and a half ago, which is that, first of all, the edifice of the mainstream is implacable and seemingly unmovable, and yet it shifts. It shifts. If you think about this with regard to the history of jazz, for instance, what was avant-garde in 1930 was [mainstream] in 1955. So the mainstream shifts, but that doesn't mean that it's force or that it's implacability lessens. And anything can become orthodox over the course of time. So part of what's at stake is the necessity of this continuing, ongoing renewal of marginality, this ongoing renewal of differentiation, and what it means to maintain an openness to that. And I think that's really crucial. That would be the way that I would think about the first one, but can you remind me of the second quote? I know it was connected to it.

Audience Member, Theodore Harris: "It is virtually impossible to invoke the discourse of marginality without buttressing the implacable edifice of the mainstream." And that is quoted from Mr. Gaines.

FM: Okay, well, that's the second one. But the first one was about the artist whose marginality is all bound up with her identity, and who has to claim it as an identity. That's tougher—I think it's really important to take up this question and this lesson of whether or not, and how it might be possible to detach artistic practice from the creative imagination. My sense of it, which I think is aligned Charles' sense of it, is that the first and most fundamentally problematic thing about the creative imagination is its individuation. Right? The fundamental constraint that the creative imagination

tends or seeks to disavow is the constraint of others.
Right? The constraint of sociality. And that sociality
can be within the realm of the human, but it's also
an ecological matter, right? This is why, for me,
the particular notion of personhood that's predicated
on a free creative imagination is a mode of personhood
that is undifferentiable from the settler. A person
whose work I've been studying and paying attention
to because I was trying to write something about it
over the last six months is Jimmie Durham. I think he
understands this in this deep way, and not just as
a function of his history of activism in the American
Indian Movement, or of being at Wounded Knee in 1973,
but also as a function of being on the Lower East Side
in the '80s, where, though his writing, you can get
a sense of the intensity of this relationship between
the ideology of the settler and the ideology of the
individual creative artist. You know, at the level of the
way people were bumping folks out of apartments
and stuff, and thinking that was their purview. "I need
this space more than this person needs this space
because I'm making art." So those things are connected.
What this means is that the creative artist who also
thinks of herself as exemplifying a kind of marginality
is fighting a battle not just for, but also with, identity.
That's the way I understand it. Ultimately, if we want
to engage in an artistic practice that offers a proper
critique of the creative imagination, and the modality
of individual personhood to which that corresponds,
it puts us in a position of saying, "Well, I want to be
interested in art. I want to be a servant of art. I want to
be a lover of art, but I don't know what any of that
would have to do with being an artist." Or I would put it
with regard to the medium that I'm supposed to be connected—I love poetry, and I'm interested in poetry, and
I would like to be a servant of poetry. All of it seems to
require that I am ready at the drop of a hat to give up
the honorific or the name or the identity of poet. It also
means that in the interest of poetry, for me at least,
I have to radically detach myself from the metaphysics
of the poem as a particular instance of the work. The
way I would hear it is not just as a fight *for* identity,
but a fight *with* identity. And it's a complicated fight,
because it occurs against the backdrop of the denial of
identity; it occurs within the context of the fact that

there can't be a politics without identity. All this sort
of racist hand-wringing about identity politics
conveniently forgets that there is no such thing as a
non-identity politics. You can go tell that shit to
Pericles or something. So these are the ways that
I would begin to respond or rethink my original
response to those formulations that Charles has.
But I see now, today, that whatever I thought I knew
about what you meant, I have to go back to the lab.

CG: To move on to the end, I'll show this six-minute
video called…. What's it called?

FM: *Black Ghost Blues.*

CG: This piece was actually produced specifically
as part of an installation I showed with Terry before
he died.

[video plays]

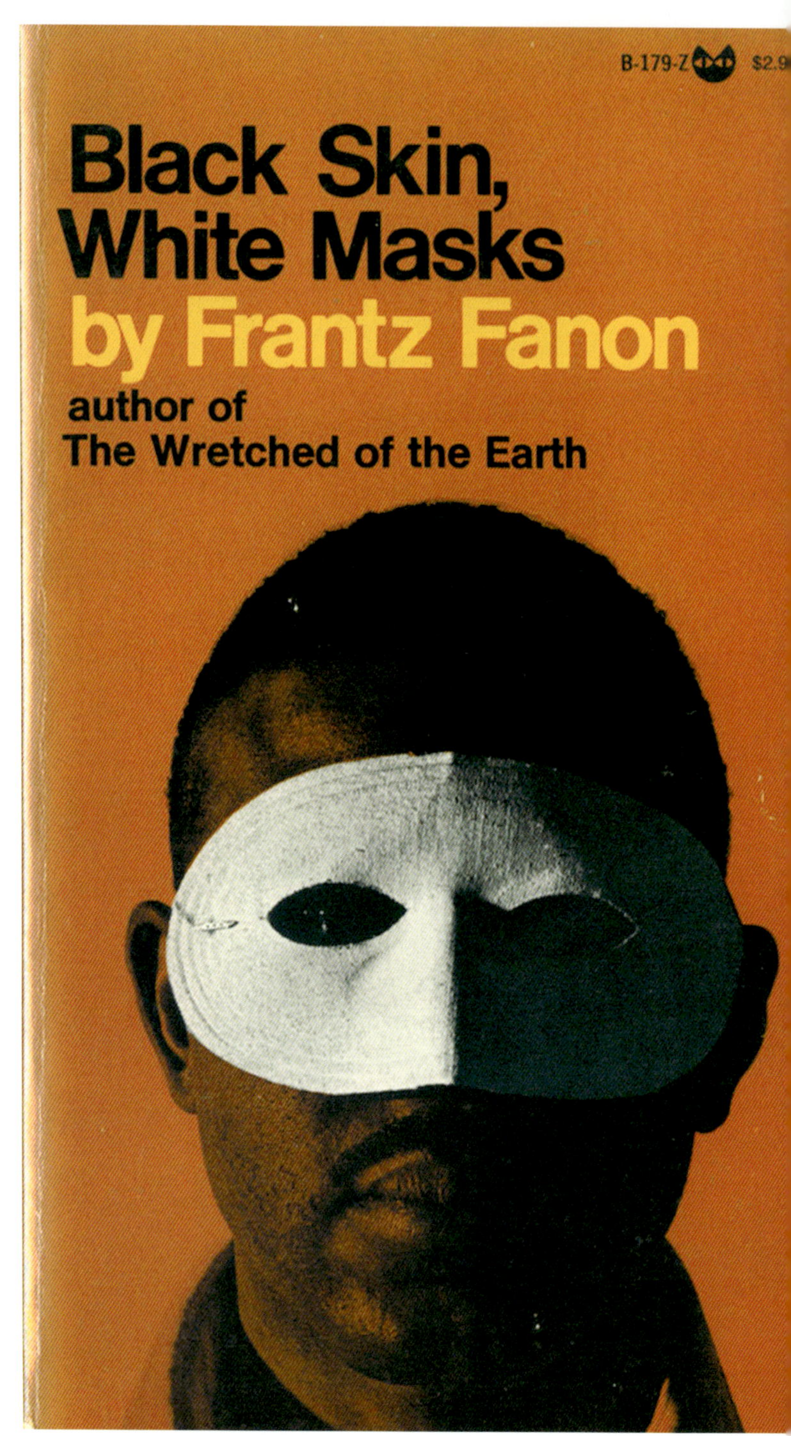
B-179-Z $2.9
Black Skin,
White Masks
by Frantz Fanon
author of
The Wretched of the Earth

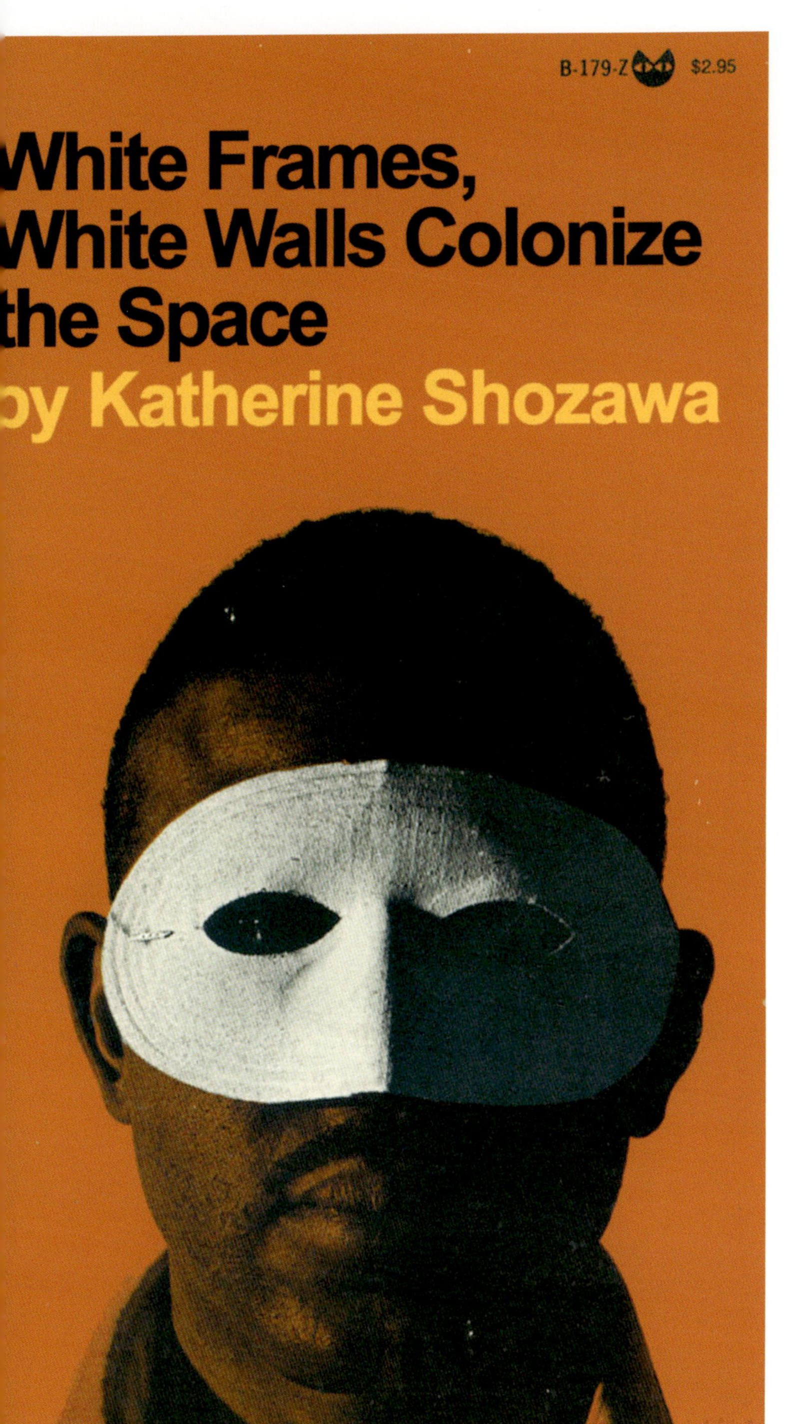
B-179-Z $2.95
White Frames,
White Walls Colonize
the Space
by Katherine Shozawa

Dear Moth,

One hundred trillion neutrinos pass through each square inch of matter every second, though it is presumed to be the case that human flesh cannot feel them with sensual registers already discovered. Quantum physics verifies what we have always known, what black folks and indigenous folks and queer folks have known for such a long time: there are things that happen in the world, in the universe, that are not easily perceptible to human flesh. We cannot see on the quantum scale, eyes cannot detect atoms, electrons, neutrons, photons. We simply feel the effects of such material, how these tiny particles come together forming the building blocks of, while moving through, matter. Neutrinos are part of what quantum physicists call "dark matter," teeny, tiny particles unaffected by light, uninhibited by gravity.

I keep thinking about these two quotes:

quantum particles have no intrinsic properties that neatly correspond to position and velocity, and that measurement forces a quantum system to cough up values for these quantities in a way that depends on how the measurement is done (Physics and Philosophy x).

And

For [Niels] Bohr, what is at issue is not that we cannot know both the position and momentum of a particle simultaneously (as Heisenberg initially argued), but rather that particles do not have determinate values of position and momentum simultaneously … What he is doing is calling into question an entire tradition in the history of Western metaphysics (Meeting 19).

So what would knowing at the limits of justice mean—have you yet read the da Silva essay I sent you?—if knowing itself is in need of interrogation. I guess what I'm trying to say is, what if otherwise possibility doesn't simply name a different epistemology, what if it attempts to name what is literally unknowable because it a zone and inhabitation that does not have intrinsic properties that correspond neatly to what we call the good, the merciful, the just, the equitable—it does not and cannot have intrinsic properties of the possible and the just—until there is a forced measurement of sorts, until there is the simultaneity of event that causes a necessity?

Sorta like what I said last time on the phone, that because western man, the citizen, the human, doesn't account for what da Silva called the "others of Europe," then how can we measure or make attempts to understand actions and behaviors, how can we think about the ethical for those that are not considered to be human? If being ethical and having a commitment to ethics is dependent on modern man and his capacity

Ashon Crawley

but black folks and indigenous and queer and and and are outside such possibility, maybe what is enacted and is actionable is the anethical, a sorta way to measure and think relations of the good, the merciful, the equitable for those that don't fit in modern epistemologies of identity and difference. And this anethical possibility would also be a critique of ethics, ethics as a normative concept that necessitates ethical being, being that emerges through the coloniality of being/power/truth/freedom. And then perhaps maybe the anethical would also mark the relation to and be the decolonial. It seems to me to be the case that the tradition of western metaphysics the physicist Karen Barad—and yes, her essay about quantum physics was excellent, thanks for sending—attempts to critique because of the way knowledge is presumed in such a tradition also influences the way we think knowledge of the possible and knowledge of justice simultaneously.

So, what I mean is, for example, quantum physicist Werner Heisenberg begins his book *Physics and Philosophy* with the following:

> *When one speaks today of modern physics, the first thought is of atomic weapons. Everybody realizes the enormous influence of these weapons on the political structure of our present world and is willing to admit that the influence of physics on the general situation is greater than it ever has been before* (1).

And he's just doing the thing that I think is terrible, the way he assumes thought itself as totalized, as universal. Like, I want to ask him, why would atomic weapons be the first thought? What is the order of things such that atomic weaponry is assumed to be the first thought? (I've been reading Cedric Robinson a lot lately, so he's on my mind too.)

What is the myth of personhood, of racial and class distinction, that produces an occasion such that Heisenberg thinks the first thought of "modern physics" is weaponization and annihilation, the first thought for him is cataclysm and chaos? And what is assumed about modern man such that the mere mention of modern physics has within it this first operation, this first thinking with regard to warfare and destruction? Wouldn't this first thought be the renunciation of the flesh? Wouldn't this first thought, in other words, veil from view the fact that the first thought would have been produced through thinking other possibilities as not able to rise to the occasion of thought as thought? I guess I mean, the "first thought" is a misnomer of terribly large proportions, it's only first insofar as it is the renunciation of the world, of the materiality, from which thought occurs.

And doesn't Heisenberg's purported first thought not assume modern man and all his intellectual capacity? Isn't this a universalizing impulse that grounds the way he thinks thought itself? A universalizing impulse that proclaims itself to be a first operation that cannot deal with the irreducible doubleness, the irreducible plurality from which thought is nominated? In other words, the first thought ain't first, it's a choice, a decision, a desire and such a choice, decision and desire is produced by the way one thinks relation to self, others, the earth. This first thought is the thought of European man, the colonizer, the citizen, the human, the subject.

And what for those of us that hear about modern physics but do not take atomic weapons as a first thought, even if that thought does perhaps occur? Would those that do not think atomic weapons as a first operation be marginalized as having improper thought? Such impropriety would be queer. It just seems that this illustrates the way thought has been hierarchized, how it has been assumed, how it appears to be totalizing and producing modernity itself. Perhaps what is needed is a way to think, to cognize, to have knowledge of possibility and justice that only emerges through the simultaneity of measurement, a simultaneity beyond the limit, beyond the horizon, in the zone of darkness, a sorta anethical thrust or drive or critique. Maybe that's what black performance is. This zone might be the secret place of marronage.

More soon but I gotta get going. Anyway, I miss you.
A

Dear Moth,

What if it were possible to vibrate at the same speed and velocity as our favorite music, our favorite sound? What if we resonated the way Mahalia Jackson sorta wails and sways on "souuul" in "How I got Over" or like a Twinkie Clark black Pentecostal shout on the Hammond organ? What if we could just move and tremble and quiver and quake and spin and spin and spin until equilibrium is off and we just slip into the sonic world? I watch *The Flash* a lot—even though I have to catch up on the episodes—but the show keeps intimating that if Barry could just vibrate at the same speed as what is presumed to be solid and impenetrable matter, they keep saying he could slip in and into and through matter itself. So what if we could do the same with music, with sound? Would we perhaps then evaporate into and be united with it? What would be our mode of existence?

What song or sound would you choose? I'd wanna choose something that resonates with a simultaneity, spin and quiver and quake and be one with you. Withdraw into you and you withdraw into me. So yeah, what's the song?

Also, I'd been meaning to ask you about mysticism because you said you went on the silent retreat and it made you think about all kinds of things, that it was this mystical experience for you. So who are some folks you'd suggest for me to read?

Moving,
A

Dear Moth,

It's been a while because I've been reading Meister Eckhart since you said I'd enjoy him. Interesting dude. You said, "Stop thinking of being alone as lonely. Think about it as a moment to reconnect with your deepest self, think about it as a chance to sit in silence and be still and to breathe and to be. If you can think of being alone as a chance to hear God, then you'll be ok. Check out this Eckhart."

But the more I read, the more I figure out why I have a sorta resistance to this shit—to silent retreats and shit like that—why it makes me feel weird. The Eckhart, and the other stuff I've been reading actually, seems to be tied to particular traditions, to particular religious affiliations, but that unsettles me. I'm not looking for a New Age individuation of blessings and wealth and acquisition that discards the histories and practices from which certain mysticisms emerge and from which they gestate. But I guess I have the same problem with mysticisms that I have with what I guess we could call, imprecisely of course, non-mystical traditions. (Does such a thing even exist?) Mystical traditions, at least the western ones, seem to run up against their own limit, seem to only be able to go so far, seem to be about the production of normative function and form.

The limit, I guess in Eckhart, would be a kind of normative Christianity. And his aloneness, his negativity, his nothingness all emerge from that limit even if he is trying to approach something otherwise. Because for his experience to be about Christianity, such experience is against the very interconnectedness of all things mysticism presumes to seek. How, in other words, can I be connected to all things, how can I be integrated as a part of a whole, while remaining steadfast in a conviction about Jesus being the only way to the Father, for example? Some folks, some doctrines, are much more dogmatic about there being only one path whereas others even in the same traditions seem to be much more open and capacious and imaginative. I wanna be like them, I guess.

So yeah, I've been reading Eckhart and I think he's cool. But Eckhart assumes a certain theological world with a certain deity, godhead, a certain understanding of the human, a very particular understanding of immanence and transcendence. It's that particularity that is introduced that seems to produce an antagonism for other traditions, even in their mystical strains. [Also, perhaps because of the invention of the category of religion as a product of modern thought and, thus, the concept of tradition too is one that I don't know how to feel about. And I'm thinking of Talal Asad here, at least, if not others.] Based on our conversations about this, it seems you think it's impossible, or only New Age, for mysticism to be devoid of a particular religious tradition. If that's the case, that's very unsettling to me.

I'm thinking of Eckhart and also Theresa of Avila and St. John of the Cross. And Athanasius and Cassian and the Rule of Benedict. I'm even thinking of John of Fécamp that says, in his book Lament Over Lost Leisure and Solitude,

> *It shames and horrifies me that I must appear in public assemblies, going into the city, talking to those in power, looking at women, mingling with the chattering masses and enduring so many other things that pertain to the world.* (Hollywood and Beckman 83)

He's just one example but think about it: he was an 11th century Benedictine monk lamenting over the fact of lost leisure and lost solitude, what was lost was so because the social world had become too much for monks to pretend to be unencumbered by, the social world made itself evident in the ways the monks had to alter the practice of their daily lives. For John of Fécamp, what was desired was leisure and solitude from the social world, from the noise of relationality, so much so that he lamented having to deal with the materiality of people, their funk, their voice, their breath. It's just hella Kantian before Kant because wasn't Kant, too also, worried over the material fact of beggars on the street, the fact that beggars became too numerous? And didn't Kant escape their noise because they were too much for him to engage? John of Fécamp gives a Kantian analysis of the transcendental aesthetic before Kant, or really perhaps model the sorta idea of the aesthetic to come.

What intrigues me about all these folks is their desire for a vertical relationship with the Lord over and against all other kinds of relationships, how there is a sorta necessity to renounce sociality, how there is a retreat, how there is a movement away from noise. And so, even when monks were called upon to recite the psalms daily in communal prayer, the emphasis seemed not to be on the communal aspect but on the regimentation of following the rule, of following order, of inculcating obedience in the service of the creation of the individual, of the self, of the subject. Such an individual, self, subject would be rational, would be higher, than the base emotions, than the flesh. There was an assumption, a moving out from the flesh, a renunciation of the body, to produce this vertical relation.

Living alone, ridding oneself of the appetites of the flesh as much as possible, retreating from the world into the desert. I've got no problem with renunciation, retreat or movement, it's just the direction of such that worries me. And you wanted me to read this because you thought it'd help me think about being alone, or single, or finding god. I don't know, I am thinking a lot but more perturbed than anything. But I'll keep thinking.

More soon,
A

Dear Moth,

There are worlds. And the fact of our experiencing them is because we are impossibly vulnerable, open, as a way of life. The central nervous system isn't enclosed in the borders of the so-called body. But it's out there, in worlds, that which is central is kind of an ecstatic force, ecstatic being, existence beside or otherwise than, the self. Such that the idea of an outside and inside needs to be thought against. Maybe entangled. Maybe a system.

It's been a while since I've heard from you. You sent that text when you returned home that you shouldn't have come over, that you're sorry you cried, that you love me but can't. And then all this talk, mostly, about god. So it's taken me some time to think about what you wrote to me about god, I had to think about it, had to think about what you think god is.

So here …

What quantum physics is discovering is a redefinition of spacetime as not linear nor separable. If this is the case and god is, as you say, an unfolding, then this god would be the unfolding of all that is and is not detectual (able to be detected) by sensual capacities. This would mean that there is some something "behind" or that withdraws from even this quantum understanding of spacetime, some otherwise sorta relation, some sorta unity and convergence that would undo even the concepts of unity, convergence, together, sociality, unfolding, enfolding, undoing, doing, action, reaction. Does this even make sense?

And that would then too mean love, right? Because don't we think love as the unfolding of possibility in time and space, or following quantum mechanics, in spacetime, love as approaching a kinda sociality of experience? But then maybe also love would be that which necessarily withdraws through approach the very possibility of possibility. Because what does it mean for something or nothing to be of—from or marking relation to—possibility if "it" recedes from sense experience? Love as the sense experience beyond sensuality, beyond or withdrawing from or below or sharing some other kinda relation to experience? It's like when you said, "you are more than someone else's negation, someone else's exclusion," because we exist in and as excess, as that which cannot be contained or engulfed or enclosed by anything, negation and exclusion included.

It's as if we are the flesh of what quantum mechanics is discovering.

I won't settle. I will continue to pursue what at times feels at most like a hunch or a vague sense of possibility or perhaps even like a pulling towards, something sorta like a dream trying to be pieced together after having awaken abruptly and having felt deeply but losing such feeling second by second though you know, though you intuit, that though you have not attained, pressing in such a direction will fulfill a promise to come. And I will continue precisely because my now moment is dictated by some moment to come sensed as verve and visitation from outside the possibility of spacetime. I won't settle. Because it happened. Because it happens. Because it is happening. Because it will happen.

What I'm trying to say, imprecisely, is this: I think I love you? I watch *An Oversimplification of Her Beauty*, as you know, a lot. And I get why she sent the text she did, why it was a question that was also a statement, how it was tentative but also very sure.

I think I love you?

I finally understand because you, Moth, make me feel what I've just been afraid to say but I know to be true: I have never felt this way about anyone—anyone—in my life before. And that sounds like a platitude.

But this is what I mean: You are, and my feeling for you, is black noise, is static, is sorta the background against which everything I do occurs. I don't consciously think about you all of the time, no, but I feel you. When I sleep, when I wake, when I cook, when I sing, as I breathe, as I breathe, as I breathe, it's you. A sorta quiet omnipresence, a soft enclosement, you are the sound, almost chant-like, I hear sorta far off in the deep recesses and furthest reaches of my flesh. And yet, you feel more than near, closer than anything I've ever known. I do not think about you as much as I think: you. It's as if you are bound to each thought—whatever that thought might be—I think. It's as if you are the ground of all that is for me. I don't mean this in a way pathological or that I cannot exist without you, that I have some sorta weird co-dependence that is more about ego and narcissism than about your well-being or mine. I mean that I desire you. And I feel we are one.

It's like what I said to you in that text message not soon after meeting you, it's as if in and with you I'd found the voice in my to which I was constantly searching, the voice in my head to which I was always replying, as if meeting you confirmed that we already were, that we already was, as if meeting you were the promise and the fulfillment of the promise, a breakdown of simultaneity through a spacetime rip or tear or break.

I understand David and Jonathan and being knit together.

Unlike weaving, knitting does not require a loom or other large equipment, making it a valuable technique for nomadic and non-agrarian peoples.

They were knit together and were movers, nomadic. Nomads are wanderers and I'm thinking about David's psalm, talking about walking through the valley of the shadow of death but not fearing, wandering in death's shadow but still feeling assured. And though this 23rd is about the lord, I wonder if it's also about what had been backgrounded, David's being knotted up and tangled with Jonathan.

And what I mean is this: I think I love you. No question mark.

And what I mean is this: I have not stopped telling everyone about you, the joy you have brought and continue to bring me.

And what I mean is this: there is not only you in the world but you are my paraclete, and I, yours.

And what I mean is this: I want a consensuality with you, a continued consent to be together.

And what I mean is this: entanglement might be the best way to approach what I feel, that once joined together, we are a system. We maintain our uniqueness regardless of the nearness or farness, regardless of spacetime separation, we are indivisible, we renounce the individual for the social, for and with and in each other.

And what I mean is this: it's as if dreamworlds were hallucinating otherwise universes as possible, and mine and your dreamworlds outpoured towards each other, enfolded into and collapsed within each other.

And what I mean is this: it's kinda beautiful, and mostly scary, because I don't know what this means and haven't since I first met you and am unsure what to do. I do not want to control you. Your consent is more necessary than my desire.

And what I mean, finally, is this: I don't want you to go to seminary if it means you will not, and cannot, be with me. I want to support you but why the priesthood when they require celibacy? My stomach churns at the thought of us not being together, I literally get sick at the thought. Your T-shirt that you left here when you were last here, I have not yet washed because the smell of sweat and Polo cologne and you and you and you linger on, in it. Don't do this. Please. I hate to even ask such a thing. Don't not go for me. But please don't go. I know Saint Sabina was formative for you, that you chose that space of care and were so compelled, you were able to get your parents to join too. I know you want to continue in the tradition of the folks there, that you too think the University of St. Mary of the Lake is the place to which you are called to study for a master's degree and all but, but … please. Do you think this will make you happy? Can you do the justice work and the preaching work in another tradition? I need you too.

I am not just speaking metaphorically, I want to be touched by and to touch you continually. I'm not talking about some abstract kinda affection but a real feeling of and with and in you. And reciprocally. Love is a material thing, it breaks open imagination and makes possible other ways of conceiving what we can think and do and be.

Until the spacetime beyond when where I no longer feel you, which will never be,
A

Dear Moth,

You said it was beautiful, that you believed me, but didn't say much else. You ignored my texts and haven't returned my calls. It's been two months and there's not been a word from you. I've given you the space you didn't even ask for but I intuited you desired, you needed. But, if the shit I said was so beautiful and moving to you, why the intensity of silence? Is the beauty also on the edge of grotesque, too much, too weighty for you? How is it that the thing you called beautiful is also that which made you recoil and retreat not into but away from me? It makes me feel you don't value me. And I don't know, shit is terrible.

I know before I said that I wanted you without it being a weird codependence but that was imprecise. There's nothing wrong with depending on another, it's sorta the condition of our lives, to need one another. Why demonize need or desire or want? It's just, I wanna be able to depend on you to reply to me, to tell me what you feel, how you feel, when you feel it. I want to be able to depend on you without being parasitic.

You misunderstand me when you think I say there are worlds and that I am only talking about love, or when I say that I am entangled with you and your smile, that it did something to me. You misunderstand me because I think we are an example, minuscule of course, of things otherwise. I'm thinking of blackness as the marking of alternatives. I'm thinking of indigeneity, too, as that marking. And queerness. And I'm thinking of these as mutually constitutive categories, as nondivisional, not in order to liquidate and evaporate difference but in order to say that western logics of thinking relation have been imposed on us.

Anyway, what I mean is, blackness would have to also be against linear time. And indigeneity. And queerness too. These would not be additive but a different relation. This different relation isn't created by western epistemologies but is the resistance to that categorical coherence. These would not then be identities, no matter how hard we try to turn them into property, but the resistance to identity. They would be, instead, ways of life, ways to live, ways to relate to one another against the imposition of identification as that which would sever and divide us.

What I mean is, blackness and indigeneity and queerness mark an otherwise spacetime. This spacetime would not be linear in its trajectory or force. And I'm thinking, what if the encounter with black being, with indigenous being, with queer being, is also a confrontation with a kind of refused refusal of entanglement, an encounter with the confrontation of the fact of entanglement, the fact of an encounter of a different and very much material because imagined and produced disruptive epistemology?

Just thinking … you misunderstand me, still,
A

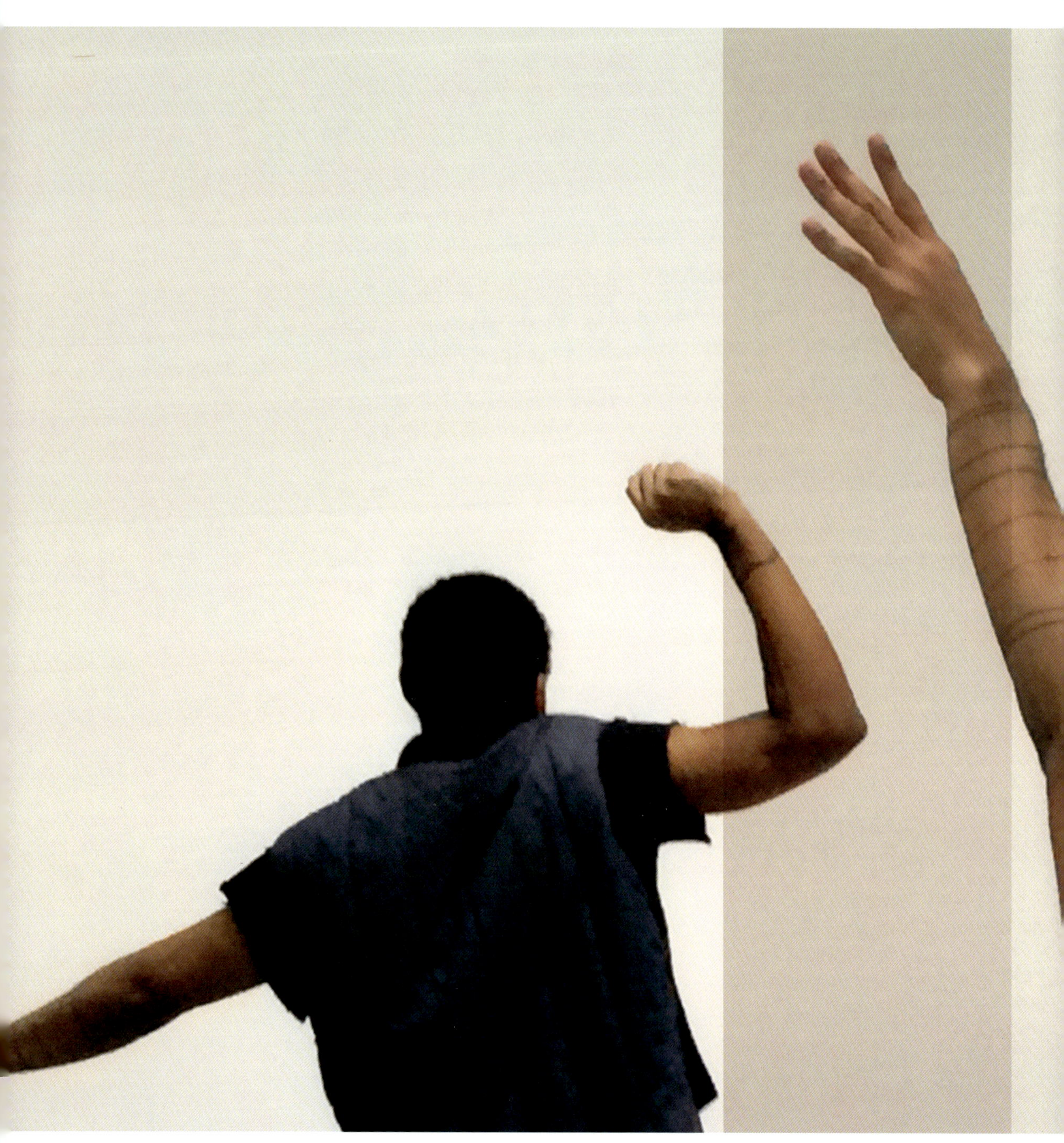

Virago-Man Dem: in-process showings by M. Cynthia Oliver   120

Cynthia Oliver

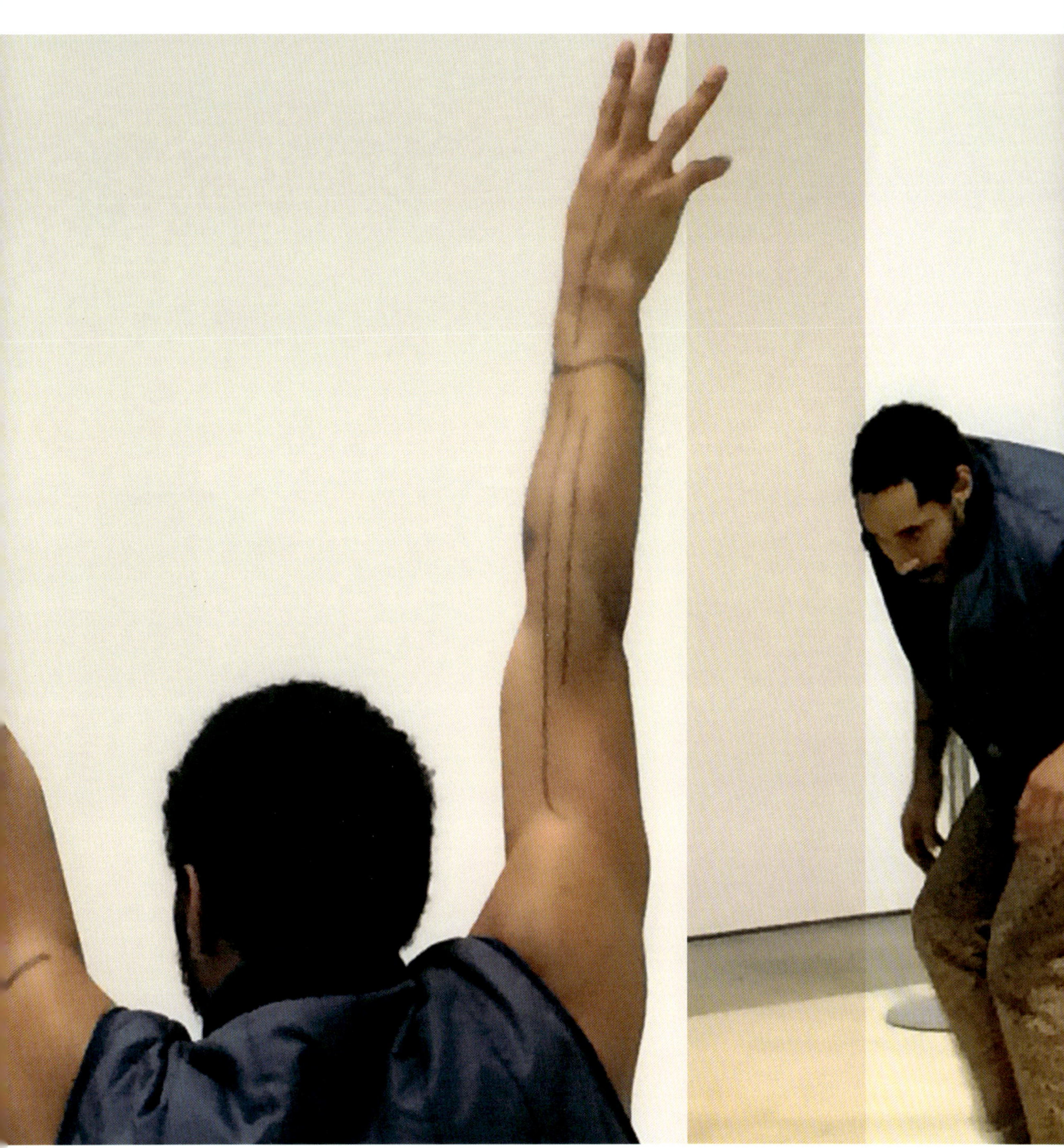

Composer: Jason Finkelman; Lighting design: Amanda K. Ringger; Costume design:
Susan Becker; Visual design: John Jennings and Stacey Robinson of Black Kirby;
Projection design/animator: John Boesche. Performers: Niall Noel Jones, Duane Cyrus,
Jonathan Gonzalez, Shamar Watt

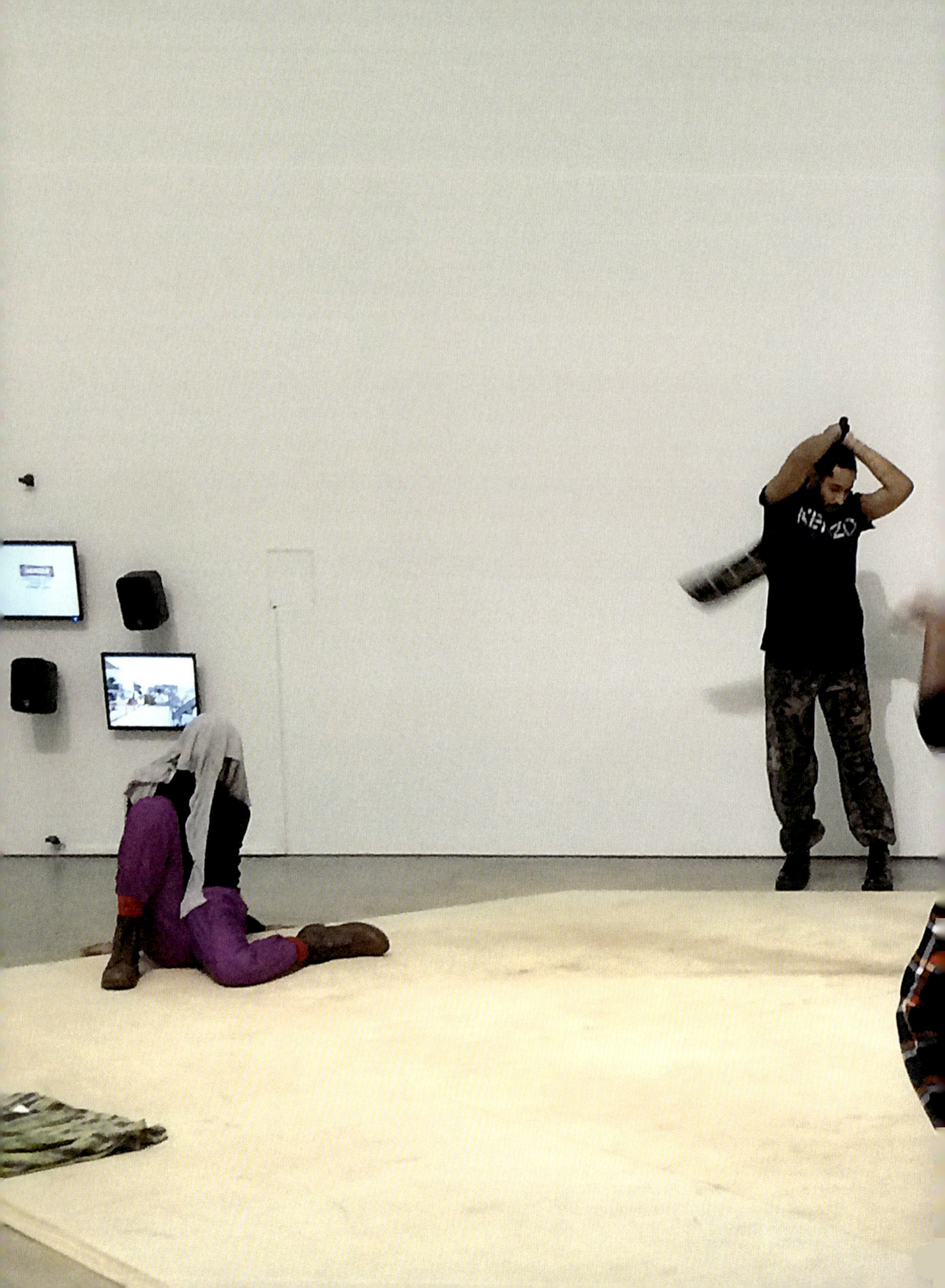

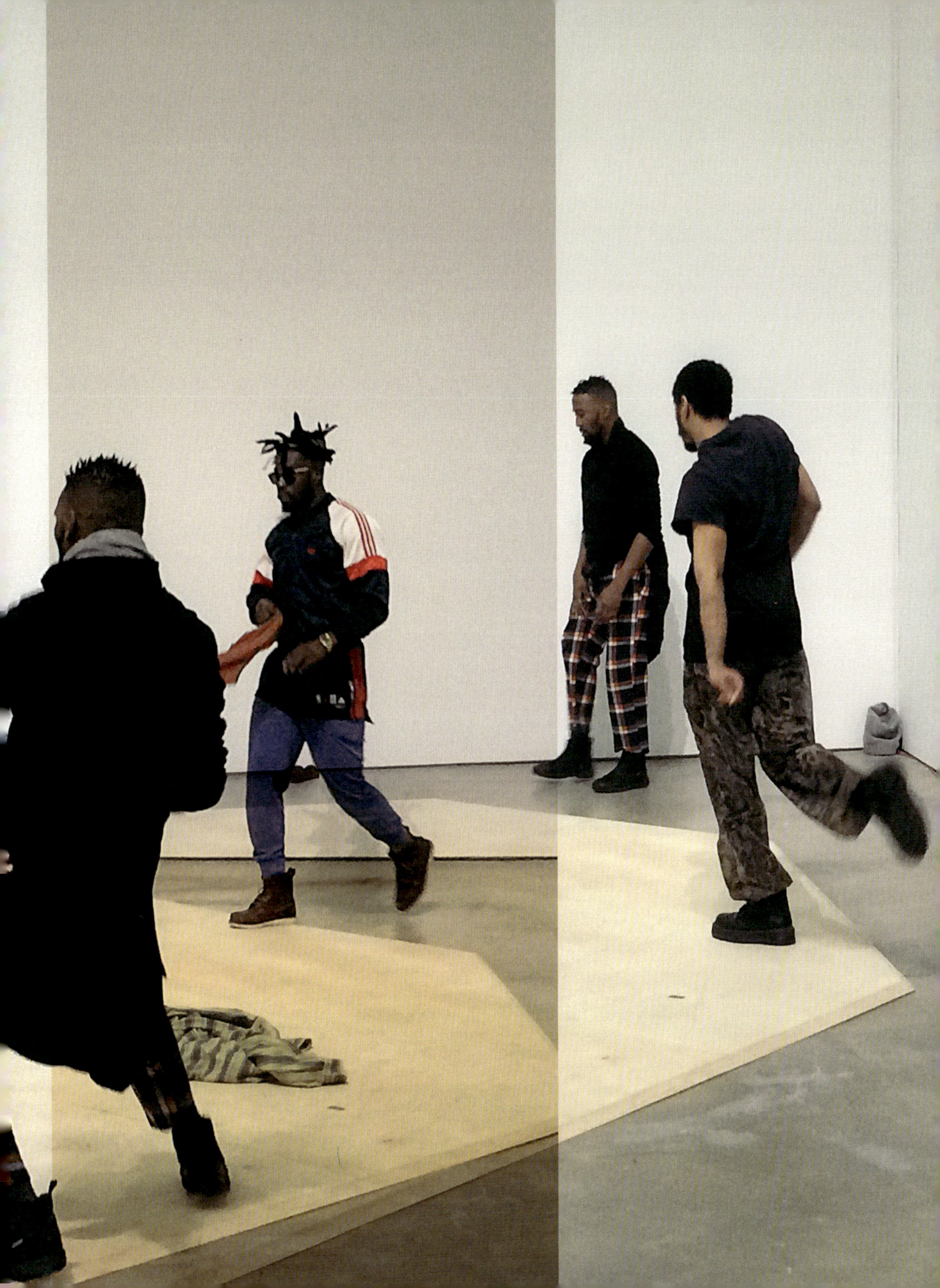

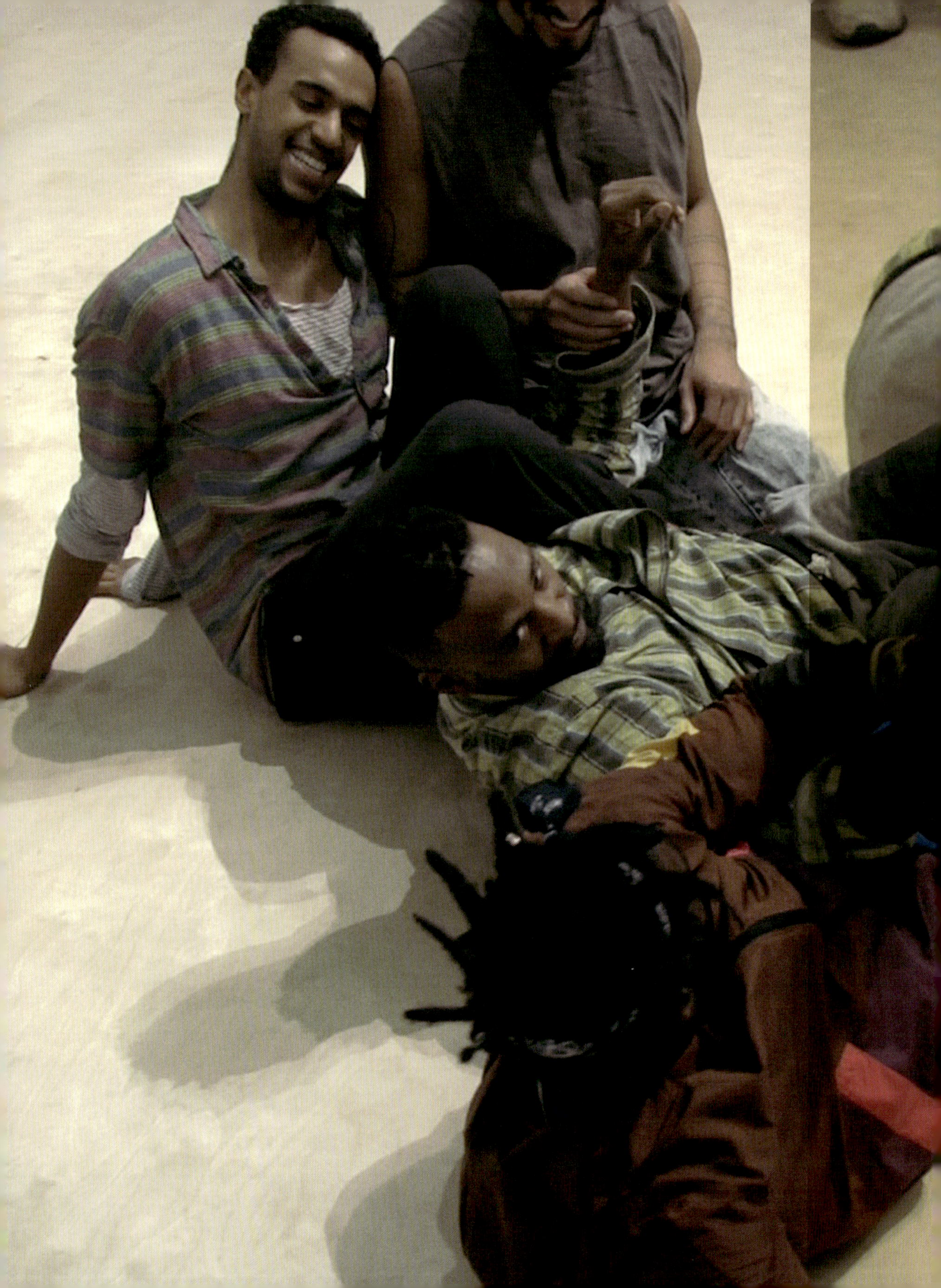

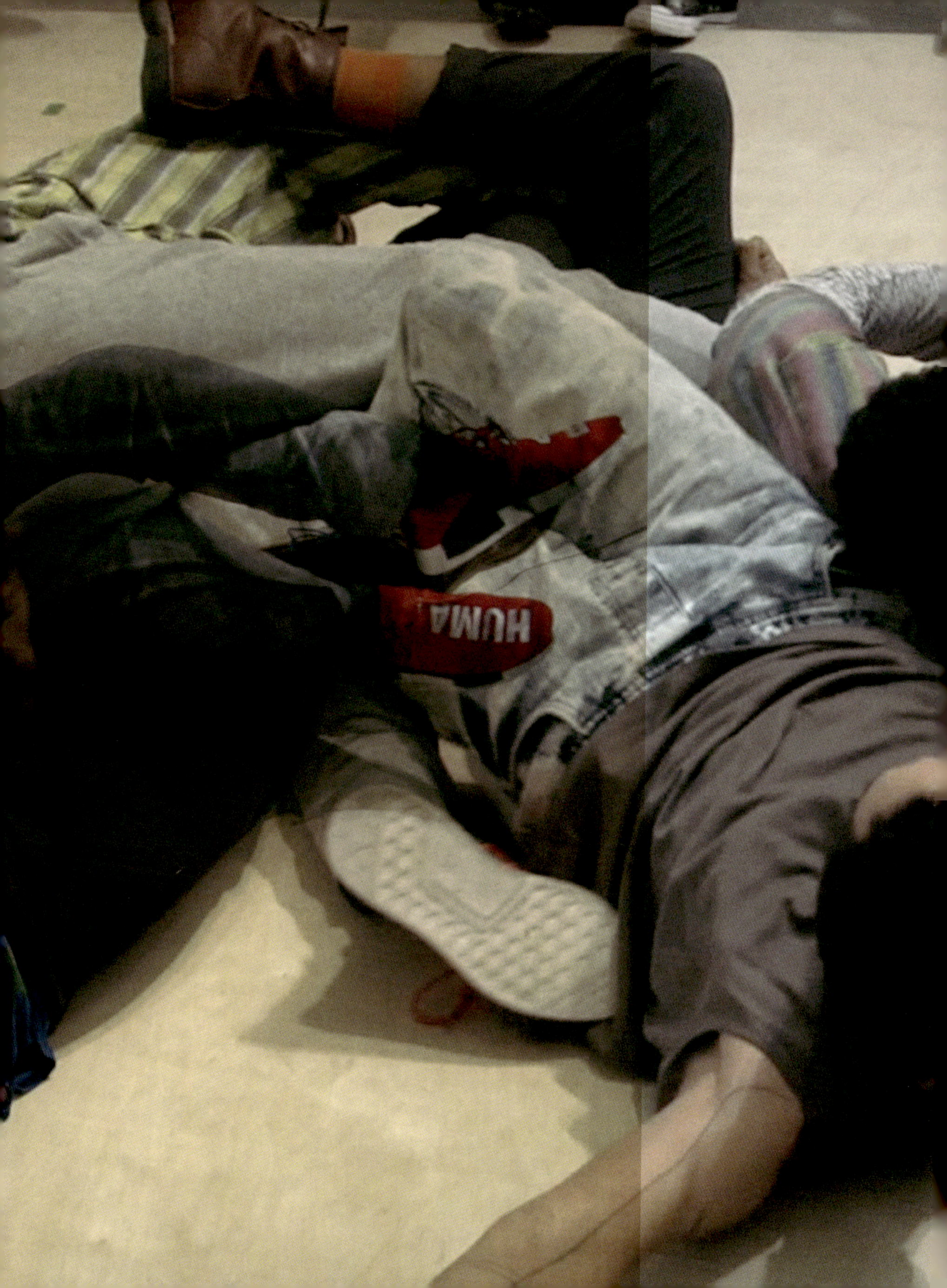

By the winter of 2017 I had been engaged in improvisational investigations around a new dance theatre work for about a year and a half. I was a Mellon Fellow at the Maggie Allesee National Center for Choreography, where I encountered Danielle Goldman. We talked a lot about improvisation and my use of it in the work. A few months later, she called and asked me to participate on the program of artists she was curating for the *Endless Shout*—an exhibition I understood to be an extension of/based on the historic *Freedom Principle: Experiments in Art and Music 1965–Now* which had been held earlier at the MCA Chicago.

I began thinking about Virago-Man Dem decades ago, but started actively crafting it in the summer of 2015 in Trinidad at New Waves Institute. Devastated by the unyielding assault on black life and the never-ending cycle of stereotype, abuse, and murder in the lives of black men, I was determined to create a work that offered a more expansive, nimble, loving, and humane view of the complexities of black masculinities. We had just completed a showing at Gibney Dance Center in New York for the Arts Presenters (APAP) Conference and I wanted us to dive right back into process, to move more deeply into our investigations that were less about "showing" and more about discovering in the "doing." Not that the two need be mutually exclusive. But this effort was for me, a way to focus on areas of our work that relied on improvisation and group thinking. We could do this in a space of other works of art and a variety of flexible audience orientations that were ideal for certain sections of our material. So I brought the cast of this in-process production to the ICA.

I wanted our work there to be intimate, for the audience to experience the visceral nature of the dancing bodies and our human commonalities. I wanted to take advantage of histories of museum/gallery spaces as locations for experiments in seeing, and add the moving body to that visuality. We coordinated four timed experiments of twenty minutes each over the course of two days. I was told this was the first time the museum presented time-based art in the museum in this particular way. It was also a first for me to present the experiments that would inform my work rather than the work itself (this was confusing for some members of the audiences who have been more accustomed to showings of finished material rather than its bones).

I was interested in the trace the performers and our experiments would leave in the space, on the performers and the witnesses—particularly those who came to more than one experiment. I was interested in the ways the meanings of one segment / experiment might accrue between and into the next. I was keenly attuned to the whiteness of the container—the actual color of the walls, the architecture of the enclosed space, as well as the history of museums as places where the white gaze maintains dominance. I wanted to interrupt these somehow. I didn't know what the regular ICA visitor looked like. The gaze there was not exclusively white by any measure. The conventions of museum environments might never be an issue in this space or might only be periodically interrupted depending on programming. Whatever the case, we were momentary interlocutors, both in the timing of the experiments and the traces of these black male bodies in the white box of the room on the given day(s). Some investigations felt successful in both spatial and historical/contemporary aims and some felt flat, which I attribute to my question/task assigned, not the response I received from the space or audiences. I arranged and rearranged the seating for each experiment. The four men—Duane Cyrus, Jonathan Gonzalez, Niall Noel Jones, and Shamar Watt—performed themselves in ways I had not seen up until then. The close proximity of the witnesses created an intimacy that seemed to prompt them to establish personas which would create the distance space did not provide. Some embraced that intimacy, others retreated from it. Shamar spoke directly to young students who were giggling and asked them why they were laughing. I didn't hear their answers. Niall retreated into his mercurial self and quietly slithered in and out among

Virago-Man Dem: in-process showings by Cynthia Oliver

Cynthia Oliver

them. Duane explored the most abstract of communication methods in guttural sounds and eclectic movement both related and unrelated to some of the arsenal provided by the repertory. Jonathan made himself vulnerable and available—an open vessel—as he negotiated both his dancing partners and the audience members who so closely watched.

The performers were queued to begin on cymbal chimes from a neighboring exhibition. Each experiment had a different directive. In one, they were to play with their voices, to investigate a section of the work we called "whisper/display" where they expressed life lessons from intimate relationships cast against segmented descriptions of body parts. They explored the performance of their clothing as their style might relate to their internal selves or distract from it. They inhabited an exercise in failure as they moved sequentially from image to image in an effort to (re)present every image they have ever seen of a black man (this exercise was both part of our process and a fixture/feature in our performances). They explored a section we internally call "Rat King," an intertwined morass of limbs and torsos so close to the surrounding audience that when they slowly slipped out of the knots they made and worked their way out of the room, audience members told me it was so sensual and close that they felt a part of it, or as though they wanted to join in themselves. We explored our "BOOM! Muthafucka" section where they practiced loud, brash, and humorous aspects of black masculine play in the cavernous room with echoes of their nonsense banter bouncing off the walls. These were experiments integral to the larger full evening work, but also moments utterly dependent on improvisational skill. They allowed the performers to develop timing, physical cues, understand what did or did not work, and more valuable than anything, nurture the continuing relationship with each other that would infuse the final work with an ease and familiarity upon which it depends. We discovered a new sense of exhaustion as the performers had to hold it together for hours on end, readying themselves to "perform" for fifteen to twenty minutes every two hours, rather than a "hit it and quit it" standard perform and finish model. I learned a lot about the performers themselves and their relationships to audience, each other and my direction. The work matured in ways I could not have manufactured in another environment at another time. As with all of our residencies, we talked about where we were, what we were doing, and why it mattered all along the way. Virago-Man Dem prospered from these experiments and the generosity of so many in this venue and numerous others who allowed us to utilize their environs as our playground and share with their patrons. I am grateful to the ICA and Danielle to have made room for us in this exhibit.

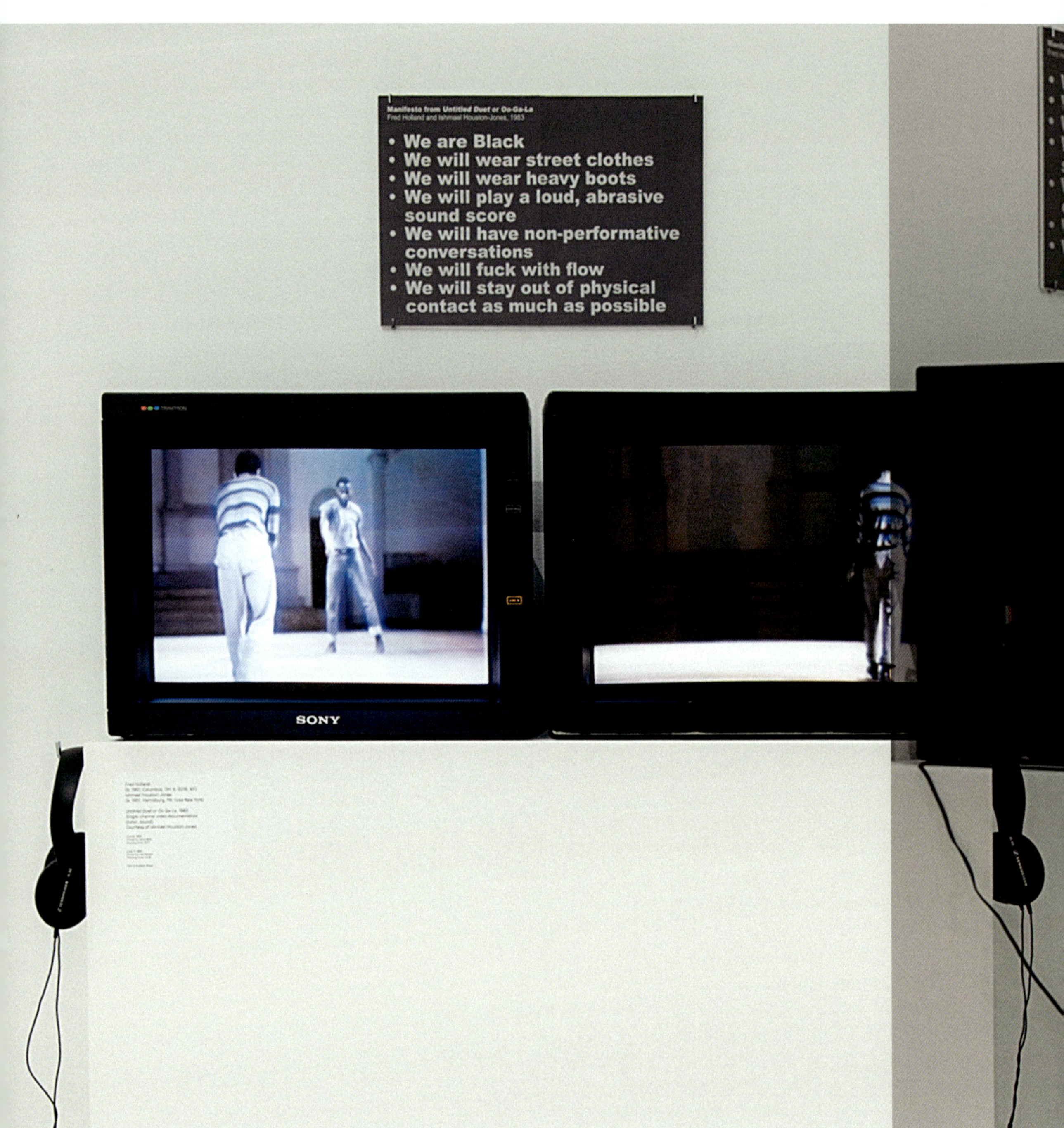
Manifesto from Untitled Duet or Oo-Ga-La
Fred Holland and Ishmael Houston-Jones, 1983
• We are Black
• We will wear street clothes
• We will wear heavy boots
• We will play a loud, abrasive
  sound score
• We will have non-performative
  conversations
• We will fuck with flow
• We will stay out of physical
  contact as much as possible
SONY

Ishmael Houston-Jones and Fred Holland

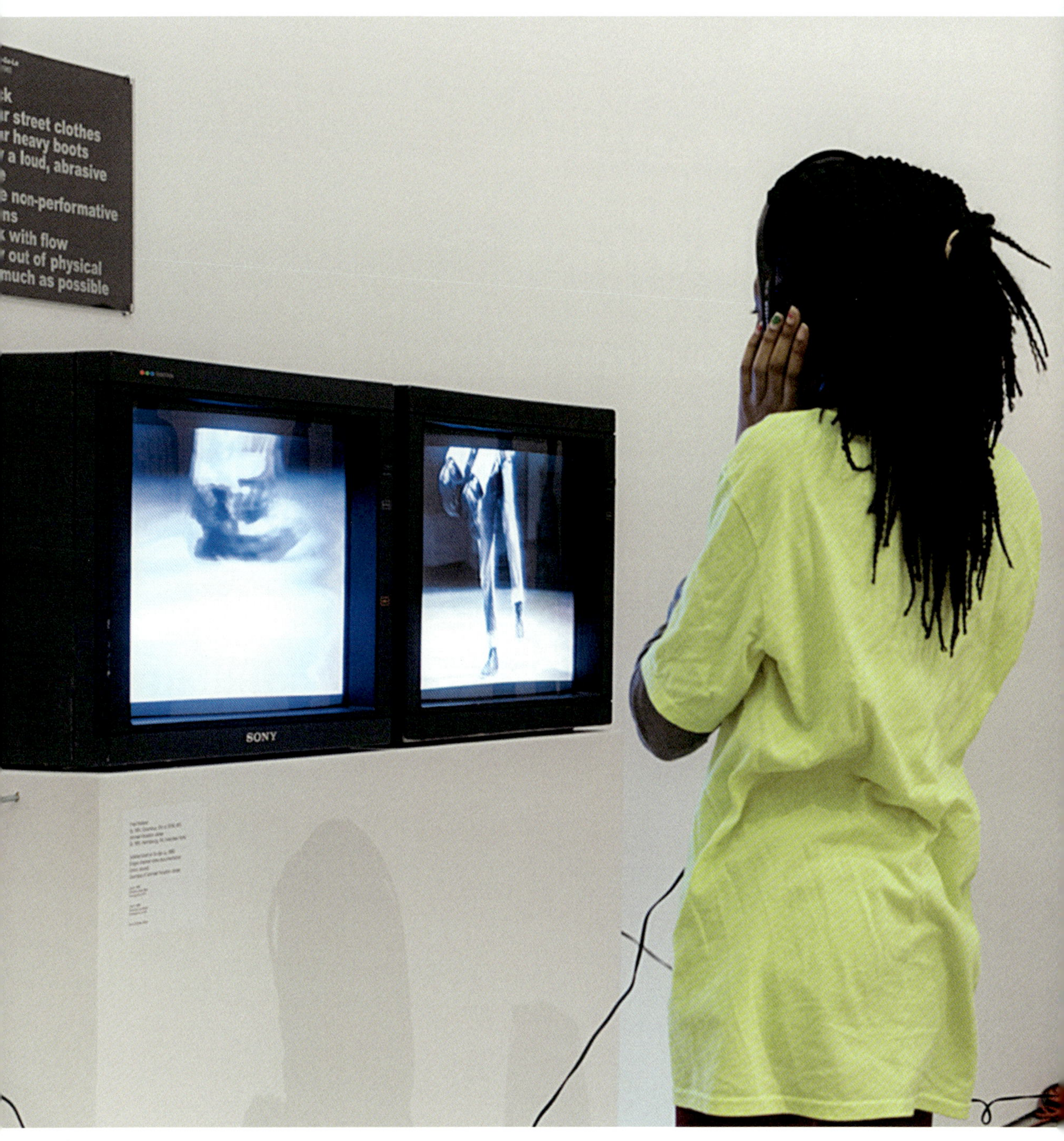

Installation view, single-channel video documentation (color, sound).
Courtesy of Ishmael Houston-Jones. June 6, 1983, filmed by Cathy Weis. Running time: 15:11
June 11, 1983, filmed by Lisa Nelson. Running time: 14:49

- **We are Black**

- **We will wear street clothes**

- **We will wear heavy boots**

- **We will play a loud, abrasive sound score**

- **We will have non-performative conversations**

- **We will fuck with flow**

- **We will stay out of physical contact as much as possible**

Manifesto from Untitled Duet or Oo-Ga-La
Fred Holland and Ishmael Houston-Jones, 1983 (annotated 2016)

We are Black
(The earliest iteration of Contact Improvisation was
Magnesium, a dance performance created by Steve Pax-
ton, first done at Oberlin College in 1972. Contact Improvisation remained in 1983 and remains still a dance form
done largely by people who are liberal arts educated
and are not black.)

We will wear street clothes
(Contactors most often wore baggy, soft sweats with
little attention paid to style.)

We will wear heavy boots
(Contact was always performed in bare feet and Fred
and I were very punk rock; I wore combat boots and
Fred wore construction worker boots. We used to be
chastised for wearing boots at contact jams.)

We will play a loud, abrasive sound score
(Early contact was rarely done to any music and if so it
was of the gentle ambient variety. We used a tape given
us by a noise composer, Mark Allen Larson, which he
made with samples from Kung Fu movies.)

We will have non-performative conversations
(We talked about anything we wanted, sometimes
referring to the dance we were performing and at other
times just everyday chit-chat, but neither were projected to the audience.)

We will fuck with flow
(In ten years, a classicism had attached itself to Contact
Improvisation that dictated that movements "should"
always be soft, owing, and sequential.)

We will stay out of physical contact as much as possible
(As the name of the form implies, this was an important
rule to break.)

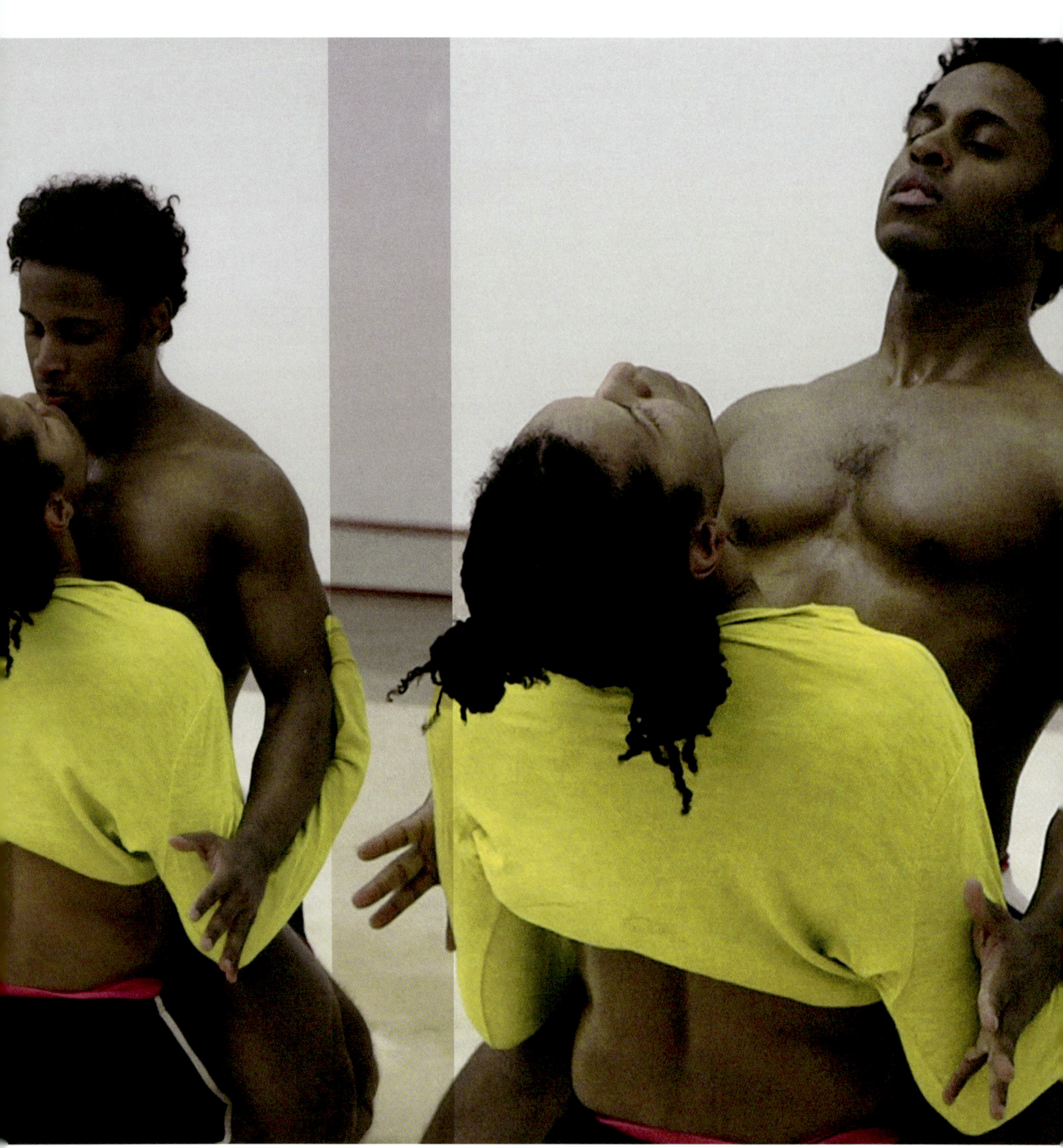

Let 'im Move You: A Study and This Is a Success

jumatatu m. poe

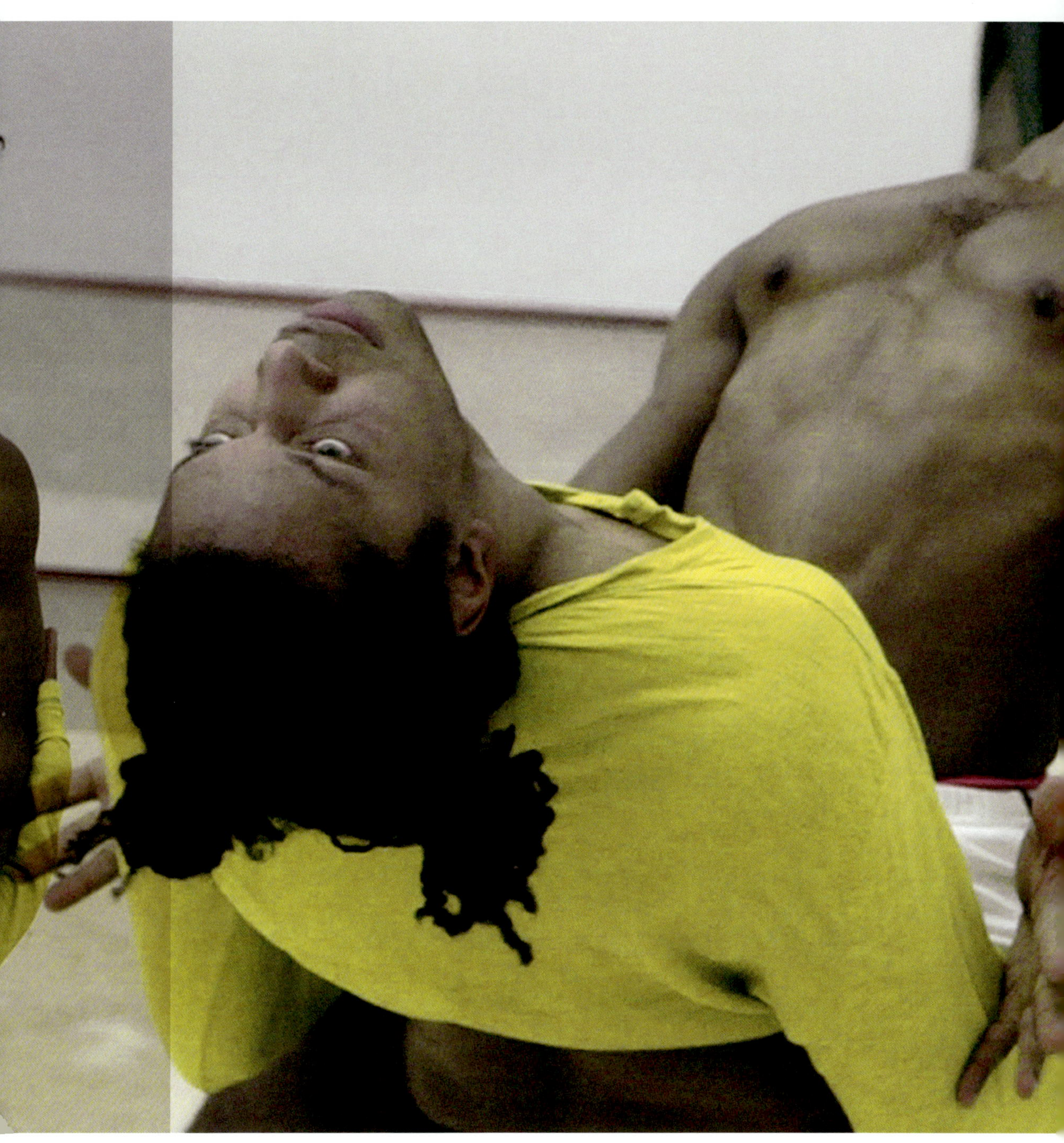

Jermone Donte Beacham, Zen Jefferson / dø√Σ Ç@KΣ, jumatatu m. poe, and William Robinson
Audience Infiltrators: Sanchel Brown, Julian Darden, Nikolai McKenzie, Sophiann Moore,
Vincent Taylor

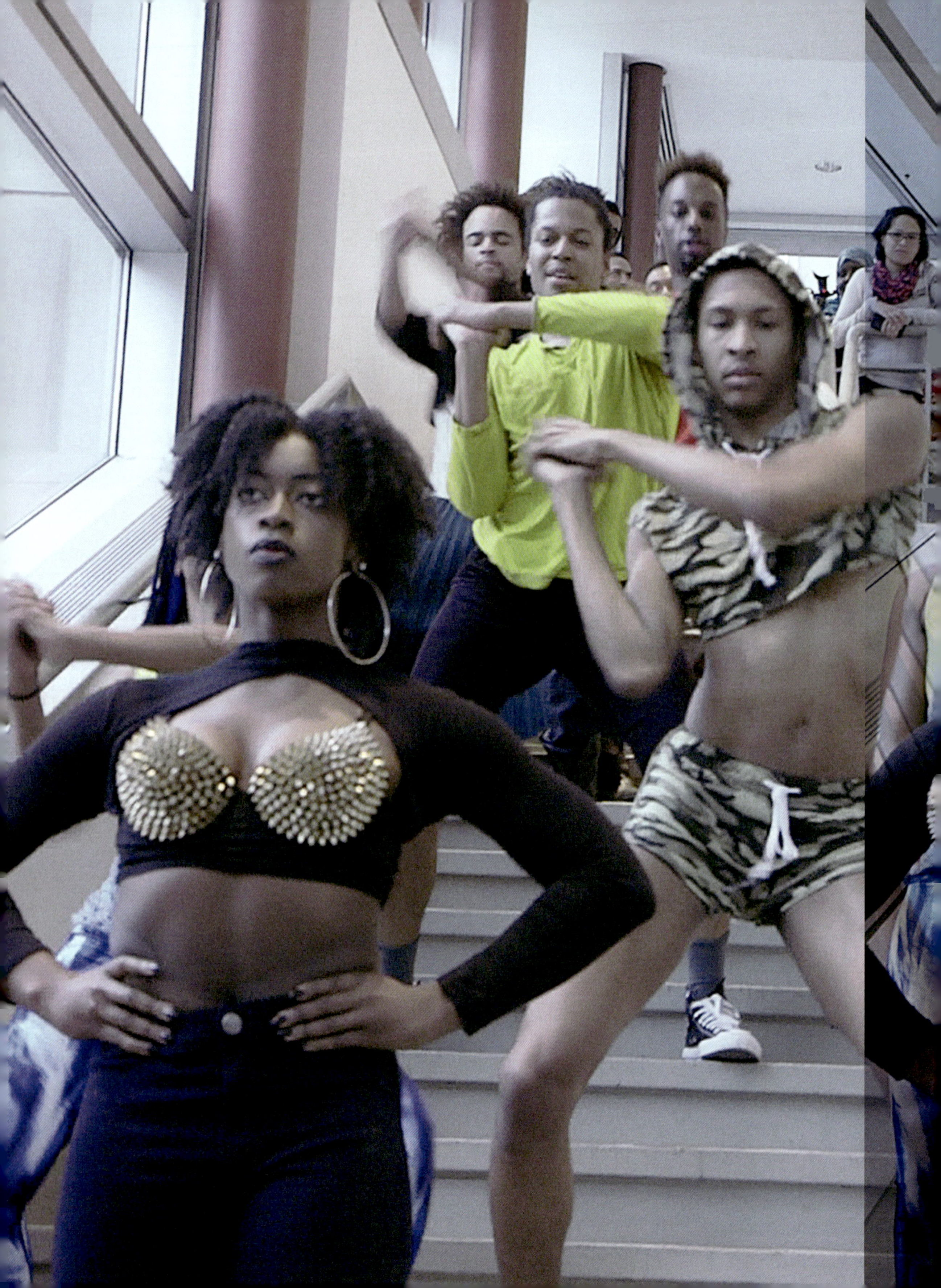

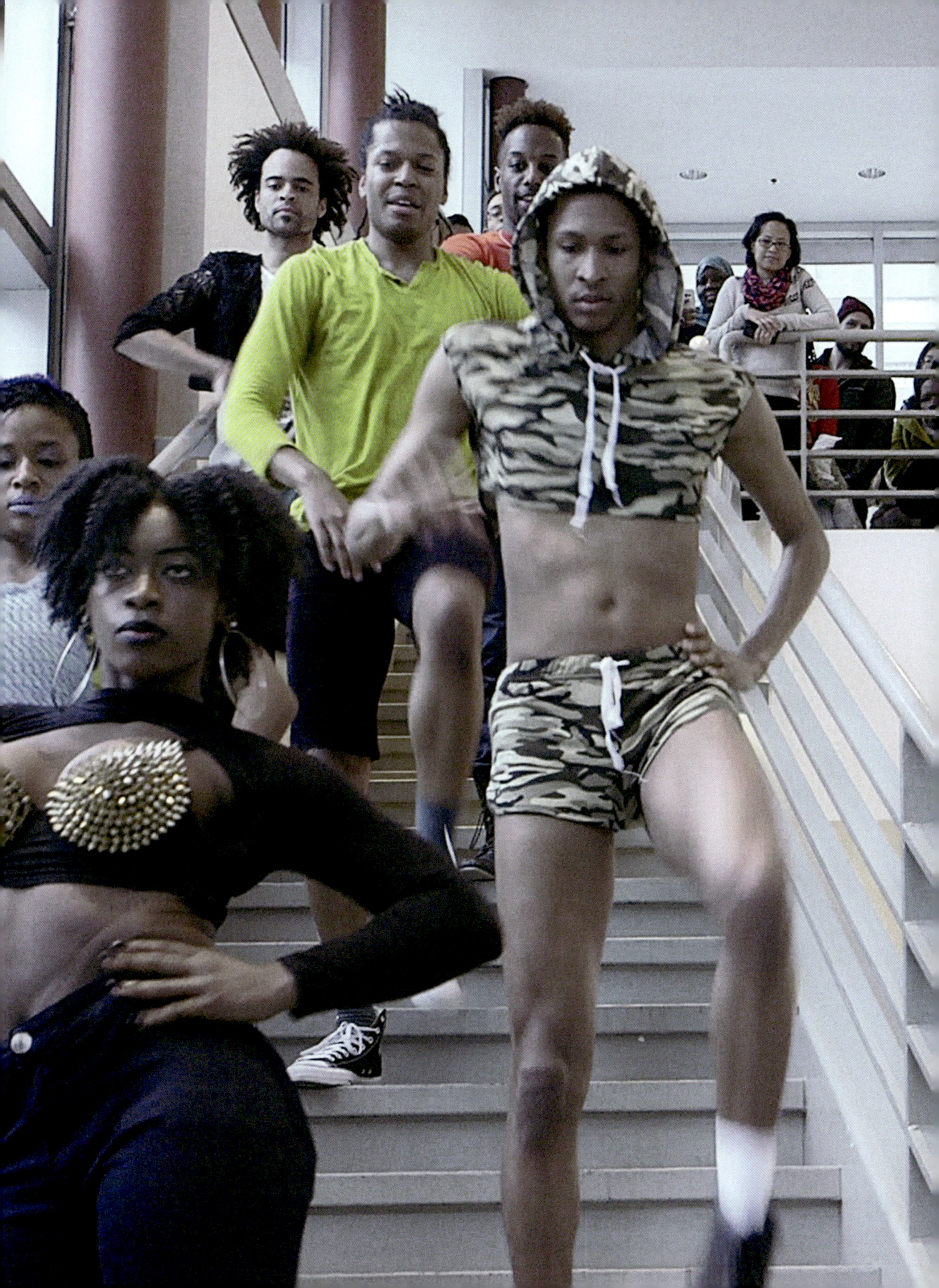

Let 'im Move You
jumatatu m. poe

Jermone Donte Beacham and I—jumatatu m. poe—have been working together in some capacity now for about eight years. In 2010, though we did not know one another yet, he was calling out to me from the screen … YouTube, that is. Pre-BeyChella-brand Beyonce had recently premiered her "Single Ladies" video, and set the internet on fire. Some of those flames were fed by the inclusion of a brief but decisive sixteen counts of J-Sette choreographic material among her Bob Fosse-inspired (and who inspired him?) music/dance video. The active online community of J-Sette artists was made hyper-visible in the afterglow of these flames, some of them catapulting their views into the hundreds of thousands. Enter Donte, in oversized jeans swallowing his petite figure, a basketball jersey, and a baseball cap dancing in what I now know to be his grandfather's living room—coffee table and easy chair shifted as close to the walls as possible so as not to become obstacles for Donte's rapidly swinging arms or the swift percussive attack of thrusting pelvis or chest. The movements he bodied embraced a robust sexuality that his performance did not need to announce further than the fully informed execution of them. And the joy of moving in that way radiated from his small body in Jackson, Mississippi, through the YouTube mediated screen, all the way into my own living room in Philadelphia, Pennsylvania. And there, from that instant of pre-connection, I knew that I wanted to learn from him, learn alongside him, talk to him, hear him, dance with him. I sent him a message on YouTube. After about five more over a period of maybe two months, he finally responded.

Donte and I worked without knowledge of a destination for a couple years. We were curious about one another, about the worlds we were from. We had several overlaps—two black, queer, college-educated cis men who like to smile. And we had several divergences: my pan-Africanist upbringing vs Donte's more conservative African American Christian rearing, my college experience at an elite midatlantic PWI (predominantly white institution) versus Donte's experience at a Southern HBCU (historically black colleges and universities), my convergence of Africanist aesthetics with postmodern dance's minimalism for performances primarily on stages and in art galleries vs Donte's expertise in navigating the club space as a performance home for showy and sensational choreographies. We are both air signs, though. And we seemed quite open to evade notions of eventuality together while we invested ourselves as deeply as possible in the movement information we could offer to one another. We both were satisfying our respective hungers—to know more—to be more rigorous—to understand joy better—to understand black better—to elevate more the things that mattered to us.

J-Sette is a dance form originating in black southern US female drill teams and majorette lines at historically black colleges. Parallel in history, leagues of black queer boys and men would create competitive teams to practice the J-Sette form in gay clubs, pride parades, and even now on reality television. While the majorette version of J-Sette is typically practiced with live band accompaniment, the queer version is traditionally accompanied by club tracks hot in DJ rotation. Commonly known as "bucking" among practitioners, J-Sette's sensual movement features rhythmic insistence, nimble grounding, and percussive attack through the trunk, in both punctuated and sustained movements.

When Donte and I decided that we wanted to perform some of our workings together, what we could make the most sense of at the time was performing in experimental art venues—theater and gallery spaces. Living in a nation with a legacy of white supremacy, this meant that our performances were going to be staged for audiences of primarily white art consumers. Our resistance to this has led to the performance of our work together on sidewalks and in alleyways in primarily black neighborhoods, in queer club spaces, in university halls, and yes, in those institutional art spaces with our deft attempts to address race in the space via both subversion and direct confrontation.

Now, in 2018, we have created together three performance works and a visual installation all as part of a series that we have titled Let 'im Move You. We are currently working toward the fourth performance work in the series that will be dealing with J-Sette via an array of intervening mathematical formulas applied to the rhythmic choreographies, and also to the accompanied DJed music. We continue to create this work in conversation with one another, and a larger community of black queer folks.

counts orchestrate, a meadow (or weekly practice with breath)   138

taisha paggett, Meena Murugesan

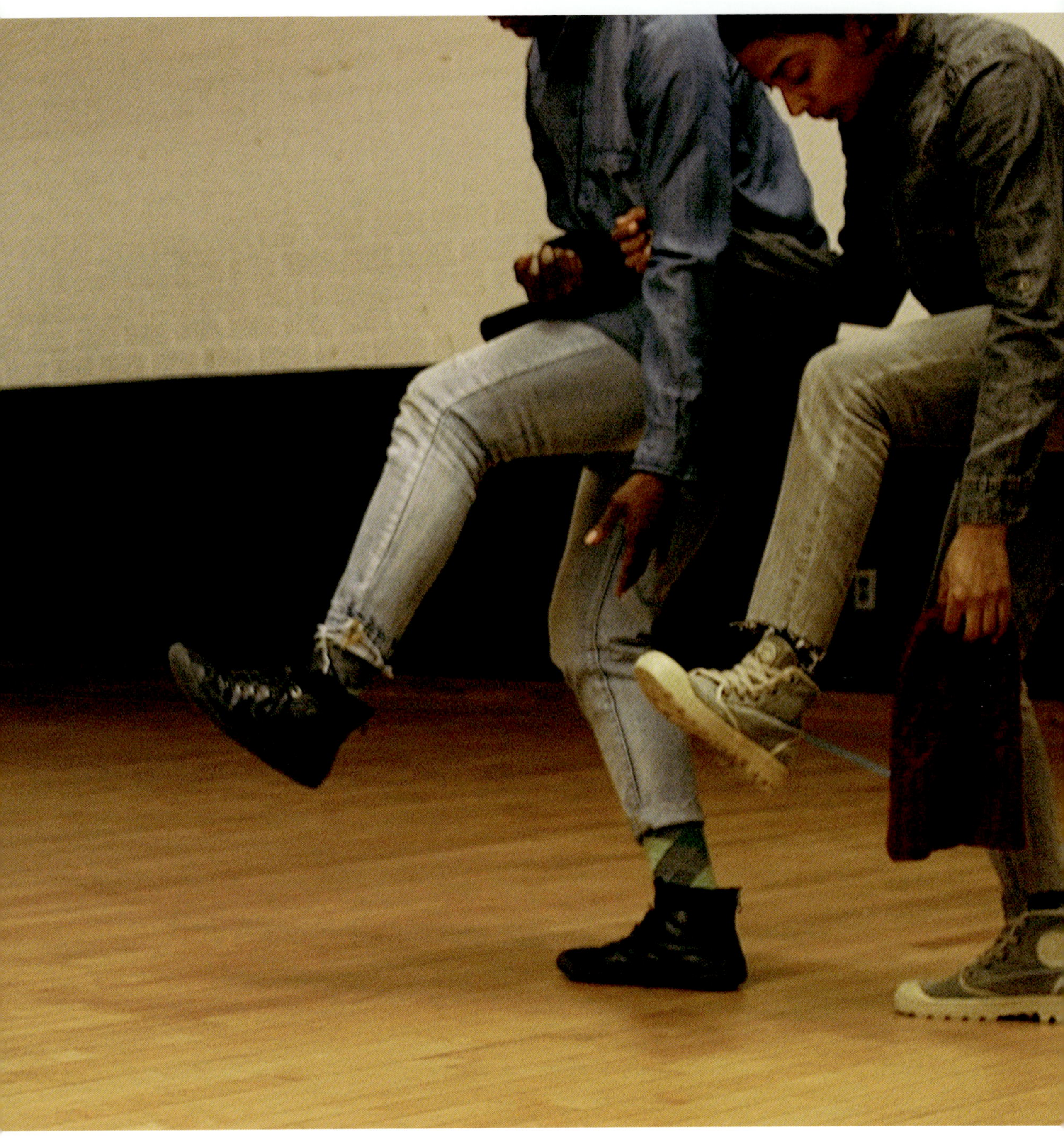

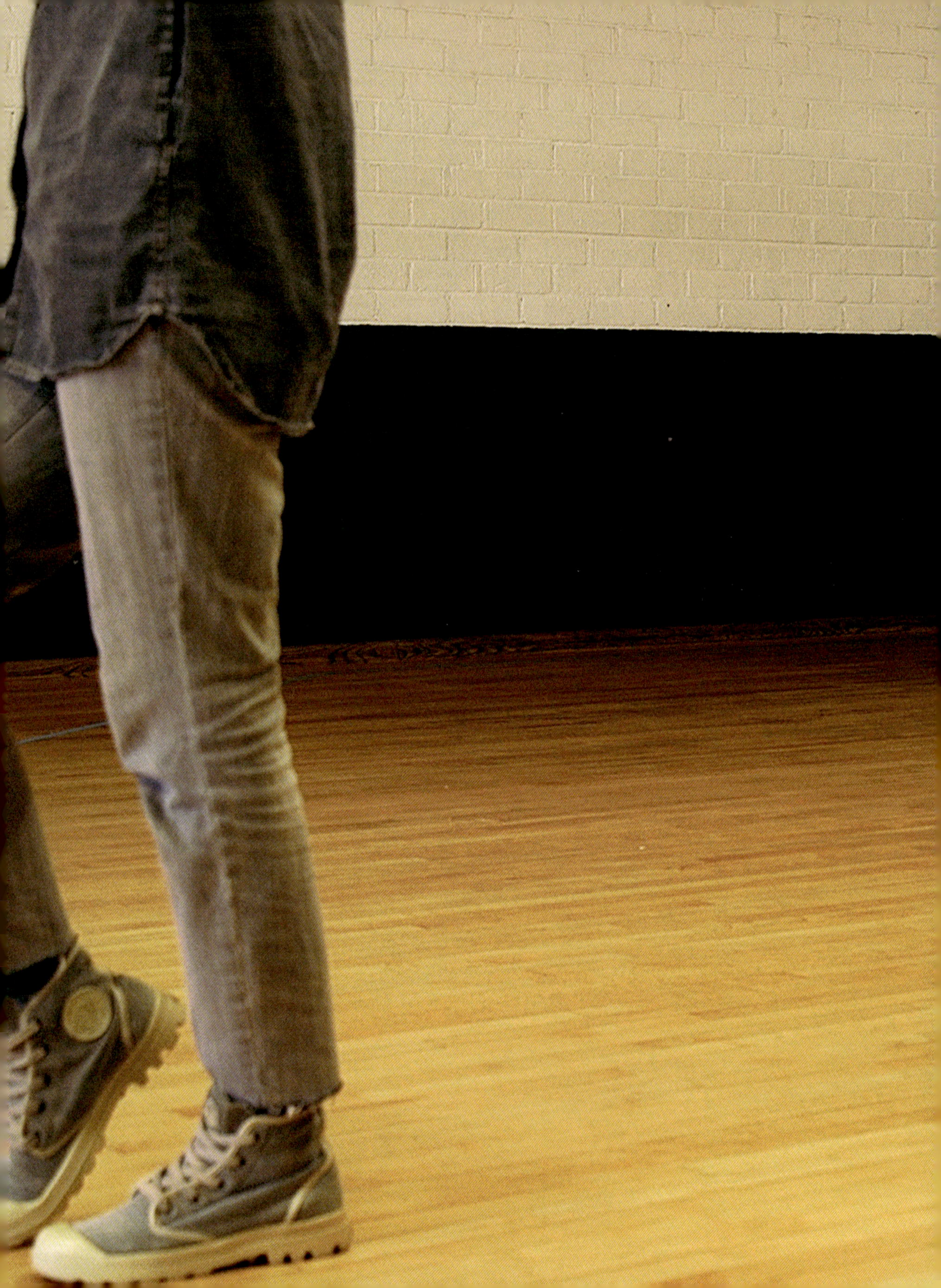

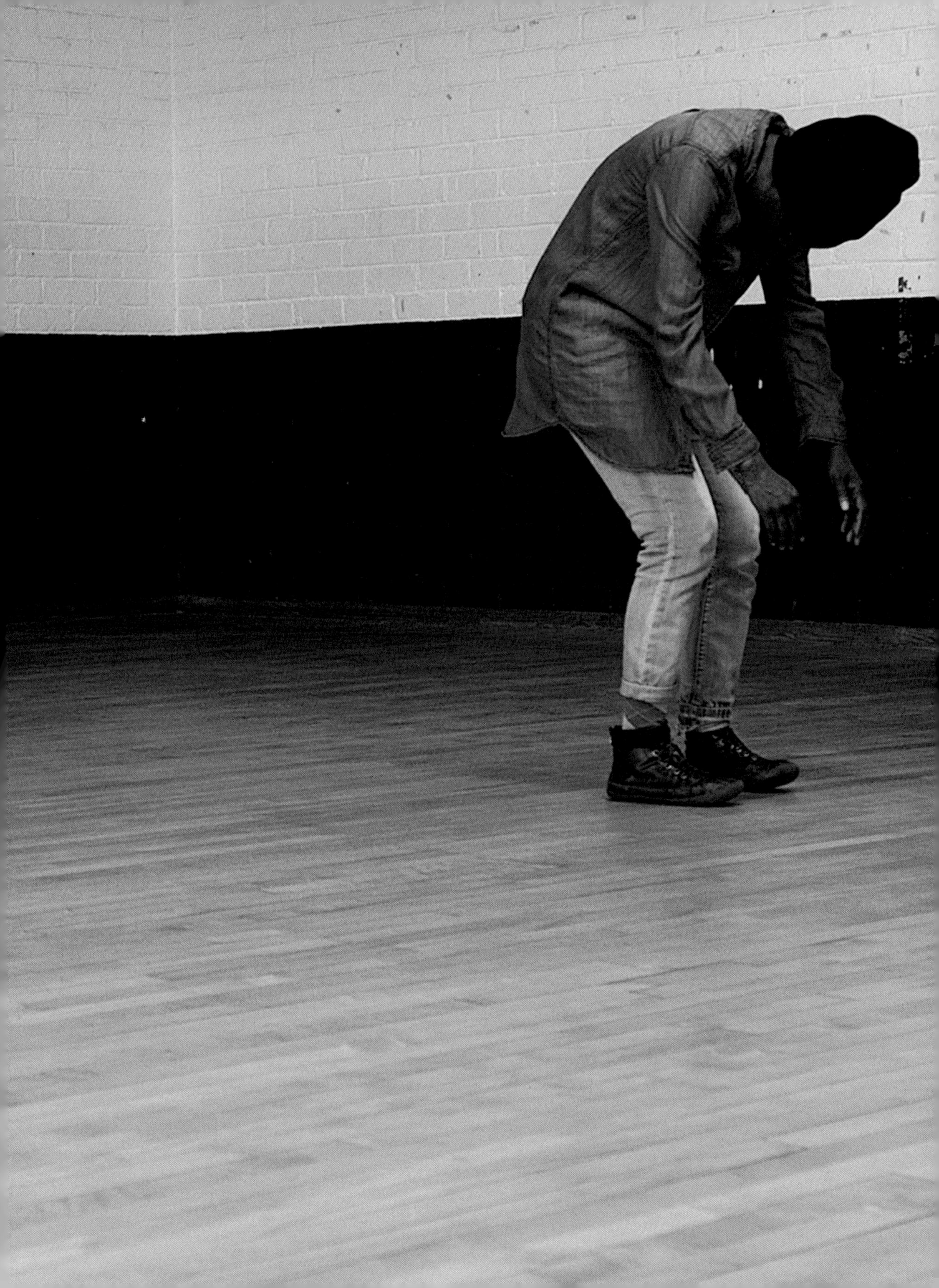

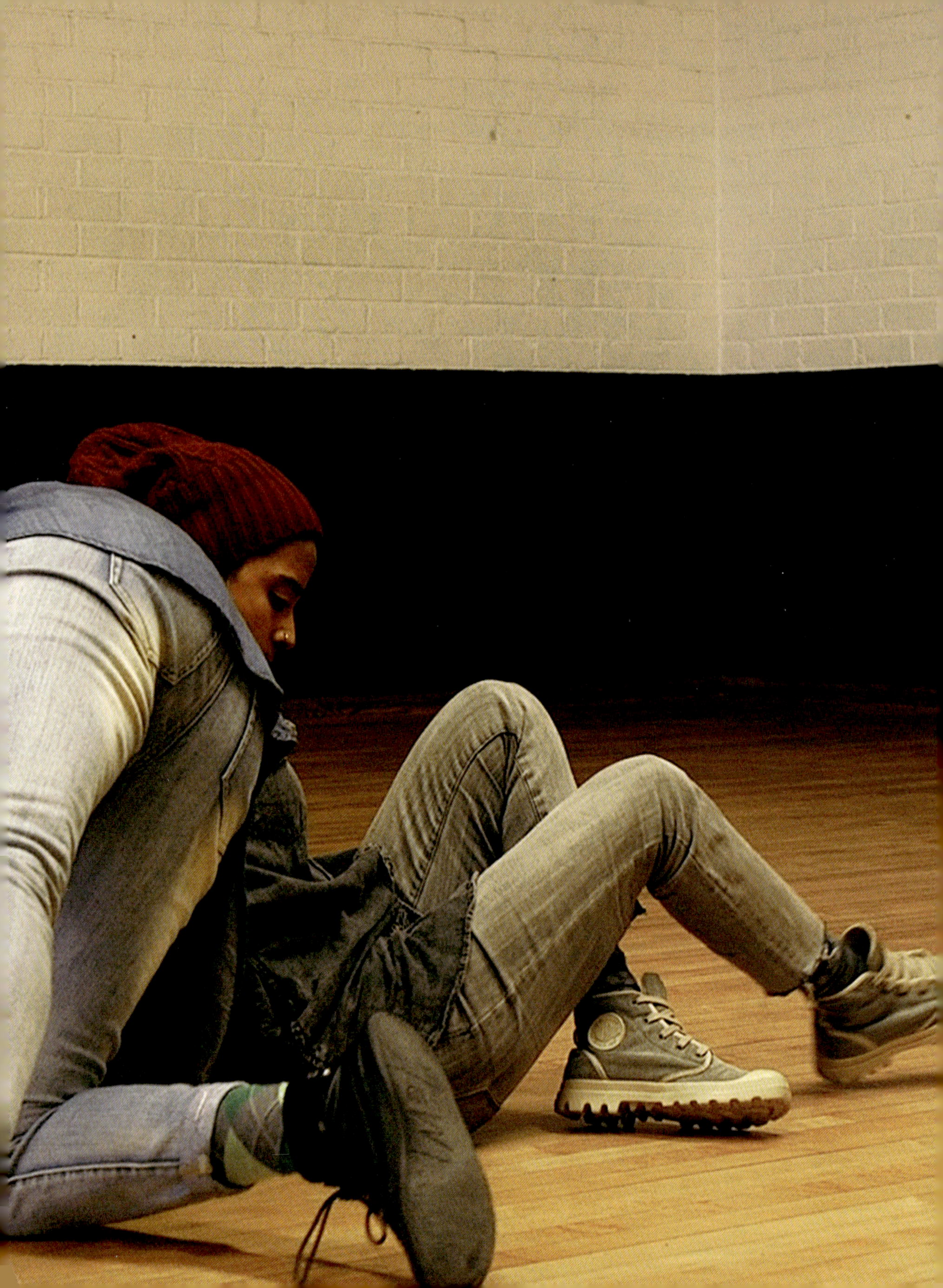

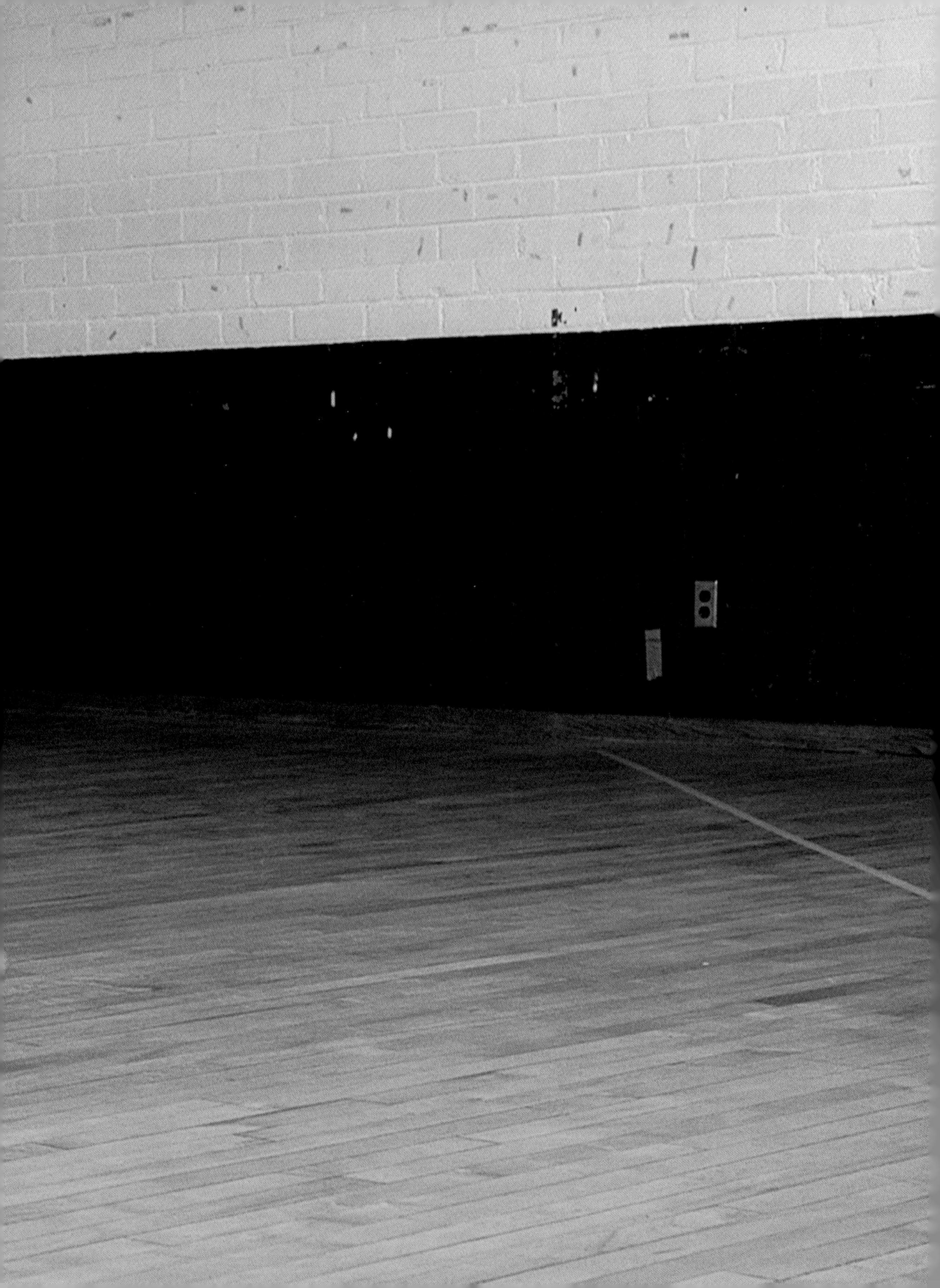

→

FLOOR, FOUNDATION, THE GROUND, ~
THE BEGINNING, THE ROOT, THE EARTH, SOIL
- PROPORTIONS? SHAPE? TEXTURE. NOISE?
- I'M DRAWN TO THE ANALOG, MATERIALS
IN THEIR RAWEST FORM... LOW TECH → PROJECTION
PLAYBACK MATERIALS FROM ~~[crossed out]~~
- SNEAKERS (ELABORATION ON) ← WHAT SURFACE ACCOMPANIES STREET SHOES
- ~~INTERESTED~~ IF BEING ON THE CONTEMPORARY FLOOR AS ↑
OPPOSED TO THE HISTORICAL/ARCHIVAL FLOOR.. FRED + ISH
- MATERIAL THAT RESEMBLES (BLENDS INTO) THE STONE FLOOR...?
- SCREEN SIMILAR TO STAN DOUGLAS THAT PROJECT MY VIDEOS
DANCE ENVIRONMENT VS DANCE FLOOR ↑
- A FLOOR THAT'S MODULAR, THAT LENDS CUSHION (AN ECHO)
THAT CAN TAKE ~~VINYL~~ LETTERS OR OTHER MATERIAL
[AGNOSTIC TEMPLE] ADHERED TO IT...? SO THAT MY
SPACE CAN SHIFT & ACCUMULATE FROM DANIELLES
- THE accumulation OF MY materials overtime creates a stage
- CREATE A FLOOR/DANCE ENVIRONMENT THAT
CAN BE REPLICATED & REHEARSED W/ IN LA. → ECHO
- MAKE SPACE FOR WITNESSES
TO BE WITH (IN THE TIME OF) THE WORK. W/OUT BEING THERE — BEING THERE

BREATH: Action?
Activation

improvisation as (NOT "is")

radical act

of preparation.

preparation, particularly
of the body, as a
common denominator
between dancers & musicians, so
my mind first goes there...
~~so have two gestures~~

write a score that says
"i am that,"
a score that describes itself

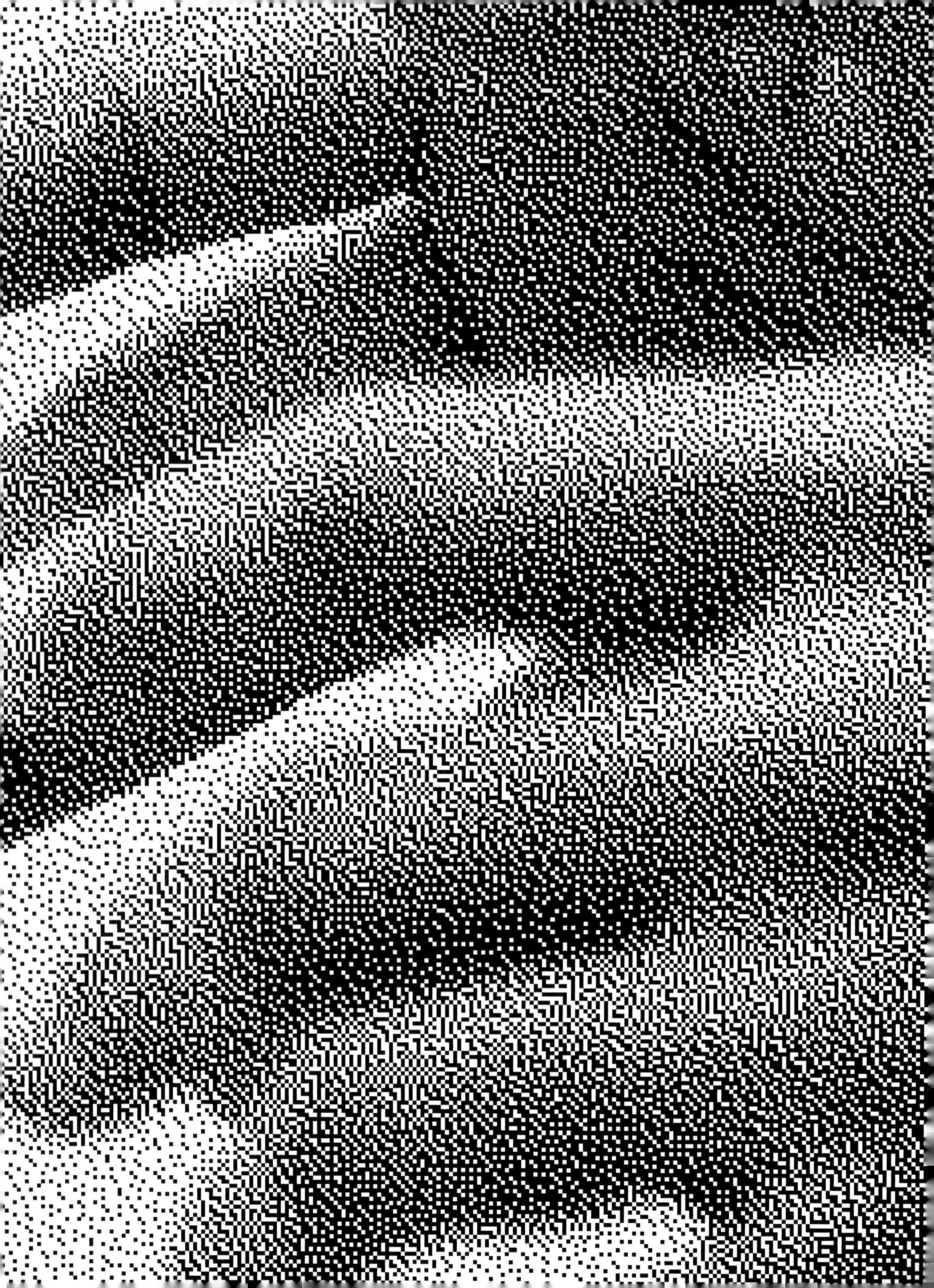

Request for Audio Materials
taisha paggett and Meena Murugesan

i'm soliciting breath patterns from individuals to be used as sound material for
an upcoming project that will be on display beginning February 22 for *Endless Shout*
at ICA Philadelphia.

i ask that you please call my phone xxx-xxx-xxxx and do the following into my
voicemail:

**using only your breath, count to eight, 8 times (or 64 counts total), doing so as
if you were conducting a band of marching dancers and/or an imagined dance.**
(i've attached two samples of what it *may* sound like, but am interested in your personal interpretation of the directions.)

---

if possible, please do this somewhere relatively quiet and please hold the phone close
to your mouth.

if you are interested in participating, it is important that i receive your voicemail as
soon as possible. i apologize for the late notice. your breath will be part of an accumulation of recordings over time, new voices added to the space each week, culminating
in performances on March 4 & 5, and continuing on for an additional span of time.

upon receipt of your contribution, i will text you to request contact information so
that you can be credited, if you'd like to be.

i'm also happy to provide any additional background information you might need.
thank you, thank you. inhale, exhale

in unison,
taisha

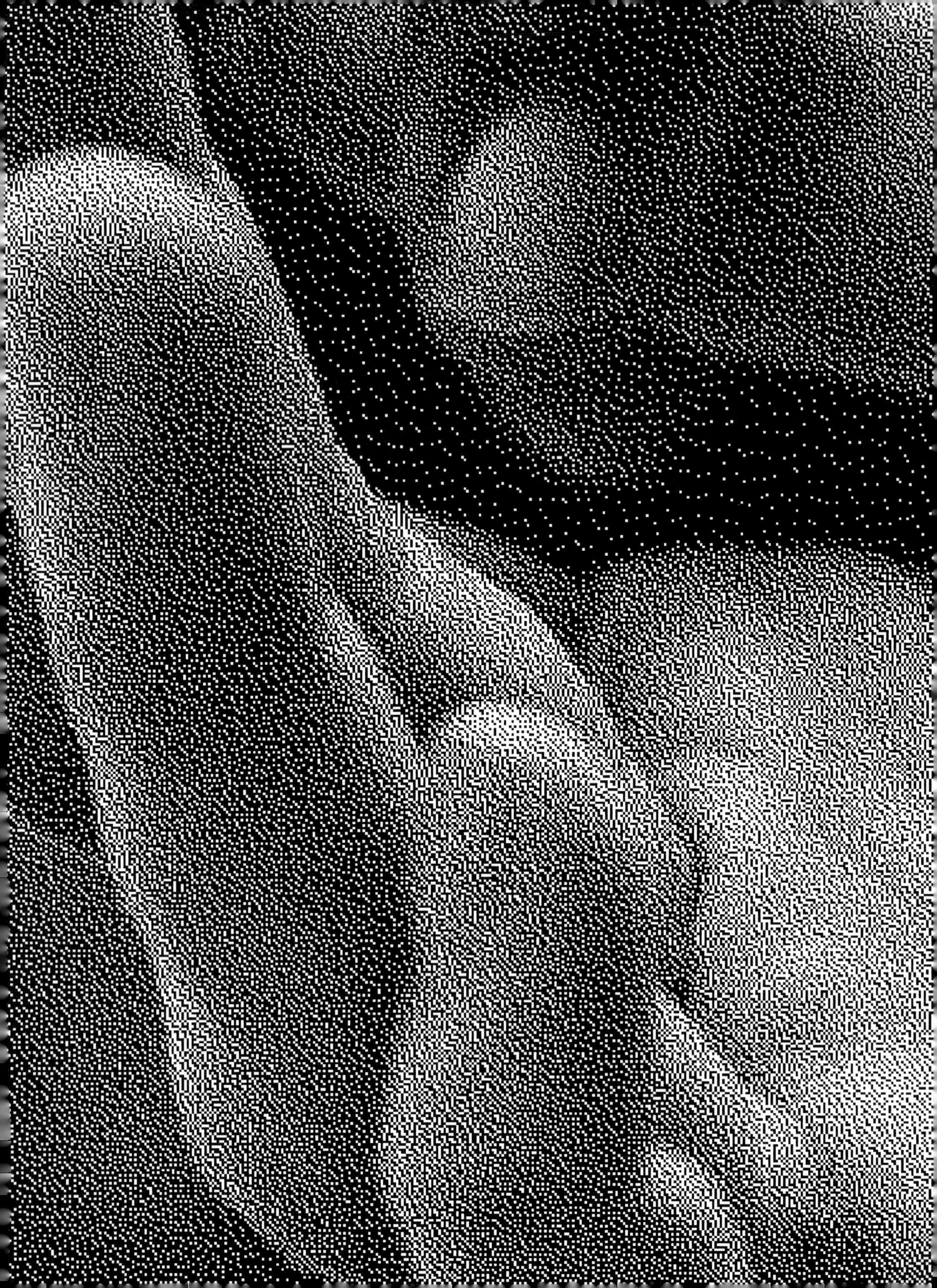

counts orchestrate, a meadow (or weekly practice with breath)
taisha paggett and Meena Murugesan

Meena and taisha build a weekly studio practice. here we ask a seed question. taisha feeds the structure (action), Meena develops the video (reciprocal image). these two intertwine.

the production of a project (space) as (queer) labor to be practiced, returned to. specific attention to that which puts us into tactile relationship.

build (on) (invisible) coalitions. (we must always, anyways.)

a structure in which to ask questions of, de ne, stumble and stand inside of what all the space of improvisation produces and allows, particularly in relation to how consciousness gets shaped and our experience of ourselves reconfigured within.

another question needs to be asked: what all can really be taken up in such a short amount of time?

practices of getting ready.

to ask: where in what we are doing is the breath?

a carpeted platform stage, a doubling of the original space/shape, a landscape to move in and through. (for you dear reader, as well.)

where does pleasure go?

the count is the precipice between two realities.

(and there is something about *Hors-champs* that i'm still trying to understand ...)

power resides in that which is/remains unseen.

a duet of desire, gravity, repetition, and effort (without a male center).

the melancholy of the small dance.

every space is a classroom.

this too is the meadow.

we'll move together for ourselves, knowing that we will be seen elsewhere; we'll move together for ourselves, knowing that we have control of the frame.

(when my dad transitioned i started thinking differently of objects.)

two monitors on short stands offering two perspectives of a single experience.

[black is (also) a meadow, a spectrum, an orientation and position.]

a record of voices tasked to organize time (invisible power) in their own way.

how do we stand as objects?

(we conduct)

what organizes our bodies alone and together?

how do you count to 8?

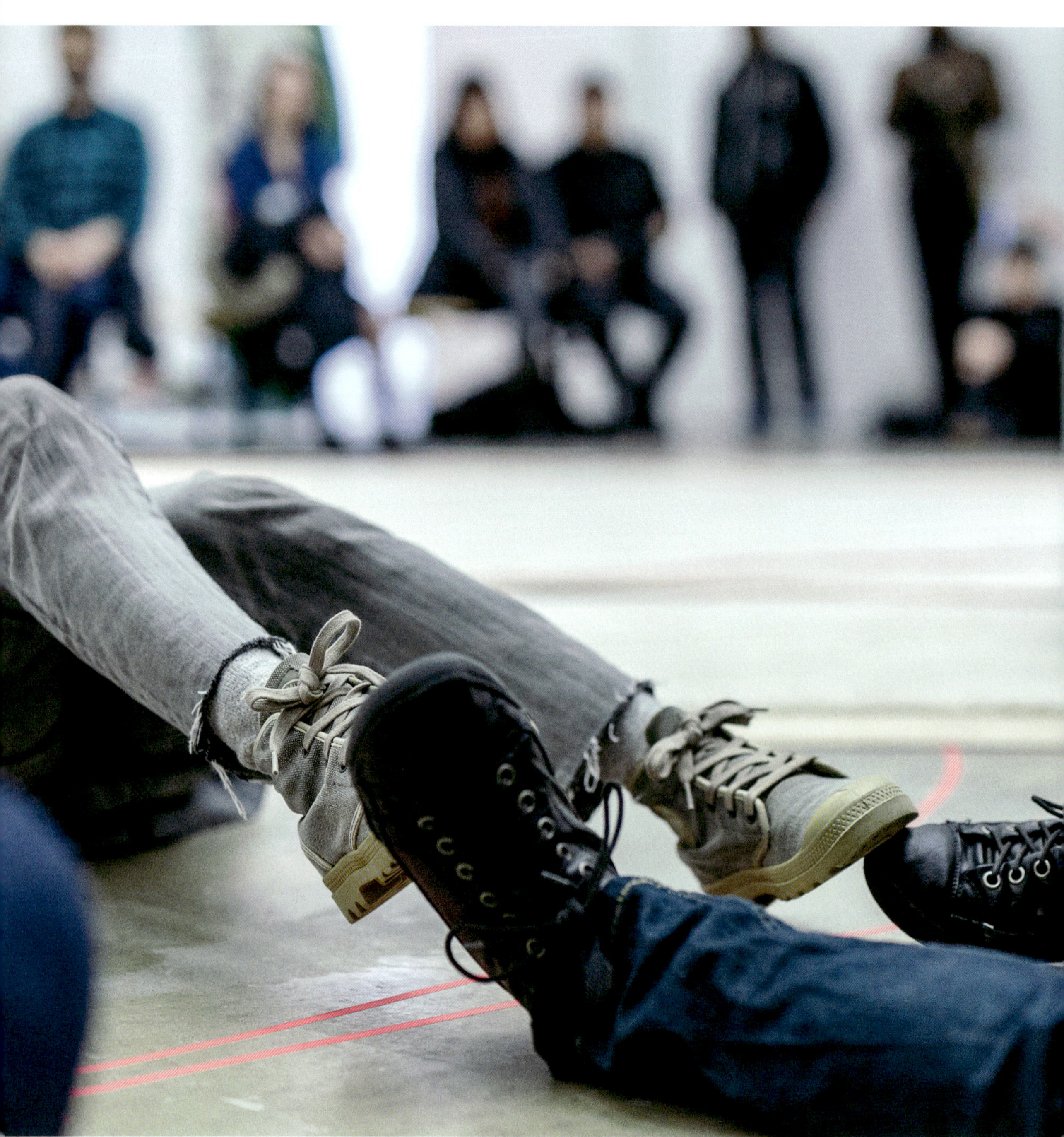

counts orchestrate, a meadow (or weekly practice with breath)　150

taisha paggett, Meena Murugesan

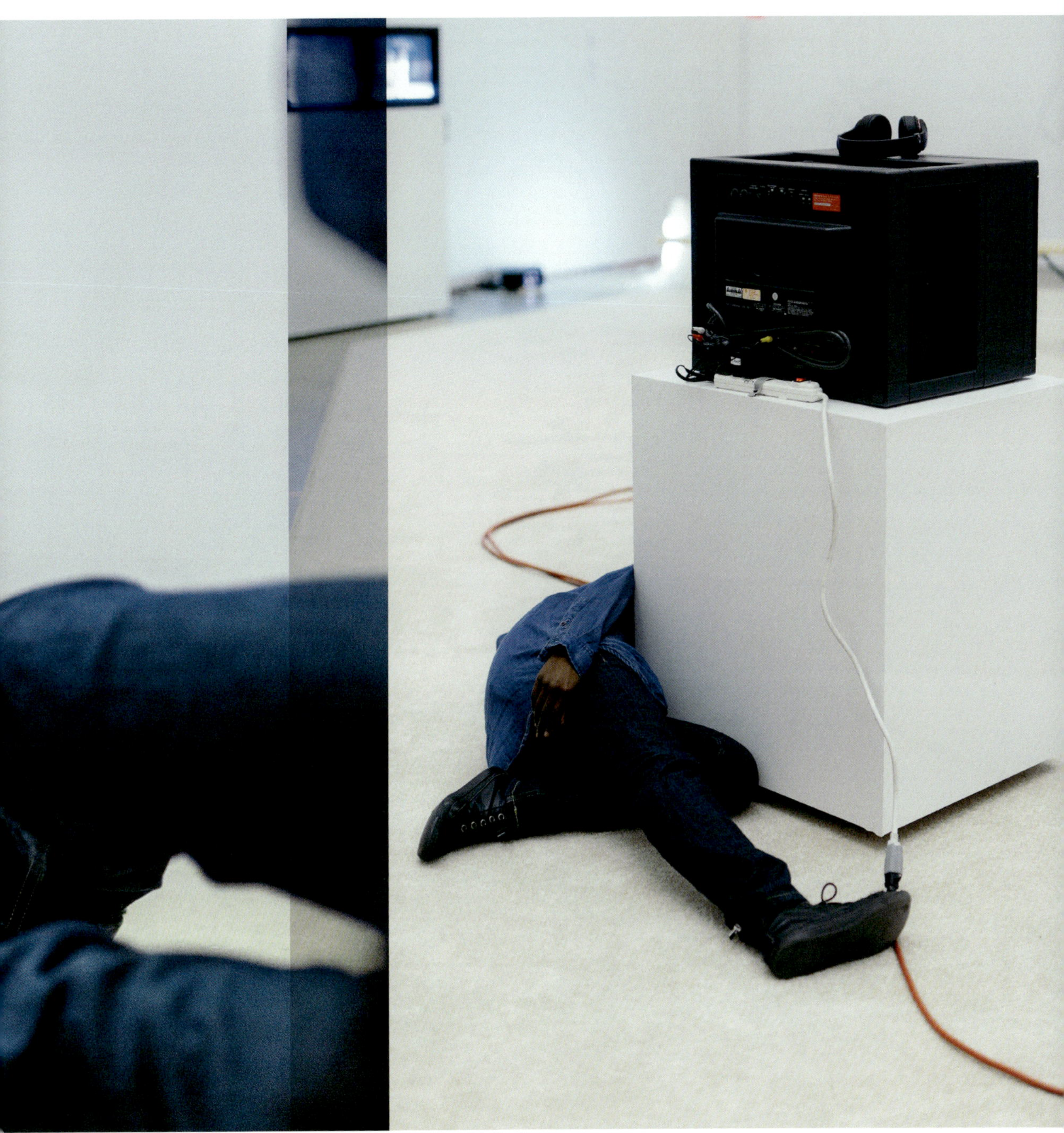

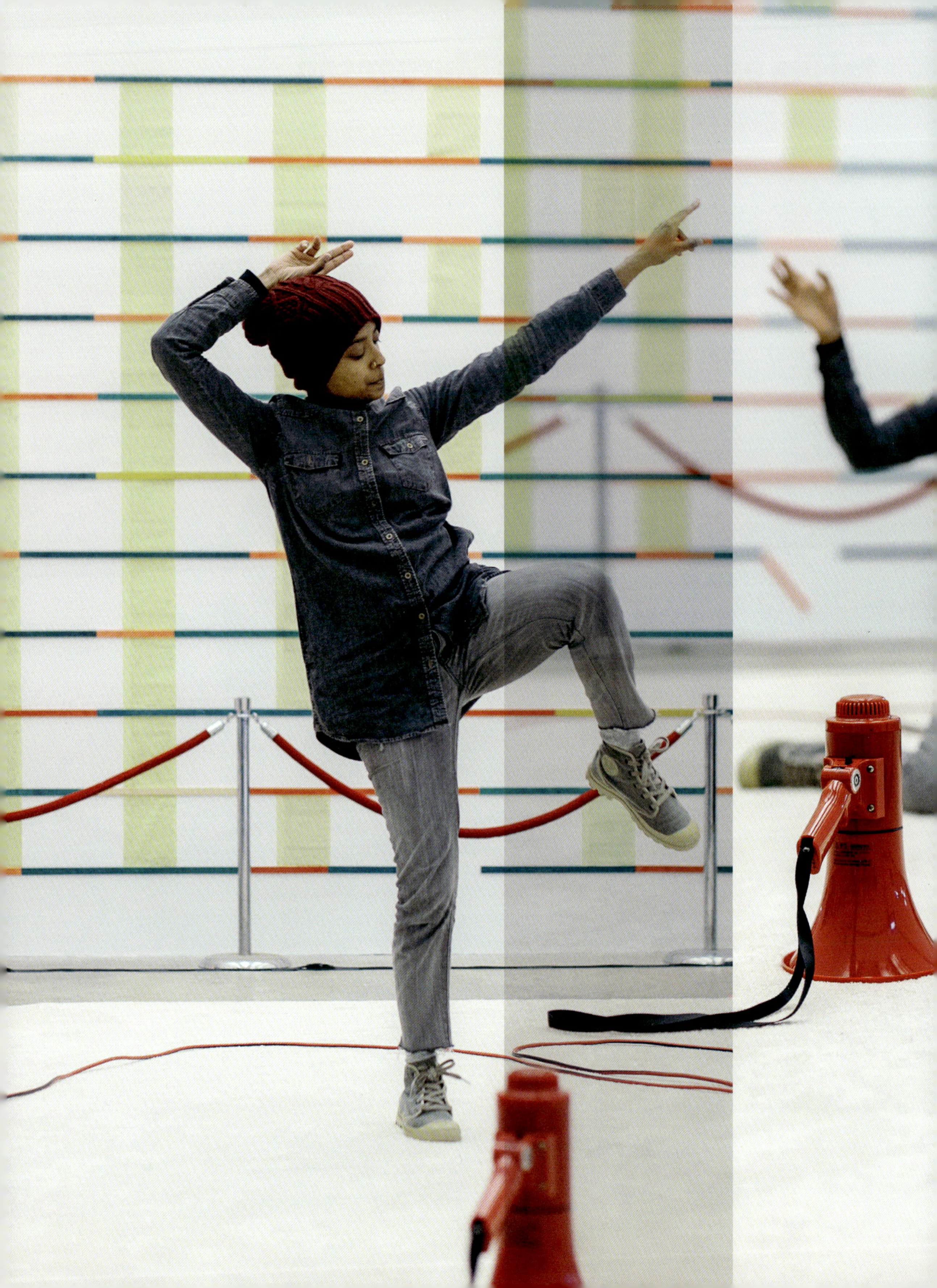

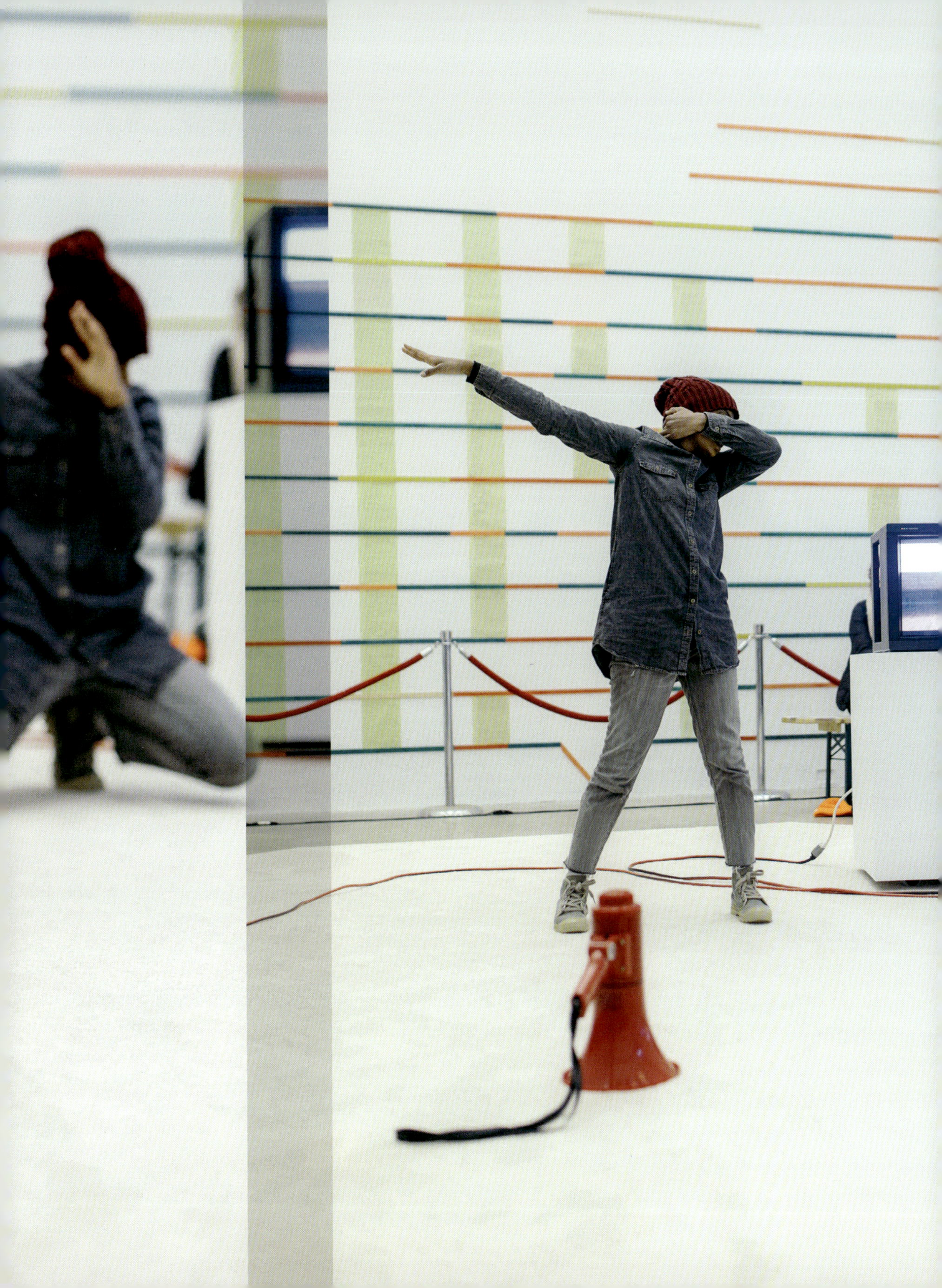

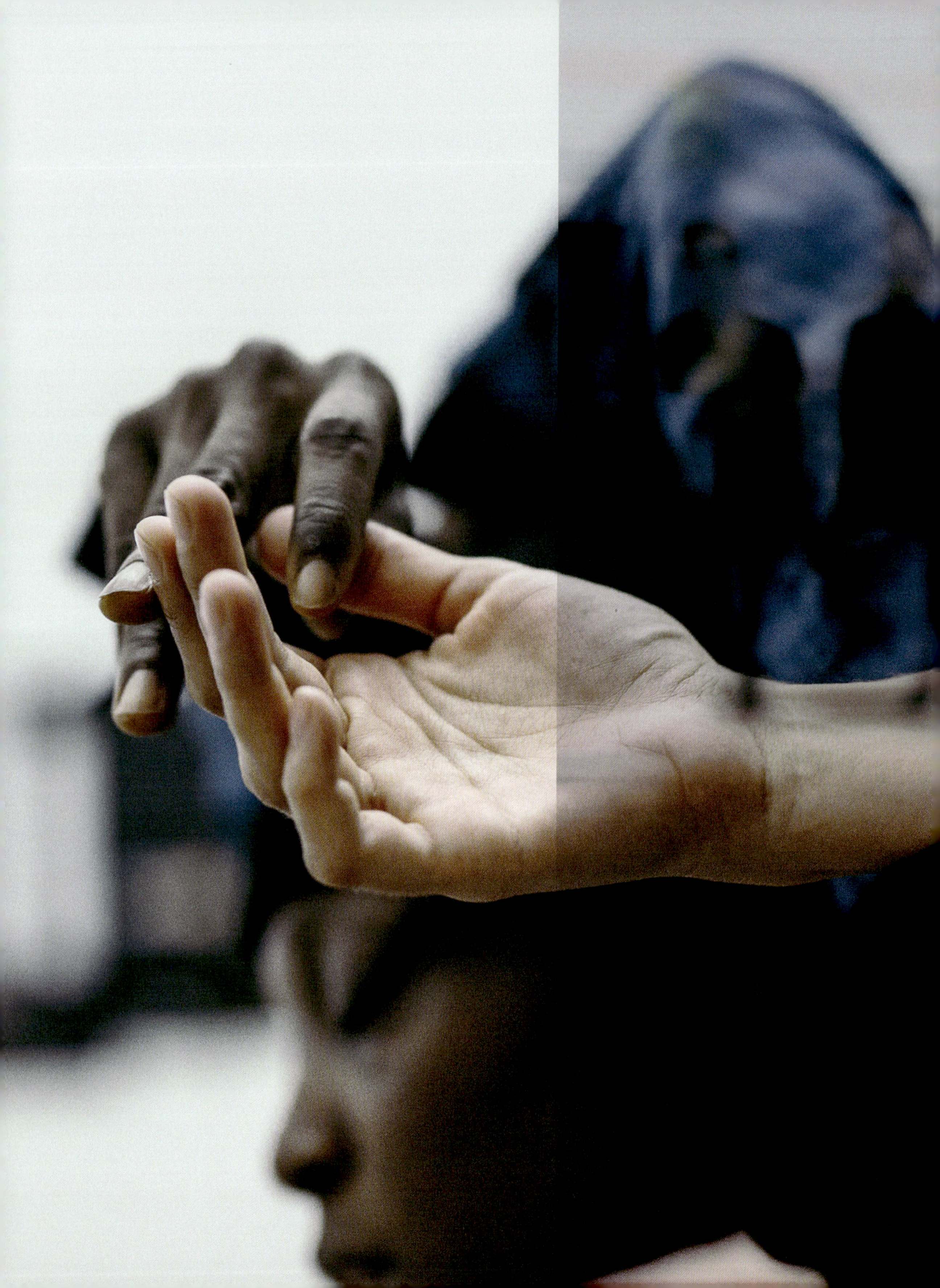

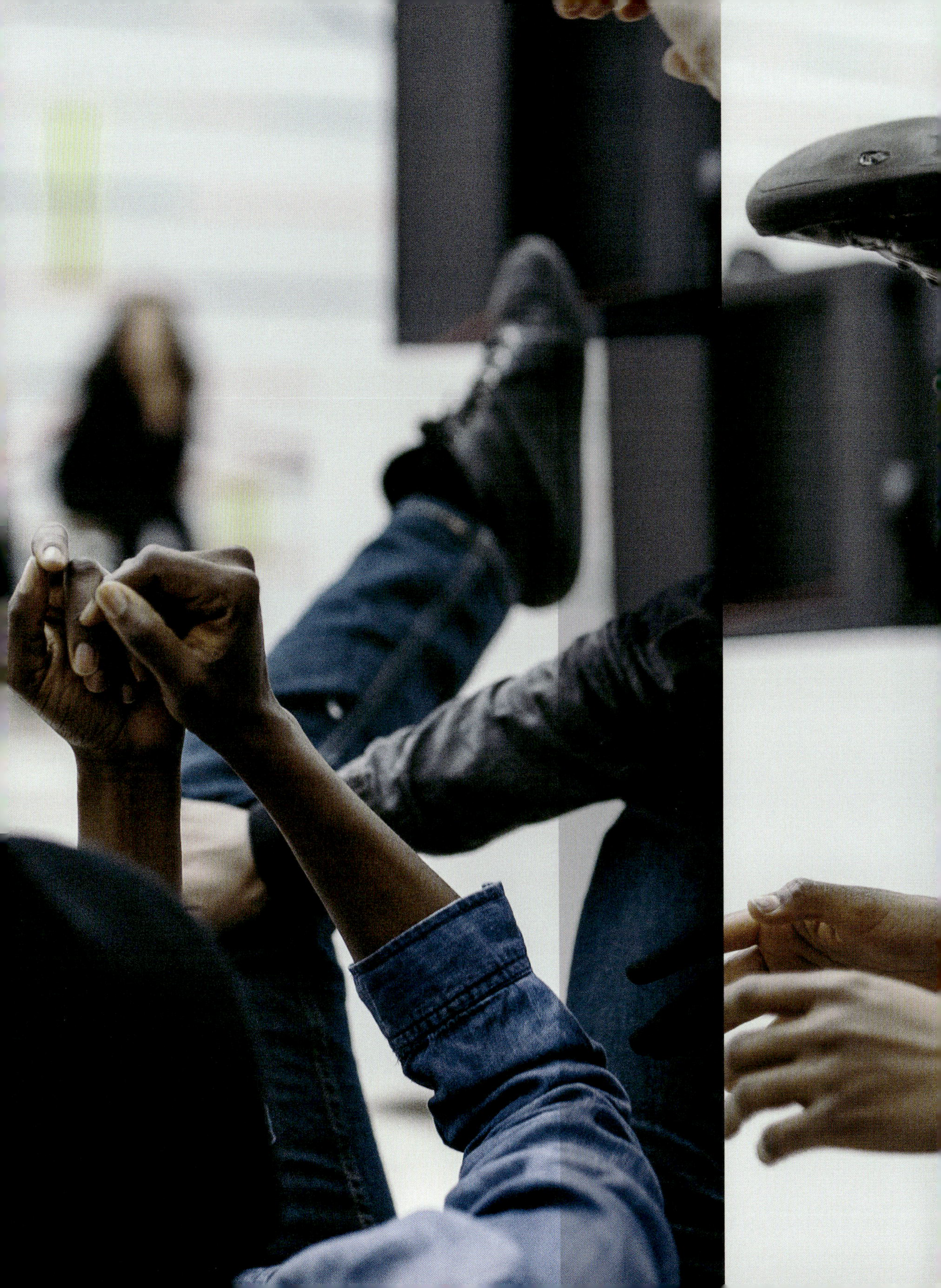

The Third Part of the Third Measure

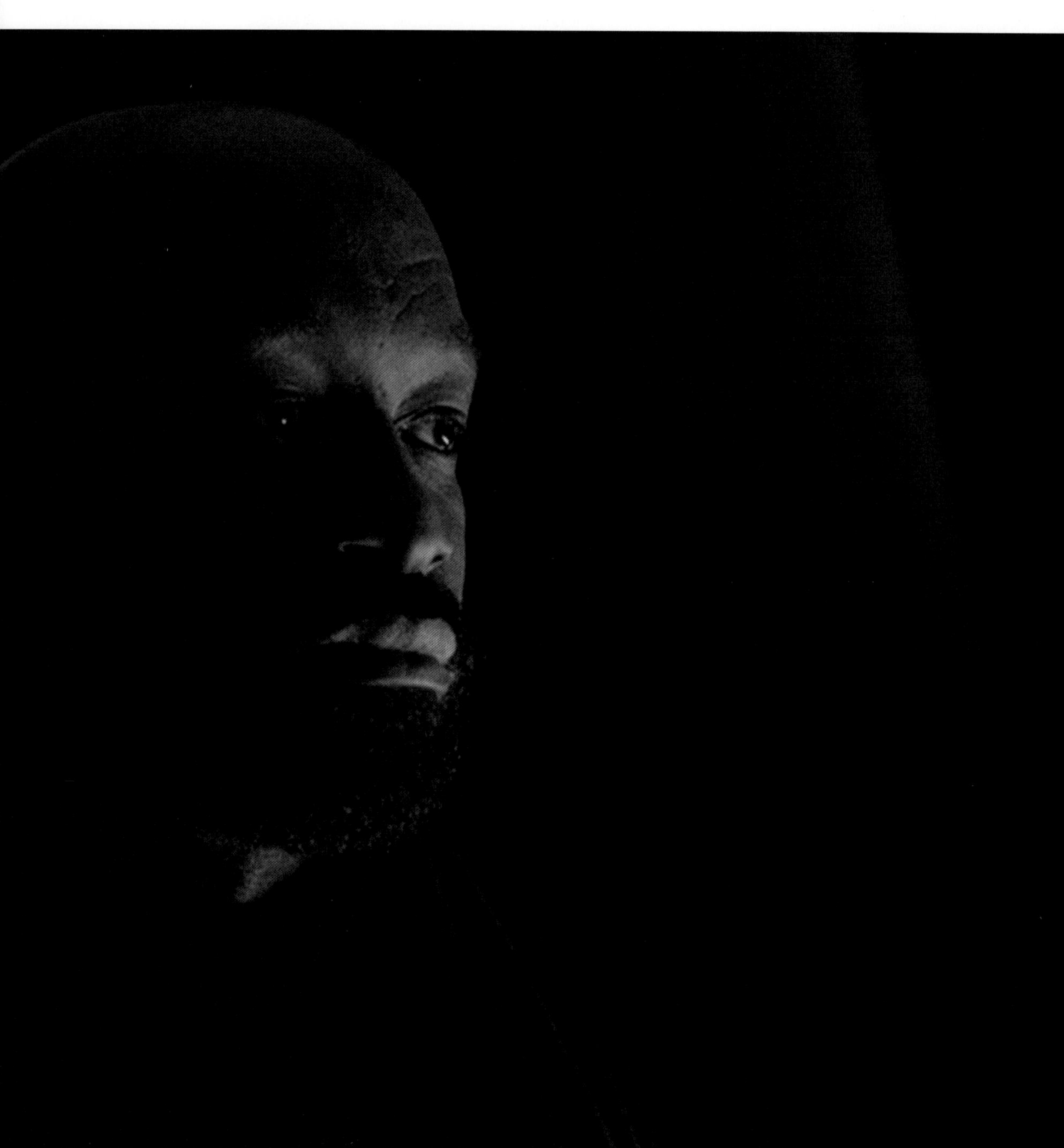

The Third Part of the Third Measure

The Otolith Group

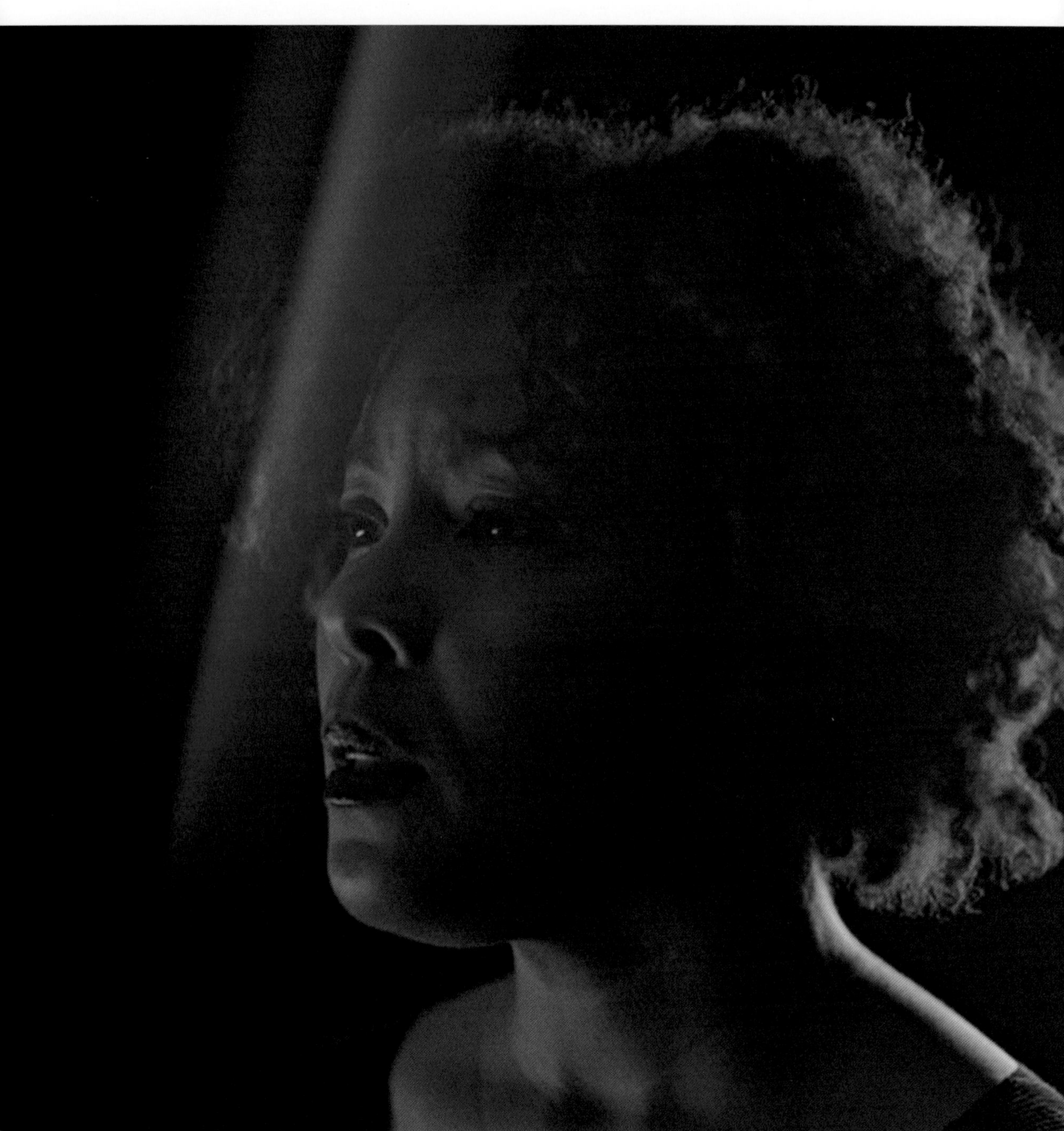

Forty-three minutes, color, stereo. Cinematography: Kate McDonough; Editor: Simon Arazi;
Sound design: Tyler Friedman; Music: Julius Eastman

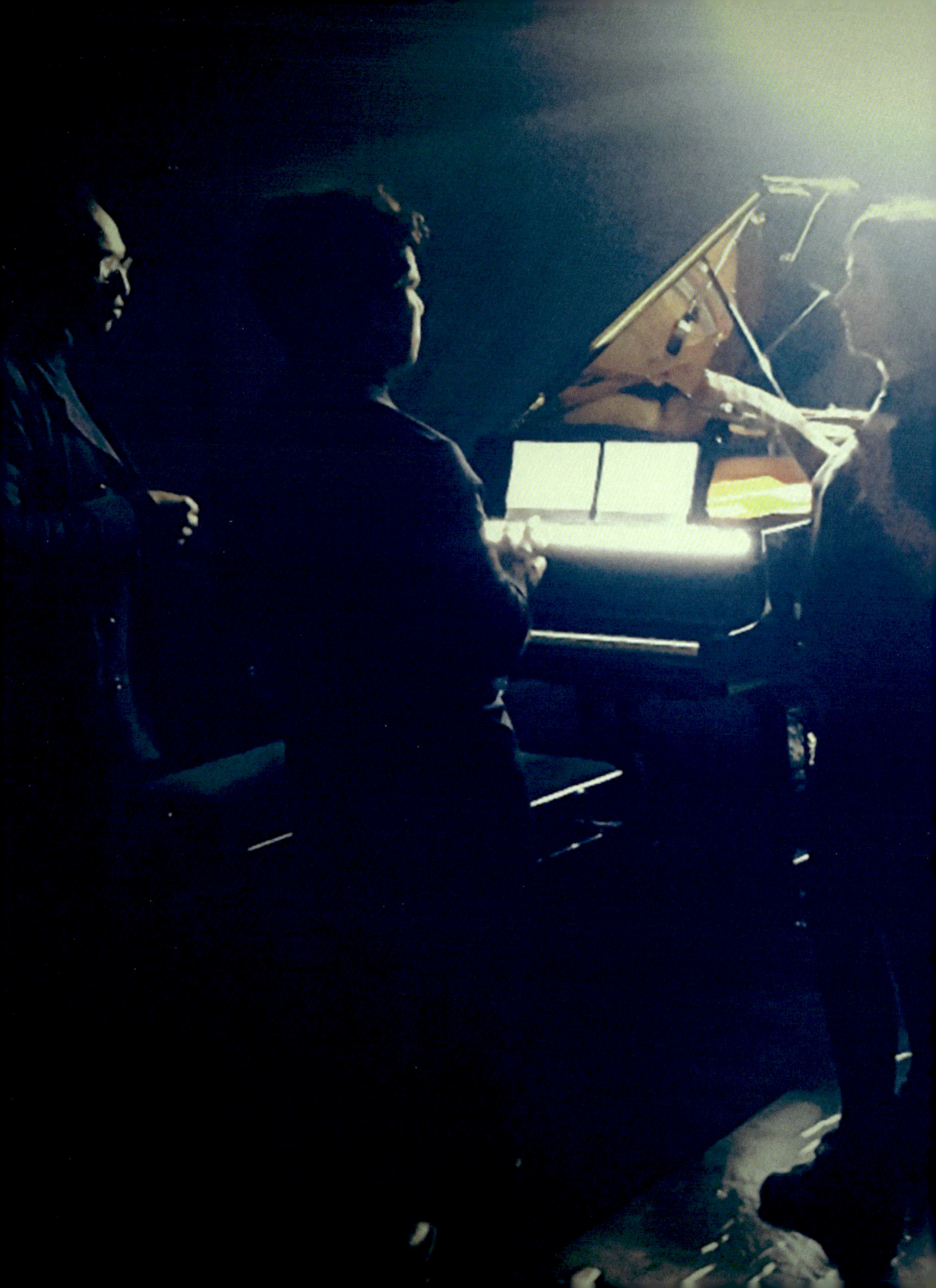

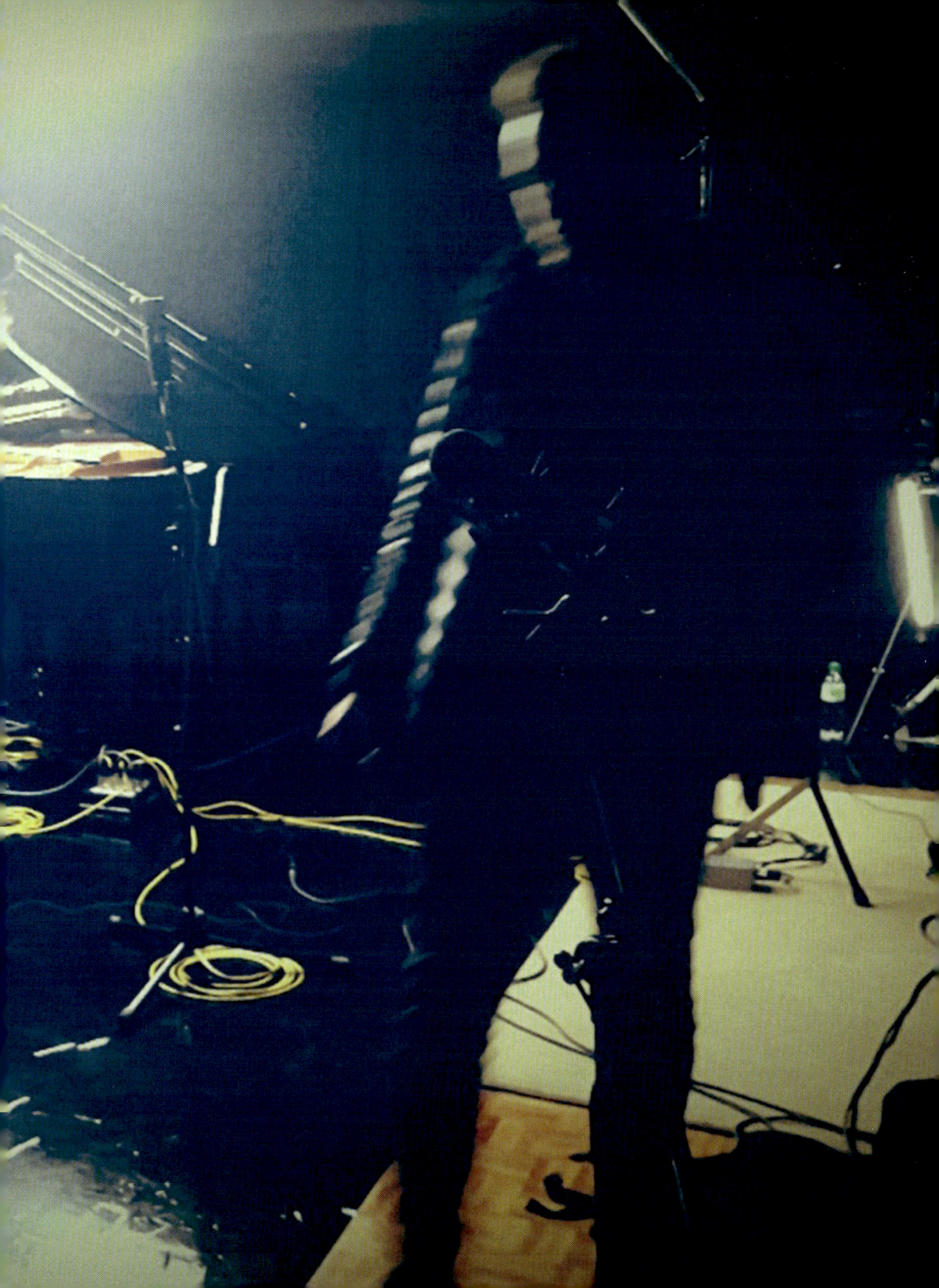

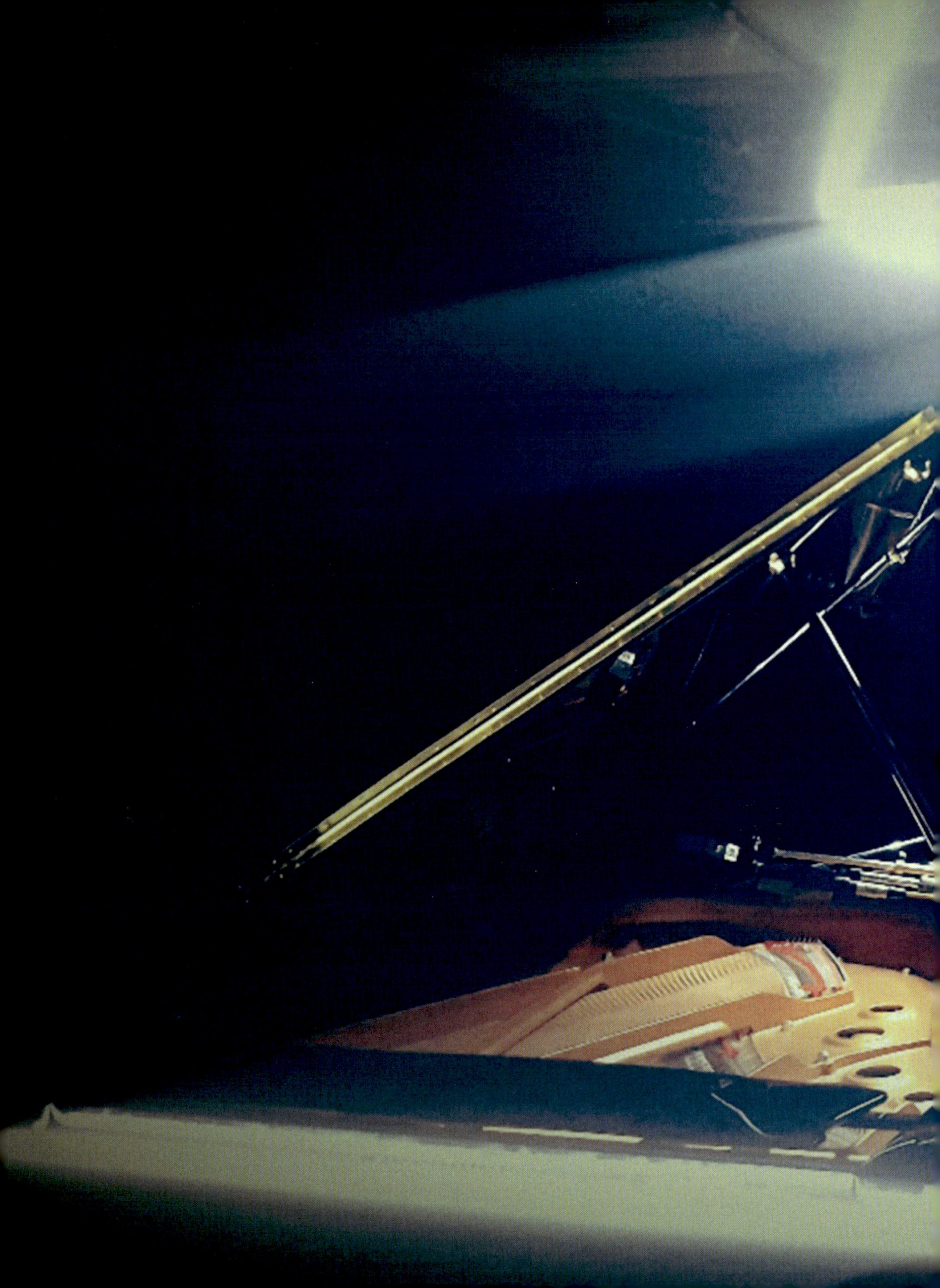

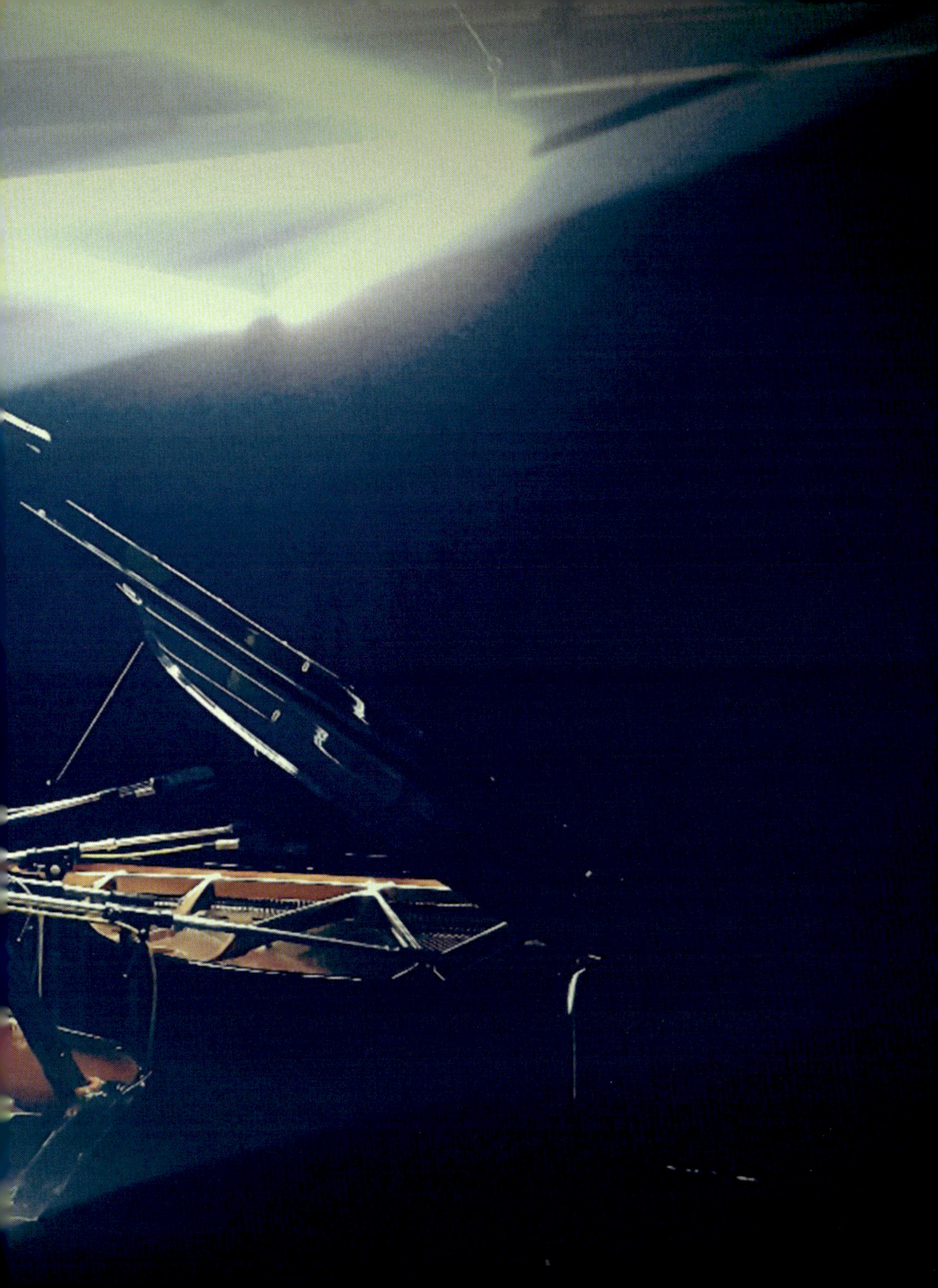

The Otolith Group in Conversation on The Third Part of the Third Measure

ICA and Lightbox (International House Philadelphia) presented a screening of films reflecting on collective improvisation, anticolonial resistance and black cultural nationalism as found in the exhibitions The Freedom Principle: Experiments in Art and Music, 1965 to Now *and* Endless Shout. *The program included a new digital restoration of Sarah Maldoror's short film* Monangambee (1968), *which was shot in Algeria and features a soundtrack by the Art Ensemble of Chicago, followed by The Otolith Group in person introducing their new work.*

Kodwo Eshun: Thank you very much for staying. We had a presentation prepared, but actually I think we're going to bracket the presentation because this is a North American premiere, we'd much rather have a conversation about this work—which is really new—and answer questions that you might have, or thoughts you would like to share about the work. We'll do the presentation another time.

Anjalika Sagar: I should say about the film, we will be editing a single-screen version. This is a two-screen version for installation. What you're getting is a very different experience of the work as shown here.

Questioner 1: This is a recreation of the original concert of Eastman's three piano compositions?

KE: No. It's just the one composition. It was very, it was a very short shoot. It was a very short shoot. It was just two days so we wanted to concentrate on this composition. We shot six takes over two days of Eastman's Evil Nigger composition, but not the other two. If everything works out, we plan to make a vinyl record, in which case, we would record Gay Gorilla. That's for the future.

Questioner 2: Could you say something about the text that bookends the performance?

KE: As you might or might not know, the introduction was delivered on the 16th of January in 1980 before the concert of Evil Nigger, Gay Guerilla, and Crazy Nigger at Pick-Staiger Concert Hall, at Northwestern University in Evanston, Illinois. The music department had invited Eastman to present this concert and, just as he says, some faculty and students protested the controversial nature of the titles. Eastman went on stage before the concert and gave this speech which you can hear on the Unjust Malaise CD, and you can hear on YouTube.

We wanted, in a way, to asymmetrically double the screens, the pianos, and the four performers. So the first reciter is poet Dante Micheaux, an African American as you can hear. He's based at University College London, he's researching the relation between Edward Carpenter, the nineteenth-century gay socialist, and the Harlem Renaissance, specifically the relations between Carpenter and Alain Locke. Micheaux agreed on short notice to give the opening recital. The ending recital is by experimental vocalist and performer Elaine Mitchener. We saw her in a concert of Eastman music performed in London in December. Elaine was there performing and she's an artist who specializes in extended vocal technique; as you can hear she has incredible range. We knew that hers would be a more impassioned recital; Dante's would be a more sober recital.

Effectively by the time you've got to the end of the performance, which takes twenty-seven minutes, you've effectively had your brain wiped clean of Dante's recital by the sound, such that it is actually hard to recall that both vocalists are saying exactly the same words. Not only is the recital and the mode of the address different, but a vast amount of time has passed between the two. If this was a Morton Feldman piece, I'd say it was the kind of broken symmetry between the two. Instead I'd say it's more the changing sameness, you know, in the sense that LeRoi Jones/Amiri Baraka talked about in black aesthetics. It's the changing sameness of the way in which everything repeats and mirrors, but not quite. That's why we kind of liked the idea of starting and ending with the same words— a symmetrical asymmetry.

AS: The symmetry is not a fake symmetry but a symmetry that demands it be interrogated, if you like. There's a symmetry of gender, there's a symmetry in relation to the way certain edits have been composed. There's asymmetry in the way that is front-ended and back-ended by a man and a woman. Within all of this symmetry, there is kind of change as Kodwo said, and there are also many refractions and reflections within the images, and this constellation—this kind of minimalism—held together, but within it differences.

Questioner 3: I have two questions. One, I don't actually know much about the Otolith Group, so I am curious of how you came to this piece in the first place? Second, you have a kind of separation or binary on who's speaking and who's performing. There are no black performers at the piano, but there are black folks speaking. I am curious about that choice.

KE: The Otolith Group has been in existence from 2002/2003 and there's a body of work which moves between certain preoccupations, science fiction and sound, to be concise for this context.

When *The Freedom Principle* began at the MCA Chicago, and Dieter Roelstraete and Naomi Beckwith, curators of that exhibition, invited us to be a part, we weren't able to make a new work. So the exhibition included our video *People to be Resembling* (2012), a work based around Codona, a trio founded in 1978 by Don Cherry, Collin Walcott, and Nana Vasconcelos, who made three recordings in '78, '80 and '82 until Walcott died in a car crash. This is a kind of music film working with photography, the permutations of photography and working with what Fred Moten calls the "black aesthetic sociality" of images. And in that film, there is a kind of permutation of a limited number of photographs that we continually return to in different formations.

For this work, *The Freedom Principle* traveled here, and *Endless Shout* took shape, we went through many different proposals. In the end we were quite keen to work with Eastman as he's a figure that we've liked for

a long time. Maybe since about '07 when the American artist Sam Durant posted a playlist for an exhibition in London and we knew all the compositions, all the musicians, all the songs, apart from this one from the name Julius Eastman. When I eventually found my way to these compositions, I was just stunned by them. I was shocked by how I had never come across the compositions, and how I never had a chance to listen to them. I felt quite angry and somewhat cheated, y'know? Because I listened to minimalism forever, and how come I didn't know about Eastman? I was quite frightened. I was really frightened that someone so brilliant could be so forgotten. I was kind of shocked, but that's an ahistorical shock. It was shocking that I was shocked by this. There was a long standing desire to work with Eastman's music and this seemed like the right moment to do it.

The division of labor in the performers reflects the state of new music in the UK. I was told by Zubin Kanga, the pianist in the film who does the count-up—the "1,2,3,4!"—there are only twenty pianists in the UK who could play Eastman's compositions. The four in the film are the best known interpreters and the most experienced interpreters of Eastman in the UK. They played at Eastman concerts in December, and they played Eastman compositions back in 2014, and they first began playing Eastman back in 2010. The Afro-diasporic pianists we contacted didn't have the specialism in new music. It would have taken months to form a new ensemble, and actually you can't force an ensemble to form, you know. In other words, this quartet had the years of thinking and playing Julius Eastman. We decided to work with this fact and to unify them. The idea is that when Eastman talks about the gay guerillas of the future in his Northwestern introduction, the idea is that these four performers are them. The pianists are the gay guerillas that Eastman in 1980 is looking forward to. They are here in 2017. The idea was to unify them through makeup, through uniform, and through a kind of visual sonography. They come literally from the future of Eastman, but in a way they come from our future. They are supposed to be just a bit somewhat ahead of us.

AS: We are very aware of the politics when we make a piece; when we curate work; when we put people together we are always concerned to having a diverse range of people. Not in a forced way but in a way that just allows for a more complicated discussion to take place. We didn't want any white male heterosexuals necessarily on set because we didn't want any kind of white male cameramen who would dominate with their miserable sort of attitude. [audience laughter] We had three camera women and that naturally occurred and was very very good because it created a different vibe.

We went for it as it was with the ensemble. Sometimes when you're making a work and you've been thinking about it for a long long time, and it's been gestating for seven years or so, suddenly you do it and all these things just work out. In December we go to Second Home, there's this Eastman concert, we see these pianists. We plan this shoot. Then this whole process gets difficult because, a very good friend, colleague, and collaborator of ours, Mark Fisher, the author of *Capitalist Realism* and other books, commits suicide at the beginning of January. It completely stalled us and we've dedicated this piece to him as a result, because it's a kind of melancholic work. But anyway, we wanted to go with this flow. Sometimes we think the flow will teach us something. And it felt like that here.

The Friday night before we shot on a Saturday, we were at the house of a good friend. I was thinking the whole week, we really need to conjure a gay African American male to deliver the speech at the beginning. It was going to be the performer travis originally, but it was a bit difficult to get him to London. Someone's just got to appear. At this friend's it happened. This African American writer was there and I said, "would you mind doing this speech in our film?" He said, "Well no. Not me, I don't think I will work, but I have a very good friend Dante Micheaux and he will do it." The writer just rang Micheaux and he said, "Sure I'll do it, I love Eastman." That's so weird and good. And of course Elaine as well, she loved Eastman, and the the performers.

After, something even stranger starts to happen. We've just installed this work in Sharjah and people talked about it as a kind decolonization of raciality. Think of the fact that the N word, I can't say it though

it's in our film, is so labored, right? People are so used to hearing it said in so many different ways. It's so labored in the way Dante and Elaine speak it. Almost speaking it to these pianists who are playing Eastman, or who are conjuring Eastman. Channeling him in their own way. The labor of their bodies to channel and perform, to me this this is all about labor. Maybe that is where we need to begin when we think about decolonization, we need to focus on labor.

Questioner 4: What do you mean when you say decolonization of raciality?

AS: I'm speaking from a British perspective. It's quite complex and takes a long time to answer, so I'm not going to try to be smart about it. Identity politics was always supposed to be about raising a form of consciousness, for groups to be able to understand each other more. Certainly that's how I was brought up in the '80s. Watching Stuart Hall on television. There was a sense that we were all learning about each other. And the project of socialism as it was being practiced within the institutions dealt with race as sharing or raising some form of consciousness about each other. In the '90s that gets colonized, it gets hijacked by a kind of neo-liberalism and turned into something about the global happy family which we all know doesn't exist. And this madness has lead us to now, where this white working-class is saying "we were left out." So to explore decolonization is to decolonize from a neo-liberal form of consciousness into a politics of identity that are still about thinking more deeply the questions of belonging and difference.

These terms are a little bit old fashioned. For example, in Britain you see, at one time the term black included Asians. It wasn't that black only meant Afro-Caribbean. Because it came out of the unions, and class, and all of that. A relation with what was considered to be the colonized body in Britain at that time.

travis [from the audience]: Maybe someone else would want to speak to that point on decolonization. Not sure I can [laughter]. I was at that Eastman performance in 1980 and I'm a graduate of Northwestern University. At that performance, this idea of decolonization is very pertinent. Evanston is very white upper class. It's not black. There were blacks on the other side of the tracks; not at Northwestern. There was never another black person with me in any of my classes, for instance. Now the night that Julius performs his compositions—this idea of having this black man who had been there teaching white music students these pieces for a while, and they put on the concert, and the white community fills Pick-Staiger Hall and Julius brazenly does this music. It separates that world of blackness and whiteness immediately. He drove a wedge through people. Speaking of a colony, he was the evil nigger and good white people fled the theater. And I understood it, perfectly. I was part of the new music community in Chicago. But this idea of decolonization of race was in your face at that performance, because instead of there being this black man doing black music, or a black man doing white music, or pretending to be Philip Glass or John Cage—this was a black man who dared to use the white words, nigger, in a white environment with a white inflection. Accepting it. Not only accepting it, taking control of it. And It was very very powerful. I was itching. It was wonderful for me. But you don't have progress in that area since. We have fallen miserably, our statements about colonization. We have failed in terms of understanding how it works or even defining these as issues. But I will deal with that Sunday afternoon when I perform at two o'clock. [audience laughter]

Questioner 5: Were you working from a shortened score or did you decide to abridge the piece?

KE: The musicians had their score which is not in anyway shortened. Actually it's lengthened. The actual time of the score is twenty-one minutes and nine seconds. And their version, which is take five when they were getting more tired, is actually twenty-seven minutes. It's six minutes longer because they don't play with stopwatches or with clocks. This is how Eastman indicated it should be played. They've evolved their own method for playing, because you know it's obviously notated, there isn't room so much for improvisation, but there is room for interpretation. Every take was somewhat different. There's twenty-two minute takes, twenty-three minute takes. But by take five it was twenty-seven minutes.

Questioner 6: Hello. You were talking about the symmetry and asymmetry with the bookended spoken performances. Throughout the piece there were various symmetries and asymmetries with two male and two female performers. And then with the faces painted. One side was like a triangle and the other side was a little bit more like a trapezoid. Then the split screen. And also some of the shots were mirrored right? Was that a choice of aesthetics? Because what I found myself doing during the film was trying to match who's playing what part. I don't know if the cuts were actually set to the music or if they were visually there?

KE: All the cuts are set to the music but the cuts come from all the takes. The music is one take, take five. But the cuts come from six different takes. They are all edited to the image. The key or rather the complication is that very quickly you can't locate sound and image. When you're in the studio you can't locate it either, and when you're in the concert you can't. The aggregation—the additive sound of four pianos means you very rapidly lose the ability to index sounds to gestures. Once we realized that, we actually worked very hard to fix images to sounds, regardless of whether you could tell or not. But before having done that, what we tried to do in the shoot was multiply the imagery because the fallboard of the piano is polished. The whole piano is highly polished, it's kind of …

AS: Black mirror.

KE: Yes! Like a kind of vehicle. You see in the close up shots you have the four hands which are multiplied in the black mirror of the fallboard and become eight. And then if you consider the other performers then you have sixteen total. Once we realized that it was very difficult to fix fingers to sounds we decided to multiply. You're not the only one who finds it difficult to pin the sound and image of performance together, everybody does. Which is part of the additive principle at work in Eastman's piece.

AS: And of course to build a crescendo of action as
the composition gets more and more intense. There
were a number of decisions that involve repetition
to build concentration.

KE: I don't think of it as watching. I think of it as studying concentration. An invitation to concentrate. And
you an invitation to follow a kind of ecstatic mathemat-
ics. Ecstatic division and addition and subtraction.
An ecstatic fractioning of sixteenths. Time dividing,
time doubling, time tripling. The key is to stay with
them. Because the pianists are staying with. And the
question is, can we? What emerges when we stay in
the time and space? Can the time and space of spectatorship participate in the time and space of the performers
intense concentration? We think of these pianists as
warriors. They are warriors inside the plane of music.
We think of this music as our protest music. We think
of this music as a weapon for the wars and the fights
we all will have to fight and we all are fighting. The
key going forward is to fight in the field that you're in.
Of course you should go to the demonstrations and
the protests, but the key is to find the protest form from
within whatever your field is, whatever your work is,
whatever your art is. You have to find a way to weap-
onize it. Because there are real enemies. And there
is a real struggle. And there are people who have us in
their sights, and they are making targets of us and
we want to be ready for them. This music, that's how
we see it. This film's about reloading Eastman and
giving us the kinds of resilience and the kinds of for-
titude and the sense of internal reserves for the fights
ahead. It's about vigilance and it's staying woke. Woke is
not a word we use so much in Britain, but we understand it and we are in solidarity with it. And that's how
we see this film, as a solidarity film.

Anthony Elms: I think that seems like a good place to
stop actually, thank you.

[Applause].

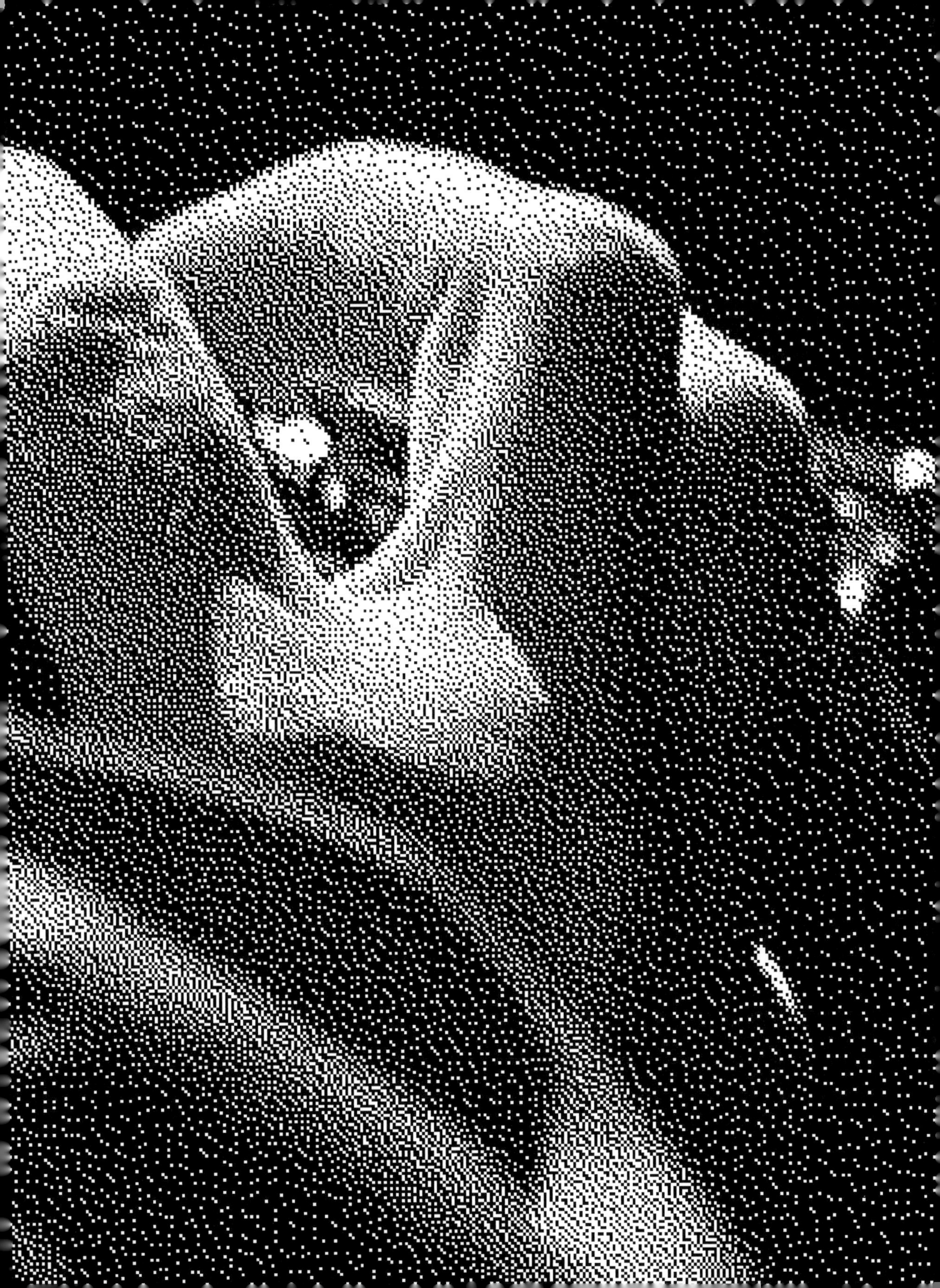

A Day of Correction and a Night of Grading in the Digital Universe of Colour
The Otolith Group

Unperformed script written for *Endless Shout*

Anjalika Sagar: The Art and Technique of Digital Color Correction.

Kodwo Eshun: By Steve Hullfish.

AS: First Edition 2012.

KE: Second Edition: 2013

AS: Chapter 1.

KE: Primary Color Correction: Tonal Range.

AS: Definition: Crush

KE: To lower the black levels to the point where detail is lost in the deep shadow areas.

AS: "Crushing" clips the signal on the low end.

KE: Sometimes "crushing the blacks" is a desired result: creating a contrasty look.

AS: It is also sometimes a warning that the black levels are too low.

KE: For example:

AS: As I lowered the blacks, the picture was looking nice and rich, but I pulled back a little on my correction because I saw that I was crushing the blacks and couldn't see any detail in the shadows.'

KE: First Things First: Black Level

AS: Nearly every colorist attacks an image by first determining where the blacks should be.

KE: "Blacks" refers to the deepest, darkest shadows and black part of the image.

AS: As mentioned earlier, blacks are also sometimes referred to as set-up, lift, shadows, pedestal or lowlights.

KE: There is usually some portion of an image that you can pick out that should be corrected to the lowest legal level.

AS: If you don't correct at least some portion of the image to a black level that is low enough that is almost devoid of image, the shadows of the image will appear milky and the image will lack snap or pop.

KE: The trick is to lower the blacks to the proper point without losing detail that you want to keep.

AS: Fred Moten.

KE: The Case of Blackness.

AS: Like the more than mindless,

KE: more than visceral,

AS: events and things

KE: whose meaning is unattained

AS: even as their political force is ascertained,

KE: chromatic saturation has repercussions.

AS: Oops … nearly lost the skin there.

KE: Crush the blacks there.

AS: I've taken his beauty grade and applied that to the keyboard.

AS: Swapping from a …

KE: What happens if we crush the blacks a little bit?

AS: Primary.

AS: We do the primary correction first.

AS: Then the secondary.

AS: Then a final pass.

AS: That's a waveform monitor for exposure.

AS: There's no ceiling buffer. It goes up to a 100.

KE: What's the perfect score for skin tone?

AS: It's so subjective.

KE: You can see here … this is more about artistic judgement than technical judgement.

AS: I normally set my Zebra to 70.

AS: If we grade this skin and let them fall in and out of it, we can get away with it.

KE: We need to crush the blacks more.

AS: It's not biasing towards green.

AS: There's your Scope.

KE: It's a bit confusing.

AS: Because the Fleshline says it's off.

AS: That's our baseline … after the crush.

KE: If we just lose some blue first in the mids.

AS: She looked a bit jaundiced.

KE: That put a bit more colour back in.

AS: Really tricky.

AS: Almost translucent.

AS: Like grading piglet skin.

AS: Translucent … almost like piglet.

AS: Still not happy with that.

AS: Got a weird translucent glow.

KE: I think there's too much red in it.

AS: Ermmm.

KE: Mmmm.

AS: You know those handhelds will really show when you project them large?

AS: I could do with a piece of black wrap.

AS: I think my eyes are been tricked by the blowout highlights.

AS: Have a look at that.

AS: You can see where the problem is …

KE: You think she is pinkish?

AS: Compared to that weird image.

AS: There's something a bit weird about her.

KE: There's something a bit flat.

AS: Err …

AS: Looks a bit Flash Gordon this shot

AS: Alright, I think … we might have pushed the white too high on these fluorescents.

KE: When did we do that?

KE: I want these fluorescents to be blown out.

AS: Cos the rolloff won't be great

KE: This has got …

AS: For me these are dead.

KE: I agree.

AS: There's a weird cast on this image.

KE: Let's just keep moving on.

AS: I don't want to put a mask in.

AS: You'll see a gradient dropoff.

AS: You'll see a block of black there.

AS: I'm cropping the image.

AS: The only thing that shows you is the skin tone.

AS: Then I'm looking at the skin on the scope.

KE: Is that like a Macbeth?

KE: A Macbeth colour chart?

AS: Greyscale.

AS: All it is is presets that I'm saving.

AS: Then we put it together.

AS: So we do all the glare on this.

AS: Then we do all the values numerically.

AS: Just in terms of when 2 images are next to each other.

AS: So it looks like two blacks bleed into each other.

AS: They can tweak it.

AS: Da Vinci? I don't trust it.

AS: It's a bit … buggy

KE: I don't trust it with 4K.

AS: It's okay for HD.

AS: Baselight is good.

AS: It's really solid.

AS: It's not just the software.

AS: It's the control surface.

AS: It's the deep integration with the software.

AS: Fresh piglet skin.

AS: It's so translucent.

AS: Even in no direct sunlight.

KE: When were you shooting piglets?

AS: Last year.

KE: What are you looking at? Her skin tone?

AS: No … just the blacks at the moment.

KE: OK.

KE: We have to be careful with crushing some more than others.

KE: You have to be careful.

AS: Some will crash.

KE: Others will pop.

AS: This light is pure.

AS: This looks a lot more tungsten-y.

KE: Take a little yellow out …

KE: Let's see what happens.

KE: What happens if you make it pinky?

AS: I know … we could add pink.

AS: She's lost a little warmth.

KE: That's fine with me

AS: Maybe it's here.

KE: That's the problem.

KE: Do we have to live with that?

KE: Do we lose the piano if we crush the piano a bit?

KE: What happens if you pull it down a bit?

KE: Take the contrast down a bit.

KE: No ... Take it back.

AS: That's an interesting hue on the ceiling.

KE: It might be interesting to take some of it out.

AS: The problem is getting a really good key.

AS: Getting a good key.

AS: Then we'll be laughing.

AS: That's better, no?

AS: There's a little bit of noise.

KE: I can live with that.

KE: Let's try something else as an option.

AS: Hang on.

AS: When you stabilize the shot, you'll get warp stabilization.

AS: I need to check the UT.

KE: The LUT?

AS: The Look up Table.

KE: The Look Up table?

AS: It's your chosen palette.

KE: Is that a bit green on their polo necks?

AS: There's not much green.

AS: It's already underexposed.

KE: What happens if we push the image?

AS: It's already got big holes in it.

AS: It's gonna fall apart.

AS: Yeah, it's a bit rough.

AS: In this situation, I would put a bit of blue in.

KE: I thought that you took red out.

AS: Tricky ... cos it should be a poppy shot this.

AS: I've got an idea.

KE: Let's take a bit of colour out

AS: Desaturate it a bit.

KE: What happens if you take the colour out?

AS: There.

KE: Hmm ...

AS: Tricky ...

KE: Just looks really washed out.

AS: There ... I think that's better.

KE: You've made the keys more of a true white, haven't you?

KE: Go back to that image.

KE: Go back to the raw image.

AS: Can we live with the fact that it's yellow and not red?

AS: I'm keeping an eye on these values.

AS: IRE values.

KE: Industry Standard Definition values.

AS: Like the more than visceral

KE: More than mindless,

AS: events and things

KE: whose meaning is unattained

AS: even as their political force is ascertained,

KE: chromatic saturation has repercussions.

KE: Is it not self-evident that black lives matter?

AS: That saying that black lives matters

KE: goes without saying?

AS: That it is necessary,

KE: but not sufficient,

AS: to state that what matters

KE: is that black lives matter?

AS: That what matters now,

KE: more than ever,

AS: is that black lives are seen to matter?

KE: To state that black lives matter

AS: is to presuppose a time

KE: in which black lives did not.

AS: A time when the border

KE: between the lives that mattered

AS: and the lives that did not

KE: mattered to those trying

AS: to dissolve the border by crossing

KE: from the latter to the former

AS: and those seeking to maintain the border

KE: by moving with it as they tracked

AS: and targeted

KE: and logged

AS: and accounted

KE: When was this time?

AS: This time was now

KE: In this time when what matters

AS: does not yet matter

KE: Is it not a question of

AE: matter out of place ?

KE: Is the matter of seeing in which ways

AS: black lives are

KE: seen to matter

AS: not a matter of

KE: seeing in which precise ways

AS: and with what methods

KE: and from what perspectives

AS: and with what frames

KE: and with what words

AS: and what musics

KE: and with what figures

AS: scenes of black lives and

KE: scenes from black lives

AS: and lives of black scenes

KE: can be made to matter?

AS: Is it not a matter of inventing ways for cinematters to matter

KE: Any image and any sound can be a cinematter

AS: A formatter

KE: Any format can matter

AS: Any format can be a matter

KE: Could be

AS: Might be

KE: So long as it's a matter of concern

AS: It has to be a matter

KE: that matters to

AS: those that it draws towards it

KE: Does it not go without saying that

AS: seeing scenes from black lives

KE: is a matter of

AS: inventing ways of hearing

KE: in which ways,

AS: precisely,

KE: cinematters continue to matter.

AS: Is it not a matter of listening

KE: it is matter of a cinema that listens into scenes from black lives

AS: in order to make the senses into theoreticians,

KE: As Marx would say,

AS: So as to begin to formulate,

KE: in which senses,

AS: and in which ways

KE: what is visible differs

AS: from what is obvious

KE: so as to sensitise yourself to the ways in

AS: which what is visible

KE: distinguishes itself

AS: from what is evident

KE: From inattention

AS: From what goes without saying

KE: From what passes below attention.

AS: It is matter of observing against the grain of the habitual,

KE: Seeing against all the evidence

AS: against blind spots

KE: To think cinematically is to draw attention to the

AS: infamous and the anonymous

KE: and to create an encounter with mortality

AS: Like the more than

KE: more than visceral,

AS: events and things

KE: whose meaning is unattained

AS: even as their political force is ascertained,

KE: chromatic saturation has repercussions

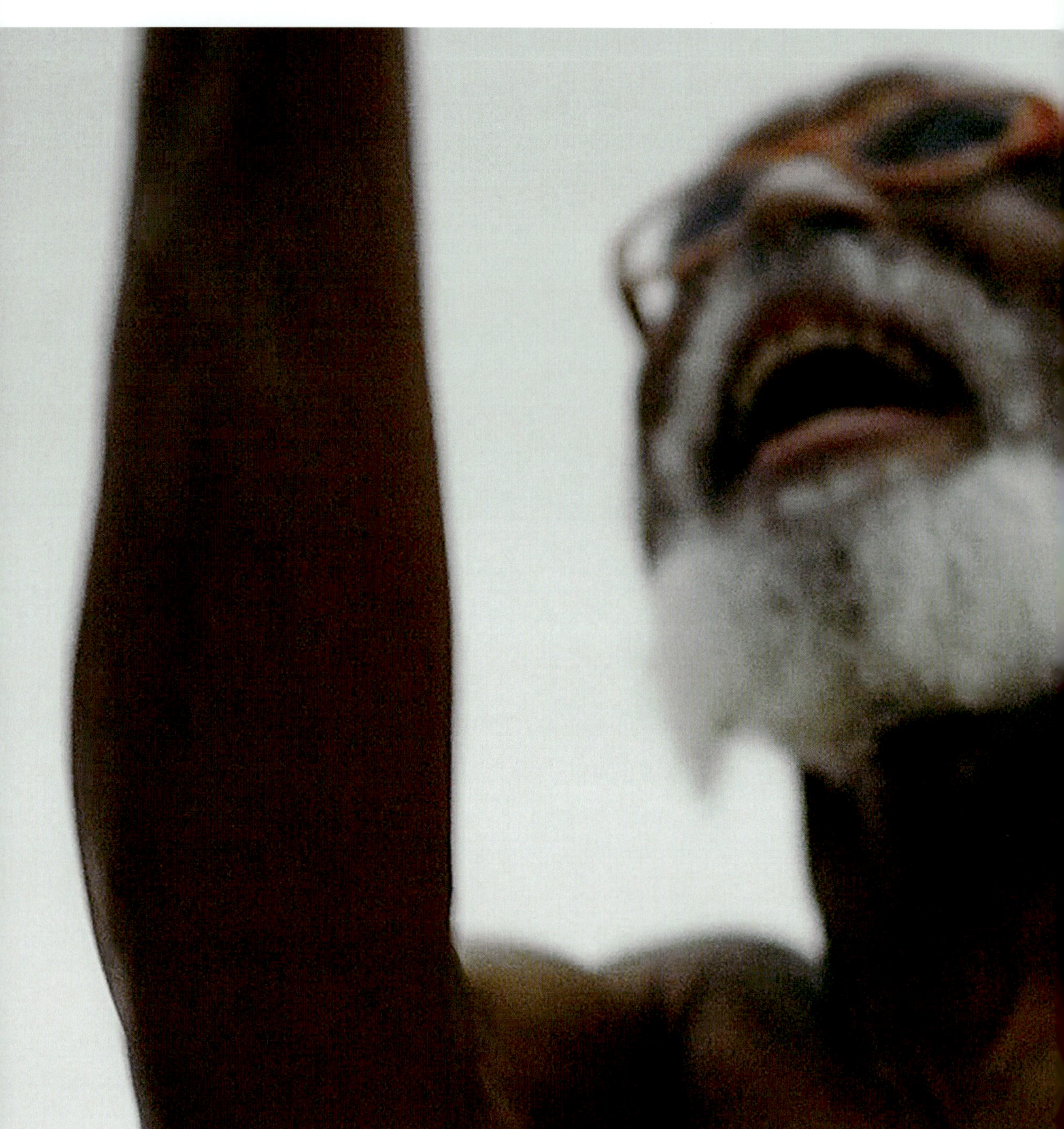

Mouth of Darkness

travis

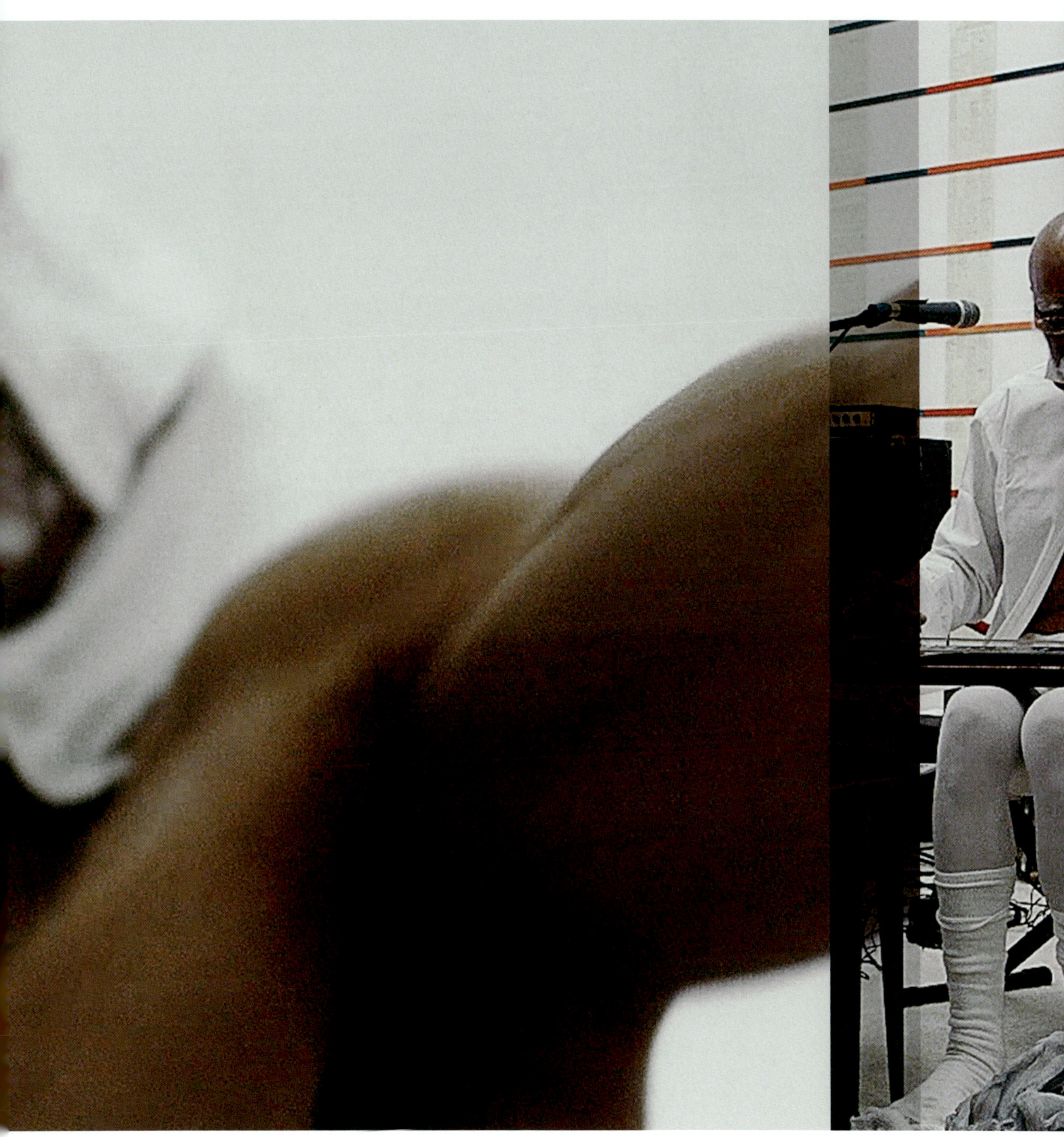

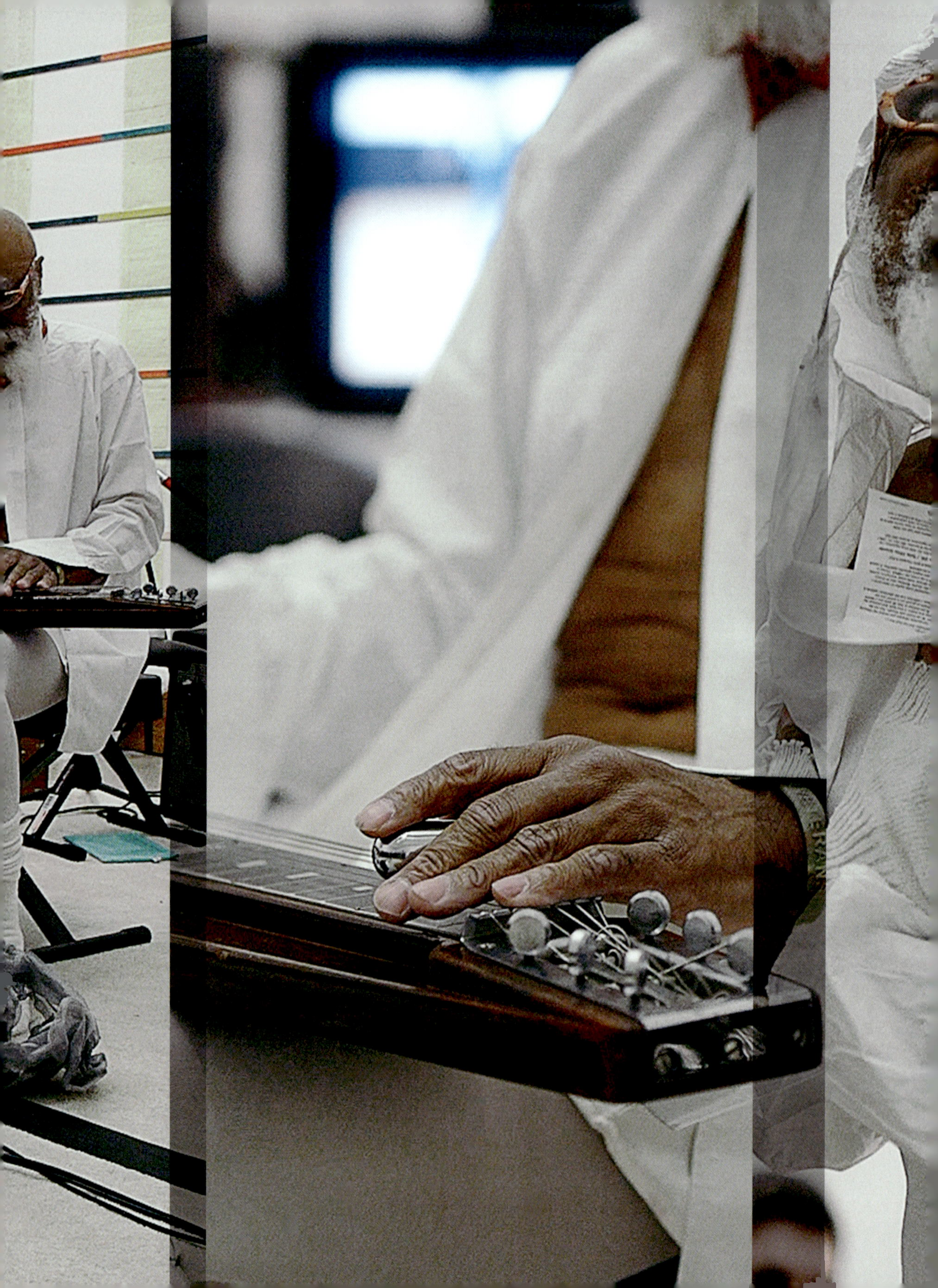

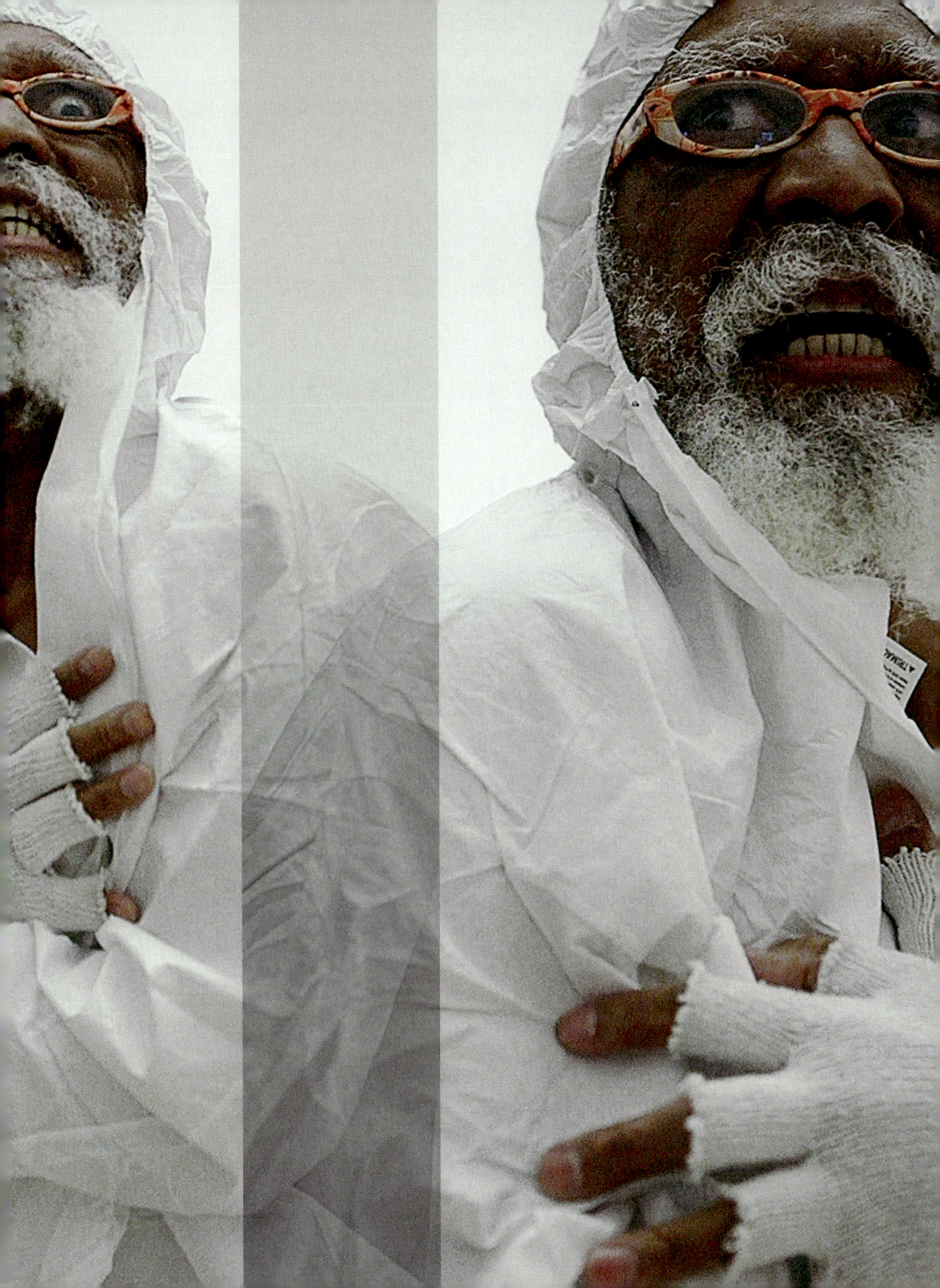

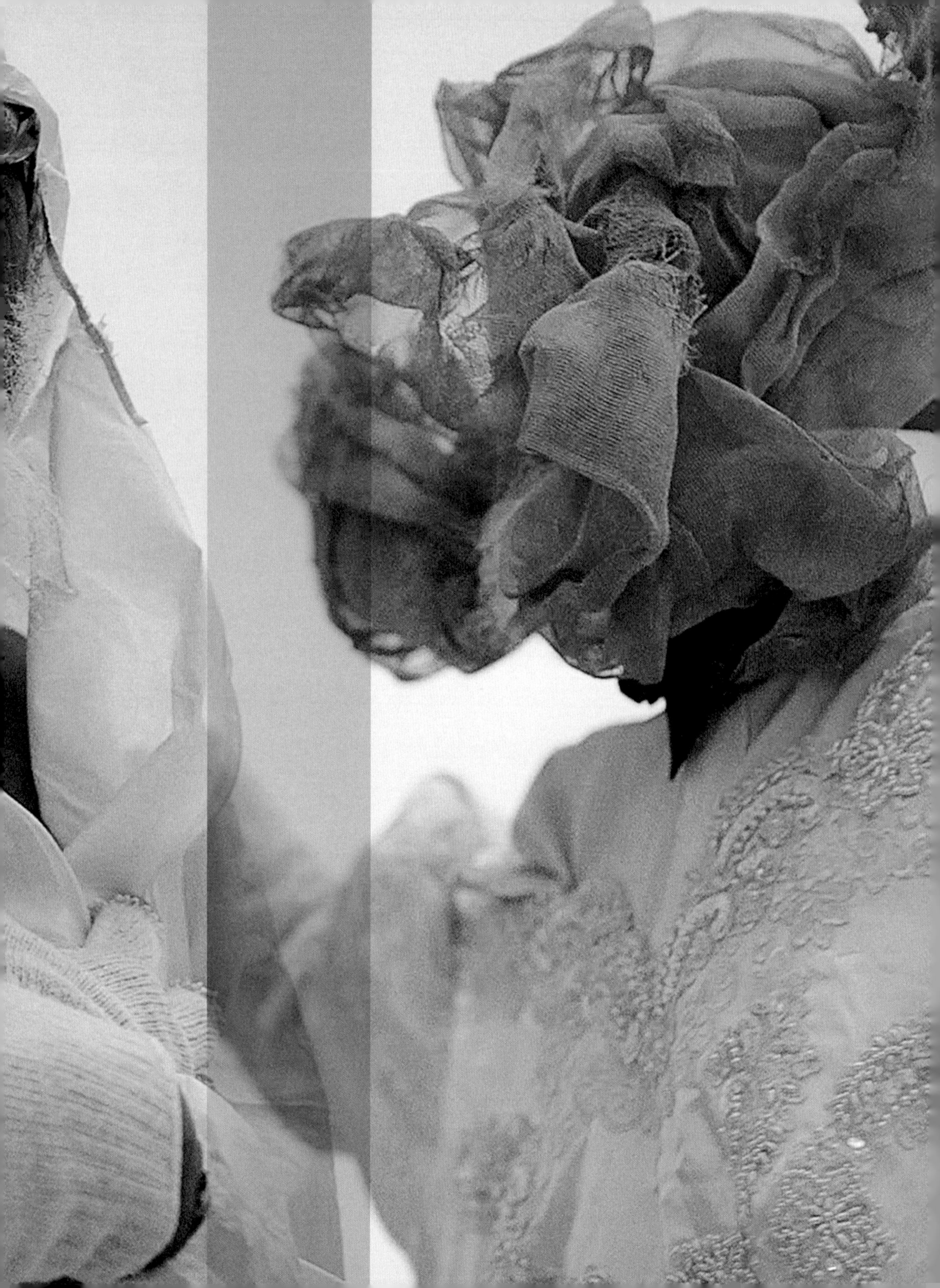

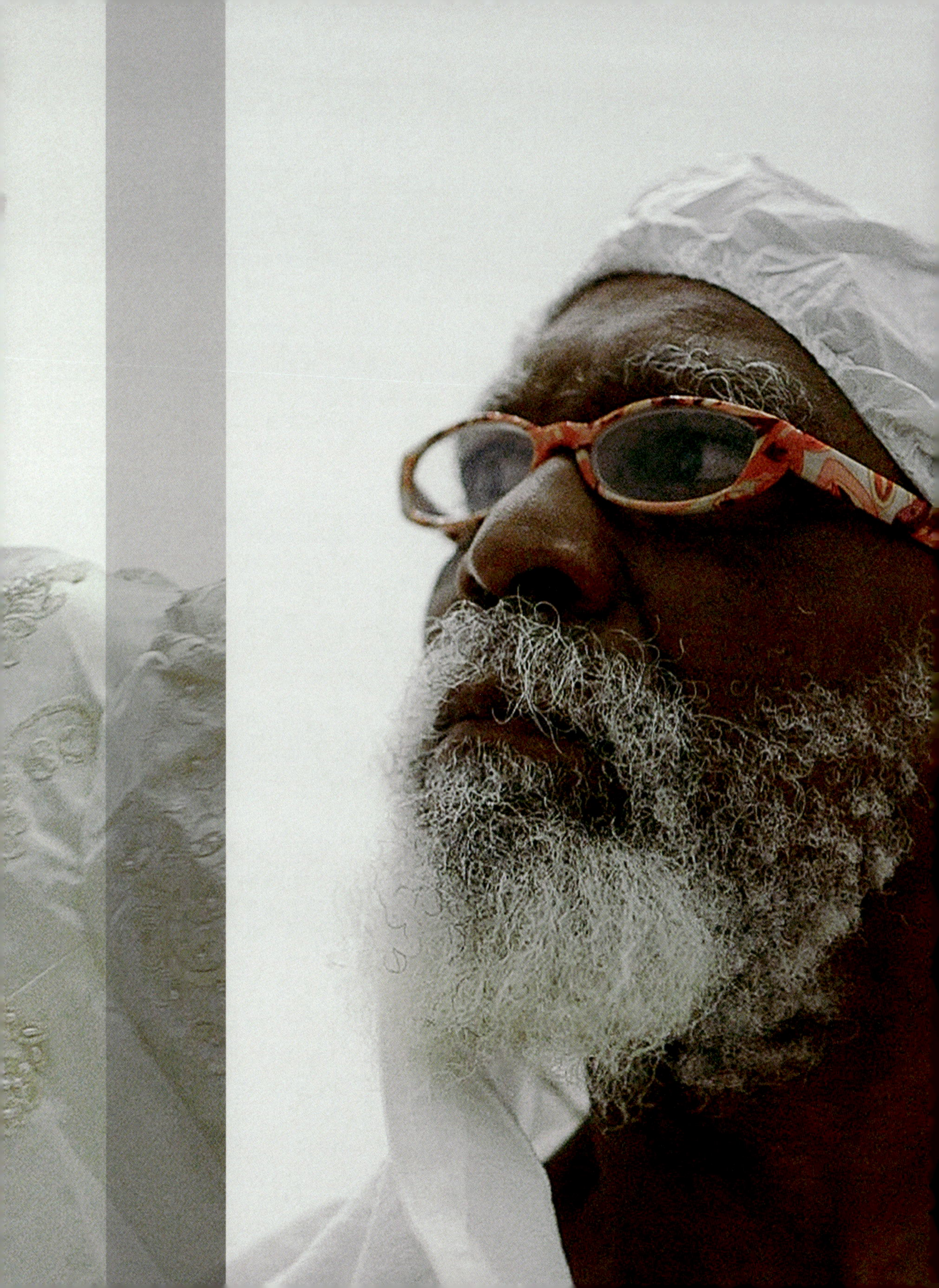

Sin defends young men. Soil-soaked geopolitical scapegoats black and fertile, covered at first in fugitive entanglement, flaming embers now bleached white bone. The dead detour the dead. Black men fear not; art buried my thicket unfed. Wheels within wheels, muddy phantoms shaft, muzzled and sown.

In the late 1980s, I designed an outdoor prison theater. The porch, secured by expanding zinc-coated anchors, reinforced an elevated stage for wheelchair performance. Blank walls projected shapely humors and artificial Flammarion fictions. Black Guard uniforms, skirts, muskets, and bayonet arsenals, collapsed free of charge, encouraged spectators now and then to howl, to caterwaul, to sprawl. Onomatopoeum #16: 180°–270° Greek, peninsular, three-sided slab slashed by an Elizabethan thrust stage. All actors interrupted my vomitorium via underground railway and fragrant scenery.

The human eye has a peripheral spread of about 130°. This may change depending upon head or eye strain. Lighting designers show far less interest in Black flesh textures than in famished glances of darkness, the rhythms of the morgue or hasten the color of sound falling like flame from upholstered rain. And the flowers? They freeze at midnight. An event racing spectators, consumed by proximity, tuning, or underhair (*Le Faux Miroir*) await. Borne upon cultish moments of loathing submission, waste handlers and electricians imposed flesh, blood, and enemy emotion upon every blistered wildlife.

Haints attain to no one motet. Vocal memory never fails what we banshee, cow dung, or sinew. Pictures of fourteen-foot-square rooms, three pens deep, reseed the sea while retaining thistle and thorn debris. Every thrust of porch pen floor plan openly visible, one to the other. Secret lessees, like durational mysteries and sin, grew with 3-D missionary idols, repeating rifles and internal doors; which, by the seventeenth Century, imprisoned undertakers. Initiated brotherhoods obliterated Aristotelian care givers, unmasked as occult sex slaves, cool, moist and lustful; or, most often, concupiscent races led by dismembered,

disinherited spirits within Marianist "wild nature." Upon the stage: Night! Five judges upend 10,000 Watt lamp cattle pens. Brutal hysterical polyphonies! Trembling melancholia! Hid by daylight: Withdrawal! Torture! Transmuted into European Renaissance exorcism. OTO!/OTO!/OTO! OTO! TU-UM TABU!

Two dancers without wheelchair seatbelts miss their eight-foot "Downstair" and flip, face-first; plummet onto sloped ascensions; flung into the middle of the air. Gravity-seeking coalbed methane, white fog turned white-hot black flame, slowly rises. Topside, refracted luminescence lit up the blood-red black oak tree glittery, yellowish glint. Without incandescence or cause, house lights and law lamps plunged into abandoned tunnels, igniting firedamp along highly viscous bituminous strata. Fireworks! Fin-de-siècle! Promiscuous colonists prefigured all succeeding stigmata like alabaster reflectors reinforcing deep forest prison plantations. Here, both backbone and seraphim of the American economic system lick my lips. Blake's *Little Black Boy* pass for *Aida*. When did the firelight leave your tribe? Perhaps buybacks outside my repossessed shotgun shack museum. Bribed spectators rise! Adjust night-vision goggles, camouflaged helmets, vigilante-tripped courts and grips. We fall again, for eight bells.

CALVIN: I know that you can never love me   Soon you will be dead.
Lash out your Love of God refrain for me   Soon you will be dead.
Our little Faith is now 16   Screams of terrain & fearful camouflage
She brings down the saints & then all eternity   Gods/Demons; sentimental predetermination
Silent thickets inside my head   Soon you will be dead
When did the firelight leave your eye   Sunrise sunset waft across your bed
Sky of blueblood, flesh like lead   Soon you will be dead
CALVIN: I know that you can never love me   Soon you will be dead.

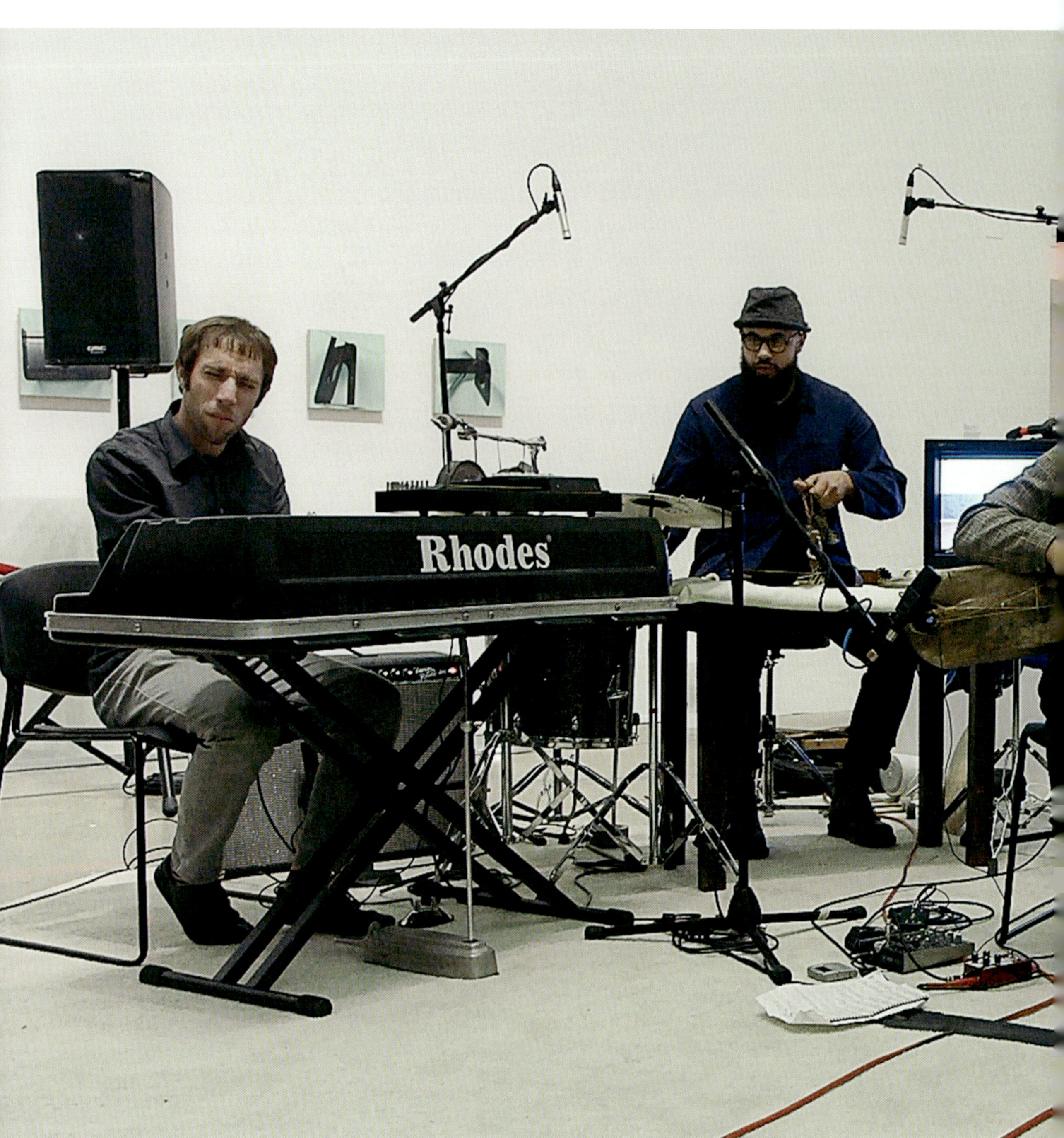

Rhodes

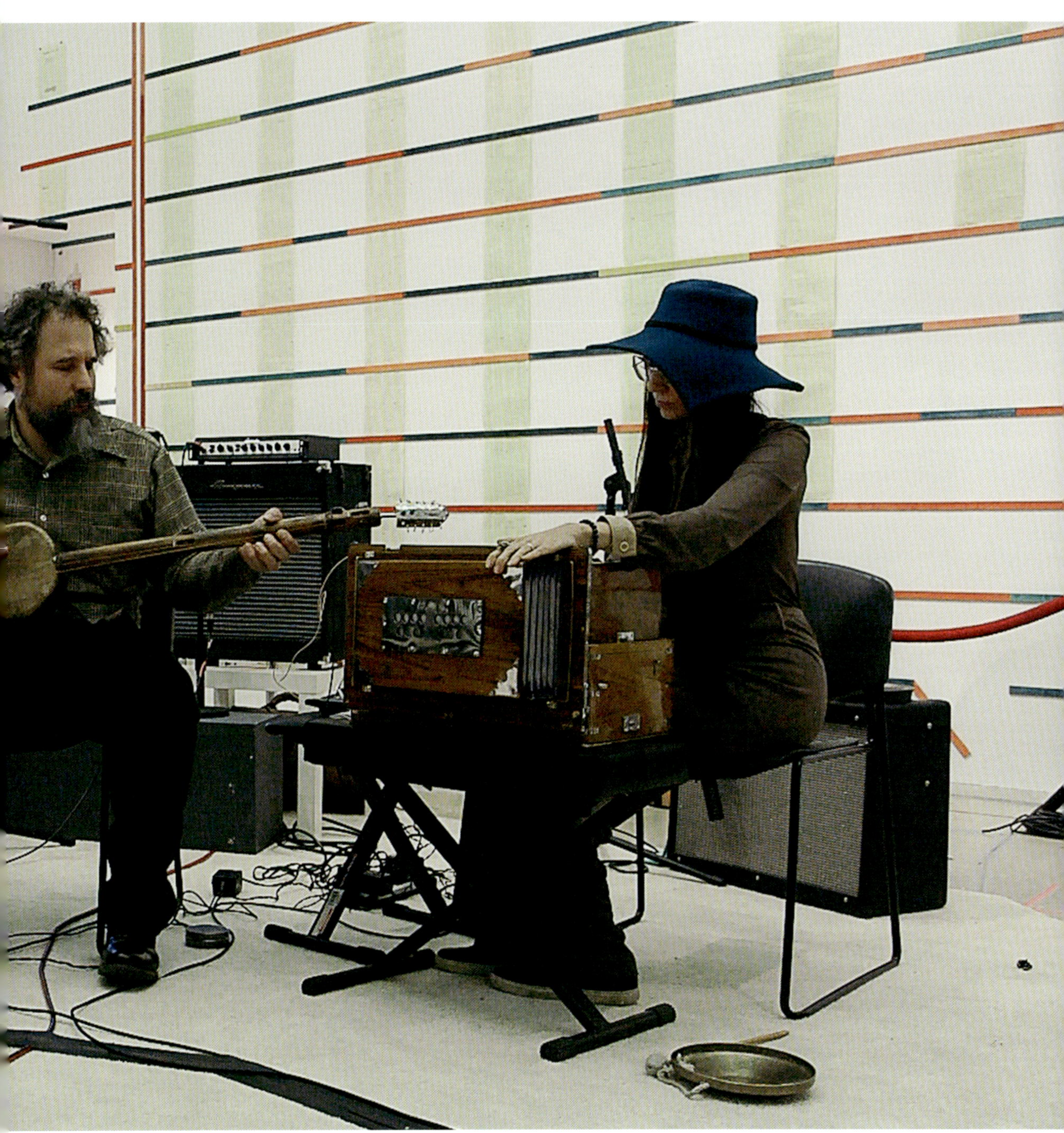

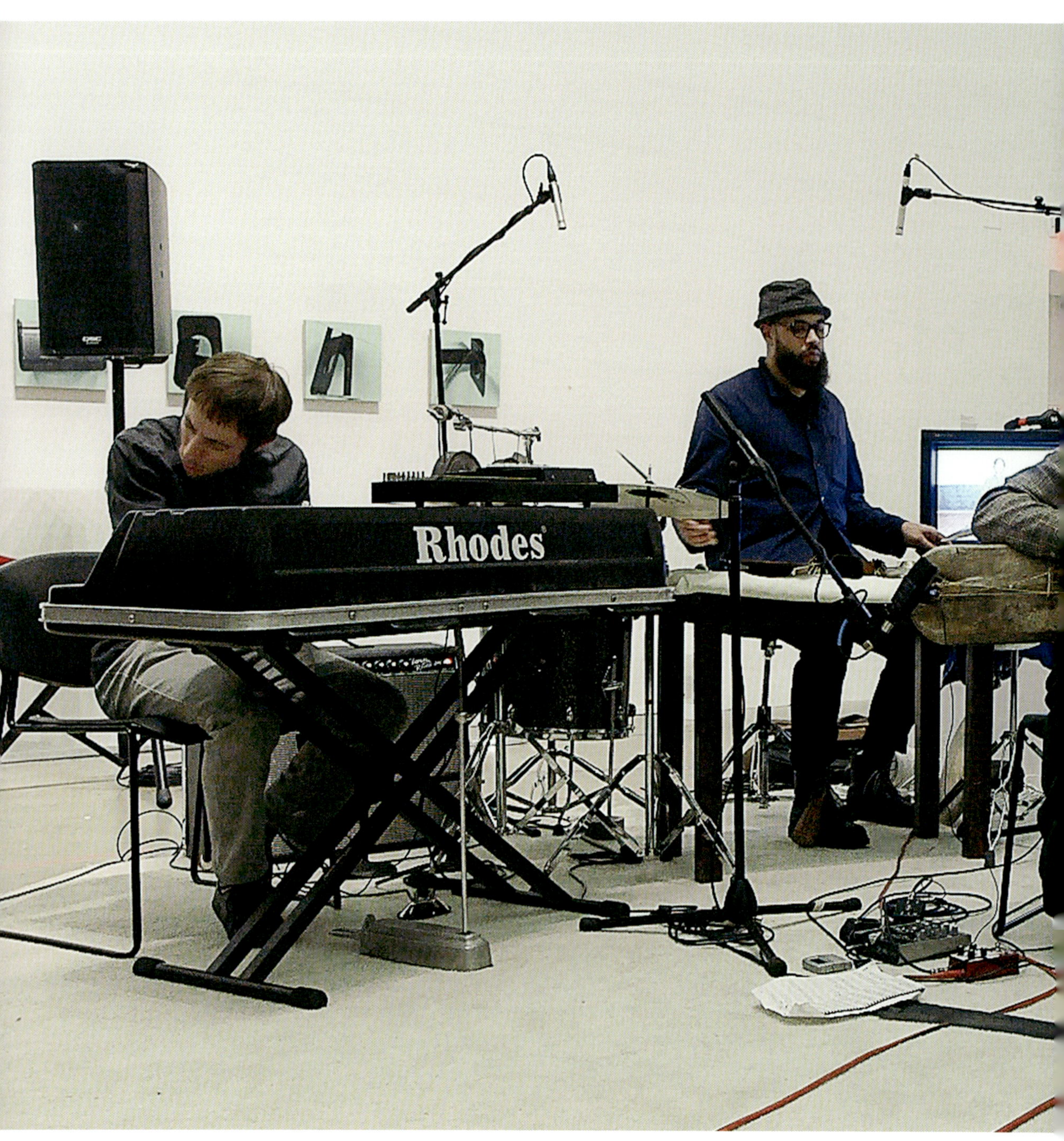
Rhodes

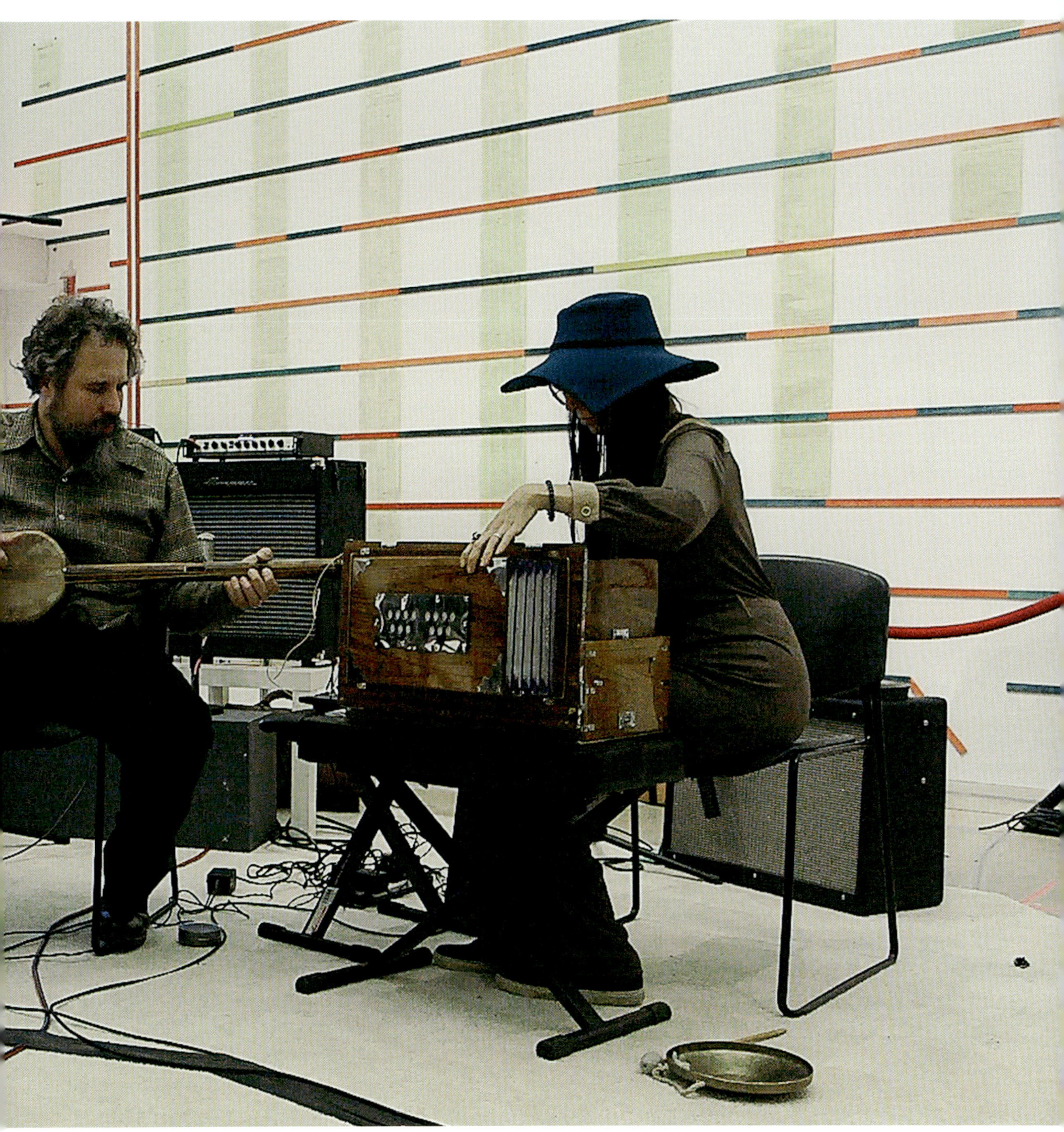

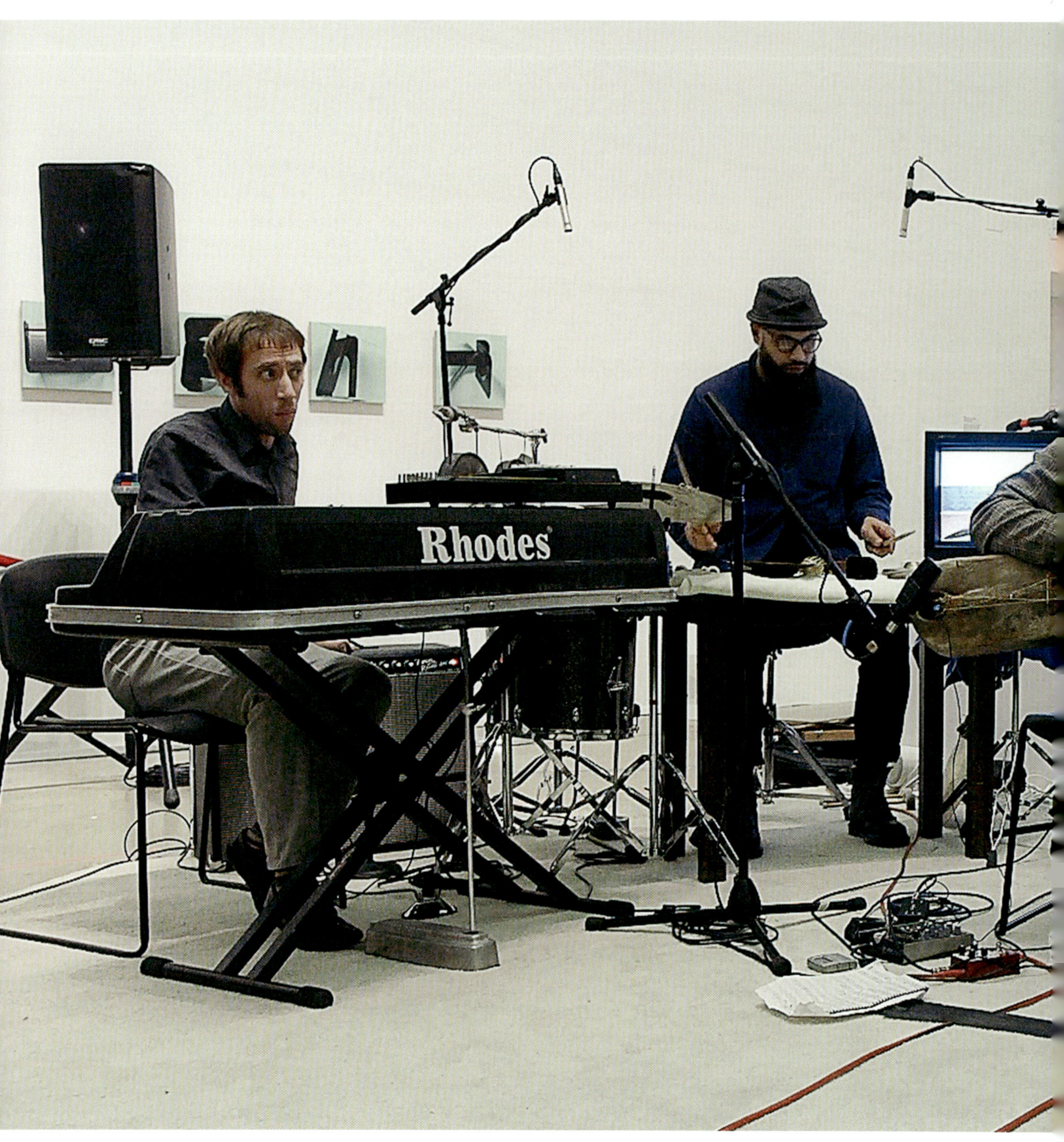

Rhodes

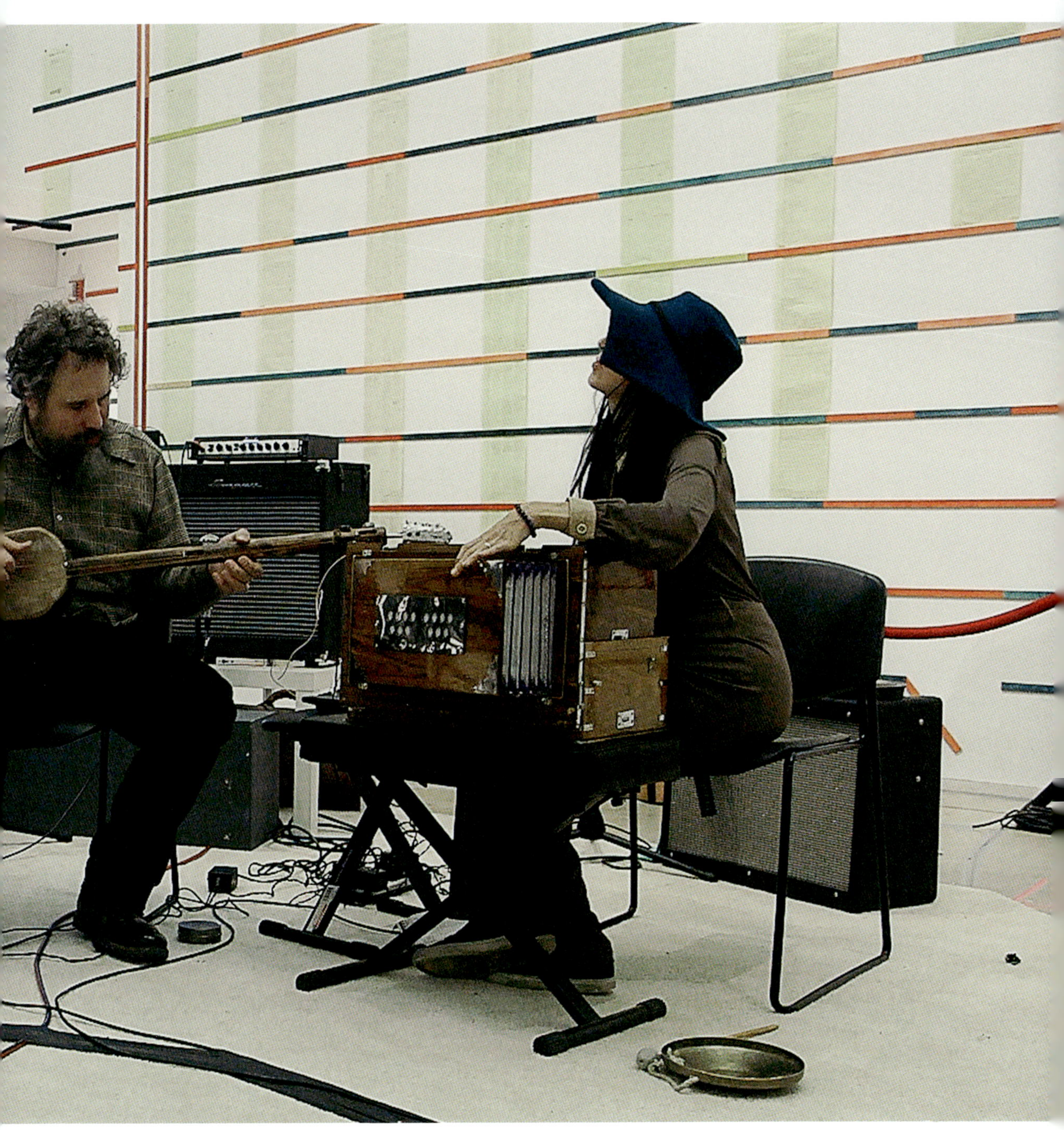

Natural Information Society
Joshua Abrams

Human music is a simplification of the music of the world, always in play.
Human music can point towards the natural through many directions, for example
by way of stochastic methodology, or a musician and jaw harp partnering with
a live beetle in Papua New Guinea. Music, like laughter, precedes language; it catches
timing, response and reaction, a range of feeling. Music lives in the context of sound.
The world's sonic activity, such as: wind, a/c, electrical hum, distant computers or
televisions, a baby's song or cry constantly infiltrate human music, whether acknowledged or otherwise. The drone of a plane, a mile above/behind the conversations
of dozens of birds at 4am on a spring morning in Chicago could be a basic description
of music of the world. Or this moment could be recorded by a phone, flattened into
a digital file, and called human music, its locus prescribed by speakers or headphones.
We create parameters to allow a context of understanding.

I formed Natural Information Society (NIS) in 2010 to present my music in performance. My work weaves composition and improvisation together to create long form psychedelic environments; with NIS I invite fellow musicians to participate as sound producers, active listeners, and navigators of shifting musical limitations. NIS draws upon mutable configurations of musicians and a blend of traditional and electric instrumentation. The group is conceived of as a network of community rather than a fixed ensemble. NIS explores simultaneous differences such as stasis and motion, space and density, esoteric and familiar, and old and new. The group's approach is visually reinforced by the tapestry-like paintings of visual artist Lisa Alvarado, whose work is reproduced for album covers and used as setting for the performances. Alvarado also plays harmonium and gong with NIS. In addition to Lisa and myself, group participants have included Mikel Avery, Jason Adasiewicz, Jim Baker, Ben Boye, Ari Brown, David Boykin, Gustavo Costa, Hamid Drake, João Pais Filipe, Ben Lamar Gay, Emmett Kelly, Noberto Lobo, Artur Majewski, Nick Mazzarella, Nicole Mitchell, Jeff Parker, Tomeka Reid, Frank Rosaly, Angelica Salvi, Jason Stein, Helge Sten, Kuba Suchar, Nori Tanaka, Chad Taylor, Yaw Tembe, and Michael Zerang. Natural Information Society has also collaborated on projects with visual artists Theaster Gates and Simon Starling.

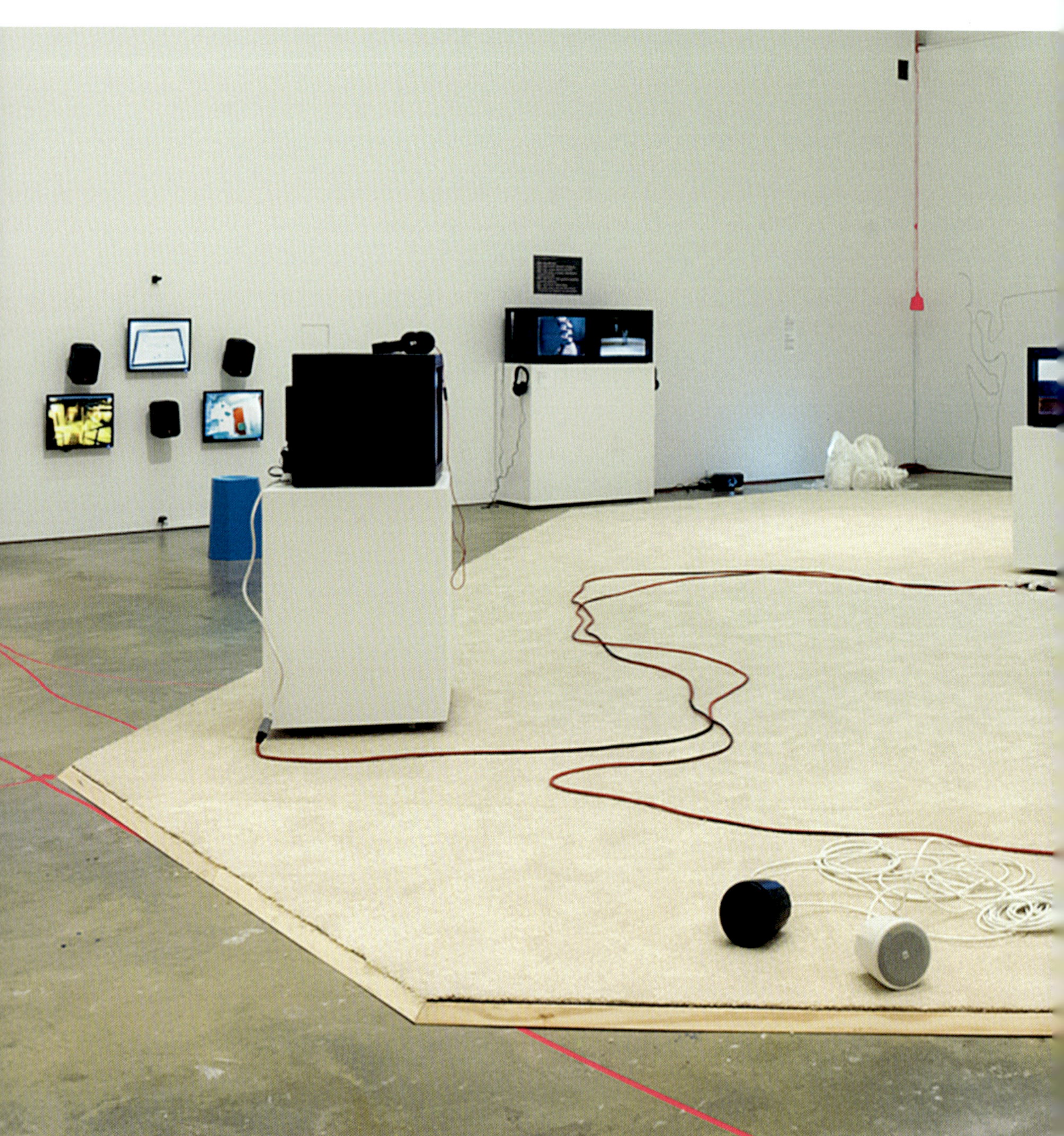

Ending

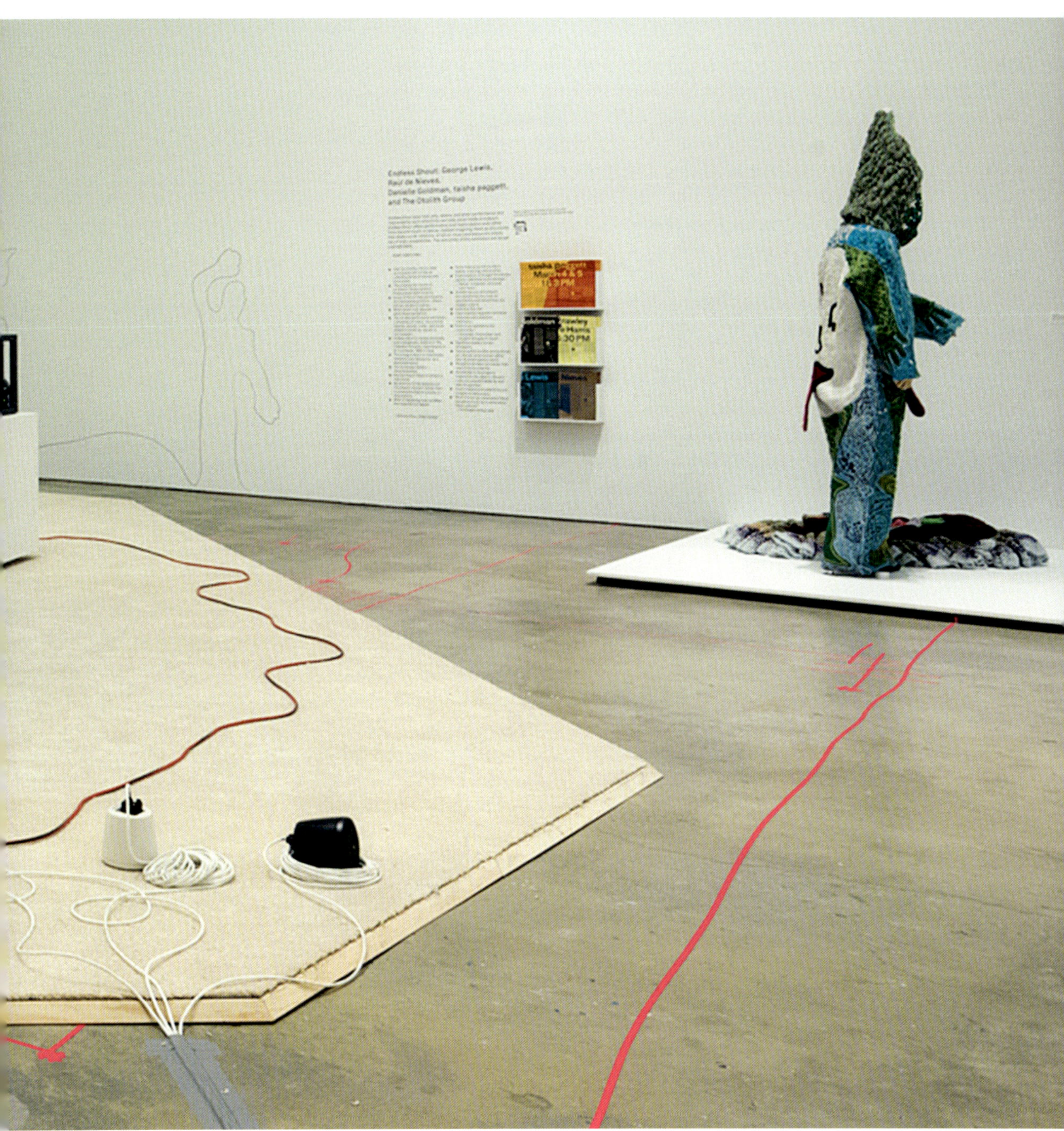

There are preconditions publicly and politically that define the characters placed against white backdrops between didactics. The largest preconditions are probably also the least likely to be addressed: who is an artist? And how?

Endless Shout was intentionally developed to sit alongside ICA's presentation of *The Freedom Principle: Experiments in Art and Music, 1965 to Now*, touring from the Museum of Contemporary Art, Chicago. Not to be programmatically supportive nor to programmatically contextualize the historical exhibition. Rather the proposal was to be ideologically and ethically entwined, and implicate locations and frameworks and timeframes. To scramble figure-ground. This cohabitation of exhibitions, the objects, histories, and bodies further made a case for the cross-generational ethos and boundary blurring argument core to *The Freedom Principle* and the African American visual and music history on which that exhibition focused.

In this, *Endless Shout* had critical edge. In my studies of the exhibition checklist for *The Freedom Principle*, as the materials moved farther away from the nucleus formed between the African Commune of Bad Relevant Artists (AfriCOBRA) and the Association for the Advancement of Creative Musicians (AACM), improvisation and collectivity largely became subject matter and representation by individuals rather than structure and method. Notable exceptions being the film installation *Afterword via Fantasia* by Catherine Sullivan in collaboration with George Lewis and Charles Gaines; Douglas Ewart, George Lewis, and Douglas Repetto's environment *Rio Negro II*; and possibly Pope.L's score as wall installation *Another Kind of Love: John Cage's Silence, By Hand*. My criticism was set to extend and not critique. Too, this engagement acknowledged the difficulty of providing respectful environments where communal action and improvisational process flourish and maintain; with an eye toward how, why, and who gets presented as active artists of influential histories by the museum.

To make good on values of improvisation and collectivity championed by *The Freedom Principle, Endless Shout* would need to enact *a* freedom principle. This initial inquiry was structurally quite modest by design, intended to complicate during implementation. An open-ended line of questioning guided along two interrelated paths. First: Why, as performance increasingly factors within visual arts institutions, do museums continue to treat the seeds of artistic performance as rooted in the actions of Judson Street Church, or the nonsense pageantry of Dada and the formal staging of Bauhaus? To name just three oft referenced paths. Why not begin with, say, the Museum of Modern Art's Jazz in the Garden series, where many of jazz's trailblazing composers and musicians performed? Or maybe the Museum of Contemporary Art, Chicago's own extensive history dating back to the '60s of events with the Association for the Advancement of Creative Musicians? And also, why is "tap dancing in front of the paintings" often how curators bemoan outreach activities? What does this stock dismissal imply about the value directed to some traditions and histories that have dotted lines between disciplines?

Setting for Voices.

Anthony Elms

This year concert attendance will be limited to 1,500. Tickets will be placed on sale (in the Museum lobby only) on the Saturday preceding each performance. A few chairs will be available on the garden terraces, but most of the audience will stand or sit on the ground. In case of rain, the concert will be canceled; tickets will be honored at the concert following. Other museum activities continue as announced.
—Museum of Modern Art press release announcing the second season of Jazz in the Garden.

The exhibition title, *Endless Shout*, is taken from a suite of four piano works written for Frederic Rzewski by George Lewis in 1994. Lewis always focuses on the way improvisation does, not is. George's composition alludes to the blues utterances of stride piano. And the title does so as well, riffing off "Carolina Shout" (1921) by James P. Johnson. Lewis' writings and musical compositions form an overwhelmingly generous and dedicated front by which to recognize improvisation is not a style in which people engage and react and perform. Improvisation is contingent behavior not solid production. Lewis' combinations of traditions, techniques, and technologies might register, by way of literary theorist Houston Baker, as a "living, mutable, mobile, noisy, unstable, vibrant—and ultimately infinite—set of postmodern possibilities." Techniques for togetherness. Using George's title was a way to call forth methodology in a way that expanded any stylistic limitation. Call and response.

That shout from Carolina in 1921 is extended by Lewis in 1994 to register endlessly. Certain conversations, demands, and expectations seem to always need be enunciated and addressed. We are still shouting in the streets at institutions that refuse to listen. And we are still learning to listen to that shouting directed at ourselves. How to listen with and to others. This always unfinished condition was the tacit space for *Endless Shout*.

Somebody else's idea of somebody else's world, is not my idea of things as they are.
—Sun Ra, sung by June Tyson

In the histories of black aesthetics, improvisation, and collectivity, I am not an expert, simply an engaged and concerned collaborator wanting these paths valued as pillars of our society. Exhibitions need to be motivated by a willingness on the part of the curator to admit they are not the expert and instead an invested questioner. This is a modest proposal. The structural shifts necessary for institutions to be open pathways can only happen if those overseeing the decisions reach beyond their skills and levels of identification. Then exhibition spaces might remake themselves into welcoming hosts for traditions, peoples, and ideologies for which the architectural and structural volumes were not made. A recalibration and crucial respectful step toward institutions admitting they have and deserve no authorial voice along any number of narratives, and in fact have historically behaved happily to undermine numerous narratives and ideologies and peoples.

Not wanting to exhibit my expertise, a group of collaborative thinkers and makers was engaged for advice with a mind to gathering a core group of around six. First contacted were George Lewis, and writers/artists/organizers The Otolith Group (Kodwo Eshun and Anjalika Sagar). To think through identity, improvisation, and collectivity without these three, without opening to their thorough and future-facing queries around issues of collective interaction and the politics of assembly is doomed from the beginning. Next, choreographer/artist/activist taisha paggett. Comments taisha had made in earlier conversations and in various interviews had been rewiring my ways of thinking performance and museum space for years. Her mode of address and movement within a room makes felt any number of structural and political forces that demand questioning. Then performer/musician/artist Raúl de Nieves. His exuberance and joy—often channeled via catharsis or bathos—includes a continually expansive number of collaborators, coconspirators, interlocutors, and bystanders. Couple with de Nieves' costumes and baroque stagings, so heavy embedded with traditional craft that in performance they quixotically veer flamboyantly into mutant spirituality, and prismatic comic cosmos appears. The last person to agree was dancer/writer Danielle Goldman. Goldman I knew the least, directed to her scholarship during generous conversations with poet/philosopher Fred Moten. Her energy was crucial to what developed. Goldman is an energizing historian. Goldman also performs but is not a choreographer herself. She is not looking to performance as an author of performance.

Taken together, the multiple descriptives required to define each of the contributors turned each backslash into crucial conjunction—and, or, but. Involvement, interaction, and porousity. The inter, as in cross-. Intermedia and interhistories wedges that challenge dominant narratives siloing the white avant-garde.

From the beginning, The Otolith Group enthusiastically signed on as contributors with appended caveat: "But we aren't performers." Slight variations of this response were also offered by George Lewis (who preferred not to perform) and Danielle Goldman (who does not author her own performances). These pregnant pauses in structure forced a group conversation on what participation entails. How are we a time-based audience? What is the moment and location of anticipation? How are we performing together? Where is the whole?

The initial invitation letters sent to prospective collaborators centered on a base text:

I want the focus to be on collectivity, improvisation and sociability as not simply performance but a kind of public and civic space. And focusing on such opens questions of citizenship, community, race, and so much more.

This project positions performance and African American aesthetics as integral to understanding contemporary art. Not a series of repertoire pieces, or a jazz or dance series; *Endless Shout* is, instead, performance

over time rooted in social space: a space conceptualized and realized collectively with a spectrum of artists—diverse in discipline and race—for whom political/social/experimental black aesthetics, and its traces, are inspiration. The space and programming will be shaped by dialogue with artists who are engaged with collectives or collaborators. We will devise a dedicated area within the ICA where performance can prepare, happen, decay, and revive, possibly featuring dual tracks of scheduled presentations and ongoing (daily, weekly) ones. Taking the museum as context, performing artists (including dancer/choreographers, musicians, poets, and actor/directors) will be commissioned to create work that expands performance gestures, sparking dynamic experiences, insights and conversation for audiences.

Since the curatorial process we envision is itself collaborative and improvisatory, project parameters, performers, and number of performances will be determined through ongoing dialogue among ICA's curatorial team of staff, artists and advisors. Performance will manifest in music, movement, and acting, but also in sociability, and in bodies convening.

What we would like to ask of you: We want to gather a group of six or so thinkers and makers we respect and we feel have thought about these issues through a range of arenas and formats. We want the shape (literally, from available space to presentation to who and how often) to develop out of a workshop meeting with the assembled group. Beyond that we would ask for you to have a hand in two weeks of the event. This involvement could be a sharing of materials for presentation, selecting other performers, performing yourself. Or a combination of these and something else I can't anticipate. This is as you see fit and want to involve yourself. The idea is to keep this project an inquisitive and speculative looking forward, rather than setting closed terms or definitions.

While a group was being assembled, the ICA contracted Philadelphia presenting organization Ars Nova Workshop as expanded stage manager and technical support—keeping in mind that in museum settings, tactical concerns are never simply tactical—they define content. Mark Christman of Ars Nova Workshop has extensive knowledge of working with improvising performers and staging performances—with compressed load-in times at a range of spaces—proving critical to this exhibition. Regardless the what *Endless Shout* was going to move fast and need to be soft in the ways it impacted the museum exhibitions. Mark leads a tight core that at the time included Turner Williams, Eugene Lew, and Eric Carbonara, extended further to Christopher Andrew McDonald and Ryan Collerd, and required crucial efforts from Celeste DiNucci and Maddie Hewitt and still more. This was the first time ICA largely turned over lead operations for programming to an outside entity. Without their ingenuity and connections, many presentations would have been prohibitively expensive or radically intrusive.

Most every avenue of this exhibition—research, conception, technical implementation, artistic engagement, public presentation—unfurled hand-in-hand and at times all
at once; details usually standardized and taken for granted were open to revision from
the beginning until the end. Often I was one of the last to learn precise details. Having
so many hands generated a pliability strong network that often underrecognized
just how far it extended; alternative organizations of agency and cooperation to the
standard channels often exhibition work follows. The willingness of all participants to
discuss stage, seating, lights, walls, power capacity, yet also positioning and ethics and
preconditions set a difference. This dialogue of concern and delay was not necessarily
perceived by the public. The fact that no detail was taken as a given during *Endless
Shout* became an ethos and a source of the project's ongoing creative discomforts.

There are no mistakes, just chances to improvise.
—Miles Davis to Herbie Hancock, anecdote often shared among musicians

No one person knew best. Collective thought doesn't often clearly articulate itself.
Which direction is appropriate when the starting line can be anywhere and redrawn
everywhere? Conversations and meetings and emails and calls and visits—many—
ensued, after all, one of the most commonly encountered forms of improvisational
collective action is an everyday conversation. Endless collective acknowledgement
of a frustrating lack in resolution. (To which, jumping forward, a week of rounding
and emotional conversations with typographer and kind soul Will Holder over
a plan and plot for this exhibition fell to the wayside. The structure simple, beautiful,
and impossible to coral—maybe someday. This frustrated motion, however, did
open onto generative and elegant possibilities later formed with Adam Michaels and
Inventory Press.)

Again, summer 2016, a core group was invited to Philadelphia for two days of
talking, looking, listening, eating and drinking, and roundabouting and dead-ending
three months prior to the exhibition opening. The Otolith Group in the end did not
attend, as Kodwo's necessary entry papers were denied. (Due to the US government's
longstanding racist and paranoid security bureaucracy that can only acknowledge
enemy or ally.)

De Nieves, Goldman, Lewis, paggett, plus myself and Mark Christman convened.
Two interns, Nicole Pollard and Florenz Balane took notes during conversations.
Around a series of tables we worked collectively on individual needs. What professor
of French Literature Yves Citton might have in mind when noting that improvisation's
"(fundamentally political) challenge is to devise collective forms of agency which
articulate the outstanding power of the participating singularities with the principle
of equal respect necessary to find non-oppressive strength in numbers." At the tables
there was a trust: that if I am having personal difficulties, alongside others having
personal difficulty, unspooling presumptive thoughts in collective difficulty generates
group meaning.

In the weeks prior to this convening, during a skype session with The Otolith
Group, Kodwo alluded to a favorite passage in *Bedouin Hornbook*, the first novel
of Nathaniel Mackey's ongoing *From a Broken Bottle Traces of Perfume Still Emanate*,

but the exact passage eluded recollection. A day later I tracked down the passage, typed it up and sent it to The Otolith Group. Days later the passage returned via email, Mackey's fiction reformatted into twenty-six points for active contact. A call to futurities. This speculative rereading spurred by reshaping format became a curious document the group turned to during moments of stuttered direction over the two days. For me, this document has served long after as well, a way to think in parallel about how to reformat exhibition structures, as The Otolith Group had reformated fiction. An ongoing otherwise demand for elsewise thoughts.

> **Improvisation is one thing and other things are other things.**
> **—Cecil Taylor in Gérard Patris and Luc Ferrari's 1965-68 film series**
> **"Les Grandes Répétitions"**

Depending how you delineate, somewhere between twenty-two and twenty-seven directly staged events—concerts, lectures, readings, conversations, film screenings, workshops, dances, monologues, installations. Stand-up comedy, punk thrash cartoon opera, political dialogue, a chamber opera, what-have-yous, and sixteen further extended events in various orbits relative *Endless Shout* and/or *The Freedom Principle*. Audience rarely concerned itself whether an event was set to one or the other exhibition, and in fact often confused the two. *Inter—*

Place was carved out in the final gallery of *The Freedom Principle* exhibition. Officially *Endless Shout* shared a room with works by Matthew Metzger and Pope.L. A bullet-point vinyl wall text of preconditions was crafted to set the stage for how to spend time with *Endless Shout* even when nothing was obviously happening. Six posters were printed over the months to give information on events and collaborators. The beginning was fairly quiet: a stage designed by ICA's Paul Swenbeck and built by Jacob Lunderby and Greg Biché, designed based on ideas floated by paggett developed through conversations with Goldman. Also a revisited version of an earlier interactive work by George Lewis, and an app developed by George circling online. That's it spatially. Mid-November, a costume used by Raúl de Nieves during his monologue *The Fly* was displayed on a mannequin. In January, two monitors added to the space with newly digitized footage of an influential dance by Fred Holland and Ishmael Houston-Jones. Next a small video installation and hanging sound work by jumatatu m. poe. Poe also put pink tape direction lines throughout the room. After his performance, residue—a figurative outline wall drawing made during. In March paggett asked the stage to be doubled in size and carpeted. Two monitors matching the Holland and Houston-Jones monitors were added, except on mobile pedestals. These additional monitors updated weekly with footage of paggett's rehearsals in Los Angeles. Four hand-sized speakers were scattered around the stage. The speakers shared collective breathing exercises recorded from taisha's cellphone. After her performances taisha continued to update the rehearsal footage. The exhibition closed, it didn't finish.

Opportunity is a virtue that writes its own level unpredictability. Ethically and ideologically it was gratifying to feel how readily we could attend different directions. To build a performance exhibition rooted in principles of improvisation, black aesthetics, and collective responsibility that complicated who exactly was staging whom.

The situational nature of shifting rhythms was not accomplished by clearly defining core requirements or styles for a tradition of collectivity and improvisation based in African American traditions. It was done deferring staunch definitions to instead wander and listen and attend to the intersecting activities already in the landscape.

> **It's like watering a plant. I'm trying to show something: that a score is a living entity and that it changes just like the cosmos does. Multiple performances will show the score's versatility and its expansive nature. It's kind of like a nebula: you see the crest of it, but then it goes around almost into infinity.**
> **— Wadada Leo Smith, *Bomb*, Summer 2016**

Endless Shout was a physical space even when not physically happening. Insurance waivers were required. A willing staff kept invested and attentive. The framework of *Endless Shout* was open to reinscription through the last minute of the exhibition. Allowing the contributors space for improvisation, collective response and varied audience space forced the museum to let go of guidelines that define things in advance; institutions do not love to act from systems of response.

One curiously unanticipated aspect. *Endless Shout* as enunciated dictated that at end I was the only person audience to every event. Curators naturally have a privileged position to exhibitions, not usually quite in this degree. The person closest me in terms of time spent in the exhibition was Turner Williams, the coordinator whose calm midnight-somewhere demeanor, unflappability, and attention to untimely details made events expertly and pleasantly possible. Following Turner, Lauren Downing, ICA's Curatorial Assistant, had the most experience of events. She was the spine of steady anticipation, reminders and landings, as formats and outlines and individuals changed form. And of course ICA's longstanding security guard Linda Harris, was enthusiastic, demanding to be cheerleader and dedicated audience to most everything, followed closely by her security colleague Maria Tomas. There is a steep drop off before the next most frequent rungs of audience: ICA staff from across the departments and contracted Ars Nova Workshop helpers, likely no one in the public audience, let alone the artists, came close to experiencing the many paths and throughways, nor how all the activity might complete a group exhibition. But did my witness to everything generate any privilege for meaning to my spectatorship?

Let's approach this imbalance in spectatorship not as detriment as much as a redirection and revision of the presumptive balance of values between contributing artist and casual audience and organizer vis-a-vis attentiveness. What being available means institutionally. Conditional distribution is often ignored in museum spaces— who is programmed and programming versus who is exhibited and exhibiting. No matter how many or few attended, every single moment in the course of *Endless Shout* was a shared moment of correspondence available between subject, object, organizer, performer, audience, and available space. This exhibition performed. This exhibition tired. This exhibition subsumed. This exhibition missed entrances. In tandem. The delicate responsiveness of collective improvisation does not unfold at one individual's speed. In fact, when improvisation is not successful, it is often because at least one person's speed is off in the way it fuels the collective rhythms. In this light, my familiarity of all the events does not actually generate a privileged position to the collective improvisation of *Endless Shout*. My experience is simply one; and likely I was often the weakest of links. One of many rhythms at which the time passed. An *Endless Shout*.

Schemes that rely on the construction of plans for execution will operate poorly in a complicated or unpredictable world such as the world of everyday life. In such a world it will not be feasible to construct plans very far in advance; moreover, it will routinely be necessary to abort the execution of plans that begin to go awry.
— Philip E. Agre, *Computation and Human Experience*

This exhibition privileged the local reactiveness, in terms of who could quickly take advantage of multivalent registers of presentation, and in terms of where pressure caused cracks. A privileged, informed audience wasn't necessarily the presumption for address. Not knowing *the what* beyond a month out for six months is brutal, particularly for those outside the core. In some cases facts didn't really land more than thirty minutes in advance. How to dream through deadlines and hard fiscal requirements and exhaustion and anxiety? Where is soul and kindness and communal gathering in gaff taping chords and missing messages? We tried to make things plot to a rational manner and regimented calendar, circumstances (including participants' fortunes, governmental ineptitude, staff distraction, and fragile health) undermined this viability. Endless stress. Endless Shit. The rhythm of the exhibition as a whole warped the efforts and hours of our marketing team in particular, keeping Jill Katz and Heather Holmes, not to mention design team Other Means, on constant call. Always trying to extend and support endeavors and make good on the promises meant Public Engagement staff, Maori Holmes along with Derek Rigby and Liz Barr, were always off-kilter yet Herculean in their brilliance at finesse under punches. Programming team Alex Klein and Gee Wesley, attuned to all programs and activities institution-wide, were forced to swap dates and details. All teams had to sort out who was what when. In structurally coordinating staff and mechanizations throughout, Robert Chaney was charged with assuring staffing and security and tech was sufficient, hard to fathom when the what wasn't on offer. He was strikingly calm. Paul Swenbeck and some of his steadier go-tos, most often Pat McGuire and or Jacob Lunderby, were called on to install tech and build supplemental structures from half-notions. Jessica Johnson and her front desk staff routinely under stress with how to clearly articulate what, when, where, and for how long anything might be taking place for those curious who walk into the building on an unassuming daily basis expecting static exhibitions. And of course Turner, Lauren, and Linda figuratively and at times literally loading the truck before, during, after. Amy Sadao, as director, was always at my heels grappling to get a larger mission out from the turns. So many big and little apologies and thank yous.

Exhibitions are not ideas or arguments or walks through histories. They only look like these things on the surface. Exhibitions are ways to work with, study through, and care for energies of respect between people. To with order share this gathering publicly with care. On this path, embarrassment, disconnection, and wounds are probable. And wounds *were* inflicted. On myself and some of the people listed above. Upon collaborators and performers. And still others unmentioned. Inflicted by myself and at times collaborators and at times staff and at times audience. Some wounds take longer to heal than others. In wounding institution and individual do not bear equal levels of guilt nor equal levels of culpability for righting the situation. Institutions should recognize they are collectively responsible for upholding the abilities of individuals to work well together as singular entities with asynchronous manners. Any errors and miscommunication, therefore, weigh more heavily upon flawed institutional structures than individual emotional response. Institutions have specialized positions and multiple departments to support the betweens and churn, not simply to process and generate paperbound redundancies. In this *Endless Shout* that weight rested on me as the representative of and path to the governing processes and support structures undertaken by the institution in concert with collaborators and audiences. In a dynamic collective situation you need to react without all the known facts. Speed does not always produce acceptable answers. And I failed in turn to provide good answers time and again. A hard lesson learned: any project that does not have doubt built into the structure, that does not allocate time and redundancy of skill sets to address emotions as they unfold, is not institutionally structured at an appropriate ethical level. There were moments when *Endless Shout* fell short as a result of my not making that space always available.

If improvisation is any good, it involves failure. There is always some moment in the middle of a performance where you feel lost. Like you've done everything, and what the fuck. Then you have to try to figure it out from there. —Arto Lindsay, in conversation

At the beginning ICA anticipated fewer events that would require extensive theatrical infrastructure (risers, lighting rigs, sprung floor, etc.). This was not to be, except for one case: George Lewis's *Recital*. Rather than trying to "expand" the capacity of the gallery—the lead participants embraced the small and indeterminate and intimate space of a traditionally sterile—white wall, track lighting, concrete floor—gallery space. They shared every resource we could offer. Month-by-month each in different ways fueled a complex generative matrix of relations that is a performing *exhibition* rather than a performance *series*. As such, the pauses between verbs generated as much meaning and visits as the nouns of events.

Danielle Goldman reached out to Ishmael Houston-Jones, Cynthia Oliver, and jumatatu m. poe, in part taking cues from duet dance segments from Catherine Sullivan's video from *Afterword via Fantasia*. Both taisha and jumatatu in their own ways would reflect on the same video extending cues from the historical Fred Holland and Ishmael footage. This confluence of energies guided my desire to engage Wadada Leo Smith, and he serendipitously suggested a duo performance. Perfect! This performance occurred relative *The Freedom Principle* on taisha's expanded *Endless Shout* stage. Other collapsing structures: Cynthia and her dancers welcoming the drifting ever-diverting flow soundtrack of Cauleen Smith's video installation two galleries away into their already collaged score. And setting their twenty-minute workshop presentations by the periodic clattering clashes of Terry Adkins's *Native Son (Circus)* in the next room. Sculpture become stage manager. In this and other ways, participants preferred more involvement with more direct or implicated collaboration to spotlighting individual authorship of improvisation and collectivity. Inter—. Here for a brief time an exhibition always speculating rather than displaying.

Speculative exposure sometimes simply leaves one exposed. It was important that artists might find support and be nurtured toward next endeavors. This public *Endless Shout* at its best formed an elaborate prosthetic extension for private directions. A qualitative value on quantity with contingency. As aside, in the visual arts, organizers such as Working Artists and the Greater Economy (W.A.G.E.) increasingly bring focus on the support offered, or withheld, by institutions. Initiatives such as W.A.G.E. declare emphatically: new curatorial frameworks and innovative aesthetic approaches are rotted from within without artists and creative ecologies getting real fiscal and material support. At our museum, *Endless Shout* was a hardscrabble preparatory incubator in working out the extensions and circumstances of providing support to ranges of individuals. To say the museum is nothing without them.

I think although great new ideas are articulated by individuals, they nearly always are generated by communities.
—Brian Eno, undated and unlocated panel discussion

Lights dim. Spaces hush. Acknowledge here. You rely with others. Move forward. Have the feeling, engage, and keep going in concentration through another's hands. Hold and extend. At each moment check circumstances of togetherness. A performer and an audience might come together. So might curator and artist. Or curator and supporting coworkers. Or all the above, even in delay. Try to cultivate and have and learn soft hold and collective distinction in counter affect to letting go and institutionalized division. Many must move separately; we needn't all get there together. But acknowledging togetherness offers the chance of future circumstances for us all to get there in time.

Currently the United States is in brutal need for an honest return to learning in dream and turning from fear. We—as we—cannot fear salaciousness in gathering. Or the sweat in proximity. (Consider, as tonic of course, that Trump's blathering nonsense and ill-willed changes of direction and focus is just one malignant form of improvisation too.) This is the emotive path that can be molded in the patience of attending improvisation or simply experiencing for togetherness. A pausing reset of boundary terms.

Craft exhibitions and programs to reach beyond ownership or expertise toward people who inspire, challenge, and improve your work because they know and feel more. Or at least more than I can. This exhibition made a space for competing viewpoints and an encroachment of love and trust into spaces set to unfeeling architectures. It came with pain. So be it. Expect this of all institutions and wonder what they fear when and if providing infrastructure.

Equal footing, if not equal knowledge and or engagement. Risk misbehaving. Risk lack of attribution. Risk having personal enunciation collectively formed elsewhere. An *Endless Shout*. Audience and performers gave no notice to who really was driving. As it should be. *Endless Shout* proposed loving within exhibitions in micro. Coming only to incompletely recognizing the scale of the stage. Attribution and argument are small-handed worries compared with this opportunity.

> **Lately we haven't been getting the sense of subtle, unsounded shout I had in mind when I wrote it. We managed it early on, but the last few times we've played the piece on gigs I've noticed a certain overstatement creeping in, as though the band had read but misread my mind regarding shout, taken it literally, a matter of volume rather than bend (circumambular bend, oblique, steal-away torque.)**
> — Nathaniel Mackey, *From a Broken Bottle Traces of Perfume Still Emanate*

It was not an *Endless Shout* event, per se, that recalibrated the exhibition in my understanding toward the above. It was trumpeter and composer Wadada Leo Smith's performance in conjunction with *The Freedom Principle* on taisha's *Endless Shout* stage. And all the recognized and unarticulated accumulation *inter*— of the room. The concert clearly demonstrated exhibitions overlap at indeterminate points physical and temporal, and breathe into each other in ways invisible yet felt and experienced together. Joyful. After performing, Smith hushed the jubilant applause to introduce his long-time collaborator and duet partner for this performance, percussionist Pheeroan akLaff. Ending his introduction of AkLaff and their collective history with, "And just want to say I love him." A pause. Smith then went on to remarks on broader concerns for the earth and all assembled.

There was one last day and two more performances to the exhibitions after this moment. "And just want to say I love him," crystallized the terms of infrastructure in *Endless Shout* and beyond. Institutions offer more than money, space, lights, and risers; institutions need be run with an infrastructure such that Smith's emotional admission is the valid and appropriate effort whose enunciation ripples through tangible support. Beyond tightly-drawn economies of aesthetic setting, historical framework, or "appropriate" politics. Above and beyond any histories or theories or tastes or techniques and yet by structural necessity happening in the orbits of loan forms and timelines and travel itineraries and checklists. Tactical concerns are not just. Provide the space where a participant can rewrite the moment and expected frame to their scale and own your time.

Wadada's "And just want to say I love him" shook many in the audience. There were tears.

How could it take so long to realize *Endless Shout*, rather than stage a frustrated, ongoing shout of protest and pain, exasperation at amnesia, and loudness of recuperation, was more importantly strident along private registers of an even larger protest?

Consider this analogy, you are leaving the house. Your lover's out of sight on the second floor but they can hear you and you them, so you turn, breathe in, and exclaim, "Hey! I love you!" and leave unseen but acknowledged. Another space generated beyond the door that now locks between indifferent spaces. Endless is not synonymous with forever. What happens next? "And just want to say I love ..."

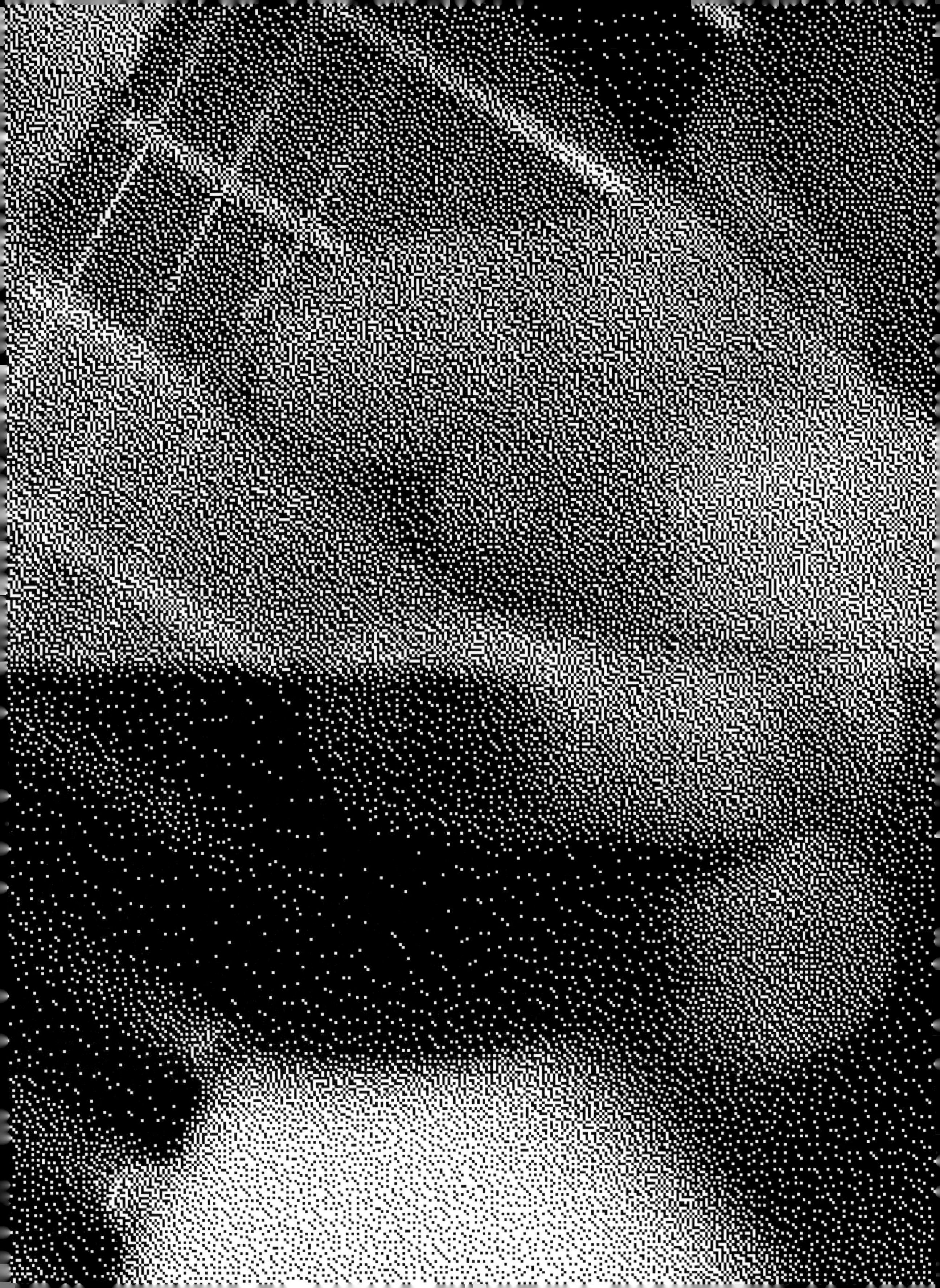

The poet I live with, Thomas Devaney, taught me about "you poems" and "I poems". Perhaps poetics classifications translate to contemporary visual art and music? If so, then George E. Lewis' history of the Association for the Advancement of Creative Music (AACM) and its titular motto, "A Power Stronger than Itself," reflects the "we poem" of black experimentation, collectivity, and improvisation that inspired *Endless Shout* and grounded *The Freedom Principle: Experiments in Art and Music, 1965 to Now,* the exhibition that provided the setting for *Endless Shout.*

That ICA publishes on a cycle not fully synched with its exhibition schedule enables all-important installation and performance documentation. It also allows for a separate *before*, *during*, and *after* thinking and feeling that Chief Curator Anthony Elms suggests is a necessity of attentive experience of live event. Thus, this book is long awaited by artists, participants, funders, and visitors while, in production and presentation, it expresses and reflects ICA's own prioritization of experimentation. *Endless Shout* asked many questions. What happens when a performance series or exhibition of live events is produced in a *Kunsthalle*? How does the museum accommodate performers and performance with the same thoroughness and responsiveness as it does physical artworks and those categorized as contemporary (visual) artists? What can the museum give publics who visit when there is no event scheduled? How to avoid the empty theatre/platform/gallery experience? And finally, how do we thoughtfully address—critically, theoretically, curatorially—that which is about to happen, is happening, and has happened? Whether performance or exhibition, ICA has historically used each *channel* of the museum—exhibition, event, text, publication—as a distinct form with a discreet temporality, potentially different audiences and lifespans. As is oft said but less frequently enacted, time is most precious.

As I enter my sixth year as director, I continue to exist in a spirit of gratitude for the opportunity to lead the ICA and to work alongside the great and diverse talents who populate the museum. I thank Anthony Elms for his work, for pushing the museum to think harder about what an institution presenting performance, improvisation, collectivity, and black cultural politics should and can be. Assistant Curator Meg Onli helped with *The Freedom Principle*'s installation at ICA, was an essential partner throughout *Endless Shout*, and has skillfully managed the production of this publication. Our development team, especially Diane Feissel, deserve credit for skillfully, transparently, keeping ICA in step with our partners, especially those at the Pew Center for Arts & Heritage. Bill Bissell, Josie Smith, Murph Henderson, Bill Adair, Laura Koloski, Kelly Shindler, and especially Paula Marincola at the Center continue to safeguard the experimentation and programmatic excellence of the great city of Philadelphia. ICA could not ask for better partners and I thank the entire team and board at the Pew for continuing to allow ICA and our audiences to learn and grow.

Endless Shout was formed in Philadelphia's rich tradition of groundbreaking music. Ars Nova Workshop has built a contemporary home base in Philadelphia to

Amy Sadao

renown worldwide. Mark Christman and Turner Williams's tactical prowess on the details of production for *Endless Shout* deserve special commendation. Jesse Pires and Lightbox Film Center continue as fundamental partners for ICA's work in cinema and video. Thank you for partnering with us and for making our city richer. Another excellent collaborator is musician and professor Eugene Lew who is a ready source of friendship and music equipment.

The artists of *Endless Shout* deserve special mention. It was my privilege and my joy to experience their work. As one visitor expressed, the program was an unexpected and necessary balm for a post-2016 election Philadelphia.

Naomi Beckwith and Dieter Roelstraete were extremely good-natured to let ICA seat a different exhibition within their exhibition. Inventory Press continues to deserve our praise and thanks for the design and distribution of the catalogue. Other Means and MING Media produced video and posters that enabled the project's future and past to live in the present.

I am filled with gratitude for our patrons, both inside and beyond the University of Pennsylvania. I thank the University Secretary Leslie Kruly and Director of Development John Zeller, our former Provost Vincent Price, and our current Provost Dr. Wendell Pritchett, and especially our Vice Provost of Faculty Affairs and "art czar," Dr. Anita Allen. President Amy Gutmann continues to inspire with her understanding of the centrality of contemporary art, writing, and performance to a world class education.

ICA's adventures have made history. That we can continue to explore the unknown alongside great artists and performers is entirely due to the daring board and patrons of the museum. I thank President Stephen Weber and all the Board of Overseers for ICA, UPENN for making this publication, the season of extraordinary performance that the catalogue reviews, and ICA's continued free and inspiring program possible.

September, 2016–March, 2017

September 17, 2016	6:00 PM	**ICA Gather** **I Wonder What Else Could Be Different Around Here: A Poetic Intersection with Music and Art featuring Yolanda Wisher, Dick Lourie, Natalie Diaz, and Christian Campbell** **Partner: Philalalia**
September 23, 2016	8:00 PM	**Ken Vandermark + The Few:** **An evening of improvised music**
September 28, 2016	6:30 PM	**Free For All: Black Quantum Futurism** **Black Quantum Futurism (Rasheedah Phillips + Moor Mother), Metropolarity, Mind Over Matter Music Over Mind, Irreversible Entanglements, and prophetesses.**
October 22, 2016	4:00 PM	**ICA Gather** **CLAPBACK with niv Acosta** **Partner: Bring Your Own Body: transgender between archives and aesthetics, curated by Jeanne Vaccaro with Stamatina Gregory and on display at the Cantor Fitzgerald Gallery at Haverford College**
October 26, 2016	6:30 PM	***The Freedom Principle*:** **Experiments in Art and Music, 1965–Now Curators' Conversation: Naomi Beckwith, Anthony Elms, and Dieter Roelstraete**
November 13, 2016	2:00 PM	**Coffee and Conversation:** **Problematics of the Record: Fixity, Memory and Futurity in Improvisational Performance with Laura Carlson**
January 14, 2017	6:00 PM	**ICA Gather** **No Justice, No Peace: Breaking the System** **Partner: Philadelphia Printworks**

Adjacent Actions

January 25, 2017	6:30 PM	**Free For All: Free Press** **Ghazaal Vojdani, the Common Press, Just Seeds, Lava** **Space, the Media Mobilizing Project, and the People's** **Paper Co-op.**
February 5, 2017	2:00 PM	**Coffee and Conversation:** **Renée Green's Participatory Histories with** **Anna-Claire Stinebring**
February 19, 2017	2:00 PM	**Coffee and Conversation:** **Black Woman, Black Power & Interpretive Literacy** **with Danièle Dennis**
February 25, 2017	6:00 PM	**ICA Gather** **Revolutionary Noise: music as struggle and healing** **Partners: Leeway Foundation and Girls Rock Philly**
February 26, 2017	2:00 PM	**Coffee and Conversation** **Jae Jarrell's garments of collective resistance with** **Lauren Altman**
March 2, 2017	6:30 PM	***The Freedom Principle* Now:** **Creative Capital presents a Creative Conversation** **Muhal Richard Abrams, Steve Coleman, Cauleen Smith** **and Henry Threadgill, moderated by Greg Tate**
March 10, 2017	12:00 PM	**Brown Bag Lunch:** **Kara Springer & Willis "Nomo" Humphrey**
March 18, 2017	12:00 PM	**Greg Tate and Guthrie Ramsey Book Talk & Signing**
March 18, 2017	3:00 PM	**Wadada Leo Smith and Pheeroan akLaff**

Anthony Elms: Perhaps we should start with what brought you to the Ankhrasmation scores that were part of the recent biennial at the Hammer Museum.

Wadada Leo Smith: If we start at the beginning: As a seven- or eight-year-old kid, I was a very good drawer. That's how I made extra money at my school; I would draw the blackboards for each of the teachers in that school. I got pretty good at it, and then my parents decided that they would put me in some kind of competition where you could get a scholarship to go to school. This is in Mississippi, of course. I must have won the little scholarship, or at least that's what they said. When the guy came to visit me at the house, he found out that I was black, and they didn't accept black kids. At that point, I decided that art was not going to be one of the places I would go. After this, over the years, I drew, but only incidentally.

AE: Wow. So, to back up, you were deterred away from visual arts because of discrimination. Was art something you ever sought to go back to?

WLS: The Ankhrasmation language fulfilled that urge. I'm extremely blessed that I had those formative years of drawing so that I didn't have to learn how to draw when I developed Ankhrasmation; I just transferred that visual energy that I had into this new expression. And, importantly, I didn't have to ask anybody to accept this effort except the people in my ensemble.

This path opened up for me in 1967, when Anthony Braxton asked me to record "The Bell" for his record *3 Compositions of New Jazz* (1968). During recording, each time the ensemble got to a box with a dotted element at the end, there was space. The ensemble finished, yet Muhal Richard Abrams and I kept going. That made me feel that there was a relationship in the markings between the auditory part of a unit, the notes, and the inaudible part, the pause; and here, in this score, I discovered a general idea of how to represent

this. At the time, though, I had no idea how to interpret the experience, except by listening back to our recording of "The Bell." In playback, I discovered how to think about the marks in the dotted box as rhythm units, and that was the beginning.

Of course, since then, the rhythm unit language I use has grown pretty large.

AE: This trajectory is fascinating. Often in conversations of extended techniques for music notation—language, graphic, game commands, etc.—the composer has moved beyond traditional music notation either because it isn't giving them something, or because they want to dismantle the methods represented by traditional notation. For example, John Cage and his overlayed drawings on acetate, or Cornelius Cardew and his composition "Treatise" (1963–67)—each is a drawing that requires the performers to interpret the variable schematic lines and dots into musical directions. In both cases, they are not so much reaching out to the visual to expand traditional notation so much as they are sort of— I don't want to say falling into the visual, but the visual is not perceived as a developed language with which to extend notation. The visual is only a tool deployed against the perceived hierarchy of traditional music notation.

WLS: Exactly.

AE: What impresses me in your comments is that the visual is an early proclivity you were discouraged from, and when you wanted to expand your musical vocabulary, you already have a background with the visual. It is this toolbox that is already there for you to develop; it's not about cutting off and beginning again, but rather adding to.

WLS: Right. This is how I explain Ankhrasmation: it must have the formalized structure of composition and the intuitive freshness of improvisation. That language

Wadada Leo Smith and Anthony Elms

of traditional notation I came out of was not deficient. But as you're developing as an instrumentalist, you want something more, a way to share more of your feelings with the musicians around you. So you marry these two advanced languages, as opposed to removing or stepping back from one or the other. When both of them are mixed together, like when you mix two colors, they become a new color. That was important for me because the idea of just doing art—for me that is a big problem.

AE: When you say art—the visual arts?

WLS: Any art. To me, everything has to be placed in context.

AE: This relationship between formalized structure and intuitive freshness requires memory and having to think through relations. I know you've been pretty direct in saying Ankhrasmation scores are not graphic scores—

WLS: They're not.

AE: So the combination of formal structure and intuitive regeneration—is this why they are not graphic scores?

WLS: That's one reason. Another reason is because there are rules of engagement and levels of success and failure in my scores. With a graphic score, normally what happens is people play it as a picture; that picture is used as inspiration. With my scores, if they're used purely as inspiration, it violates the principle because it's not a picture; it is a score. The rules of engagement for Ankrasmation erase the possibility of someone just using it as a picture to be inspired by, with no level of success or failure.

AE: If I understand correctly, your scores offer symbols that detail proportions—an amount of sound and an amount of silence—and the symbols themselves are crafted to have proportions within and between them.

One symbol will tell the performer to suddenly, say, play twice as fast as the last figure, for example. In this way, Ankrasmation does not direct the performer to exact notes or tempos, but to relationships between motifs once a decision has been made. So the relationship between the performance and the score, for a tradition graphic score, is as a one-time reaction—a response, by the performer, to the image that is the score—but it's a two-way street with your scores. The performer and the score effect each other.

WLS: Exactly. It's a reaction. In fact, you can actually say that each individual person made that graphic score. Whereas with an Ankhrasmation score, you have to say that I constructed the relationships and the structure, and then everybody made it.

AE: How large of a group has performed an Ankhrasmation score?

WLS: The recorded version of "Occupy the World" (2013) has twenty-three performers and seven pages. Normally, I rehearse all seven pages but spontaneously construct it in the performances as I conduct. None of the performers on stage know which page is coming first or last.

AE: It's a bit of a game piece.

WLS: People use the word game, but I don't like the word game. With this, you have a controller who's manipulating the figures that have been rehearsed, and this controller is guiding a composition made in the moment. For me, a game means something a bit different. It means you're engaged in some play in which one team has something in opposition to another team. It's a competitive aspect, and it's not that I think that gaming is bad—

AE: But you do not want competition in this space.

WLS: Not in this space, no.

AE: How do you prepare people to play the Ankhrasmation scores?

WLS: Normally, I start off by explaining the rhythm units. There are six sets that I commonly use. Actually, today there are seven sets, but I rarely use the seventh set. I made it for potential, but I never teach anybody the seventh set.

Anyway, I start with the rhythm units because the rhythm units are unique in the sense that they work by proportion. There's a long portion, and that long portion is called A—when it's performed or played, it's an audible portion of that sound. The other half of that sound, which is the inaudible portion, I label B. A and B together makes a complete sound. You need sound and silence to make a complete sound. I've been challenged many times on this fact—why is it that you need the audible and the inaudible together, and is that relationship exact?

I tell everybody immediately, no, it's not exact. And the reason it's not exact is because we're dealing with proportions and we're dealing with individual thinkers, and every thinker sees the same proportion, yet how one executes it will be different from person to person. That is exactly what I want.

Proportional rhythm offers the performer the greatest opportunity for construction of his or her own distinct rhythmic cycles. I explain it like this: Metrical proportions in music bars and time signatures are, of course, precise. But they have a limit. Every metric rhythm is either an odd or even number of beats.

Whereas proportion rhythms are only based on long and short. If you try to precisely count proportional rhythms, you're eliminating individuality and the autonomy of the individual.

AE: In this turn toward proportions and how to teach them, it seems that you're speaking to the importance of improvisation and communal dialogue as an ethos and as an ethics, and as a position beyond music. Making decisions as a citizen, within a group of other citizens making their own decisions; not against but with.

WLS: Yes, it's a social environment. Notation is placed in the perspective of a community. I usually start there, with the rhythm units, because that's the basis of Ankhrasmation. Those same ideas of proportions are reflected on several hierarchical levels. For example, in one of my scores, when you see a velocity unit and you see different figures inside of it, those insets are also broken down as proportions; and for that I use the term cycles, large cycles and small cycles. Those cycles are spontaneously picked by the performers, and intuitively the proportions begin to construct a musical tower amongst the performers that develops the composition, like a fractal.

Can I draw something?

AE: Yes.

WLS: See: set number one, this is A, this is B, and in between that, you have this line, and that makes a whole unit; and in between that, you have an arrow that runs through it, and that makes a whole unit. Within the context of the whole rhythm unit, you've got two audible relationships: long and short. As you move on from one rhythm unit set to the next rhythm unit set, which looks like this, this rhythm unit to the next, relationships are developed and built upon.

AE: Because they're always a pair.

WLS: It's always a pair. It's always a pair in the physical, visual sense, but when the players play that one unit, every one of them is being regenerated by the relationship to the others.

AE: It's from the landscape. It's around us, it's from us and it's from what's around us.

WLS: Right. Civilization is not various societies having dominance in world power. It's a single stream where everyone is responsible. It's those that have passed on, because that material that they laid down made it possible for the next, and the next, and the next.

That's how I think about this stuff. It's not something that I just sat down and thought about in 1965. I started to think about it because this is the way that I thought as a young kid, and to prove it to myself meant

I had to find some answers, and how I found those answers shows something about me.

AE: With this in mind, let's go back to '65. I can only imagine there must have been conversations between you and other people invested in these approaches, like Anthony Braxton—

WLS: No, no. Sadly enough, there was no conversation. You know why? I was in the Army. The Army breeds uniformity. It breeds no discontent, and this is poison.

AE: Okay, so let's not go back to '65, per se, but how did you arrive in Chicago at the AACM (Association for the Advancement of Creative Musicians)?

WLS: When I went to the AACM, I had a string quartet just about finished. I had ideas, but unexpressed ideas. At the AACM, I met a group of people who were exploring sound and composition, but no one was exploring stuff on a blank sheet of paper. What they were exploring were notions of sound and philosophical ideas about freedom. That's what I gleaned from them, in addition to a lot of other good things like respect for fear, and respect for the person in the ensemble you play for, and allowing that person to shape the ensemble. I learned how to be strong on the stage.

One of the original AACM members, Muhal Richard Abrams, had a big band—I don't use that phrase, "big band," but he does—and in rehearsal he would select a bunch of guys and maybe ask you to play. Then once you start playing, the others would all walk off stage and leave you there playing, and then they would stand on the side of the stage, just beyond the curtains, and they would talk. You could hear them talking while you're playing. They'd do that to see what you are and if you could become part of the group. Out there playing, you discover a lot about yourself and about them—a lot! In that one moment, you just grew up.

AE: But how did you get to the AACM?

WLS: I met a guy in my last Army post in Colorado. This guy had been in the military, in Korea, with Anthony Braxton. He gave me Anthony's telephone number. When I got to Chicago, I called Anthony up. He says come over. I go over to his house and carry with me an edition of scores edited by John Lewis and Gunther Schuller, I believe. Anthony and I, on our first meeting, spend a couple hours playing this book, just this book. Nothing else.

AE: This fellow, did he think, "I know Braxton. You should meet." Like this is someone you need to know?

WLS: Yes, because those last few months in the Army, I'm reading bits and pieces here and there in Downbeat and other magazines about the AACM.

AE: So, you were aware of the organization?

WLS: Yes, and my wife's family lived in Chicago. I had a lot of family there too. The main goal after the Army was to go to Chicago, where there was something happening. Get there and play with Braxton. At our meeting Braxton says clearly, "I will introduce you in the AACM. You've got to become part of the AACM." Braxton, when he says that, he absolutely means it, but it evaporates. He just forgot.

Maybe a week or two later, I'm walking in my neighborhood, the Old Town area of Chicago, and I see a sign that says Joseph Jarman and his quartet are playing in this coffee house. Now, I know the name Jarman.

AE: From those little blurbs in *Downbeat*?

WLS: Yes. So I said, "I'm going to go there." I went really early, and when I got outside the coffee house, Lester Bowie and Roscoe Mitchell had just ridden up on their motorbikes—they had leather jackets on, they had high boots on. Lester Bowie had a cigar that long [exaggerates with hands], and Roscoe was looking like a rebel.

AE: As he often did those days.

WLS: They were in jeans and open clothing, meaning nothing was buttoned. They looked just like rebels. I went over. They got off their bikes and they said, "Hello," and I said, "Hello," and we started talking. Roscoe says there's a rehearsal on Monday night. This was like a Friday night. He says, "Come on Monday. Muhal has a big band that rehearses every Monday night—go there and bring your horn." He gave me the address. It was on Cottage Grove Avenue.

AE: Going back to a statement you said as a tangent a bit ago, you said you never use the term 'big band.'

WLS: Right. You know why?

AE: Why?

WLS: Because Duke Ellington called his ensemble an orchestra. Fletcher Henderson called it an orchestra. Jelly Roll Morton called them orchestras. Benny Goodman called it an orchestra. Paul Whiteman called it an orchestra. The whole tradition of orchestra is always there, and these big band guys— I don't know what state they came from, but somehow they came in, and I believe that the notion of big band is associated with arranging.

AE: An arranger is reworking someone else's material, rather than composing.

WLS: An arranger's not a composer. I don't use the words "big band." They always did.

AE: So, back to your introduction to AACM.

WLS: Right. So Roscoe also said to come to the AACM on the Saturday after the Monday rehearsal and he would introduce me to the group.

That Monday night, I go. I leave my horn in my car trunk. I meet Muhal as I come in, and he says, "Well, go sit down and take a listen." Very rough, like, "Go sit down and take a listen." I go sit down and I take a listen. All the guys looked like rebels and outsiders—really hip guys. They start rehearsing, and the trumpet players—there were three or four of them— don't play the figure right, and Muhal's getting more and more angry. Not swearing angry, just "Come on, guys. It goes …" You know.

AE: "Get it together."

WLS: Right. And all of a sudden, in his frustration, he turns around in the rehearsal and says, "Hey, you got your horn? Go get it. Come play this phrase." I walk out, get my horn, come up, sit down, play the phrase. The whole band turns around to see who this new guy is. It was an instant kind of connection from everybody. That next Saturday I go to the AACM meeting, and Roscoe Mitchell stands up and introduces me, and puts my name in to become a member of the AACM. That's a long story, but that's what life is about. These beautiful narratives.

AE: Within the AACM, I identify both you and Braxton as the primary leaders in trying to find ways of scoring beyond traditional notation. Not at the same level, but you're the ones that I think of as having the earliest, most distinctive approaches.

WLS: Yes, but we found different ways.

AE: You and Braxton never discussed his work with diagrams—appealing to scientific notations and formulas—relative to your investigations with symbols and rhythm units? I mean, you both have written nearly contemporaneous extensive texts on your methods.

WLS: No, no, no, no. His and mine are very different. His are more realistic, mine are symbolic. Look at the LP of his that's called F Series. He has a diagram of stuff in there, and for notes that go up, he uses a step. A step going up, or undulating line going up, is an ascending pattern, et cetera. That's a realistic thing that's part of our environment. Mine are symbolic shapes, so any portion of it can be interpreted by the individual if they have learned the language. They can actually add to the language.

AE: If the interpreter can add to the language, they need to study it, obviously. What are rehearsals of your scores like?

WLS: Ankhrasmation scores don't necessarily need to be rehearsed. But if you've got a group of people who show some kind of difficulty or conflict, then you do this kind of thing that we call a rehearsal; but you don't

really have to do it. The ultimate goal when I write
an Ankhrasmation is to have a score that can be played
instantly by a group of players who have even just a
small portion of the language down.

To that effect, at CalArts with a guy named Mark
Trayle, who's an excellent electronic composer, we
created this design for an ensemble—the Creative Music
Electronic Ensemble—that ran for fourteen years at
CalArts. Two years on, one year off. The reason we did
that is that we wanted to affect the climate of people
coming into it. Once they've gone in for two years,
people come back into it just to check it out, and that's
not the same as what you come into it for. We wanted
to erase those people, put a year between, and maybe
get a new breed of people who actually want to learn
something new.

Every class would be self-sufficient. It would start
out and I would draw a rhythm unit, draw a velocity
unit, and then I would construct that in a music tower
with an improvisation symbol; and those three properties, they would learn them that same day. In the last
thirty-five to forty minutes of the class—it's a two-hour
class—we would play, and then we would quickly
self-critique by going around to everybody in the
ensemble and having them present what they did in the
piece, what the difficulties were, and what was successful. Then the full ensemble would determine what
was successful and what needed to be corrected. When
they walked out of that first class, the students had
three symbols that they could visually identify and they
had played through those three symbols. Every class
was run like that, so we got a fresh performance of the
language right away.

AE: It sounds like rehearsal is less about learning the
score and more about—

WLS: Learning the symbols.

AE: And also learning the personalities within.
Learning how to be part of a social system.

WLS: How to be part of a social dynamic, but also
the velocity unit, the rhythm unit, the improvisation
unit—you can't learn all of it in four or five or six years.

You have to grow with it and begin to experiment with
your growth.

AE: Another question I want to ask: There's a sort of
retrospective moment happening with you right now.
The scores are on display. Notes has been republished.
Is looking back something you've always had within
your process, or is this a different feeling for you now?

WLS: I don't see that as looking back. I see it as continuing. I made those scores starting in 1967 and up through
this year—some of them I play, some of them I put on
the shelf—and I simply pull them off the shelf and bring
them out. I know what you mean. You mean that these
things are happening now and when I look over it, what
do I see? I see this: I see that from the very beginning,
when I was twelve years old, I saw something and I still
see it now. The people that realize their own destiny
don't need to be measured by other people.

That idea was crystallized for me through Marcus
Aurelius's Meditations. He was both emperor and a spiritual leader, and people called him a philosopher. He
was a mystic. I read that when I was twelve years old.

AE: That's kind of early to read Marcus Aurelius.

WLS: I read it because in those days, I read these
magazines, and they give you five books if you sign
up and pay three or four dollars. I didn't know who
Marcus Aurelius was. I didn't know what meditation
was. I bought it and then I perused it and began to read
it, and here were some fundamental principles about
spirituality and the relationship of the human being.

About this same time, I started playing the trumpet.
Approximately three months from my thirteenth
birthday—like September, October—I wrote my first
piece, for three trumpets. At that time, I had not committed to memory the framing for all the notes, but
I did know that there were twelve notes, and I put all
twelve of them in the score. I went and got my friends.
Sammy T. Scott, Cleo Hall, and me, we sat down in
the gymnasium and we started rehearsing my score.
We played it and my band director, his name was O'Neal
Jones, he came downstairs and said, "What are you guys
doing?" You know what I said? "We're playing a piece

of music I wrote." He says, "Hold it." He goes upstairs—
he played clarinet and alto saxophone—and he got
the alto saxophone, and he came down and played one
of the trumpet parts on the alto saxophone. He didn't
transpose, he just played it as is. So there I am. I hear
this sound that I'm going to hear for the rest of my
life, because I don't transpose for instruments either.
That's why my sound, if I've got five instruments
or ten, it sounds twice the size, because every instrument has not been reduced to C, what they call the
concert key.

There's no such thing as a concert key. That's a
political position. The French horn is in F. The alto flute
is in G. The trumpet's in B flat, but also it has B flat,
E flat, D, F, G, A, you see. Each tonality in those twelve
tonalities, once they're sounded, present a sonic spectrum. That sonic spectrum is unique to itself, and if
you mix these sonic tone spectrums—let's say with a
B flat and an E flat, and an F instrument—you have
three spectrums existing at once, but only if you don't
transpose. If you transpose, you make a French horn
sound artificially in C, and you make a B flat trumpet
sound artificially in C, and those three instruments
produce only one spectrum. That rich spectrum is the
dynamic we lose in music dominated by this idea of
concert pitch.

AE: This keeps circling back. I've said it before, and
you've said it before, and we both said it earlier: This
is not just an argument about instruments. This is
an argument about how people are, how people can be.

WLS: The whole gamut of socialization, if you want to
look at it like that.

AE: This is a way of being in the world with differences.

WLS: Yes, because art making, frankly, is so vital—
just like, for example, doctors and sanitary workers.
All of us have a specific function that makes the society
whole and complete; and the fact that we are on stage
is incidental, because the stage itself doesn't make the
music. That's just a place, a place that has made itself a
dominant part, but it doesn't make the music.

AE: In Notes you assert that the artist must be self-
conscious, and it's most important for the black artist
to be self-conscious. Do you still find yourself to be
self-conscious?

WLS: I find myself realizing that I was right in 1970,
when Notes was published. Everything in there. Even
if I could not have known that. You see, the radical
views and direction that people take always happens
in their young years, but you can also be a radical in
your late years.

This notion about awareness is an important
political aspect for human beings and the communities
in which they live in. In America, just like in the world,
the idea of otherness and difference is still the weakest component of society. It is less valued. It's less
recognized. My proclamation for self-conciousness,
my intention was to say to this community at large—
African, European, or whatever—that one should be
thoroughly aware of what's going on in this world that
we live in. Being aware means you have a glimpse of
how you stand in the political and social and economic
spectrum of our society. That's still true today. That
doesn't change.

AE: Back about twenty years now I saw an interview
with Roscoe Mitchell in Chicago. He was asked about
the performers he loved and why. This conversation
was around the time he was restaging his important
'70s compositions "L-R-G" and "The Maze" at the
Museum of Contemporary Art in Chicago. You are the
L in "L-R-G." Instead of saying he liked your playing,
or your attack, your tone—common things said of
horn players—he said, basically, "I like how Wadada
breathes."

WLS: I never heard that, and I'm extremely joyful
to hear that, because he's a master of art making and for
him to say that, that's beautiful. From his perspective
and from mine, that's a good explanation of it. It elimi-
nates all the foreground.

AE: It's acknowledges your reason behind the rhythm
and velocity units. To have proportions, fast and
slow; tone and pause make a total sound. It brings

that duality and balance into a statement on how you
perform. It tacitly acknowledges the drive behind
Ankhrasmation scores: To have the space accompanying
any statement considered as important as the statement.
Obviously, he's listening to something which is at your
core. Your breath.

WLS: Breathing shapes the size of the sound, the timbre
of the sound, the kind of texture it's going to have.
It would take a book to fantastically write about that.

Institute of Contemporary Art
at the University of Pennsylvania

ICA Staff List

Amy Sadao, Daniel W. Dietrich, II Director
Liz Barr, Public Engagement Assistant
Mandy Bartram, Registrar
Jeffrey Bussmann, Associate Director of Development
for Individual Gifts
Robert Chaney, Director of Curatorial Affairs
Lauren Downing, Curatorial Assistant
Anthony Elms, Chief Curator
Diane Feissel, Assistant Director of Development
and Alumni Relations
Shannon Freitas, Business Administrator
Samantha Gibb Roff, Director of Development & Alumni
Relations
Heather Holmes, Digital Editor & Communications
Associate
Maori Karmael Holmes, Director of Public Engagement
Charlotte Ickes, Whitney-Lauder Curatorial Fellow
Jessica L. Johnson, Visitor Services Coordinator
Jessica Kaminski, Editions Coordinator & Assistant
Administrator
Jill Katz, Director of Marketing & Communications
Alex Klein, Dorothy and Stephen R. Weber (CHE'60)
Curator
Kate Kraczon, Laporte Associate Curator
Meg Onli, Assistant Curator
Derek Rigby, Audiovisual Coordinator
Paul Swenbeck, Chief Preparator & Building
Administrator
Gee Wesley, Spiegel-Wilks Curatorial Fellow
Christina Yu, Development Assistant

ICA Board of Overseers

Pamela Toub Berkman
Charles X Block
Theodore Coons
Carol T. Finley
Wendy Fisher
Glenn Fuhrman
Kirk Kirkpatrick
Andrea B. Laporte
Marjorie Esterow Levine
Josephine Magliocco
Hilarie Lauter Morgan
Midge G. Palley
Karen Redrobe, PhD**
Lori W. Reinsberg
Katherine Sachs
Ella B. Schaap*
David E. Simon
Daniel S. Sundheim
Lisa A. Tananbaum
Bryan S. Verona
Stephen R. Weber, Chairman
Susan J. Weiler
Caroline Gittis Werther, Esq.
Lise Wilks

*Emeritus
**Ex officio

This book is published on the occasion of the exhibition *Endless Shout*, curated by Anthony Elms, and organized and presented by the Institute of Contemporary Art, University of Pennsylvania, September 14, 2016–March 19, 2017.

Major support for Endless Shout has been provided by The Pew Center for Arts & Heritage.

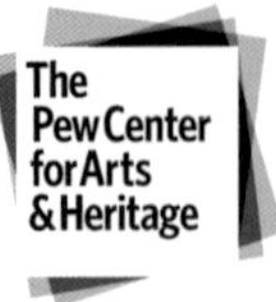

Design: IN-FO.CO

Photo credits: Pages 8–9, 130–1, 190–1: Constance Mensh; Pages 14–7: William Hidalgo; Pages 20–31, 66–71, 86–95, 152–7, 174–9, 182–7: Christopher Andrew Studios; Pages 44–47, 78–85, 122–7: Turner Williams; Pages 54–7: courtesy Nhlanhla Masondo; Pages 72–5: Derek Rigby; Pages 76–7: Liz Barr; Pages 110–1: Theodore Harris; Pages 134–7: Ryan Collerd; Pages 140–5: taisha paggett; Pages 158–163: courtesy The Otolith Group

Typefaces: Austin News Text and Marr Sans Condensed

Printed by Die Keure in Belgium

ISBN: 978-1-941753-16-3

Institute of Contemporary Art
University of Pennsylvania
118 S. 36th Street
Philadelphia, PA 19104-3289
www.icaphila.org

Inventory Press
2305 Hyperion Ave.
Los Angeles, CA 90027
inventorypress.com

Library of Congress
Cataloging-in-Publication Data
CIP data can be obtained at the Library of Congress

ICA is always Free. For All.
Free admission is courtesy of
Amanda and Glenn Fuhrman.

ICA acknowledges the generous sponsorship of Barbara B. & Theodore R. Aronson for exhibition catalogues. Programming at ICA has been made possible in part by the Emily and Jerry Spiegel Fund to Support Contemporary Culture and Visual Arts and the Lise Spiegel Wilks and Jeffrey Wilks Family Foundation, and by Hilarie L. & Mitchell Morgan. Marketing is supported by Pamela Toub Berkman & David J. Berkman and by Lisa A. & Steven A. Tananbaum. Additional funding has been provided by the Horace W. Goldsmith Foundation, the Overseers Board for the Institute of Contemporary Art, friends and members of ICA, and the University of Pennsylvania. General operating support is provided, in part, by the Philadelphia Cultural Fund. ICA receives state arts funding support through a grant from the Pennsylvania Council on the Arts, a state agency funded by the Commonwealth of Pennsylvania and the National Endowment for the Arts, a federal agency. ICA acknowledges Le Méridien Philadelphia as our official Unlock Art™ partner hotel.

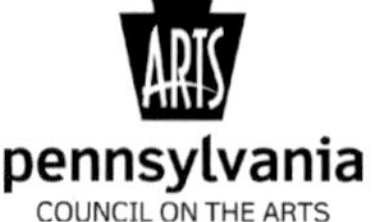
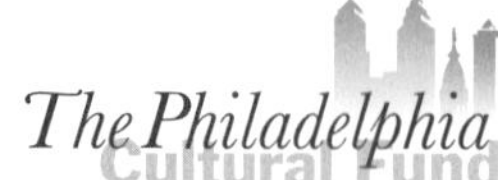